J.P. MARTIN.

CW00816298

A Fuzzy PROLOG
Database System

ELECTRONIC & ELECTRICAL ENGINEERING RESEARCH STUDIES

COMPUTING SYSTEMS SERIES

Series Editor: **Dr. P. W. Foulk**
Heriot-Watt University, Edinburgh, U.K.

1. A Fuzzy PROLOG Database System
   Deyi Li* *and* **Dongbo Liu***

* 6 Wan Shou Road, Beijing 100036, People's Republic of China

A Fuzzy PROLOG
Database System

Deyi Li, Ph.D.
and
Dongbo Liu, M.Sc.

Institute of Computer Engineering
People's Republic of China

RESEARCH STUDIES PRESS LTD.
Taunton, Somerset, England

JOHN WILEY & SONS INC.
New York · Chichester · Toronto · Brisbane · Singapore

RESEARCH STUDIES PRESS LTD.
24 Belvedere Road, Taunton, Somerset, England TA1 1HD

Marketing and Distribution:

Australia and New Zealand:
JACARANDA WILEY LTD.
GPO Box 859, Brisbane, Queensland 4001, Australia

Canada:
JOHN WILEY & SONS CANADA LIMITED
22 Worcester Road, Rexdale, Ontario, Canada

Europe, Africa, Middle East and Japan:
JOHN WILEY & SONS LIMITED
Baffins Lane, Chichester, West Sussex, England

North and South America:
JOHN WILEY & SONS INC.
605 Third Avenue, New York, NY 10158, USA

South East Asia:
JOHN WILEY & SONS (SEA) PTE LTD.
37 Jalan Pemimpin #05-04
Block B Union Industrial Building, Singapore 2057

Library of Congress Cataloging in Publication Data

Li, Deyi, 1944–
    A fuzzy PROLOG database system / Deyi Li and Dongbo Liu.
      p. cm. — (Electronic & electrical engineering research
  studies. Computing systems series; 1)
   Includes bibliographical references (p.).
   ISBN 0 471 92762 7 (Wiley)
   1. Data base management.   2. Prolog (Computer program language)
  3. Logic programming.   4. Fuzzy systems.   I. Liu, Dongbo.
  II. Title.   III. Series.
  QA76.9.D3L52   1990
  005.75—dc20   90-8345
                                       CIP

British Library Cataloguing in Publication Data

Li, Deyi, *1944–*
   A fuzzy PROLOG database system. — (Electronic and
  electrical engineering research studies. Computing systems
  series; no. 1).
  1. Computer systems. Applications of mathematics. Fuzzy
  sets
  I. Title   II. Liu, Dongbo   III. Series
  004

   ISBN 0 86380 102 1
   ISBN 0 471 92762 7 Wiley

   ISBN 0 86380 102 1 (Research Studies Press Ltd.)
   ISBN 0 471 92762 7 (John Wiley & Sons Inc.)

Printed in Great Britain by SRP Ltd., Exeter

Series Editor's Foreword

This book follows on from Dr Deyi Li's earlier successful book "A PROLOG Database System". In that book Dr Li detailed the development of his ILEX relational database system and its support of several different query languages in a uniform way. These query languages, and the database itself, only dealt with 'crisp' or nonfuzzy concepts. Such concepts may have been adequate for many of the earlier database applications of computers, for instance a stock ordering and control system, where exact data are usually stored and exact queries usually made. However, as Dr Li and Dongbo Liu show, database applications have advanced into areas where exactness is no longer relevant. For these applications, the authors show how fuzzy set theory and its developments can be applied to databases so that their data more closely resemble the data stored in the human mind. Hence the database is able to handle data and queries expressed as humans would like to express them and not how some database limitations decree that they should be expressed. Databases then take on a much more user-friendly aspect, and hence we can expect to see a great expansion of their use in the near future. It is our hope that you will find this book a valuable introduction to fuzzy databases, and that it encourages you to experiment with their use, and develop them for the use of others.

P.F. Foulk

February 1990

Foreword

In the year 1965, Professor Lotfi A. Zadeh presented a new theory, the theory of fuzzy sets. This theory provides a mathematical basis for dealing with imprecision and uncertainty associated with human thinking and cognitive faculty.

Since then, the theory has been generalized to provide many mathematical bases to human-like reasoning and the theory was applied to many engineering problems, especially to problems dealing with control systems and decision making processes. Also, based upon this theory, special software tools have been developed for representing knowledge base and for the solution of decision-making problems in engineering and management science.

The present book entitled "A Fuzzy PROLOG Database System" by Professor Deyi Li and Lecturer Dongbo Liu provides a computational basis for dealing with the modelling of human knowledge and its applications to decision making problems. This is the first book of its kind, and it provides a basic tool for dealing with the natural languages and natural expressions which cannot be modelled or described using conventional mathematical and computational tools.

The human brain has a large tolerance for imprecision, uncertainties and incompleteness. One of the most important attributes of the human mind is its ability to manipulate the imprecise data that are acquired by our natural sensors such as visual, auditory and tactile, etc.

The engineers and scientists who are engaged in debate of the new generation of computing systems have basically two computing tools: the natural computers (the carbon-based organic brain in humans and other animals) and the silicon-based artificial computers. Recent technological advances in computer hardware have made it possible to carry a very powerful computer in a briefcase; these computers are ultrafast and efficient for numerical computations.

The biological brain acts upon the non-numerical cognitive information acquired by the biological natural sensors. The cognitive process is very efficient in processing such non-numerical information, while the artificial computers fail to process such information.

Scientists and engineers are in the process of developing a new generation of computers which can compute the cognitive information and provide an output which is equivalent to human **perception**. For this purpose, we are learning from the biological processes. The mathematical aspects of our thinking and mental processes, and the hardware aspects of "neurons"—the basic element of the brain—may help in the design of the new generation of computing tools.

The cognitive activity of the brain, unlike the computational function of the binary computer, is based upon **relative grades** of the information acquired by the natural sensory system. The perception and action of the cognitive processes also appear in the form of **relative grades**. No computer scientist has yet understood the beauty of the cognitive functions of the brain.

The theory of fuzzy logic is based upon the notion of **relative grades** and so are the functions of mental cognition and perception. During the past, studies in cognitive uncertainty and its cognate—the cognitive information—were hindered by the lack of suitable mathematical theory for modelling such a formless uncertainty. However, with the introduction of the theory of fuzzy logic, it is possible to expand studies in this important field of cognitive information, neural networks and neural-like computing tools.

Recent progress in information-based technology has significantly broadened the capabilities and applications of computers. This book on Fuzzy PROLOG Database Systems is an attempt to develop computer models for their applications to decision making processes. Deyi Li and Dongbo Liu have done an extremely good job in introducing the basic notion of relative grades via the fuzzy set theoretic approach. Also, they have used the PROLOG language for developing the basic tools of fuzzy logic programs. The next part of the book covers fuzzy relational databases and the fuzzy relational (structured) query language (FSQL) and the calculus of fuzzy relational databases. In the last part of the book, Li and Liu have given methods for treating the incomplete information in fuzzy PROLOG database (FPDB) systems. The theory has been illustrated by means of several examples of knowledge representation, expert systems, fuzzy control, and fuzzy clustering and information retrieval.

The material presented in this book provides a basis for dealing with fuzzy data in developing fuzzy algorithms. The book provides some useful material both for students in their classrooms, and for researchers for developing new fuzzy algorithms.

The authors deserve to be congratulated on producing seminal work in this important field of fuzzy knowledge representation and computation. In addition to acknowledging the significance of the contents of this book, we admire the way Dr. Li and Mr. Liu have introduced the subject: it starts from the basic theory of fuzzy logic and finishes the book with system examples.

Dr. Madan M. Gupta
Intelligent Systems Research Laboratory
University of Saskatchewan
Saskatoon, Saskatchewan
Canada

Preface

The ability to handle uncertainty is one of the most fundamental attributes of intelligent behaviour. Consequently, progress in the theory and computer modelling of fuzzy information processing is of great significance to fields concerned with understanding intelligence. Such fields include cognitive science, artificial intelligence, information science, knowledge engineering, expert systems, and related disciplines. The eighties have witnessed a significant breakthrough in the foundations of fuzzy set theory from various point of views. There have been many contributions to that theory, and some of them began to enjoy wide application in engineering and applied science. At the same time, the technology of database has been extensively employed in a large number of applications. We attempted, therefore, to develop a linguistic calculus 'fuzzy calculus' which should be applicable to various sorts of systems. The present book is concerned with many facets of fuzzy sets in fuzzy relational database systems in this genuine sense. There are not so many books devoted to this kind, and anyone who has spent time in even an excellent industrial or university library can verify the problem.

The main purpose of this book is to provide a sound exposition of the basic theoretical and practical aspects involved in fuzzy database systems. It gives the impression that fuzzy set theory should no longer be viewed as a stand-alone island of research, and that is very important for eventually reaching a general consensus among engineers about the relevance and usefulness of this field. Our principal motivation in writing this book has been to collect together many of the ideas which have been devised for implementing a fuzzy database system. Our approach is a pragmatic one, being more concerned with the application and implementation of fuzzy information processing than its theoretical foundation. A key feature of the book is the inclusion of an extended sample database throughout. All the queries and answers related to the sample database are collected at the end of the book as an appendix. The reader may find it helpful to refer it from time to time in order to supplement his understanding of the precise meaning of some concepts.

This book may be considered as an extension of the treatment of the subject recorded in a previous book entitled 'A PROLOG Database System' by Deyi Li, to cover additional aspects. It concentrates on fuzzy information processing by surveying the means of analysing fuzzy data and appraising their potential advantages and possible defects in implementation. In this respect the book should be useful in particular to anyone involved in planning, designing and implementing fuzzy database systems. For students in computer science and related disciplines, this book may serve as a supplementary textbook. Due to the potential impact of fuzzy relational database technique on a variety of disciplines, this book may be of interest to a diverse range of readers, including artificial intelligence researchers, knowledge engineers, data analysts and linguists.

Finally, we would like to thank Dr. P. Foulk and Ms. V. A. Wallace for editing the book. We also owe a debt of gratitute to Prof. M. M. Gupta for writing an excellent foreword. We acknowledge the support and access to technical facility provided by the Beijing Astronomical Observatory, Chinese Academy of Sciences. We cannot omit from this preface our indebtedness to Prof. Yanyu Xiang, Ms. Ziqin Lou, Ms. Tingyu Gong and Ms. Lei Zhang for their assistance in preparing the book.

October, 1989   Deyi Li
                                                        Dongbo Liu

Table of Contents

CHAPTER 3   FUZZY LOGIC PROGRAMMING WITH PROLOG

CHAPTER 4   FUZZY RELATIONAL DATABASES

CHAPTER 5   A FUZZY RELATIONAL QUERY LANGUAGE—FSQL

CHAPTER 6   THE OPERATIONS ON
FUZZY RELATIONAL DATABASES

Chapter 1

INTRODUCTION

1.1 Uncertainty, Probability and Possibility

Most of our tools now available for formal modelling, reasoning, and computing in computer engineering are precise, deterministic and complete in character. In conventional database systems and binary logic, for instance, a piece of information or a statement can be true or false—and nothing in between. The 'exact' science plays an important role. Parameters of a model represent exactly either our perception of the phenomenon modelled or the features of the real system that has been modelled. Rigorous demands for numerical precision and measurability of variables and relations produce simplifications, approximations and distortions. Generally precision implies that the model is unequivocal, that is, that it contains no ambiguities. Many well-known decision making methods more and more often demand more exact information than the decision maker has [Holsapple and Whinston, 1987]. Certainty eventually indicates that we assume the structures and parameters of the model to be definitely and totally known, and that there are no doubts about their values, occurrence, and their completeness.

However, situations in real-life application systems are very often not crisp and deterministic and they cannot be described precisely. There is an unavoidable and uncontrollable loss of information and a discrepancy between a model and the reality. In everyday life, we often deal with imprecisely defined properties or quantities by using a fuzzy language. For example, we say:

- Smith is *very young* and *tall*, and his intelligence is *about* average

- John has a temperature *a little above* normal

- *Big* trucks must go *slowly*

- The *smaller* the drink, the *cooler* the blood, the *clearer* the head

- If it is *almost* 5 p.m. then get ready to go home

- Loss in competition *usually* tends to arouse anger

- It takes a *moderately high* level of education to earn a *high* income

- Having a *bad* cough, a *high* temperature and feeling *lifeless* gives a *likely* diagnosis of having flu

In natural language we find numerous quantifiers (e.g., *many, few, most, some, nearly all*, etc.) which are used effectively by human beings when conveying vague information. They are also important for the reasoning in soft sciences. In many cases it is not useful nor even possible to make such statements more precise by trying to extract a numerical percentage. The complete simulation of a real system often would require far more detailed data than a human being could ever recognize, process and understand simultaneously. The so-called exact solution is not exact at all, but in fact represents an idealized special case which never arises in nature. The uncertainty handling approach, on the other hand, far from being a poor substitute for exactness, is the method which most nearly represents physical reality. It includes the deterministic result as a special case. Furthermore, as the complexity of a system increases, our ability to make precise and yet significant statements about its behaviour diminishes until a threshold is reached beyond which precision and significance (or relevance) become almost mutually exclusive characteristics. Problem solving and decision making by humans is often done in environments where information concerning the problem is partial or approximate. For example, a baby can recognize his/her mother easily without the exact measurement of the mother's face or appearance. Almost all doctors diagnose diseases with fuzzy characteristics. It is usually true that much human knowledge is neither totally certain nor totally consistent. Here we argue that uncertainty, imprecision, and incompleteness are not simply "necessary evils" or unfortunate predicaments which are to be overcome and controlled by mathematical transformations. As a matter of fact, for many purposes, an approximate characterization of a collection of data is sufficient because most of the basic tasks performed by humans do not require a high degree of precision in their execution. The human brain takes advantage of this tolerance for imprecision by encoding the "task-relevant" information into labels of fuzzy sets which bear an approximate relation to the primary data. In this way, the stream of information reaching the brain via the visual, auditory, tactile and other senses is eventually reduced to the trickle that is needed to perform a specified task with a minimal degree of precision. For example, on the basis of general knowledge of the characteristic age profile of recent M.Sc. graduates, if we know:

> Mary *recently* obtained her M.Sc. degree

then we may conclude:

> Mary is *probably young.*

The inference involves some fuzzy representations such as recently, probably, but we are quite comfortable about that. Thus, the ability to manipulate fuzzy sets and the consequent summarizing capability constitute one of the most important assets of the human mind as well as a fundamental characteristic that distinguishes human intelligence from the type of machine intelligence that is embodied in current computers.

In some cases a scientific model containing fuzzy predicates is much better than a corresponding model containing only crisp predicates. The former can be sometimes a step towards greater precision. Uncertainty, imprecision and incompleteness are indispensable and fundamentally positive valuable human "inventions" which make the spontaneity, autonomy, self-coordination and self-management of systems possible. One can easily see that the use of terms which are usually considered vague or fuzzy can yield a relatively precise sentence, while the intrusion of terms usually considered standard examples of precision—like predicates containing numerical parameters—can cause a higher degree of fuzziness. Consider the following two examples:

(a) Lewis ran fast during the latter part of the race.
(b) Lewis ran at an average speed exceeding 24.413 km/h during the latter part of the race.

We can reasonably understand and give a truth value to the first sentence, while the pairing of "at an average speed exceeding 24.413 km/h" and of "during the latter part of the race" makes it much harder to evaluate the import of the second one.

It is now appropriate to discuss the types of situations in which fuzzy concepts arise in engineering. The examples presented here emphasize situations that arise in system studies, but they also serve to illustrate the essential point that engineering applications of fuzziness tend to be the rule rather than the exception.

Artificial intelligence researchers have been attempting to simulate this capability in information processing [Gupta and Sanchez, 1982; Malvache and Willaeys, 1981] and knowledge engineering [Prade and Negoita, 1986; Kanal and Lemmer, 1986]. During the last two decades one has become more and more aware of the fact that not all this uncertainty, imprecision and incompleteness can be modelled appropriately by the computer. It is very difficult and sometimes tedious to do everything with a binary system. This becomes more obvious the more we want to represent human knowledge formally. Human thinking is not always—perhaps rarely even—binary. It is subtle, not necessarily as mechanical as George Boole had in mind. Otherwise we would be simple or complex robots. Fortunately natrue has endowed man with imagination.

On the other hand, computing machinery is much more efficient at information processing than man. In order to use this advantage, together with the superior knowledge of human experts to the benefit of mankind, we must be able to communicate conveniently with such machines and set up various theories and approaches which are suitable to them in dealing with imprecision, uncertainty and incompleteness.

As far as uncertain data are concerned, there exist two main kinds of uncertainty, $i.e.$, randomness and fuzziness, in daily life, such as in medicine and in psychology, especially in the soft sciences. Randomness is the uncertainty concerned with the uncertain relationship between cause and effect, while fuzziness is the uncertainty concerned with an object's uncrisp boundary and vague character. It reflects that class of objects in which the transition from membership to non-membership is gradual rather than abrupt. Indeed, the pervasiveness of fuzziness in human thought processes suggests that much of the logic behind human reasoning is not the traditional two-valued or even multivalued logic, but a logic with fuzzy truths, fuzzy connectives, and fuzzy rules of inference. Probability theory [Kalbfleisch, 1985] is the fundamental tool for observing randomness while possibility theory is used to study fuzziness.

Some people claim that probability theory is the only correct way of dealing with uncertainty and that anything that can be done with other techniques can be done equally well through the application of probability theory. Some others dissent from this view. What we believe to be the case is that classical probability theory is insufficiently expressive to cope with the multiplicity of kinds of uncertainty which one encounters in computer engineering and artificial intelligence.

Probability theory is based on classical binary logic. This means that all predicates and concepts in probability theory have certainty, i.e. any object x in the sample space is either an instance of a predicate or it is not. As a case in point, consider one of the most basic concepts in probability theory—the concept of an event. An event, E, considered as a measurable subset of the sample space, either occurs or does not occur; it cannot occur to a degree. This restriction rules out events defined by fuzzy predicates, fuzzy quantifiers, *etc.* In addition to its inability to represent the meaning of fuzzy facts and rules, classical probability theory has no facilities for inference from fuzzy premises.

Since L. A. Zadeh proposed the concept of a fuzzy set in 1965, the relationships between probability and possibility have been discussed. They seem to be similar in the sense that they both use the interval for their measurements as the range of their respective functions. The comparison between probability and possibility is difficult primarily for two reasons: on one hand, there are certain formal similarities between fuzzy set theory and probability theory; on the other hand, probabilities have been the only means for expressing "uncertainty" in the past. Therefore, it seems appropriate and helpful to shed some more light on this question.

For a long time, probability theory was the only well-established approach employed for handling uncertainty.

A probability measure M is a function from P to $[0, 1]$ such that

(1) $M(F) = 0$,   where F is the false proposition ($F \in P$).

(2) $M(T) = 1$,   where T is the true proposition ($T \in P$).

(3)   If $p \in P$, $q \in P$,   then $M(p \vee q) = M(p) + M(q)$.

These axioms have the following consequences:

- For any $p \in P$, $M(p) + M(\neg p) = 1$

- If p implies q (*i.e.* $p \to q = T$), then $M(q) \geq M(p)$.

In applications, probabilities are usually interpreted as objective physical constants which may be measured, or estimated, by repetitions of experiments. Some examples of experiments are: tossing a coin, rolling a dice, observing whether a certain telephone subscriber places a call during a one-minute interval, recording the number of hours of life of a television set. The essential features of such experiments are that they have more than one possible outcome, and they may be considered repeatable. Of course, repeating the experiment will not necessarily result in repeating the outcome. The second toss of the coin may produce tails whereas the first toss resulted in heads, but each possible outcome is crisp. Although we can never determine the exact value of a probability, we can obtain it as accurately as we wish by repeating the experiment sufficiently often. Probability theory is the fundamental tool for observing randomness, and much work has been done using the theory of probability for reasoning under uncertainty.

The appearance of alternative approaches, such as certainty theory [Short-liffe, 1976], Dempster/Schafer theory of evidence [Schafer, 1976], or plausibility theory [Rescher, 1976], especially Zadeh's possibility theory [Zadeh, 1978(a)] has introduced new points of view on uncertainty. Possibility theory is based on Zadeh's earlier work on fuzzy sets. For a given frame of discernment a possibility distribution may be defined in a way very similar to that of a probability distribution. But there is a qualitative difference between the probability and possibility of an event which will be illustrated by an example given later.

In general, the primary distinction between the two different uncertainties—probability and possibility—are as follows:

1. Probability theory is based on classical binary logic, *i.e.* an event, E, considered as a measurable subset of the sample space, either occurs or

does not occur; it cannot occur to a degree. Possibility theory is based on fuzzy logic, namely, an element can belong to a fuzzy set with a degree of membership.

2. In applications, probabilities are usually objective physical constants. A frequential interpretation on probability is used to estimate the frequency of the outcome of a random event. However, the possibility of class membership comes from the definition of the class and is not directly related to any notion of "frequency of occurrence". Possibilities are used to measure personal or subjective belief in a fuzzy set or proposition.

3. Probability corresponds to "what may happen"; possibility corresponds to "what can be done".

4. Probability theory is used to observe randomn phenomena; possibility theory is a tool for studying fuzziness. More specifically, probability theory does not provide a general computational system for representing the meaning of fuzzy propositions containing fuzzy predicates, fuzzy quantifiers, and fuzzy probabilities [Zadeh, 1984; Negoita, 1987], and does not provide a general computational system for inference from fuzzy propositions, whereas possibility theory does.

On the other hand, the two different kinds of uncertainty—probability and possibility—have some things in common:

1. Both probability and possibility are concerned with some type of uncertainty and both use the [0, 1] interval for their measurements of the range of their respective functions.

2. Probability and possibility are both relative to a certain frame of reference directly or indirectly.

3. The intuitive concept that possibility is a quantitative mathematical concept analogous to probability. A high degree of probability always implies a high degree of possibility, but not the converse, i.e. a high degree of possibility does not imply a high degree of probability, nor does a low degree of probability imply a low degree of possibility. However, if an event is impossible, it is bound to be improbable.

To illustrate the difference between probability and possibility more specifically, an example is presented below.

Consider the statement "Hans ate X eggs for breakfast," with X taking values in $U = \{1, 2, 3, \ldots\}$. We may associate a possibility distribution with X by interpreting $\Pi_X(u)$ as the degree of ease with which Hans eats u eggs. We may also associate a probability distribution with X by interpreting $P_X(u)$ as the probability of Hans eating u eggs for breakfast. Assuming that we employ some explicit or implicit criterion for assessing the degree of ease with which Hans can eat u eggs for breakfast, the values of $\Pi_X(u)$ and $P_X(u)$ might be as shown in Figure 1–1.

u	1	2	3	4	5	6	7	8
$\Pi_X(u)$	1	1	1	1	0.8	0.6	0.4	0.2
$P_X(u)$	0.1	0.8	0.1	0	0	0	0	0

Figure 1–1 The Possibility and Probability
Distributions Associated With X

We observe that whereas the possibility that Hans may eat 3 eggs for breakfast is 1, the probability that he may do so might be quite small, *e.g.* 0.1. Thus, a high degree of possibility does not imply a high degree of probability, nor does a low degree of probability imply a low degree of possibility. However, an impossible event must also be improbable.

In fact, we have to distinguish between, on the one hand "It is possible for Hans to eat four eggs for breakfast" and on the other hand "It is probable that Hans eats three eggs for breakfast". The first example deals with Hans' ability and the second one with what may actually happen. It must be clear that what may happen can be done—but not *vice versa*. Thus, in this example, Hans is definitely able to eat four eggs for breakfast, although it has never happened. The values are complementary information to the frequency histogram of the number of eggs Hans ate for breakfast which tells us about Hans' actual behaviour.

This heuristic connection between possibilities and probabilities may be stated in the form of what might be called the possibility/probability consistency principle [Zadeh, 1978(a)]. It plays a particularly important role in decision making under uncertainty.

The intuitive concepts of probability and possibility play a central role in human decision making and underlie much of the human ability to reason in approximate terms. The crucial requirement is for the characterization of what we shall understand by "a fuzzy event has occurred". For instance, what is the probability/possibility of a warm day tomorrow? Consequently, it is essential to develop a better understanding of the interplay between probability and possibility—especially in relation to the roles which these concepts play in natural languages—in order to enhance our ability to develop machines which can simulate the remarkable human ability to attain imprecisely defined goals in a fuzzy environment.

1.2 Real Databases Are Fuzzy Systems

The initial applications of computers were in the exact sciences and corporate commercial areas such as accountancy. The emergence of database technology as a distinct applied science of computing during the past two decades is one of the most significant features of the transition in computer applications. Computers were extensively used for building powerful, integrated database systems, since Codd proposed the relational model in 1970. The technology of database systems has its theoretical foundations, and has been tried in a large number of applications. It has become the foundation of information processing and even knowledge processing.

Conventional database systems can only deal with "ideal" data. In such database systems, most processing assumes that the information represented is exact, correct, well-formulated, with no provisions for considering otherwise. In addition, the answer to a query must definitely be either this or that.

In the real world, however, there exist a great deal of uncertain or vague data, which can never be formulated in certain and well-defined form. In fact, complexity in systems stems from too large a size and the difficulty in gathering precise information or data to describe their behaviour. In many cases, information is found naturally to be imprecise or fuzzy as when representing personalities, physical features of individuals and subjective opinions and judgements in situations such as medical decision making, economic forecasting and personal evaluations. In addition, even when quantitative information is available, this precision can give rise to too great a restriction to facilitate qualitative comparisons. The required reliability of a product cannot be given in precise terms. If this is done then designs which almost satisfy the reliability constraint and which satisfy very well other conflicting constraints will not be chosen. A fuzzy boundary exists between designs which satisfy and those which do not satisfy any particular design constraint. Most likely no design will satisfy all constraints and the final design will lie in the fuzzy region of satisfactory performance. For example, instead of specifying a person's salary as $4505 per month, one may specify it as "about $4500 per month", or "a fairly good salary". All these are informative statements that would be useful in answering queries or making inferences dependent on the salary, but they are a different form of data than is normally considered in relational database literature. Hence the requirements of queries in vague statements arise frequently.

Viewed as above, the conventional quantitative techniques of the database are intrinsically unsuited for dealing with humanistic systems since they fail to come to grips with the reality of the fuzziness of human thinking and behaviour. Therefore, to handle such database systems realistically, we need a way which does not make a fetish of precision and mathematical formalism, and which employs instead a model which is tolerant of fuzzy and partial truths.

In order to bridge the gap between classical relational databases and real databases, a lot of research has been devoted to improve the interaction between databases and users. Keeping in mind user orientation and practical application, the best way, however, is to incorporate the fuzzy relations and fuzzy attribute values into database systems, and allow natural linguistic values in the queries, because the ability to summarize information finds its highest manifestation in the use of natural languages by humans.

The linguistic technology enables us to take a core of basically algebraic interactions between people and database systems and coat it with the sugar of the English language. It should help the user to retrieve relevant information relatively easily and use it effectively and efficiently. Actually the significance of this goes far beyond the sweetening of the naive user's pill. It is far easier for us to see the weaknesses of current systems when they appear as the lack of power to interpret "obvious" English constructions than as algebraic/logical weaknesses. Indeed, since algebraicists and logicians have never come anywhere near expressing the range and variety of semantic structure and reasoning patterns exhibited by people, it would be surprising if an approach based on classical formal structures did not give a mis-match to what people actually require.

The human brain might be thought of as an extremely complex database which contains fuzzy and incomplete data as its attribute values. In addition, various learning strategies can update this database with experience. This particular modelling concept is relevant to scientific, technological, medical, political and economic fields and even to daily life itself. Decisions are made by analysing pre-selected rules. This analysis takes account of various forms of uncertainty and conflicting goals and necessarily includes fuzzy reasoning to avoid high dimensional computational problems. In our view, fuzzy logic plays a basic role in what may well be one of the most important facts of human thinking, namely, the ability to summarize information—to extract from the collections of masses of data impinging upon the human brain those and only those subcollections which are relevant to the performance of the task at hand.

Since in everyday life we often make decisions based on such fuzzy and even incomplete data, particularly for macroscopic decision makers, the formulation and construction of a database which can represent and manipulate fuzzy data will increase the application areas of database systems and improve the interface between men and machines. There is little doubt that the soft sciences require formal and even mathematical frameworks for handling graded categories with vague boundaries. Not only are the phenomena of human thought and behaviour inherently fuzzy, but researchers in these fields must use concepts and theoretical schema which themselves are fuzzy. Natural language allows vague terms and concepts. Far from being a difficulty, fuzziness is often a convenience. The theory of fuzziology may well have a substantial impact on scientific methodology, particularly in the areas of knowledge engineering and soft sciences. It may benefit these fields in at least three ways:

(1)   by providing the basis for 'translatable' statistical techniques;

(2)   by linking qualitative with quantitative concepts and techniques;

(3)   as an aid to conceptualization and theory construction.

1.3 Background of Setting up a Fuzzy Database System

The subject of information processing and decision making, especially using the data arising from human thought and the cognition process, has occupied a prominent place in modern science and technology.

The rapid expansion of relational databases, both in theory and technology, provided a fundamental mechanism for information-processing and decision support systems. Codd's relational model generalized and made far more flexible the forms of data structure and retrieval specification allowed. It is now widely used throughout the world. We may think of database technology as the beginning of a process whereby the computer, as a powerful information processing "engine", begins to be given access to information structures that are of significance to us.

However, available implementations of conventional relational databases are in terms of hard, static and deterministic relations, whereas in real-world applications data are often imprecise, inherently dynamic and non-deterministic. Many well-known database design methods often demand more information than the database owner has. It then becomes necessary to change such methods and make them appropriate for using qualitative information.

Fortunately, as a new and developing subject, fuzziology, particularly fuzzy set theory, has been vigorously studied. The concept of fuzziness and the theory of fuzzy sets proposed by Zadeh have been the object of increasing attention as potential mathematical tools for representing and manipulating imprecise information. They are being studied widely and applied to various fields such as pattern recognition, decision making, natural language processing, question-answering, artificial intelligence, *etc.*, where fuzzy data play an important role.

Roughly speaking, fuzzy set theory in the last two decades has developed along two lines. First, as a formal theory which, as it matured, became more sophisticated and better specified and which was enlarged by original ideas and concepts by "embracing" classical mathematical areas such as algebra, graph theory, topology, and so on, by generalizing or fuzzifying them. Secondly, as a very powerful modelling language, which can cope with a large fraction of the uncertainties of real life situations. Because of its generality it can be adapted well to different circumstances and contexts. In many cases this will mean, however, the context-dependent modification and specification of the original

12

concepts of the formal fuzzy set theory. Regrettably this adaptation has not yet progressed to a satisfactory level, leaving an abundance of challenges for the ambitious researcher and practitioner.

In fact, many basic problems involved in fuzziology have not been solved properly:

- As a new development, the theoretical system of fuzziology, even fuzzy set theory itself, has not been formed as completely as classical theories. So it is unable to cast off the trammels of the theory of classical mathematics completely.

- The notion of degrees of membership and membership functions is obviously the cornerstone of fuzziology. Unfortunately, we lack a truly generalizable method for measuring grades of membership. The essence of membership functions, how to concretely define membership functions, and the significance of fuzzy operations, *etc.*, have not been studied satisfactorily so far. That is why there are still many difficulties in the concrete applications of fuzziology.

- **min–max** operators, for the theory of fuzzy sets, were suggested by Zadeh. They are, however, not the only possible way to extend classical set theory consistently, and it seemes that the **min–max** operators are not always appropriate in an application field. For this reason, other operators [Dubois and Prade, 1980; Silvert, 1979; Yager, 1980; Giles, 1976; Hamacher, 1978] have been suggested. These suggestions vary with respect to the generality or adaptability of the operators as well as to the degree to which and how they are justified. However, this is still an unsolved problem in fuzziology.

Recently, the evolution in database technology has been moving towards the use of logic. Some researchers [Baldwin and Zhou, 1984; Buckles and Petry, 1982(a)(b); Raiu and Majumdar, 1987; Umano, 1982] have examined database theory in the light of fuzzy logic with the objective to accommodate a wider range of real world requirements and to provide closer man-machine interaction. Zadeh has extended classical relational algebra operators such as join, projection, *etc.* to fuzzy relations [Zadeh, 1978(b)].

Artificial intelligence (AI) is an emerging technology that has recently attracted considerable publicity. Many applications are now under development.

A simple view of AI is that it is concerned with devising computer programs to make computers smarter. Thus, research in AI is focused on developing computational approaches to intelligent behaviour. This research will make computers more useful, inherently understanding intelligence.

Knowledge engineering is one of the most advanced subfields in AI research. It is a discipline devoted to integrating human knowledge in computer systems. A knowledge-based system is an information system that can pose and answer questions relating to information borrowed from human experts and stored in the system's knowledge base. The fact that answers are extracted automatically from the data descriptions, by a user-invisible inference procedure, results in a great degree of data independence. Not only can users represent data in a high-level, human-oriented manner, but they are also spared the effort of describing the operations used to retrieve those data.

Because the knowledge base in such a system is put there by human experts, and because much human knowledge is imprecise, uncertain, and incomplete, it is usually the case that facts and rules are neither totally certain nor totally consistent. For this reason, a basic issue in the design of knowledge-based systems is how to equip them with a computational capability for the treatment of vagueness and uncertainty.

A promising approach is based on fuzzy logic and fuzzy reasoning. A variety of models of fuzzy logic, which propose a logical treatment of vagueness or uncertainty, have been used, such as Zadeh's fuzzy linguistic logic [Zadeh, 1975(a)(b)], Lee's fuzzy logic [Lee, 1972], and some of others [Liu and Li, 1988(a); Baldwin, 1979]. Fuzzy logic is a generalization of classical binary logic, in which the truth values are not only true, represented by 1, and false, represented by 0, but a continuous interval $[0, 1]$.

An obvious advantage of the fuzzy logic approach is the possibility of representing numeric and linguistic variables in a uniform way and of using a sound formalism to handle them.

The purpose of knowledge representation is to organize required information into a form such that the AI program can readily access it for making decisions, recognizing objects and situations, analyzing scenes, drawing conclusions, and other cognitive functions. Thus knowledge representation is especially central to knowledge-based systems.

14

The treatment of fuzziness, however, is a critical issue in knowledge representation. To say that a word is fuzzy is to say that sometimes there is no definite answer as to whether or not the word applies to something. The indeterminacy is due to an aspect of the meaning of the word rather than to the state of our knowledge. In all expert systems based on semantic manipulation and approximate reasoning, the emphasis is on fuzziness viewed as an intrinsic property of natural language.

In recent years there has been a range of developments concerned with representing and using data that can be only represented in the *softer* terms. Some of the work has been explicitly concerned with database systems, but much of it, whilst highly relevant, has been in other application areas.

Many scientists, mathematicians, and social scientists have contributed to the progress of the subjects mentioned above. While there has been a rapid expansion in the theoretical development of fuzzy set theory, there has been an equally rapid interest in logic programming and its applications to databases, and even to knowledge bases. However, until now, there has been no book about, or an implementation of, an integrated system, which has a combination of both ideas, particularly from the engineering viewpoint.

This book is solely concerned with the application of fuzzy logic and fuzzy reasoning to relational databases, and with its use in knowledge engineering, decision support systems, and so on. It is our hope that this book will demonstrate the usefulness of applying fuzzy set theory and a fuzzy logic programming language in databases and knowledge engineering for coping with vagueness and uncertainty.

1.4   Objectives and Benefits of the FPDB System

If research is to be worthwhile, it must be directed toward the discovery of general principles, which can then be translated into the specifics of particular system design. This demand is the general basis of this work. Every effort has been made to balance theory and practice.

We list below some more detailed objectives for the project.

The primary objective is to show, through illustrations, what can be incorporated into relational database systems to allow for a wider range of real-world requirements and closer human-computer interaction.

In order to illustrate the project from all sides, and therefore form an integrated system, a fuzzy intelligent relational database system is created, which is entirely implemented in the fuzzy logic programming language f-PROLOG, and provides a user-friendly query language FSQL. It is important for the reader to know that the whole book has been written under the pragmatical spirit of looking at the Fuzzy PROLOG Database (FPDB) primarily as a tool. The material will be of direct interest to engineers who are involved in research and development. We pay much attention to the foundations, principles, implementations and engineering applications of FPDB. Throughout the book we have demonstrated each new idea by examples in a particular environment. Only by solving a large number of queries can the reader be expected to develop an understanding of the basic concepts of fuzzy PROLOG relational database systems. The complex calculations of mathematical formulae, however, have not been concentrated upon. Topics which are of high mathematical interest but which require a very solid mathematical background and those which are not of obvious applicational relevance are not discussed.

The FPDB model can be seen as the generalization of conventional relational model proposed by Codd, which allows the fuzzy linguistic attribute values and consequently provides a link between quality and quantity.

Qualitatively oriented researchers are fond of castigating quantitative researchers for their inability to translate sophisticated theories of human behaviour convincingly into mathematical form, while quantitative proponents berate "anti-positivists" for the vagueness of their concepts and techniques.

Essentially, our contention is that the traditional quantitative methods are intrinsically unsuited for dealing with complex systems such as humanistic systems. The basis for this contention rests on what might be called the principle of incompatibility.

However, it should be noted that, so far, the great majority of the literature on fuzzy set theory and its applications is highly quantitatively oriented, emphasizing numerical membership values rather than linguistic values, fuzzy set operations that require ratio-scaled membership functions rather than ordinal scales, and generally an "engineering" rather than a "humanistic" approach. While this fact does not necessarily obviate the possibility that fuzzy set applications could reverse those trends, it does mean that many developments in fuzzy set theory and applications cannot be directly used to build bridges between quantitative and qualitative research styles.

We propose a systematic approach in the FPDB system. In such an environment, we can either transform the qualitative into the quantitative and obtain quantitative results with the degree of confidence thereby, or transform the quantitative into the qualitative description to satisfy the needs of macroscopic decision making.

This book is concerned with some of the uncertainties that arise when attempting to make the logic of database systems more closely match that of human practical reasoning. From a database system or an expert system, users often want to know not only whether a thing possesses a certain property or not; if it does, they may be interested to what extent this property is exhibited. Therefore, this project is also an extension of classical two-valued logic. By using fuzzy logic reasoning on the interval $[0, 1]$, the results of manipulation on the FPDB system are no longer merely alternatively "yes" or "no". It may produce the results with the degree of certainty, or evaluate the degree of truth of the results.

The relational query language SQL (Structured Query Language) has become widely used. It consists of a set of facilities for defining, manipulating and controlling data in a relational database. However, available implementations of standard SQL did not incorporate an automated fuzzy inference mechanism, whereas in real world applications data are often fuzzy, uncertain and incomplete. For this reason, the conventional SQL language is generalized by the authors in the FPDB system. The new style fuzzy relational query language FSQL is a general query language which can be used as easily as the standard one. It incorporates an automatic fuzzy inference mechanism based on fuzzy relational algebra. In brief, FSQL presents a very natural way for improving the interface essential between man and machine, and thereby satisfies the needs of knowledge engineering and decision support systems.

Database consistency is enforced by integrity constraints which are assertions that database instances are compelled to obey. Data dependencies, including functional dependency, multivalued dependency and join dependency, *etc.*, are special cases of integrity constraints. In the logic design of the FPDB system, fuzzy functional dependencies play a crucial role. They are given as part of the structure of the model, that is, they are specified by the database designer, based on the semantics of the attributes. For conventional relational databases, the existing dependencies are clear once one has an understanding of the attributes. Sometimes the process of identifying them is not straightforward for fuzzy relational databases.

Fortunately for fuzzy relations in the FPDB system, the concept of particularization proposed by Zadeh can be used to deal with fuzzy data constraints. In this book, a useful approach is presented by the authors in the light of Zadeh's possibility theory.

For various reasons, the information contained in a real-world database is usually incomplete. Something may be undecided, while something else may be undefined. This creates a need for developing methods to handle situations where a database does not contain all the information a user would like to know.

In the FPDB system, the idea of incomplete information has been captured by the use of a value called NULL, even taking a further step to divide the incomplete attribute value into three types: UNDECIDED, UNDEFINED and NULL.

In addition, linguistic operators of fuzzification (fuzzifiers), such as *about*, *very, much, fairly, slightly, more or less*, etc., make it possible to modify the meaning of atomic as well as composite terms and thus serve to increase the range of values of a linguistic varlable. Taking the point of view described by Zadeh, a reasonable finite set of fuzzifiers is allowed in the FPDB system. Each fuzzifier may be regarded as an operator which transforms a fuzzy set into a new fuzzy set. Furthermore, the fuzzifier serves the function of generating a larger set of values for a linguistic variable from a small collection of primary terms. To define a fuzzifier as an operator, it is convenient to employ some of the operations, such as concentration, dilation, fuzzification, and so on.

Finally, the FPDB system provides high flexibility and high expediency to the designer and user, and enables him to define fuzzy sets to his personal needs in different situations.

It is widely predicted that Knowledge Engineering will be a major area of computer applications in the 1990's, where expert systems and decision support systems will play a central computing role. Along this line, the foundation of

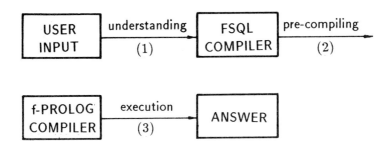

Figure 1-2 Query Modification

this work is to combine concepts from the principal research fields of computer science and engineering: Artificial Intelligence (AI) and Fuzzy Logic Programming (FLP), and Fuzzy Relational Data Base Systems (FRDBSs). From AI and FLP we use the concept of fuzzy set theory, and the concept of knowledge representation in deductive question-answering systems, and the concept of first order predicate calculus; from FRDBS we build on the concept of a fuzzy relational database. These ideas are married to form a fuzzy intelligent relational database system, yielding a novel and powerful collection of facilities in the system-user interface, and giving great benefits in reduced cost and increased flexibility of implementation and application.

1.5 The System Design Outline

These considerations led us to develop a database system entirely implemented in fuzzy PROLOG. The fuzzy relational model is described for representing and manipulating uncertain, fuzzy or even incomplete information. A fuzzy relational inference language FSQL is also implemented in fuzzy PROLOG.

The FPDB system has been entirely implemented in f-PROLOG, a fuzzy PROLOG language, on a VAX-11/780, under the operating system VAX/VMS. It processes a query in three main stages (see Figure 1-2).

Figure 1-2 gives a general overview of the information processing in FPDB, and corresponds roughly to:

(1) What does the query mean?—An intuitive understanding of the problem which may involve uncertainty.

(2) How shall I answer it?—Uncertainty handling and query optimization.

(3) What is the answer?—Execution in f-PROLOG to produce a user-friendly result.

This book can be considered as a sister book of the one entitled "*A PROLOG Database System*" [Li, 1984] in the sense that PROLOG is extended to fuzzy PROLOG, and relational databases are extended to fuzzy and incomplete ones.

In Chapter 2 the theory of fuzzy sets, which are the foundations of the forthcoming chapter, is defined and explained in detail. It provides a comprehensive and clearly presented introduction to the theory. Chapter 3 presents a fuzzy logic programming language—f-PROLOG—which allows inference under uncertainty and incompleteness in addition to the purely deductive reasoning process of PROLOG. The relation between fuzzy logic and two-valued logic in the context of first order predicate calculus is discussed. Chapter 4 contains definitions of the basic notions of a fuzzy relational model and provides the general framework for the development of fuzzy relational database systems. The chapter ends with a basic fuzzy database example which will be used extensively and constructively in the following chapters. By introducing the fuzzy structured query language FSQL, in Chapter 5, the fuzzy query patterns can be set up. Chapter 6 is devoted to all the different operations on fuzzy relational databases. Throughout this chapter we have demonstrated each new idea by query examples in a particular environment. The use of fuzzy logic as a single tool for formalizing and implementing different aspects of such a fuzzy database in a uniform manner is discussed in Chapter 7. An experimental FSQL query compiler, implemented in f-PROLOG, is presented as an illustration of these concepts. Chapter 8 has a discussion of handling incomplete information in the FPDB system. Also included here is a treatment of soft integrity constraints. Applications of the FPDB model in knowledge representation, decision making, expert systems, fuzzy control, fuzzy clustering and so on are suggested in Chapter 9. Finally we conclude our approach, together with future work, in Chapter 10.

Chapter 2

FUZZY SET THEORY

In Chapter 2, basic definitions of fuzzy sets and algebraic operations are introduced. Some fundamental concepts of fuzzy set theory are discussed including membership functions, and operations on fuzzy sets. The nature and properties of membership functions, and the significance of operations on membership functions are investigated. We eventually focus on the digital characteristics of possibility distributions. The formal framework of fuzzy mathematics developed in this chapter will serve for the foundations of fuzzy relational database systems throughout the book. We first review some basic concepts of classical set theory.

2.1 Classical Set Theory and Its Limitations

The foundations of classical mathematics are laid in the theory of sets, and since the beginning of this century mathematicians have investigated the basic assumptions that have to be made about sets (*i.e.* axioms) and the ways in which all of mathematics can be built upon these assumptions. The advantage of reviewing the classical theory of sets lies in providing an opportunity to criticise it and illustrate its primary limitations.

In classical set theory, a set is defined normally as a collection of objects, which can be finite, countable, or uncountable. Each single object can either belong to or not belong to a set A, $A \in \Omega$ (Ω is the universe of discourse). In the former case, the statement "x belongs to A" is *true*, whereas, in the latter case, this statement is *false*. Usually, an object x, which belongs to a set A, is called an element of the set A. A set which includes no element is called an **empty set**, denoted by $\emptyset$, whereas a set including all elements of the universe of discourse is called a **complete set** denoted by Ω.

Such a classical set can be described in different ways; one can enumerate the elements that belong to the set, for instance

$$N = \{1, 2, 3, \ldots\}$$

one can describe the set A analytically, by stating a property or condition $P(x)$ for membership, hence

$$A = \{x|P(x)\}$$

for example,

$$A = \{x|x^2 - 4 = 0\} = \{-2, 2\}.$$

One can also define the member elements by using the so-called characteristic function, in which 1 indicates membership and 0 nonmembership denoted by

$$f_A(x) = \begin{cases} 1, & x \in A; \\ 0, & x \notin A. \end{cases} \tag{2.1}$$

where, (2.1) implies such an assumption: for any element x and a set A, either $x \in A$, or $x \notin A$, one and only one of them must be *true*.

The alternative definition of an element x belonging to a set A or not is the scientific abstraction of membership among crisp objects. A class of crisp objects is a classical set.

Given sets A and B, A is called a subset of B denoted by

$$A \subseteq B \quad \textbf{or} \quad B \supseteq A$$

If, for all x, $x \in A$, then $x \in B$ (see Figure 2–1).

Given sets A and B, we say that A is equivalent to B, denoted by $A = B$, if $A \subseteq B$ **and** $B \subseteq A$.

Using the symbols $\wedge$ for **and**, $\vee$ for **or** and for **not**, we have

$$\emptyset = \{x|P(x) \wedge \overline{P(x)}\} \tag{2.2}$$

and

$$\emptyset \subseteq A \subseteq \Omega$$

22

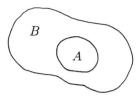

Figure 2–1 $A \subseteq B$

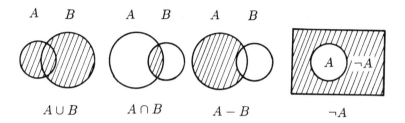

Figure 2–2 Some Operations on Classical Sets

Given sets A and B, the **intersection** of A and B, denoted by $A \cap B$, is

$$A \cap B = \{x | x \in A \wedge x \in B\} \qquad (2.3)$$

the **union** of A and B, denoted by $A \cup B$, is

$$A \cup B = \{x | x \in A \vee x \in B\} \qquad (2.4)$$

the **difference** of A and B, denoted by $A - B$, is

$$A - B = \{x | x \in A \wedge x \notin B\} \qquad (2.5)$$

the **complement** of A, denoted by $\neg A$ is

$$\neg A = \Omega - A = \{x | x \in \Omega \wedge x \notin A\} \qquad (2.6)$$

Figure 2–2 illustrates these operations.

In classical set theory, the following properties follow from the definitions of **union, intersection** and **complementation.**

Idempotency

$$A \cup A = A \qquad (2.7)$$

$$A \cap A = A \qquad (2.8)$$

Commutativity

$$A \cup B = B \cup A \qquad (2.9)$$

$$A \cap B = B \cap A \qquad (2.10)$$

Associativity

$$(A \cup B) \cup C = A \cup (B \cup C) \qquad (2.11)$$

$$(A \cap B) \cap C = A \cap (B \cap C) \qquad (2.12)$$

Distributivity

$$A \cup (B \cap C) = (A \cup B) \cap (A \cup C) \qquad (2.13)$$

$$A \cap (B \cup C) = (A \cap B) \cup (A \cap C) \qquad (2.14)$$

Absorption

$$A \cup (A \cap B) = A \qquad (2.15)$$

$$A \cap (A \cup B) = A \qquad (2.16)$$

De Morgan's Laws

$$\neg(A \cup B) = \neg A \cap \neg B \qquad (2.17)$$

$$\neg(A \cap B) = \neg A \cup \neg B \qquad (2.18)$$

Involution

$$\neg(\neg A) \;=\; A \qquad\qquad (2.19)$$

Complementation

$$A \cup \neg A \;=\; \Omega \qquad\qquad (2.20)$$
$$A \cap \neg A \;=\; \emptyset \qquad\qquad (2.21)$$

$$A \cup \Omega \;=\; \Omega \qquad\qquad (2.22)$$
$$A \cap \Omega \;=\; A \qquad\qquad (2.23)$$

$$A \cup \emptyset \;=\; A \qquad\qquad (2.24)$$
$$A \cap \emptyset \;=\; \emptyset \qquad\qquad (2.25)$$

As a mathematical model, classical set theory is a basic tool for describing crisp objects precisely. It is due to this assumption, however, that classical set theory cannot be used to describe fuzzy objects.

First of all, to use classical set theory to treat fuzzy objects, particularly in human sciences, one has to simplify the problem and draw demarcation lines artificially among objects which originally have no such distinct lines. Hence the inherent fuzzy characters of objects are lost. For example, ordinarily we do not distinguish sharply between the meaning of the word city and that of the word town, but for statistical purposes the Bureau of the Census must draw a line somewhere, so it draws it at 25000. If a child is born in a town of 24999 people, the town becomes a city. In common usage, we do not draw such a sharp line because we see no justification for it. Artificially drawing demarcation lines is a distortion of the original characters of objective events. Especially near the demarcation lines, the distortion is more obvious. Any attempt to rid our natural language of vagueness is chimerical. An essential characteristic of a vague concept is that the boundaries of the domain of its applicability are not fixed.

Secondly, the parameters of crisp objects can be precisely determined, and exact mathematical models can be formed. However, there is no way to require the necessary precise data in a fuzzy environment, so that its mathematical model cannot be built properly using classical theory. Particularly in humane studies, the measures of objects are often nonnumeric, for "cultural level", "living standard", "political consciousness", "degree of skill", and so on; intrinsically we are not able to measure them as physical entities. Human systems usually include a great many subjective factors with heavy fuzziness. In such situations, conventional precise methods based on classical set theory are not available. In general, conventional mathematics is not a universal method to achieve the quantification of social and human sciences.

Lastly, we would say that, for complex events, precision is usually contradictory to usefulness. For any approach, the precision of results frequently comes at the price of complexity. In complex systems, precision of fuzzy events must reduce artificially the significance of the approach which we use. So, in such situations, classical set theory is almost useless.

To surmount the difficulties, we need a new theory to replace classical set theory.

2.2   Fuzzy Sets

The original interpretation of fuzzy set introduced by Zadeh as a generalization of the classical subset has been applied to the description of imprecise, vague notions. To present an appropriate set description for fuzzy objects, the most important step is to propose a new assumption: for all elements x and a set A, the characteristic function f_A of A allows various degrees of membership for all x, instead of the binary assumption in classical set theory. That is to say that:

(1)   "an element belongs to a set" becomes to a fuzzy concept;
(2)   the concept of membership is quantified.

In other words, the key idea in fuzzy set theory is that an element has a grade of membership in a fuzzy set. Thus a proposition need not be simply *true* or *false*, but may be partly *true* to any degree.

We usually assume $\tilde{A}$ is a fuzzy set in the universe of discourse Ω. For any $x \in \Omega$, the grade of membership μ of x, which definitely belongs to $\tilde{A}$, is 1, whereas the grade of membership μ of x, which does not belong to $\tilde{A}$ absolutely, is 0. Apart from those cases, the grade of membership of x, which partly belongs to $\tilde{A}$, is in the interval $[0,1]$.

The value of the membership function of the fuzzy set $\tilde{A}$, $\mu_{\tilde{A}}(x) \in [0,1]$, is also interpreted in this case as a grade in which an element $x \in \Omega$ has a property $\tilde{A}$, or a grade in which x is consistent to $\tilde{A}$.

Consider the fuzzy set labelled *young*. The elements are men's ages, and their grades of membership depend on their ages. For example, a man who is 50 years old might have degree 0, a man who is 22 years old might have degree 1, and men of intermediate ages might have intermediate grades. Different individuals will have differing opinions as to whether a given man should be described as *young*. A possible representation could be

Age	Grade of membership
20	1.00
25	1.00
26	0.96
28	0.74
30	0.50
35	0.20
40	0.10
50	0.04

According to this representation, the fuzzy set *young* is defined by its domain—the range of values for ages $\{20, 25, 26, 28, 30, 35, 40, 50\}$—and the grades of membership $\{1.00, 0.96, 0.74, 0.50, 0.20, 0.10, 0.04\}$.

In this book, fuzzy sets are denoted by $\tilde{A}$, $\tilde{B}$, $\tilde{C}$ and so on, where "$\sim$" is called the mark of fuzzification.

It is clear that a fuzzy set is an association between objects and decimals, a correspondence that assigns to a given object, one and only one number in the unit interval $[0,1]$. It may be thought of as an evaluation, a subjective evaluation, applied to the objects to obtain grades of membership. Now we introduce the strict definition.

Definition 2.1

A fuzzy set $\tilde{A}$ in a universe of discourse Ω is characterized by the function

$$\mu_{\tilde{A}}(x): \quad \Omega \rightarrow [0,1].$$

$\mu_{\tilde{A}}(x)$ is called the membership function or grade of membership of x in $\tilde{A}$.

The above-mentioned example is symbolized as

$$young: \quad Age \to [0,1].$$

where Age is the domain of $young$, and $[0,1]$ is the codomain or target.

The discussion about fuzzy sets is always made in a universe of discourse Ω, so many authors use fuzzy subsets (of Ω), instead of fuzzy sets. A fuzzy subset of Ω is a function from Ω to $[0,1]$. Note that, when the function can take on only the values 0 and 1, it can be regarded as the characteristic function of a conventional, crisp subset of Ω.

There are different ways of denoting fuzzy sets in the literature:

1. A fuzzy set is denoted by an ordered set of pairs, the first element of which denotes the element and the second the grade of membership.

Example 2.1

Let $\tilde{A}$ be "Real numbers considerably larger than 10", we have

$$\tilde{A} = \{x|x >> 10\} = \{(x, \mu_{\tilde{A}}(x))|x \in \Omega\}.$$

where

$$\mu_{\tilde{A}}(x) = \begin{cases} 0, & x < 10; \\ \left[1 + (x - 10)^{-2}\right]^{-1}, & x \geq 10. \end{cases}$$

2. A fuzzy set is represented solely by stating its membership function.

Example 2.2

Let $\tilde{A}$ be "Real numbers close to 10", we have

$$\tilde{A} = \{(x, \mu_{\tilde{A}}(x))|\mu_{\tilde{A}}(x) = \left[1 + (x - 10)^4 \right]^{-1}\}.$$

See Figure 2–3.

3. For a given finite universe of discourse
$$\Omega = \{x_1, x_2, \ldots, x_n\},$$
a fuzzy set $\tilde{A}$ in Ω is denoted as

$$\tilde{A} = \mu_1/x_1 + \mu_2/x_2 + \cdots + \mu_n/x_n.$$

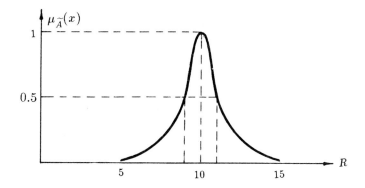

Figure 2–3   Real Numbers Close to 10

where μ_i denote the grade of membership of x_i, $i = 1, 2, \ldots, n$. The elements with a *zero* grade of membership are normally not listed.

Example 2.3

$$\tilde{A} \triangleq \text{"Integers close to 10"}$$

$$\tilde{A} = 0.1/7 + 0.5/8 + 0.8/9 + 1/10 + 0.8/11 + 0.5/12 + 0.1/13.$$

4.   For given infinite universe of discourse Ω, a fuzzy set $\tilde{A}$ in Ω can be denoted in the form of

$$\tilde{A} = \int \mu_{\tilde{A}}(x)/x,$$

where $\mu_{\tilde{A}}(x)$ is the grade of membership of x.

Example 2.4

Let $\Omega = [0, 200]$, and Young and Old, denoted by $\tilde{Y}$ and $\tilde{O}$ respectively, be all fuzzy sets in Ω, we have,

$$\tilde{Y} = \int_{25}^{200} \left[1 + \left(\frac{x-25}{5}\right)^2\right]^{-1} /x.$$
$$\tilde{O} = \int_{50}^{200} \left[1 + \left(\frac{x-50}{5}\right)^{-2}\right]^{-1} /x.$$

A fuzzy set is obviously a generalization of a classical set and the membership function a generalization of the characteristic function. Since we are generally

29

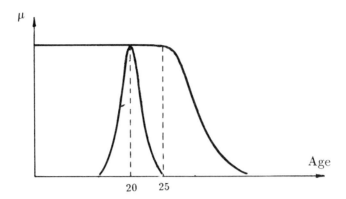

Figure 2–4 The Membership Functions of "young people" and "people with the ages about 20"

referring to a universal set Ω, some elements of a fuzzy set may have the grade of membership *zero*. Often it is appropriate to consider those elements of the universe which have a *nonzero* grade of membership in a fuzzy set.

By the definition of a fuzzy set, we have

(1) $\tilde{A} = \tilde{B}$ **iff** $\forall x \in \Omega,\ \mu_{\tilde{A}}(x) = \mu_{\tilde{B}}(x).$

(2) $\tilde{A} \subseteq \tilde{B}$ **iff** $\forall x \in \Omega,\ \mu_{\tilde{A}}(x) \leq \mu_{\tilde{B}}(x).$

For example, let

$$\widetilde{A_1} \triangleq \text{``young people''},$$
$$\widetilde{A_2} \triangleq \text{``people with the ages about 20''},$$

and $\mu_{\widetilde{A_1}}(x),\ \mu_{\widetilde{A_2}}(x)$, be shown in Figure 2–4, then we have

$$\widetilde{A_2} \subseteq \widetilde{A_1}.$$

See Figure 2–5.

So far, the definition is based on a mathematical universe of discourse. But fuzzy subsets can be defined on a variety of universes. For instance, the fuzzy subset modelling the concept "intelligent" can be defined on a set of individuals:

$$intelligent\ =\ 0.8/John + 0.7/Peter + 0.7/Mary + 0.4/Harry.$$

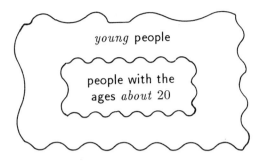

Figure 2–5

In this case, the universe of discourse Ω, may be { *John*, *Peter*, *Harry*, *Mary*, ... }.

As usual, the grade of membership is an assignment of a value in the unit interval to each point in an underlying set: in this case, a set of names, so that we have

$$\mu_{intelligent}(John) \quad = \quad 0.8$$
$$\mu_{intelligent}(Peter) \quad = \quad 0.7$$
$$\mu_{intelligent}(Mary) \quad = \quad 0.7$$
$$\mu_{intelligent}(Harry) \quad = \quad 0.4$$

and so on.

The generalization can go further if the unit interval $[0,1]$ is replaced by a lattice, by an object in a category, by the subobject classifier in a topos, and so on. In the sense of Zadeh, the grade of membership in a fuzzy set may itself be a fuzzy set. For example, if

$$\Omega \; = \; TOM + JIM + DICK + BOB$$

and *agile* is the fuzzy subset, then we may have

$$agile \; = \; medium/TOM + low/JIM + low/DICK + high/BOB$$

In this representation, the fuzzy grades of membership *low*, *medium*, and *high* are fuzzy subsets of the universe Ω'

$$\Omega' \; = \; 0 + 0.1 + 0.2 + \cdots + 0.9 + 1$$

31

which are defined by

$$
\begin{aligned}
low &= 0.5/0.2 + 0.7/0.3 + 1/0.4 + 0.7/0.5 + 0.5/0.6 \\
medium &= 0.5/0.4 + 0.7/0.5 + 1/0.6 + 0.7/0.7 + 0.5/0.8 \\
high &= 0.5/0.7 + 0.7/0.8 + 0.9/0.9 + 1/1
\end{aligned}
$$

See Figure 2–6.

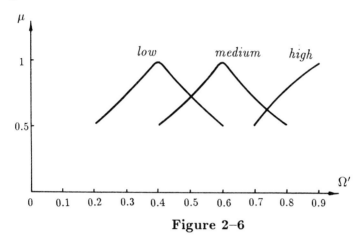

Figure 2–6

Such a fuzzy set is called a **Type 2** fuzzy set, which will be discussed specifically in Section 2.3.

2.3   Operations on Fuzzy Sets

The basic operations are **union** ($\cup$), **intersection** ($\cap$) and **complement** ($\neg$), as in the classical set theory. At the beginning of the development of fuzzy set theory, the **min–max** operations and the corresponding assumptions seemed to be sufficient to ensure the uniqueness of the choice of **intersection** and **union** operators. In this section, therefore, we will first present those concepts. They constitute a consistent framework for the theory of fuzzy sets. However, it is not the only way to extend classical set theory consistently. A lot of research both from mathematical and empirical fields has produced many other proposals [Zimmermann, 1985; Dubois and Prade, 1980; Zadeh, 1965].

Definition 2.2

The membership function of the **union** $\tilde{A} \cup \tilde{B}$ is pointwise defined by

$$\mu_{\widetilde{A}\cup\widetilde{B}}(x) = \max\{\mu_{\widetilde{A}}(x), \mu_{\widetilde{B}}(x)\}, \qquad x \in \Omega. \tag{2.26}$$

Definition 2.3

The membership function of the **intersection** $\widetilde{A} \cap \widetilde{B}$ is defined by

$$\mu_{\widetilde{A}\cap\widetilde{B}}(x) = \min\{\mu_{\widetilde{A}}(x), \mu_{\widetilde{B}}(x)\}, \qquad x \in \Omega. \tag{2.27}$$

Figure 2–7 sketches the situation mentioned above.

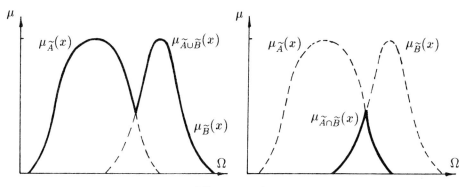

Figure 2–7

Definition 2.4

The membership function of the **complement** of a fuzzy set $\widetilde{A}$, $\mu_{\neg\widetilde{A}}(x)$ is defined by

$$\mu_{\neg\widetilde{A}}(x) = 1 - \mu_{\widetilde{A}}(x), \qquad x \in \Omega. \tag{2.28}$$

Example 2.5

Let $\quad \widetilde{A} = 0.8/x_1 + 0.2/x_2 + 0.1/x_3 + 0.4/x_4 + 0.7/x_5$

$\qquad \widetilde{B} = 0.2/x_1 + 0.4/x_2 + 0.6/x_4 + 0.9/x_5$

Then $\quad \widetilde{A} \cup \widetilde{B} = 0.8/x_1 + 0.4/x_2 + 0.1/x_3 + 0.6/x_4 + 0.9/x_5$

$\qquad \widetilde{A} \cap \widetilde{B} = 0.2/x_1 + 0.2/x_2 + 0.4/x_4 + 0.7/x_5$

$\qquad \neg\widetilde{A} = 0.2/x_1 + 0.8/x_2 + 0.9/x_3 + 0.6/x_4 + 0.3/x_5$

Example 2.6

Let us assume that

33

$$\tilde{A} = \text{``x considerably larger than 10''},$$
$$\tilde{B} = \text{``x approximately 11''},$$

characterized by

$$\tilde{A} = \{(x, \mu_{\tilde{A}}(x)) | x \in \Omega\}$$

where

$$\mu_{\tilde{A}}(x) = \begin{cases} 0, & x < 10; \\ \left[1 + (x - 10)^{-2}\right]^{-1}, & x >= 10. \end{cases}$$

$$\tilde{B} = \{(x, \mu_{\tilde{B}}(x)) | x \in \Omega\}$$

where

$$\mu_{\tilde{B}}(x) = \left[1 + (x - 11)^4\right]^{-1}$$

Then $\tilde{A} \cap \tilde{B}$ means that x considerably larger than 10 and approximately 11, and we have

$$\mu_{\tilde{A} \cap \tilde{B}} = \begin{cases} \min\{\left[1 + (x - 10)^{-2}\right]^{-1}, \left[1 + (x - 11)^4\right]^{-1}\}, & x >= 10 \\ 0, & x < 10. \end{cases}$$

$\tilde{A} \cup \tilde{B}$ means that x considerably larger than 10 or approximately 11, we have

$$\mu_{\tilde{A} \cup \tilde{B}}(x) = \max\{\left[1 + (x - 10)^{-2}\right]^{-1}, \left[1 + (x - 11)^4\right]^{-1}\}, \qquad x \in \Omega.$$

Figure 2–8 depicts the above.

The basic operations on fuzzy sets can be also generalized to the situations of n fuzzy sets, where n is any natural number.

Definition 2.5

Let $\widetilde{A_1}, \widetilde{A_2}, \ldots, \widetilde{A_n}$ be n fuzzy sets in Ω, the **intersection** and **union** of them are specified by the following membership functions respectively:

$$\mu_{\bigcup_{i=1}^{n} \widetilde{A_i}}(x) = \max\{\mu_{\widetilde{A_1}}(x), \mu_{\widetilde{A_2}}(x), \ldots, \mu_{\widetilde{A_n}}(x)\} \qquad (2.29)$$

$$\mu_{\bigcap_{i=1}^{n} \widetilde{A_i}}(x) = \min\{\mu_{\widetilde{A_1}}(x), \mu_{\widetilde{A_2}}(x), \ldots, \mu_{\widetilde{A_n}}(x)\} \qquad (2.30)$$

It was previously mentioned that **max** and **min** are not the only operators that could have been chosen to model the **intersection** or **union** of fuzzy sets respectively. The question arises, why those and not others?

34

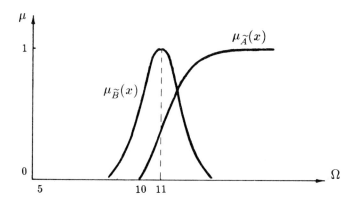

Figure 2–8 The Membership Functions of Compound
Fuzzy Sets By **union** and **intersection**

It is simple to justify the choice of **min–max** operators to define the **union** and the **intersection**, respectively. They are the only ones that exhibit the following necessary properties:

(1) The grade of membership in a compound fuzzy subset depends on the grade of membership in the elementary fuzzy subsets that form it, but on nothing else.

(2) The operators **min** and **max** are commutative, associative, and mutually distributive operators.

(3) The operators **min** and **max** are continuous and nondecreasing with respect to each of their arguments.

(4) $\min\{1,1\} = 1$ and $\max\{0,0\} = 0$.

Bellman and Giertz have addressed this question axiomatically [Bellman and Giertz, 1973]. They argued from a logical point of view, interpreting the **intersection** as "logical **and**", the **union** as "logical **or**" and the fuzzy set $\tilde{A}$ as the statement "The element x belongs to set $\tilde{A}$" which can be accepted as *more or less true*. It is very instructive to follow their line of argument, which is an excellent example for an axiomatic justification of specific mathematical models.

We shall therefore sketch their reasoning: consider two statements, S and

35

T, for which the truth values are μ_S and μ_T, respectively, where μ_S, μ_T belong to $[0,1]$. The truth value of the **and** and **or** combination of these statements, $\mu_{(S \text{ and } T)}$ and $\mu_{(S \text{ or } T)}$, both from the interval $[0,1]$, are interpreted as the values of the membership functions of the **intersection** and **union**, respectively, of S and T. We are now looking for two real-valued functions f and g such that

$$\mu_S \text{ and } \mu_T = f(\mu_S, \mu_T)$$

and

$$\mu_S \text{ or } \mu_T = g(\mu_S, \mu_T).$$

The following restrictions are reasonably imposed on f and g:

(1) f and g are nondecreasing and continuous in μ_S and μ_T.

(2) f and g are symmetric, that is,

$$f(\mu_S, \mu_T) = f(\mu_T, \mu_S)$$

and

$$g(\mu_S, \mu_T) = g(\mu_T, \mu_S).$$

(3) $f(\mu_S, \mu_S)$ and $g(\mu_S, \mu_S)$ are strictly increasing in μ_S.

(4) $f(\mu_S, \mu_T) \leq \min\{\mu_S, \mu_T\}$ and $g(\mu_S, \mu_T) \geq \max\{\mu_S, \mu_T\}$. That implies that accepting the truth of the statement "S **and** T" requires more, and accepting the truth of the statement "S **or** T" less, than accepting S or T alone as *true*.

(5) $f(1,1) = 1$ and $g(0,0) = 0$.

(6)   Generally speaking, we have

$$f(\mu_{S_1}, f(\mu_{S_2}, \mu_{S_3})) = f(f(\mu_{S_1}, \mu_{S_2}), \mu_{S_3}); \qquad (2.31)$$

$$g(\mu_{S_1}, g(\mu_{S_2}, \mu_{S_3})) = g(g(\mu_{S_1}, \mu_{S_2}), \mu_{S_3}); \qquad (2.32)$$

$$f(\mu_{S_1}, g(\mu_{S_2}, \mu_{S_3})) = g(f(\mu_{S_1}, \mu_{S_2}), f(\mu_{S_1}, \mu_{S_3})); \qquad (2.33)$$

$$g(\mu_{S_1}, f(\mu_{S_2}, \mu_{S_3})) = f(g(\mu_{S_1}, \mu_{S_2}), g(\mu_{S_1}, \mu_{S_3})). \qquad (2.34)$$

To formalize the above assumptions, we use the symbols $\wedge$ for **and** (= intersection) and $\vee$ for **or** (= union); this amounts to the following seven restrictions being imposed on the two commutative and associative binary compositions $\wedge$

and ∨ on the closed interval $[0,1]$ which are mutually distributive with respect to one another.

1.
$$\mu_S \wedge \mu_T = \mu_T \wedge \mu_S \tag{2.35}$$

$$\mu_S \vee \mu_T = \mu_T \vee \mu_S \tag{2.36}$$

2.
$$(\mu_S \wedge \mu_T) \wedge \mu_U = \mu_S \wedge (\mu_T \wedge \mu_U) \tag{2.37}$$

$$(\mu_S \vee \mu_T) \vee \mu_U = \mu_S \vee (\mu_T \vee \mu_U) \tag{2.38}$$

3.
$$\mu_S \wedge (\mu_T \vee \mu_U) = (\mu_S \wedge \mu_T) \vee (\mu_S \wedge \mu_U) \tag{2.39}$$

$$\mu_S \vee (\mu_T \wedge \mu_U) = (\mu_S \vee \mu_T) \wedge (\mu_S \vee \mu_U) \tag{2.40}$$

4. $\mu_S \wedge \mu_T$ and $\mu_S \vee \mu_T$ are continuous and nondecreasing in each component.

5. $\mu_S \wedge \mu_S$ and $\mu_S \vee \mu_S$ are strictly increasing in μ_S.

6.
$$\mu_S \wedge \mu_T \leq \min\{\mu_S, \mu_T\} \tag{2.41}$$

$$\mu_S \vee \mu_T \geq \max\{\mu_S, \mu_T\} \tag{2.42}$$

7.
$$1 \wedge 1 = 1 \tag{2.43}$$

$$0 \vee 0 = 0. \tag{2.44}$$

Then the mathematical forms f and g can be uniquely determined by

$$f(\mu_S, \mu_T) = \min\{\mu_S, \mu_T\}. \tag{2.45}$$

$$g(\mu_S, \mu_T) = \max\{\mu_S, \mu_T\}. \tag{2.46}$$

Analogous to f and g for **intersection** and **union**, let the function h be **complement**. For the complement it would be reasonable to assume that

(a) If statement S is *true*, its complement "**non** S" is *false*, that is
$$h(0) = 1, \qquad h(1) = 0;$$

(b) $h(\mu_S)$ should be continuous and monotonically decreasing.

(c) For all μ_S, $\mu_S \in [0,1]$, we have
$$h(h(\mu_S)) = \mu_S.$$

(d) For all μ_S, $\mu_S \in [0,1]$, we have
$$h(1 - \mu_S) = 1 - h(\mu_S).$$

Then h can be uniquely determined by

$$h(\mu_S) = 1 - \mu_S. \tag{2.47}$$

We now consider addition operations on fuzzy sets which have been defined in the literature [Zadeh, 1965, 1975(c); Giles, 1976; Dubois and Prade, 1980; Hamacher, 1978].

Definition 2.6

The **algebraic product** of two fuzzy sets $\tilde{C} = \tilde{A} \bullet \tilde{B}$ is defined as

$$\tilde{C} = \int_\Omega \mu_{\tilde{C}}(x)/x$$

where

$$\mu_{\tilde{C}}(x) = \mu_{\tilde{A}\bullet\tilde{B}}(x) = \mu_{\tilde{A}}(x) \cdot \mu_{\tilde{B}}(x).$$

Definition 2.7

The **algebraic sum** $\tilde{C} = \tilde{A} + \tilde{B}$ is defined as

$$\tilde{C} = \int_\Omega \mu_{\tilde{C}}(x)/x$$

where

$$\mu_{\tilde{C}}(x) = \mu_{\tilde{A}+\tilde{B}}(x) = \mu_{\tilde{A}}(x) + \mu_{\tilde{B}}(x) - \mu_{\tilde{A}}(x) \cdot \mu_{\tilde{B}}(x).$$

Definition 2.8

The **bounded sum** $\tilde{C} = \tilde{A} \oplus \tilde{B}$ is defined as

$$\tilde{C} = \int_\Omega \mu_{\tilde{C}}(x)/x$$

where

$$\mu_{\tilde{C}}(x) = \mu_{\tilde{A}\oplus\tilde{B}}(x) = \min\{1, \mu_{\tilde{A}}(x) + \mu_{\tilde{B}}(x)\}.$$

Definition 2.9

The **bounded difference** $\tilde{C} = \tilde{A} \ominus \tilde{B}$ is defined as

$$\tilde{C} = \int_\Omega \mu_{\tilde{C}}(x)/x$$

where

$$\mu_{\tilde{C}}(x) = \mu_{\tilde{A}\ominus\tilde{B}}(x) = \max\{0, \mu_{\tilde{A}}(x) + \mu_{\tilde{B}}(x) - 1\}.$$

Definition 2.10

The **intersection** of two fuzzy sets $\tilde{A}$ and $\tilde{B}$ is defined as

$$\tilde{A} \cap \tilde{B} = \int_\Omega \mu_{\tilde{A}\cap\tilde{B}}(x)/x$$

where

$$\mu_{\tilde{A}\cap\tilde{B}}(x) = \frac{\mu_{\tilde{A}}(x)\cdot\mu_{\tilde{B}}(x)}{\gamma + (1-\gamma)(\mu_{\tilde{A}}(x)+\mu_{\tilde{B}}(x)-\mu_{\tilde{A}}(x)\cdot\mu_{\tilde{B}}(x))}, \qquad \gamma \geq 0.$$

Definition 2.11

The **union** of two fuzzy sets $\tilde{A}$ and $\tilde{B}$ is defined as

$$\tilde{A}\cup\tilde{B} = \int_{\Omega}\mu_{\tilde{A}\cup\tilde{B}}(x)/x$$

where

$$\mu_{\tilde{A}\cup\tilde{B}}(x) = \frac{\mu_{\tilde{A}}(x)\cdot\mu_{\tilde{B}}(x)(1-\gamma') + \gamma'(\mu_{\tilde{A}}(x)+\mu_{\tilde{B}}(x))}{\gamma' + \mu_{\tilde{A}}(x)\cdot\mu_{\tilde{B}}(x)}, \qquad \gamma' \geq 0.$$

All the operators mentioned so far treat the case of binary logic as a special case.

Some of these operators and their equivalence to the logical **and** and **or** respectively have been justified axiomatically. We will sketch the axioms on which the Hamacher-operator [Hamacher, 1978] rests in order to give the reader the opportunity to compare the axiomatic system of Bellman-Giertz (**min–max**) on the one hand with that of the Hamacher-operator (which is essentially a family of product operators) on the other.

Hamacher wanted to derive a mathematical model for the **and** operator. His basic axioms are:

(A_1) The operator $\wedge$ is associative, that is,

$$\tilde{A}\wedge(\tilde{B}\wedge\tilde{C}) = (\tilde{A}\wedge\tilde{B})\wedge\tilde{C}.$$

(A_2) The operator $\wedge$ is continuous.

(A_3) The operator $\wedge$ is injective in each argument, that is[1]

$$(\tilde{A}\wedge\tilde{B}) = (\tilde{A}\wedge\tilde{C}) \implies \tilde{B} = \tilde{C}$$

$$(\tilde{A}\wedge\tilde{B}) = (\tilde{C}\wedge\tilde{B}) \implies \tilde{A} = \tilde{C}$$

(A_4) $\mu_{\tilde{A}}(x) = 1 \implies \mu_{\tilde{A}\wedge\tilde{A}}(x) = 1.$

He then proved that a function $f : R \to [0,1]$ exists with

$$\mu_{\tilde{A}\wedge\tilde{B}}(x) = f(f^{-1}(\mu_{\tilde{A}}(x)) + f^{-1}(\mu_{\tilde{B}}(x))).$$

---

[1] This is the essential difference from the Bellman-Giertz axioms.

If f is a rational function in $\mu_{\widetilde{A}}(x)$ and $\mu_{\widetilde{B}}(x)$, then the only possible operation is that shown in Definition 2.10[2].

The question may arise: why are there unique definitions for **intersection** and **union** in binary logic and classical set theory but many suggestions for fuzzy set theory? The answer is simply that many operators (for instance **product** and **min**-operator) amount to exactly the same if the grades of membership are restricted to the values 0 or 1, while they lead to different results if that is no longer true.

This raises yet another question: are the only ways to "combine" or aggregate fuzzy sets the **intersection** or **union** or the logical **and** or **or**, respectively, or are there other possibilities of aggregation? The answer to this question is definitely yes. There are other ways of combining fuzzy sets to fuzzy statements, and **intersection** and **union** are only two limiting special cases. A number of authors have therefore suggested "generalized connectives", which are (so far) of particular importance for decision analysis and for other applications of fuzzy set theory.

Here we only mention some of these generalized connectives:

1. A straightforward approach for aggregating fuzzy sets, for instance in the context of decision making, would be to use those aggregating procedures which are frequently used in utility theory or multi-criteria decision theory. Operators such as the weighted or unweighted arithmetic or geometric mean are examples of them. In fact, they have empirically performed quite well [Zimmermann and Zysno, 1980].

2. Yager used another procedure [Yager, 1980]. He "softened" the **min–max** operators in order to render the models for **and** and **or** more adaptable to the context in which the **and** and **or** is used. He suggested the following operators:

Definition 2.12

The **intersection** of fuzzy sets $\widetilde{A}$ and $\widetilde{B}$ is defined as

$$\widetilde{A} \cap \widetilde{B} = \int_{\Omega} \mu_{\widetilde{A} \cap \widetilde{B}}(x)/x$$

where

---

[2] For $\gamma = 1$, this reduces to the algebaric product.

40

$$\mu_{\tilde{A} \cap \tilde{B}}(x) = 1 - \min\{1, ((1 - \mu_{\tilde{A}}(x))^p + (1 - \mu_{\tilde{B}}(x))p)^{\frac{1}{p}}\}, \qquad p \geq 1.$$

Definition 2.13

The **union** of fuzzy sets $\tilde{A}$ and $\tilde{B}$ is defined as

$$\tilde{A} \cup \tilde{B} = \int_{\Omega} \mu_{\tilde{A} \cup \tilde{B}}(x)/x$$

where

$$\mu_{\tilde{A} \cup \tilde{B}}(x) = \min\{1, (\mu_{\tilde{A}}^p(x) + \mu_{\tilde{B}}^p(x))^{\frac{1}{p}}\}, \qquad p \geq 1.$$

His **intersection** operator converges to the **min**-operator for $p \to \infty$ and his **union**-operator to the **max**-operator for $p \to \infty$.

For $p = 1$ the **Yager-intersection** becomes the **bold-intersection** of Definition 2.8. The **union**-operator converges to the maximum operator for $p \to \infty$ and to the **bold-union** for $p = 1$. Both operators satisfy the De Morgan laws, and are commutative, associative for all p, monotonically nondecreasing in $\mu(x)$, and include the classical cases of binary logic. They are, however, not distributive.

The variety of operators for the aggregation of fuzzy sets mentioned above might make it difficult to decide which one to use in a specific model or situation. In our view, it is not only important that the operators satisfy certain axioms or have certain formal qualities from a mathematical point of view. The operators must in this case also be appropriate models of real system behaviour, which can normally only be proven by empirical testing. It is equally important that the selected operators have to be adaptable to the context and the semantic interpretation. In practice the computational efficiency may also be taken into consideration when large problems have to be solved. It is therefore not surprising that different definitions of an operator will result in different outcomes.

2.4 Membership Functions and Possibility Distributions

The concept of membership functions is a cornerstone of fuzzy set theory. But, up to now, their meaning in nature and how membership functions are derived is not yet clear explicitly. In this section we investigate in detail the determination, the nature and properties of membership functions. But we first review different universes of discourse on which a membership function is defined.

2.4.1 Numerical Values and Linguistic Values

Usually, the definition of a membership function is based on a universe of mathematical discourse, say the real line, a string of numbers. Generally speaking, it may be a set of real lines to form a multi-dimensional situation. In what follows, we use one-dimensional functions for simplicity, unless stated to the contrary. For instance, the fuzzy subset modelling the concept "old" can be defined on numerical values of ages. The membership function is an assignment of numbers to numbers. However, a lot of fuzzy subsets can be defined on a variety of universes. For example, the fuzzy subset modelling the concept of "beautiful flowers" can be defined on a set of flower names:

$$\text{beautiful}$$

Peony	0.95
Rose	0.9
Lotus	0.8
Dandelion	0.6

How can one determine $\mu_{beautiful}(Lotus) = 0.8$? In fact, the concept of "beautiful flowers" is a combination of qualities that give pleasure or delight to the mind or sense, which can only described by linguistic values. It seems to be that there is a set of hidden and fuzzy standards in one's mind in justification for "beautiful flowers", say on the basis of colours, shapes, and so on. Before having $\mu_{beautiful}(Lotus) = 0.8$, there was a transfer processing based on the set of standards (see Figure 2–9).

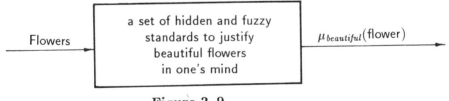

Figure 2–9

If we want to study correspondences between fuzzy subsets defined on different universes of discourse, we have to transform the underlying set mappings of these universes. A better way is to set up a unified universe of discourse, the real space, allowing interpretation of the human description of a process, with the goal of grasping a class of very complex factors which still require a human operator's presence. Again for simplicity we assume that the real space is one-dimensional. The interval of the real space is chosen from $[-1, 1]$, $[0, 1]$ or $[0, 10]$, as desired, and can be divided into a series of nondisconnected fuzzy subsets representing linguistic values. Therefore, there is a clear link or mapping between quantitative (numerical values) and qualitative (linguistic values) concepts.

Let X be a real space. Let a series of linguistic values be the fuzzy discretization on the real space. The problem is then to "code" the fuzzy sets representing the series of linguistic values. When a process is considered, a human operator having a good knowledge of it is generally able to describe the different linguistic values. For instance, the series of linguistic values may be: *almost negative, medium negative, almost null, medium positive, large positive*. The number of linguistic values is a function of the degree of precision of the description, it usually varies from 3 to 8, or more, if adverbs, such as *very, rather*, etc., are added. The membership functions of these linguistic values may be defined by values at a certain number of points, which amounts to chopping the real space of its values (see Figure 2–10).

Therefore, we can find a connection between the use of linguistic values in natural language on the one hand, and numerical values on the other hand. The method is applicable in general to the representation of a human operator's subjective evaluation with linguistic values.

2.4.2 Construction of Membership Functions

The problem of practical estimation of membership functions has not been systematically studied in the literature. Nevertheless, some ideas and methods have been suggested.

Here is an example showing one of the methods for constructing a membership function. If we wish to describe the following concepts on $[\alpha, \beta]$:

$$\{SHORT, MEDIUM, TALL\}$$

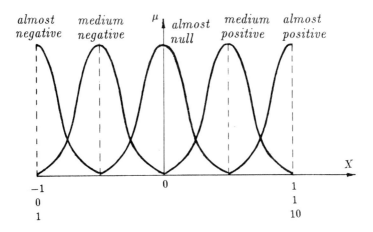

almost   medium μ almost   medium   almost
negative negative   null   positive positive

0

X

−1		1
0		1
1		10

Figure 2–10 Fuzzy Discretization of a Real
Space with Linguistic Values

We select two points ξ_1 and ξ_2 such that

$$SHORT \quad = \quad [\alpha, \xi_1)$$
$$MEDIUM \quad = \quad [\xi_1, \xi_2)$$
$$TALL \quad = \quad [\xi_2, \beta]$$

In classical logic the definition could be:

$$\mu_{SHORT}(x) \;=\; \begin{cases} 0, & x \notin [\alpha, \xi_1)\,; \\ 1, & x \in [\alpha, \xi_1)\,. \end{cases}$$

$$\mu_{MEDIUM}(x) \;=\; \begin{cases} 0, & x \notin [\xi_1, \xi_2)\,; \\ 1, & x \in [\xi_1, \xi_2)\,. \end{cases}$$

$$\mu_{TALL}(x) \;=\; \begin{cases} 0, & x \notin [\xi_2, \beta]\,; \\ 1, & x \in [\xi_2, \beta]\,. \end{cases}$$

See Figure 2–11.

However, in fuzzy logic the terms $SHORT$, $MEDIUM$, and $TALL$ are
represented as "soft" curves, as opposed to the block curves of classic logic,
and they show a given process value in principle as $SHORT$, $MEDIUM$ and
$TALL$ in various degrees between 0 and 1. The idea behind the "soft" definition

44

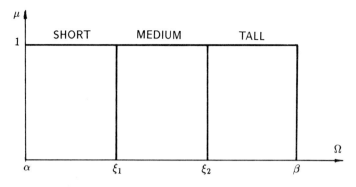

Figure 2–11

curves is to present as realistically as possible the gradual transition between the human conception of values being, *e.g.*, "*SHORT*" and not "*SHORT*", and to avoid the sudden jumps at definite values.

Suppose that ξ_1, ξ_2 are independent random variables having density functions $P_{\xi_1}(x)$ and $P_{\xi_2}(x)$ that satisfy

$$P_{\xi_1}(x) = 0, \qquad x \notin (a_1, b_1).$$
$$P_{\xi_2}(x) = 0, \qquad x \notin (a_2, b_2).$$

here $\alpha < a_1 < b_1 < a_2 < b_2 < \beta$; then we have

$$\mu_{SHORT}(x) = \begin{cases} 1, & \alpha \le x \le a_1; \\ \int_x^{b_1} P_{\xi_1}(u)du, & a_1 < x \le b_1; \\ 0, & b_1 < x \le \beta. \end{cases} \tag{2.48}$$

$$\mu_{MEDIUM}(x) = \begin{cases} 0, & \alpha \le x \le a_1; \\ \int_{a_1}^x P_{\xi_1}(u)du, & a_1 < x \le b_1; \\ 1, & b_1 < x \le a_2; \\ \int_x^{b_2} P_{\xi_2}(u)du, & a_2 < x \le b_2; \\ 0, & b_2 < x \le \beta. \end{cases} \tag{2.49}$$

$$\mu_{TALL}(x) = \begin{cases} 0, & \alpha \le x \le a_2; \\ \int_{a_2}^x P_{\xi_2}(u)du, & a_2 < x \le b_2; \\ 1, & b_2 < x \le \beta. \end{cases} \tag{2.50}$$

See Figure 2–12.

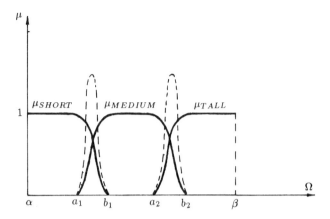

Figure 2–12 Constructing the Membership Functions
of $SHORT$, $MEDIUM$ and $TALL$

Note that

$$\mu_{SHORT}(x) + \mu_{MEDIUM}(x) + \mu_{TALL}(x) \equiv 1 \qquad (\alpha \leq x \leq \beta)$$

Fuzzy statistical experiments show that there exists a stability in the observation of the frequency of a movable interval, say (a_1, b_1), that covers a fixed point, say ξ_1, in the real line.

Figures 2–13 and 2–14 illustrate the representation of other frequently applied fuzzy terms. Note the normalized axis of abscissa generally used. The process value intervals are usually scaled to $[-1, 1]$, $[0, 1]$ or $[0, 10]$ as desired.

The method presented above may lack generality, but it seems more important, in our view, to become aware of how the human mind manipulates names of fuzzy sets than to estimate precise numerical grades of membership, since the perception process is itself fuzzy.

2.4.3 The Maximal Membership Principle

Let Ω be a universe of discourse, $\widetilde{A}_i$ $(i = 1, 2, \ldots, n)$ be a series of fuzzy sets on Ω. An issue of considerable interest is how to determine the fuzzy set $\widetilde{A}_j$ to which a given element a should belong, given all grades of membership $\mu_{\widetilde{A}_i}(a)$

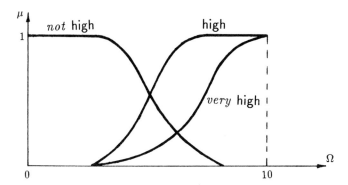

Figure 2–13   Representation of the Basic Term **high**, and the
Related Terms *very* **high** and *not* **high**. (Note the
Normalized $[0, 10]$ Abscissa Scale is Used.)

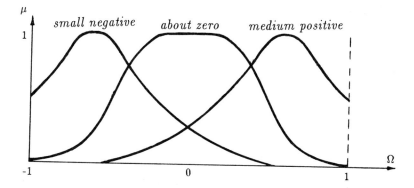

Figure 2–14   Representation of Three Fuzzy Terms *small negative*,
about zero and *medium positive*. (Note the Normalized
$[-1, 1]$ Abscissa Scale.)

of the element α.

The maximal membership principle gives the answer. If

$$\max_{i=1}^{n}(\mu_{\widetilde{A_i}}(\alpha)) = \mu_{\widetilde{A_j}}(\alpha). \tag{2.51}$$

then the fuzzy set $\widetilde{A_j}$ is considered as the set that the element α belongs to.

The concept of a fuzzy set first arose from the study of problems related to pattern classification. This is not surprising since the recognition of patterns is an important aspect of human perception, which is a fuzzy process in nature. The maximal membership principle is one of the most intuitive ways of defining a fuzzy pattern class.

As an example, let us consider the recognition of triangles. Given a certain triangle, it can be classified into "approximate right triangle $(\widetilde{R})$", "approximate isosceles triangle $(\widetilde{I})$", "approximate isosceles right triangle $(\widetilde{IR})$", "approximate equilateral triangle $(\widetilde{E})$", "ordinary triangle $(\widetilde{O})$", and so on. Given a triangle with internal angles A, B and C, such that

$$\Omega = \{(A, B, C)|A \geq B \geq C > 0, A + B + C = 180\} \tag{2.52}$$

$$\mu_{\widetilde{I}}(A, B, C) = (1 - \frac{1}{60}\min\{A - B, B - C\})^2 \tag{2.53}$$

$$\mu_{\widetilde{R}}(A, B, C) = (1 - \frac{1}{90}|A - 90|)^2 \tag{2.54}$$

$$\mu_{\widetilde{E}}(A, B, C) = (1 - \frac{1}{180}(A - C))^2 \tag{2.55}$$

then

$$\mu_{\widetilde{IR}}(A, B, C) = \min\{\mu_{\widetilde{I}}(A, B, C), \mu_{\widetilde{R}}(A, B, C)\} \tag{2.56}$$

$$\mu_{\widetilde{O}}(A, B, C) = \tag{2.57}$$
$$\min\{(1 - \mu_{\widetilde{I}}(A, B, C)), (1 - \mu_{\widetilde{E}}(A, B, C)), (1 - \mu_{\widetilde{R}}(A, B, C))\}$$

since

$$\widetilde{IR} = \widetilde{I} \cap \widetilde{I} \tag{2.58}$$

and

$$\widetilde{O} = \neg(\widetilde{I} \cup \widetilde{E} \cup \widetilde{R}) = \neg\widetilde{I} \cap \neg\widetilde{E} \cap \neg\widetilde{R} \tag{2.59}$$

Suppose $t_1 = (95, 50, 35)$ and $t_2 = (120, 40, 20)$, we have

$$\mu_{\widetilde{T}}(95, 50, 35) = (1 - \frac{1}{60}\min\{95 - 50, 50 - 35\})^2 = 0.562,$$

$$\mu_{\widetilde{R}}(95, 50, 35) = (1 - \frac{1}{90}|95 - 90|)^2 = 0.892,$$

$$\mu_{\widetilde{E}}(95, 50, 35) = (1 - \frac{1}{180}(95 - 35))^2 = 0.444,$$

$$\mu_{\widetilde{IR}}(95, 50, 35) = \min\{\mu_{\widetilde{T}}(95, 50, 35), \mu_{\widetilde{R}}(95, 50, 35)\} = 0.562,$$

$$\mu_{\widetilde{O}}(95, 50, 35) = \min\{1 - 0.562, 1 - 0.892, 1 - 0.444\} = 0.108.$$

According to the maximal membership principle, t_1 is classified as an approximate right triangle. Similarly, t_2 is classified as an ordinary triangle, since

$$\mu_{\widetilde{T}}(120, 40, 20) = (1 - \frac{1}{60}\min\{120 - 40, 40 - 20\})^2 = 0.444,$$

$$\mu_{\widetilde{R}}(120, 40, 20) = (1 - \frac{1}{90}|120 - 90|)^2 = 0.444,$$

$$\mu_{\widetilde{E}}(120, 40, 20) = (1 - \frac{1}{180}(120 - 20))^2 = 0.198,$$

$$\mu_{\widetilde{IR}}(120, 40, 20) = \min\{\mu_{\widetilde{T}}(120, 40, 20), \mu_{\widetilde{R}}(120, 40, 20)\} = 0.444,$$

$$\mu_{\widetilde{O}}(120, 40, 20) = \min\{1 - 0.444, 1 - 0.444, 1 - 0.198\} = 0.556.$$

2.4.4 The Nature and Properties of Membership Functions

The cornerstone of fuzzy set theory is the membership function. Other names for the same function from the attribute universe of discourse to the real interval $[0, 1]$ are:

> Possibility distribution function
> Compatibility function
> Fuzzy restriction
> Degree of belief

and so on. Although all these names are good conceptual definitions, they leave us with a considerable feeling of uncertainty as to a more precise meaning of the membership function, and as to their numerical values. This situation is quite serious in applied fuzzy systems in which the value of the grade of membership must be specified as an input to the system. For the time being we cannot expect consistency in the interpretation of the membership concept.

Now we are in a position to take account of these issues and to try and present some ideas which seem worthy of consideration.

The Nature of Grades of Membership

As the originator of fuzzy set theory, Zadeh's big achievement has been to draw our attention to the fact that in everyday communication we are presented with imprecise information. Because of the inherent imprecision, Zadeh suggested the revolutionary idea of defining classes with fuzzy boundaries such that an object, instead of either being an element of a set or not being an element of a set, can be an element to a certain degree which lies in the unit interval $[0, 1]$. This degree is called the grade of membership. This concept is a useful tool for describing the key elements in human thinking. These key elements are classes of objects in which the transition from membership to nonmembership is gradual rather than abrupt.

However, what is the meaning of the grades of membership in the fuzzy set theory?

The relation between the two concepts, "grade of membership" and "degree of truth", is given by the postulate that the grade of membership $\mu_{\tilde{A}}(x)$ of an element x to a fuzzy set $\tilde{A}$ is numerically equal to the degree of truth v of the fuzzy predicate "x is $\tilde{A}$" describing the fuzzy set $\tilde{A}$ applied to the element x

$$\mu_{\tilde{A}}(x) \; = \; \alpha \quad \textbf{iff} \quad v(x \text{ is } \tilde{A}) \; = \; \alpha.$$

For instance if $\tilde{A}$ is the fuzzy set of young men, the grade of membership $\mu_{young}(Harry)$ of $Harry$ to the set $\tilde{A}$ is numerically equal to the degree of truth of the proposition "$Harry$ is $young$". The presentation could have been based on both approaches. Whatever is deduced for degrees of truth can be applied to grades of membership when fuzzy logic is used.

For any object $x \in \Omega$ the grade of membership of $x \in \tilde{P}$ is the truth value of the fuzzy sentence $\tilde{P}(x)$, "x has the property $\tilde{P}$". For example, the grade of membership of $Harry$ in the fuzzy set of $young$ is identified with the truth value of the fuzzy sentence, "$Harry$ is $young$".

Another topic is whether there exists a connection between grades of membership and probabilities. Hisdal [Hisdal, 1988] believes that a grade of membership value should be interpreted as an estimate by the subject of the probability of assigning the given label. And her *TEE* model for grades of membership does make use of probabilities. Giles identifies grades of membership with subjective probabilities determined in a betting situation [Giles, 1988].

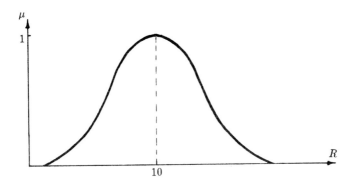

Figure 2–15

Dubois and Prade have made a comparison between possibility and probability [Dubois and Prade, 1980]. Similarities between possibility and probability theory are emphasized. A possibility distribution function is another name for the corresponding membership function, as we mentioned at the beginning of the subsection. It does not underlie the idea of a replicated experiment, nor does a possibility measure satisfy the additivity property. In this sense, the "grade of membership" is different from the probability. However, possibility distributions and probability distributions are loosely related through a consistency principle. In addition, membership functions can be determined by probabilistic approaches, such as set-valued statistics.

The Properties of Membership Functions

We have mentioned that a classical set is associated with a character function, while a fuzzy set is characterized by a membership function. The membership function is obviously one of the fundamental concepts in the theory of fuzzy sets, even in the whole of fuzziology. It is used for describing the procedure of gradual transition of objects from membership to nonmembership. That is, a membership function is a distribution of grades of membership in the universe of discourse.

Let us, now, look at the example of *about* 10. In order to formalize the example in the framework of fuzzy sets, one might use the shape in Figure 2–15.

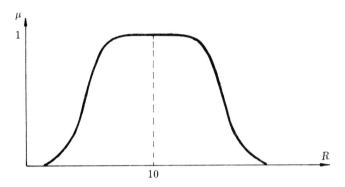

Figure 2–16

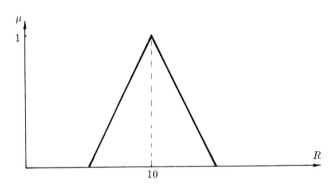

Figure 2–17

However, depending on the authors, the shape might also be one of the figures shown in Figure 2–16 and 2–17.

Considerable research has been performed in order to find methods to determine the precise shape the fuzzy set should have. Some techniques are based on statistical observations (if at all possible); others are more subjective. However, none of these techniques is very satisfactory since in the process of determining the fuzzy sets, the actual meaning of the numerical value of the fuzzy set at particular points becomes indeterminate.

We may ask: when should the grade of membership function have the value 1, when should it have the value 0, and when 0.5? And why should the function have the S or bell shape usually assumed in fuzzy set theory? These shapes seem intuitively reasonable, but we would like to support our intuition with theory.

If one looks at the shape of the different fuzzy sets modelling *about* 10 then they do have a number of features in common. Firstly, each of them attains the numerical maximum 1 at the point 10. Secondly, in all cases the numerical value decreases as the distance from the 10 increases. That is

(1) $\mu(10) = 1$

(2) if $|x - 10| \geq |y - 10|$ then $\mu(x) \leq \mu(y)$

where $\mu(x)$ is the membership function of the fuzzy set *about* 10. In another example, the fuzzy set *young people*, we find its membership function with shapes like any of the Figures 2–18, 2–19 and 2–20.

Again, there are a number of common features characterizing these fuzzy sets. Firstly, in all cases a threshold, α, is determined which determines a kind of "ideal set", $[0, \alpha]$, of all numbers which correspond to the ages of people considered *definitely young*. Secondly, if the distance from the ideal set increases then the grade of membership decreases. If we again use $\mu(x)$ for the fuzzy set we are considering, then we have

(1) if $x \in [0, \alpha]$ **then** $\mu(x) = 1$;

(2) if $|x - \alpha| \geq |y - \alpha|$ **then** $\mu(x) \leq \mu(y)$.

In general, given a basic set X, what seems to be required is a kind of metric structure on X giving a distance between points or more generally a distance from points to sets. Once such a structure is given, the determination of a

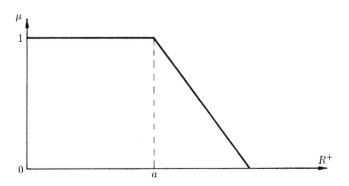

Figure 2–18

53

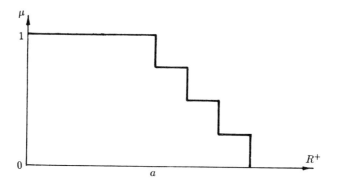

Figure 2–19

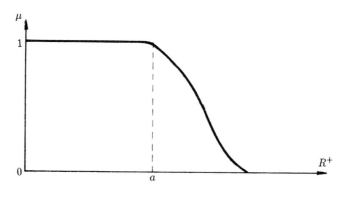

Figure 2–20

particular fuzzy set then depends on at least two further choices:

(a)   the determination of an ideal set I, a set of points absolutely (with degree 1) fulfilling the fuzzy proposition.

(b)   the determination of a shape for the fuzzy set on $X - I$ subject to the condition that the numerical values decrease with increasing distance to I.

Keep in mind that whether or not a membership function tallies with the real situation is mainly determined by the integral character of the gradual transition from membership to nonmembership, but not the numerical values of individuals of grade of membership. It is insufficient to ignore the membership function as a whole, and merely discuss the grade of membership at a certain point.

The membership function is perceived more as a continuum than a discrete set of membership values, although it may be sampled for practical purposes. The choice of continuous fuzzy set theoretic operators is consistent with fuzzy knowledge of membership functions: a slight modification of the membership value does not drastically affect the rough shape of the result of a set operation. Hence, overaccurate computation is unnecessary; that is, for the grades of membership, a high precision of computation is often insignificant.

Now we turn to the topic of comparing membership functions. In our opinion, it is not sufficient and even not scientific, to compare two membership functions merely using their extreme values, or values at the point of the **intersection**, since they cannot reflect the distributive situations of membership functions. As a result, we prefer to use areas or centres of gravity, *etc.*, in fuzzy comparison. Actually, like probabilistic approaches, we may examine the distribution characters and integral situations of membership functions by means of digital characteristics, such as mean values, mathematical expected values, fuzzy expected values and fuzzy expected intervals, *etc.*

2.5   The Extension Principle and Its Applications

2.5.1   The Extension Principle

One of the basic concepts of fuzzy set theory, which can be used to generalize classical mathematical concepts to fuzzy sets, is the extension principle.

Definition 2.14   (The Extension Principle I)

Let Ω_1 be a universe of discourse and $\tilde{A} = \int_{\Omega_1} \mu_{\tilde{A}}(x)/x$ be a fuzzy set in Ω_1, f is a mapping from Ω_1 to a universe Ω_2, $y = f(x)$, then a fuzzy set $\tilde{B} = f(\tilde{A})$ in Ω_2 is defined by

$$\tilde{B} = f(\tilde{A}) = \int_{\Omega_2} \mu_{\tilde{A}}(x)/f(x).$$

Example 2.7

Let $\Omega = \{0, 1, 2, \ldots, 9\}$, N is the set of natural numbers, f is a mapping from Ω to N,

$$f : \quad x \rightarrow 2x.$$

A fuzzy set $\tilde{S}$ in Ω is defined by

$$\tilde{S} = 1/0 + 1/1 + 0.7/2 + 0.5/3 + 0.2/4.$$

We obtain

$$\tilde{T} = f(\tilde{S}) = 1/0 + 1/2 + 0.7/4 + 0.5/6 + 0.2/8.$$

by applying Definition 2.14.

Definition 2.15   (The Extension Principle II)

Let Ω be a cartesian product of universes $\Omega = \Omega_1 \times \Omega_2 \times \cdots \times \Omega_n$, and $\widetilde{A_1}$, $\widetilde{A_2}$, $\ldots$, $\widetilde{A_n}$ be n fuzzy sets in Ω_1, Ω_2, $\ldots$, Ω_n respectively, f is a mapping from Ω to a universe $\hat{\Omega}$, $y = f(x_1, x_2, \ldots, x_n)$, then a fuzzy set $\tilde{B}$ in $\hat{\Omega}$ is defined by

$$\tilde{B} = \int_{\hat{\Omega}} \mu_{\tilde{B}}(y)/y$$

where

$$\mu_{\tilde{B}}(y) = \begin{cases} \max \min_{(x_1, x_2, \ldots, x_n) \in f^{-1}(y)} \{\mu_{\widetilde{A_1}}(x_1), \ldots, \mu_{\widetilde{A_n}}(x_n)\}, & f^{-1}(y) \neq 0; \\ 0, & \text{otherwise} \end{cases}$$

and $y = f(x_1, x_2, \ldots, x_n)$, where f^{-1} is the inverse of f.

Example 2.8

Let $\Omega = 1, 2, 3, \ldots, 10$, $\tilde{2} \triangleq about2$ and $\tilde{6} \triangleq about6$ are fuzzy sets in Ω:

$$\tilde{2} = 0.6/1 + 1/2 + 0.7/3,$$
$$\tilde{6} = 0.8/5 + 1/6 + 0.7/7,$$

56

$f(x, y) = x \times y$, then we obtain

$$
\begin{aligned}
\tilde{2} \times \tilde{6} &= (0.6/1 + 1/2 + 0.7/3) \times (0.8/5 + 1/6 + 0.7/7) \\
&= \min\{0.6, 0.8\}/(1 \times 5) + \min\{0.6, 1\}/(1 \times 6) \\
&\quad + \min\{0.6, 0.7\}/(1 \times 7) + \min\{1, 0.8\}/(2 \times 5) \\
&\quad + \min\{1, 1\}/(2 \times 6) + \min\{1, 0.7\}/(2 \times 7) \\
&\quad + \min\{0.7, 0.8\}/(3 \times 5) + \min\{0.7, 1\}/(3 \times 6) \\
&\quad + \min\{0.7, 0.7\}/(3 \times 7) \\
&= 0.6/5 + 0.6/6 + 0.6/7 + 0.8/10 + 1/12 \\
&\quad + 0.7/14 + 0.7/15 + 0.7/18 + 0.7/21 \\
&= \widetilde{12} \; (\stackrel{\triangle}{=} \; about \; 12)
\end{aligned}
$$

by Definition 2.15.

Example 2.9

Let $\quad \tilde{A} = 0.5/-1 + 0.8/0 + 1/1 + 0.4/2,$

$\qquad f(x) = x^2,$

then by applying the extension principle we obtain

$$
\tilde{B} = f(\tilde{A}) = 0.8/0 + 1/1 + 0.4/4.
$$

Figure 2–21 illustrates the relationship.

2.5.2 Operations on Type 2 Fuzzy Sets

So far, the membership space has been assumed to be the space of real numbers, and we considered fuzzy sets with crisply defined membership functions. It is doubtful whether human beings can have a crisp image of membership functions in their minds. Therefore it is necessary to consider the notion and properties of a fuzzy set whose membership values themselves are a fuzzy set. We call such sets **Type 2** Fuzzy Sets.

Definition 2.16 (**Type 2** Fuzzy Set)

A **Type 2** fuzzy set is a fuzzy set whose membership values are **Type 1** fuzzy sets on $[0, 1]$.

This corresponds to the case that the decision maker is not able (or not willing) to characterize the grade of membership by an exact number, but gives

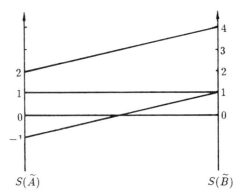

Figure 2–21 The Extension Principle

an evaluation such as the grade of membership at this point is *high* (*low*, *medium*, etc.). Such a procedure seems more suitable for many applications. It is typical for situations when questions are answered in an indeterminate manner.

The operations **intersection, union** and **complement** defined so far are no longer adequate for **Type 2** fuzzy sets. Fortunately, the extension principle can be used to define set theoretic operations for **Type 2** fuzzy sets.

To facilitate the discussion, we will consider only **Type 2** fuzzy sets with discrete domains. Let two fuzzy sets of **Type 2** be defined by

$$\tilde{A}(x) = \{(x, \mu_{\tilde{A}}(x))\}$$
$$\tilde{B}(x) = \{(x, \mu_{\tilde{B}}(x))\}$$

where

$$\tilde{A}(x) = \{(u_i, \mu_{u_i}(x)) | x \in \Omega, u_i, \mu_{u_i}(x) \in [0,1]\}$$

and

$$\tilde{B}(x) = \{(v_j, \mu_{v_j}(x)) | x \in \Omega, v_j, \mu_{v_j}(x) \in [0,1]\}$$

The u_i and v_j are grades of membership of **Type 1** fuzzy sets while the $\mu_{u_i}(x)$ and $\mu_{v_j}(x)$ are their membership functions respectively. Using the extension principle the set theoretic operations can be defined as follows [Mizumoto and Tanaka, 1976]:

Definition 2.17

Let two fuzzy sets of **Type 2** be defined as above. The membership function of their **union** is then defined by:

$$\mu_{\widetilde{A}\cup\widetilde{B}}(x) = \mu_{\widetilde{A}}(x) \cup \mu_{\widetilde{B}}(x)$$
$$= \{(w, \mu_{\widetilde{A}\cup\widetilde{B}}(w))|w = \max\{u_i, v_j\}, u_i, v_j \in [0,1]\}$$

where

$$\mu_{\widetilde{A}\cup\widetilde{B}} = \sup_{w=\max\{u_i,v_j\}} \min\{\mu_{u_i}(x), \mu_{v_j}(x)\}.$$

Their **intersection** is defined by

$$\mu_{\widetilde{A}\cap\widetilde{B}}(x) = \mu_{\widetilde{A}}(x) \cap \mu_{\widetilde{B}}(x)$$
$$= \{(w, \mu_{\widetilde{A}\cap\widetilde{B}}(w))|w = \min\{u_i, v_j\}, u_i, v_j \in [0,1]\}$$

where

$$\mu_{\widetilde{A}\cap\widetilde{B}} = \sup_{w=\min\{u_i,v_j\}} \min\{\mu_{u_i}(x), \mu_{v_j}(x)\}.$$

and the **complement** of $\widetilde{A}$ by

$$\mu_{\neg\widetilde{A}}(x) = \{((1-u_i), \mu_{\widetilde{A}}(u_i))\}.$$

Example 2.10

Let $\Omega = 1, 2, \ldots, 10$, $\widetilde{A} \triangleq$ "small integers" and $\widetilde{B} \triangleq$ "integers close to 4" denoted by:

$$\widetilde{A} = \{(x, \mu_{\widetilde{A}}(x))\}$$

and

$$\widetilde{B} = \{(x, \mu_{\widetilde{B}}(x))\}$$

where for $x = 3$:

$$\mu_{\widetilde{A}}(3) = \{(u_i, \mu_{u_i}(3))|i = 1,2,3\} = \{(0.8,1), (0.7,0.5), (0.6,0.4)\};$$
$$\mu_{\widetilde{B}}(3) = \{(v_j, \mu_{v_j}(3))|j = 1,2,3\} = \{(1,1), (0.8,0.5), (0.7,0.3)\}.$$

Compute $\mu_{\widetilde{A}\cap\widetilde{B}}$:

u_i	v_j	$w = \min\{u_i, v_j\}$	$\mu_{u_i}(3)$	$\mu_{v_j}(3)$	$\min\{\mu_{u_i}(3), \mu_{v_j}(3)\}$
0.8	1.0	0.8	1.0	1.0	1.0
0.8	0.8	0.8	1.0	0.5	0.5
0.8	0.7	0.7	1.0	0.3	0.3
0.7	1.0	0.7	0.5	1.0	0.5
0.7	0.8	0.7	0.5	0.5	0.5
0.7	0.7	0.7	0.5	0.3	0.3
0.6	1.0	0.6	0.4	1.0	0.4
0.6	0.8	0.6	0.4	0.5	0.4
0.6	0.7	0.6	0.4	0.3	0.3

Now we have to compute the supremum of the grades of membership of all pairs (u_i, v_j) which yield w as minimum:

$$\sup_{0.8 = \min\{u_i, v_j\}} \{1, 0.5\} = 1$$

$$\sup_{0.7 = \min\{u_i, v_j\}} \{0.3, 0.5, 0.5, 0.3\} = 0.5$$

$$\sup_{0.6 = \min\{u_i, v_j\}} \{0.4, 0.4, 0.3\} = 0.4$$

So we obtain the membership function of $x = 3$ as the fuzzy set:

$$\mu_{\tilde{A} \cap \tilde{B}}(3) = \{(0.8, 1), (0.7, 0.5), (0.6, 0.4)\}.$$

The example above is a good indication of the computational effort involved in operations with **Type 2** fuzzy sets. Note that, in this example, the grades of membership of only one element of the **Type 2** fuzzy set are computed. For all other elements, such as $x = 4, x = 5, \ldots$, etc., of the sets $\tilde{A}$ **op** $\tilde{B}$ the corresponding calculations would be necessary. Here "**op**" can be any set theoretic operation mentioned so far.

2.6 Operations on Membership Functions

2.6.1 The Significance of Operations

The membership function is the key to fuzzy sets, because operations with fuzzy sets are all defined via their membership functions. This section is devoted to the significance of operations on membership functions.

We have mentioned that overaccurate computation is useless as long as information of the object cannot be precisely described. That is, for grades of membership, high precision of computation is often not relevant. A slight modification of the membership value does not affect drastically the rough shape of the result of a set operation. Moreover, excessive concern with precision has become a stultifying influence in computer systems; in so doing, the advantage of high speed computation of computers ceases to exist. In fact, the human ability to perceive complex phenomena stems from the use of fuzziness to summarize information.

In addition, the operations on membership functions or grades of membership are not always meaningful. For example, the fuzzy set modelling the concept *intelligent people* can be defined on a set of individuals:

$$\tilde{I} = 0.8/John + 0.7/Peter + 0.4/Harry + 0.7/Mary$$

Here, we have $\mu_{\tilde{I}}(John) = 0.8$, and $\mu_{\tilde{I}}(Harry) = 0.4$. $\mu_{\tilde{I}}(John) = 0.8 > \mu_{\tilde{I}}(Harry) = 0.4$ reflects that the grade of membership of $John$ in the fuzzy set $\tilde{I}$ is greater than the grade of membership of $Harry$ in $\tilde{I}$. That is, $John$ is more intelligent than $Harry$. On the other hand, however, we have $0.8 = 2 \times 0.4$. Could we say that $John$'s degree of intelligence is twice as high as $Harry$'s? This statement is obviously meaningless in real life.

When humans deal with fuzzy events, **intersection** ($\cap$), **union** ($\cup$), and **complement** ($\neg$) of fuzzy sets are often used. For examples,

Young-girl	$=$	*Young $\cap$ Female.*
Higher-education	$=$	*University $\cup$ Post-graduate.*
Unsatisfactory	$=$	$\neg$ *(Satisfactory).*

We have shown that **min, max** and **non** are basic meaningful operations with fuzzy sets defined via their membership functions. They correspond to **inter-**

section, **union** and **complement** respectively

$$\mu_{\widetilde{A} \cap \widetilde{B}}(x) = \min\{\mu_{\widetilde{A}}(x), \mu_{\widetilde{B}}(x)\}, \qquad x \in \Omega;$$
$$\mu_{\widetilde{A} \cup \widetilde{B}}(x) = \max\{\mu_{\widetilde{A}}(x), \mu_{\widetilde{B}}(x)\}, \qquad x \in \Omega;$$
$$\mu_{\mathbf{non}\,\widetilde{A}}(x) = 1 - \mu_{\widetilde{A}}(x), \qquad x \in \Omega.$$

Although we cannot say that **min**, **max** and **non** are the only operators that could have been chosen to model the **intersection**, **union** and **complement** of fuzzy sets respectively, many mathematical and set operations on membership functions are not meaningful, **as in the example above.**

Note that, when the basic operations are used, the fuzzy sets used in each operation must be compatible. That is, they must be in the same universe of discourse.

2.6.2 λ-level-set

A more general and even more useful notion is that of a λ-level-set. This is a bridge between fuzzy sets and ordinary (crisp) sets.

Definition 2.18

The ordinary (crisp) set of elements which belongs to the fuzzy set $\widetilde{A}$ ($\subseteq \Omega$) at least to the degree λ is called the λ-level-set:

$$\widetilde{A}_\lambda = \{x | x \in \Omega, \mu_{\widetilde{A}}(x) \geq \lambda\} \tag{2.61}$$

where λ is called threshold value.

Example 2.11

Let $\widetilde{A} = 0.5/1 + 0.7/2 + 1.0/3 + 0.2/4 + 0.4/5$, we have

$$\widetilde{A}_{0.2} = \{1, 2, 3, 4, 5\};$$
$$\widetilde{A}_{0.4} = \{1, 2, 3, 5\};$$
$$\widetilde{A}_{0.5} = \{1, 2, 3\};$$
$$\widetilde{A}_{0.7} = \{2, 3\};$$
$$\widetilde{A}_{1.0} = \{3\}.$$

By Definition 2.18,

$$\widetilde{A}_{1.0} = \{x | x \in \Omega, \mu_{\widetilde{A}}(x) \geq 1.0\} = \ker \widetilde{A} \tag{2.62}$$

$$\widetilde{A}_{0.0} = \Omega \tag{2.63}$$

The kernel of a fuzzy set can be the empty set, ker $\tilde{A} = \emptyset$, that is, for any element x, in the universe of discourse Ω, $\mu_{\tilde{A}}(x) < 1$. These kinds of sets are called irregular fuzzy sets. Otherwise, if ker $\tilde{B} \neq \emptyset$, then $\tilde{B}$ is called a regular fuzzy set.

The following properties follow from Definition 2.18:

$$(\tilde{A} \cup \tilde{B})_\lambda = \tilde{A}_\lambda \cup \tilde{B}_\lambda \tag{2.64}$$

$$(\tilde{A} \cap \tilde{B})_\lambda = \tilde{A}_\lambda \cap \tilde{B}_\lambda \tag{2.65}$$

$$\textbf{If} \quad \lambda_1 \geq \lambda_2, \quad \textbf{then} \quad \tilde{A}_{\lambda_1} \subseteq \tilde{B}_{\lambda_2} \tag{2.66}$$

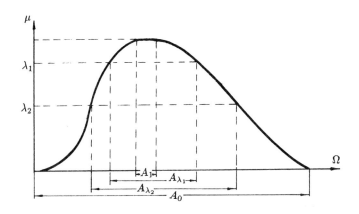

Figure 2–22

Figure 2–22 shows different λ-level-sets with corresponding λ cuts.

Convexity also plays a role in fuzzy set theory. In contrast to classical set theory, however, convexity conditions are defined with reference to the membership function rather than the **support** of a fuzzy set[3].

Definition 2.19

A fuzzy set $\tilde{A}$ is convex if

$$\mu_{\tilde{A}}(\lambda x_1 + (1 - \lambda))x_2 \geq \min\{\mu_{\tilde{A}}(x_1), \mu_{\tilde{A}}(x_2)\},$$

where $x_1, x_2 \in \Omega$, and $\lambda \in [0,1]$.

---

[3]The support of a fuzzy set $\tilde{A}$ is the set of points in the universe of discourse Ω at which $\mu_{\tilde{A}}(x)$ is positive, where $x \in \Omega$

Alternatively, a fuzzy set is convex if all λ-level-sets are convex. Figure 2–23 depicts a convex fuzzy set, whereas Figure 2–24 illustrates a nonconvex fuzzy set.

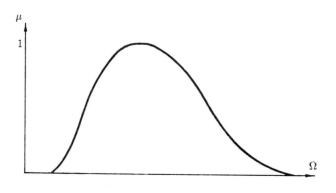

Figure 2–23   Convex Fuzzy Set

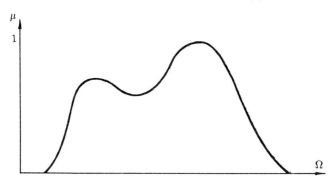

Figure 2–24   Nonconvex Fuzzy Set

2.7   Digital Characteristics of Possibility Distributions

2.7.1   The Mathematical Expected Values of Possibility Distributions

To represent fuzzy values properly, it is necessary to introduce the concepts of digital characteristics of possibility distributions, such as expected values, variance, moments, and so on. The mathematical expected value of $\tilde{A}$ is called the mean value, and is usually denoted by $E(\tilde{A})$; it reflects the location of the "centre" of the possibility distribution in the sense of a centre of gravity or balance point in mechanics. The expected value of $\left[\tilde{A} - E\left(\tilde{A}\right)\right]^{2}$ is called the variance, and is usually symbolized by σ^{2}.

Although various other measures of location and spread are possible, the mean and variance have the advantage that thay are easily calculated for sums and linear combinations of fuzzy values.

Definition 2.20

Let $\tilde{A}$ be a discrete fuzzy value with universe of discourse $\Omega = \{x1, x2, \ldots\}$ and discrete possibility distribution $\pi = \mu_{\tilde{A}}(x)$. The **mathematical expected value** of $\tilde{A}$ is a number defined by

$$E(\tilde{A}) = \frac{\sum_{x \in \Omega} x \cdot \mu_{\tilde{A}}(x)}{\sum_{x \in \Omega} \mu_{\tilde{A}}(x)}$$
$$= \frac{x_1 \cdot \mu_{\tilde{A}}(x_1) + x_2 \cdot \mu_{\tilde{A}}(x_2) + \cdots}{\mu_{\tilde{A}}(x_1) + \mu_{\tilde{A}}(x_2) + \cdots}$$

provided that this series converges absolutely (see discussion below). $E(\tilde{A})$ is also the first moment of the possibility distribution.

Example 2.12

Let $\tilde{A}$ be the fuzzy value "integers close to 10" defined as:

$$\tilde{A} = 0.1/7 + 0.5/8 + 0.8/9 + 1/10 + 0.8/11 + 0.5/12 + 0.1/13.$$

According to Definition 2.20, we have

$$E(\tilde{A}) = \frac{0.1 \times 7 + 0.5 \times 8 + 0.8 \times 9 + 1 \times 10 + 0.8 \times 11 + 0.5 \times 12 + 0.1 \times 13}{0.1 + 0.5 + 0.8 + 1.0 + 0.8 + 0.5 + 0.1}$$
$$= 10.$$

If $\tilde{A}$ has only a finite number of possible values, as in the preceding example, then $\sum x \cdot \mu_{\tilde{A}}(x)$ is a sum of a finite number of terms. In this case $E(\tilde{A})$ is finite and uniquely defined. However, if $\tilde{A}$ has an infinite number of possible values, then $\sum x \cdot \mu_{\tilde{A}}(x)$ may diverge, or its value may depend on the order in which the summation is performed. In order that $E(\tilde{A})$ be well defined, it is necessary that the series $\sum x \cdot \mu_{\tilde{A}}(x)$ be convergent to the same finite value regardless of the order of summation. By a standard result from calculus, all rearrangements of a series are convergent to the same value if and only if the series is absolutely convergent. Thus, in order that $E(\tilde{A})$ be well defined, the series of absolute values

$$\sum |x \cdot \mu_{\tilde{A}}(x)| = \sum |x| \cdot \mu_{\tilde{A}}(x)$$

must be convergent. If this is not so, we say that $\tilde{A}$ has no finite expected value.

Definition 2.21

Let $\tilde{A}$ be a discrete fuzzy value with universe of discourse $\Omega = \{x_1, x_2, \ldots\}$ and possibility distribution $\pi = \mu_{\tilde{A}}(x)$, and let n be a non-negative integer. The n-th **moment** of $\tilde{A}$ is defined by

$$E(\tilde{A}^n) = \frac{\sum_{x \in \Omega} x^n \cdot \mu_{\tilde{A}}(x)}{\sum_{x \in \Omega} \mu_{\tilde{A}}(x)} \qquad (2.67)$$

provided that the series converges absolutely.

Moments are numbers which describe the possibility distribution, and the most important moments of $\tilde{A}$ are those given by $n = 1$, which is the mean value discussed above, and by $n = 2$, which leads to the mean-square value.

$$E(\tilde{A}^2) = \frac{\sum_{x \in \Omega} x^2 \cdot \mu_{\tilde{A}}(x)}{\sum_{x \in \Omega} \mu_{\tilde{A}}(x)} \qquad (2.68)$$

Many practical situations call for a comparison of two or more possibility distributions. It often happens that the two distributions to be compared have nearly the same shape, and then the comparison can be made in terms of the first two moments only. Somewhat less frequently, a comparison of third and fourth moments may also useful.

Definition 2.22

The **variance** of $\tilde{A}$ is a non-negative number defined by

$$var(\tilde{A}) = E\{[\tilde{A} - E(\tilde{A})]^2\} = \frac{\sum_{x \in \Omega} [x - E(\tilde{A})]^2 \mu_{\tilde{A}}(x)}{\sum_{x \in \Omega} \mu_{\tilde{A}}(x)} \qquad (2.69)$$

The positive square root of the **variance** is called the **standard deviation** of $\tilde{A}$, and is often denoted by σ. The **variance** is then denoted by σ^2.

Since $\mu_{\tilde{A}}(x) \geq 0$, $var(\tilde{A})$ is clearly non-negative. Furthermore, $var(\tilde{A}) > 0$ unless $[x - E(\tilde{A})]^2 \mu_{\tilde{A}}(x) = 0$ for all $x \in \Omega$; that is, unless $\mu_{\tilde{A}}(x) = 0$ whenever $x \neq E(\tilde{A})$. If $var(\tilde{A}) = 0$, then the distribution of $\tilde{A}$ is singular, with all the possibility being concentrated at the single point $E(\tilde{A})$.

The standard deviation measures the spread or dispersion of the possibility distribution. If the distribution is tightly clustered about the **mean**, then $\mu_{\tilde{A}}(x)$ will be very small whenever $[x - E(\tilde{A})]^2$ is large, and hence σ will be small. On the other hand, σ will be large whenever the possibility is spread over a wide interval.

The variance can also be expressed in an alternative form by using the rules for the expected values of sums; that is,

$$E(\tilde{A}_1 + \tilde{A}_2 + \cdots + \tilde{A}_m) = E(\tilde{A}_1) + E(\tilde{A}_2) + \cdots + E(\tilde{A}_m). \qquad (2.70)$$

Thus,

$$var(\tilde{A}) = E\{[\tilde{A} - E(\tilde{A})]^2\} = E\left[\tilde{A}^2 - 2\tilde{A}E(\tilde{A}) + E(\tilde{A})^2\right]$$
$$= E(\tilde{A}^2) - 2E(\tilde{A})E(\tilde{A}) + E(\tilde{A}) = E(\tilde{A}^2) - E\left(\tilde{A}\right)^2$$

and it is seen that the variance is the difference between the mean-square value and the square of the mean value.

Example 2.13

Let $\tilde{A}$ be the fuzzy value "integers close to 10" defined as:

$$\tilde{A} = 0.1/7 + 0.5/8 + 0.8/9 + 1/10 + 0.8/11 + 0.5/12 + 0.1/13.$$

According to Definition 2.22, we have

$$E(\tilde{A}^2)$$
$$= \frac{0.1 \times 7 + 0.5 \times 8 + 0.8 \times 9 + 1 \times 10 + 0.8 \times 11 + 0.5 \times 12 + 0.1 \times 13}{0.1 + 0.5 + 0.8 + 1 + 0.8 + 0.5 + 0.1}$$
$$= 101.95$$

$$var(\tilde{A}) = 101.95 - 10^2 = 1.95.$$

There are many fuzzy values which naturally we think of as continuous ones; that is, as fuzzy values with continuous membership functions (or possibility distribution functions). Although the discussion in the above is restricted to discrete distributions, one need merely replace sums by integrals to adapt the definitions and results to the continuous case.

Definition 2.23

Let $\tilde{A}$ be a continuous fuzzy value with a continuous possibility distribution $\pi = \mu_{\tilde{A}}(x)$, the **mathematical expected value** (mean value) of $\tilde{A}$ is defined by

$$E(\tilde{A}) = \frac{\int_{-\infty}^{\infty} x \cdot \mu_{\tilde{A}}(x)dx}{\int_{-\infty}^{\infty} \mu_{\tilde{A}}(x)dx} \qquad (2.71)$$

provided that the integral converges absolutely; that is,

$$\int_{-\infty}^{\infty} |x \cdot \mu_{\tilde{A}}(x)| dx < \infty \qquad (2.72)$$

Otherwise we say that $\tilde{A}$ has no finite expected value.

Definition 2.24

Let $\tilde{A}$ be a continuous fuzzy value with possibility distribution $\pi = \mu_{\tilde{A}}(x)$, and let n be a non-negative integer. The n-th **moment** of $\tilde{A}$ is defined by

$$E(\tilde{A}^n) = \frac{\int_{-\infty}^{\infty} x^n \cdot \mu_{\tilde{A}}(x) dx}{\int_{-\infty}^{\infty} \mu_{\tilde{A}}(x) dx} \qquad (2.73)$$

provided that the integral converges absolutely.

Definition 2.25

The **variance** of $\tilde{A}$ is a non-negative number defined by

$$var(\tilde{A}) = E\{[\tilde{A} - E(\tilde{A})]^2\} = \frac{\int_{-\infty}^{\infty} [x - E(\tilde{A})]^2 \mu_{\tilde{A}}(x) dx}{\int_{-\infty}^{\infty} \mu_{\tilde{A}}(x) dx} \qquad (2.74)$$

2.7.2 Cumulative Distribution Functions and Fuzzy Expected Values

In the past, imprecision was considered only to be statistical, and thus was manipulated by the methodology of probability theory. Investigation shows, however, that in the real world, a frequent source of imprecision is not only the presence of random variables, but also the impossibility of dealing with exact data as a result of the complexity of both the system and the problem domain. Also, in many cases, classes of data do not have clear boundaries. So some data may have intermediate memberships to a class. From this point of view, probability and possibility are similar.

Probability is an objective characteristic and thus can be tested by experience. The grade of membership is subjective, although it is natural to assign a low grade of membership to an event that is considered to have low probability. In many cases the decision to assign a membership grade to an event is more or less the same whether we use probability or some fuzzy measure. But in other cases it is impossible to use probability. The event "*Smith is young*" is a fuzzy event and cannot be expressed by probability methods, since *young* is a fuzzy value and has subjective interpretation.

The motivation for the development of fuzzy statistics is its philosophical and conceptual relation to subjective probability. This subjective probability represents the degree of belief that a given person has in a given event on the basis of given evidence. This view can match the definition that probability is the degree of confidence and varies from individual to individual. The difficulty in applying subjective probability stems from the vagueness associated with judgments made through subjective analysis.

The fuzzy expected value is a fuzzy measure of typicality [Schneider and Kandel, 1988(a)(b)]. It is different from the notion of mathematical expected value. But in order to compute the fuzzy expected value (FEV), as well as any other measure of typicality, it is necessary to know how the population is distributed and what is the grade of membership of each group.

Here we first discuss the concept of the cumulative distribution function and then we show how to approximate the fuzzy expected value in a fuzzy environment by using the cumulative distribution function.

Given a fuzzy set $\tilde{A}$ (see Figure 2–25), there are many situations where

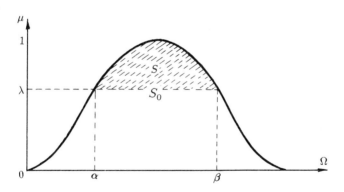

Figure 2–25

one wishes to know the relative population above the threshold λ.

Definition 2.26

The **cumulative distribution function** $f_{\tilde{A}}$ of a fuzzy set $\tilde{A}$ represented by the possibility distribution $\pi = \mu_{\tilde{A}}(x)$ is defined as follows:

$$f_{\tilde{A}}(\lambda) = \frac{S}{S_0}$$

69

$$= \frac{\int_\alpha^\beta \mu_{\tilde{A}}(x)dx}{\int_{-\infty}^\infty \mu_{\tilde{A}}(x)dx} \qquad (2.75)$$

where $\mu_{\tilde{A}}(\alpha) = \mu_{\tilde{A}}(\beta) = \lambda$, and $\alpha \le \beta$.

It is shown approximately in Figure 2–26.

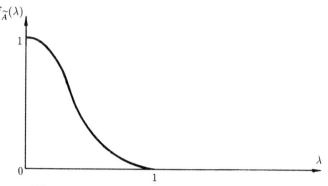

Figure 2–26 Cumulative Distribution Functions

By the use of cumulative distribution functions, the fuzzy expected value (FEV) was developed to evaluate fuzzy data. The following is a formal discussion on the properties of the FEV.

Definition 2.27

The FEV of the fuzzy set $\tilde{A}$, with respect to the cumulative distribution function $f_{\tilde{A}}(\lambda)$, is defined as

$$FEV(\tilde{A}) = \sup_{\lambda \in [0,1]} \{\min\{\lambda, f_{\tilde{A}}(\lambda)\}\} \qquad (2.76)$$

where λ is the threshold value in the interval $[0,1]$.

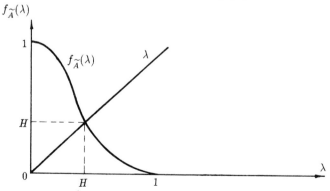

Figure 2–27 The Evaluation of $FEV(\tilde{A})$

70

The actual calculation of $FEV(A)$ consists of finding the **intersection** of the curves $\lambda = f_{\tilde{A}}(\lambda)$, which will be at a value $\lambda = H$, so that $FEV(\tilde{A}) = H \in [0,1]$. Figure 2–27 depicts this procedure, while the following example illustrates how the FEV can be computed.

Example 2.14

Using the fuzzy value "hourly wages," assume a given population and a given possibility distribution curve such that

$$
\begin{array}{llllll}
1 & person & earns & 3.00 & \longrightarrow & = & 0.40 \\
3 & persons & earn & 4.00 & \longrightarrow & = & 0.50 \\
4 & persons & earn & 4.20 & \longrightarrow & = & 0.55 \\
2 & persons & earn & 4.50 & \longrightarrow & = & 0.60 \\
2 & persons & earn & 10.00 & \longrightarrow & = & 1.00 \\
\end{array}
$$

As can be seen we have five different thresholds $\{0.40, 0.50, 0.55, 0.60, 1.00\}$. The first step in the process is to check how many persons are above each threshold (in percentage terms). As can be seen, 12 persons are above or equal to 0.4, 11 persons are above or equal to 0.5, 8 persons are above or equal to 0.55, 4 persons are above or equal to 0.6 and 2 persons are above or equal to 1.00.

Pairing these data and rearranging in increasing order (of the measure of belief, μs), we obtain the following five $[\lambda, \mu]$ pairs:

$$
\begin{array}{l}
(0.40, 1.00) \\
(0.50, 0.91) \\
(0.55, 0.66) \\
(0.60, 0.33) \\
(1.00, 0.16) \\
\end{array}
$$

The minimum value of each pair is:

$$
\begin{array}{lll}
\min\{0.40, 1.00\} & = & 0.40 \\
\min\{0.50, 0.91\} & = & 0.50 \\
\min\{0.55, 0.66\} & = & 0.55 \\
\min\{0.60, 0.33\} & = & 0.33 \\
\min\{1.00, 0.16\} & = & 0.16 \\
\end{array}
$$

and, therefore, according to Definition 2.27, the FEV, which is the maximum of all these minima, is:

$$\max\{0.40, 0.50, 0.55, 0.33, 0.16\} = 0.55$$

Thus the FEV is 0.55. From this result we can obtain that the fuzzy expected hourly wage is 4.20.

2.8 Fuzzifiers: *about*, *very* and *fairly*

In addition to the basic operations defined in Section 2.3, there are other operations that are of use in the representation of linguistic hedges in a natural language. The hedges *very*, *fairly*, *about* and other terms which enter in the representation of linguistic values may be viewed as signs of various operations defined on the fuzzy sets of Ω.

This section is devoted to defining fuzzifiers *about*, *very* and *fairly* as operators for **concentration**, **dilation**, and **fuzzification** respectively. Taking the point of view given by Zadeh [Zadeh, 1973], a fuzzifier f may be regarded as an operator which transforms the fuzzy set $\widetilde{M}(u)$, representing the meaning of u, into the fuzzy set $\widetilde{M}(fu)$. Fuzzifiers serve the function of generating a larger set of values for a linguistic variable from a small collection of primary terms.

Although in its everyday use the hedge *very* does not have a well-defined meaning; in essence it acts as an intensifier, generating a subset of the set on which it operates. A simple operation which has this property is that of concentration. This suggests that *very* $\tilde{A}$, where $\tilde{A}$ is a fuzzy term, could be defined as the square of $\tilde{A}$, that is

$$very\ \tilde{A} = \tilde{A}^2$$

or, more explicitly

$$very\ \tilde{A} = \int_\Omega \mu_{\tilde{A}}^2 (x - \delta)/x, \qquad \delta > 0. \tag{2.77}$$

Applying this operation to $\tilde{A}$ results in a fuzzy subset of $\tilde{A}$ such that the reduction in the magnitude of the grade of membership of x in $\tilde{A}$ is relatively small for those x which have a high grade of membership in $\tilde{A}$ and relatively large for the x with low membership. For example, if

$$\mu_{possible}(x) \; = \; \begin{cases} 0, & 0 \leq x \leq 0.5; \\ 2\left(\frac{x-0.5}{0.2}\right)^2, & 0.5 < x \leq 0.6; \\ 1 - 2\left(\frac{x-0.7}{0.2}\right)^2, & 0.6 < x \leq 0.8; \\ 2\left(\frac{0.9-x}{0.2}\right)^2, & 0.8 < x \leq 0.9; \\ 0, & 0.9 < x \leq 1. \end{cases}$$

then

$$\mu_{very\ possible}(x) \; = \; \mu_{possible}^2(x-0.1) \; = \; \begin{cases} 0, & 0 \leq x \leq 0.6; \\ 4\left(\frac{x-0.6}{0.2}\right)^4, & 0.6 < x \leq 0.7; \\ \left[1 - 2\left(\frac{x-0.7}{0.2}\right)^2\right]^2, & 0.7 < x \leq 0.9; \\ 4\left(\frac{1-x}{0.2}\right)^4, & 0.9 < x \leq 1. \end{cases}$$

Figure 2–28 illustrates the effect of fuzzifer *very*.

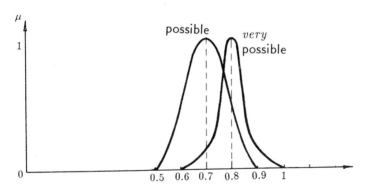

Figure 2–28   Effect of Fuzzifer *very*

Viewed as an operator, *very* can be composed with itself. Thus

$$very very \; \tilde{A} \; = \; \left(very \; \tilde{A}\right)^2 \; = \; \tilde{A}^4.$$

The operation of *fairly* is defined by

$$fairly \; \tilde{A} \; = \; \tilde{A}^{\frac{1}{2}} \; = \; \int_\Omega \mu_{\tilde{A}}^{\frac{1}{2}}(x+\delta)/x, \qquad \delta > 0.$$

Consider again the preceding example; we have

$$\mu_{fairly\ possible}(x) = \mu_{possible}^{\frac{1}{2}}(x+0.1) = \begin{cases} 0, & 0 \leq x \leq 0.4; \\ \sqrt{2}\left(\frac{x-0.4}{0.2}\right), & 0.4 < x \leq 0.5; \\ \sqrt{1-2\left(\frac{x-0.6}{0.2}\right)^2}, & 0.5 < x \leq 0.7; \\ \sqrt{2}\left(\frac{0.8-x}{0.2}\right), & 0.7 < x \leq 0.8; \\ 0, & 0.8 < x \leq 1. \end{cases}$$

As its name implies, the fuzzification operation of *about* has the effect of transforming a nonfuzzy set into a fuzzy set or increasing the fuzziness of a fuzzy set. The result of application of fuzzification to n_0 will be denoted by *about* n_0. Thus $x = $ *about* 25 means "x is a fuzzy set which approximates to 25". In general, we define

$$\mu_{about\ n_0}(x) = e^{-\alpha(x-n_0)^2}, \qquad \alpha > 0. \qquad (2.78)$$

74

Chapter 3

FUZZY LOGIC PROGRAMMING WITH PROLOG

Based on the fuzzy set theory described in the preceding chapter and production systems to be introduced in this chapter, a symbolic representation of fuzzy quantities coupled with axiomatic evaluation is proposed. This is incorporated into the PROLOG language to produce a fuzzy version, f-PROLOG, enabling fuzzy reasoning in a fuzzy environment with truth values. Processing these fuzzy truth values during reasoning is also considered. This will prove to be very useful for fuzzy relational databases.

3.1 Production Systems

In recent years we have witnessed great progress in techniques for designing production systems. The new approach may be called an axiomatic approach, where facts and rules are stored as axioms and the original problem to be solved, or the original question to be answered, is stated as a theorem to be proved.

A production system usually consists of the three components illustrated in Figure 3–1:

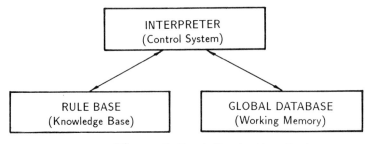

Figure 3–1 A Production System

- a global database (working memory)
- a rule base (knowledge base)
- an interpreter (control system)

The global database is used to store data about the problem in hand. For example, it may contain information about candidates who are going to be employed. This is a principal data structure in production systems. It can either be very simple like a matrix, or complex like an index file, according to the application area. Note that the global database is different from the notion of an ordinary database. The rule base contains a set of production rules, which represent general knowledge about the problem domain. For example, the rule base might contain rules which are used in the selection of candidates. Each rule consists of a condition part *Conditions* and an action part *Actions*, and is of the form:

IF *Conditions*
THEN *Actions*

Where *Conditions* may be C_1 & C_2 & $\cdots$ & C_n, and *Actions* may be A_1 & A_2 & $\cdots$ & A_n. As an example, consider the following naive rule:

IF the candidate has a university education
& young
& intelligent
& speaks two languages at least
THEN the candidate can be a manager.

76

Whether or not the condition part of a rule is satisfied can be established by reference to the database and/or by questioning the user of the production system. The action part of a rule can denote different things. For example, it can denote a command to add something to the database about the problem in hand, to suggest undertaking a task to the user such as asking the candidate a question, and so on.

The interpreter selects and applies rules which may yield changes and/or additions to the database. In conventional production systems the interpreter uses a data-driven approach whereby it cycles through the rules looking for one whose condition part is satisfied by the database. When it finds such a rule, it invokes the action part. In many cases, the action results in changes to the database which enable other rules. The interpreter continues cycling until either (i) the problem is solved (the goal is achieved), or (ii) a state is reached where no more rules may be invoked.

The condition parts of several production rules may be satisfied simultaneously. The set of satisfied rules is called a conflict set. And one rule must be selected by a conflict resolution. One of the simplest conflict resolution strategies is the rule order strategy that the rule appearing earliest in the list of rules is selected.

Examples of production systems are discussed below.

Example 3.1

A simple example of the production system in Figure 3–2 is given, where [DB] and [RB] mean the database and rule-base respectively, and the action 'deposit(x)' will put x to the tail of the database, the 'delete(x)' will remove x from the database, the 'stop' will stop the execution of the production system. The execution profile is shown in Figure 3–3. We have adopted the rule order strategy for conflict resolution.

Example 3.2

Consider a car fault diagnosis system which is implemented as a production system containing the following rules:

[DB] x is A_1, y is B_3

[RB] R_1 :   **IF** $(x$ is $A_1)$ & $(y$ is $B_2)$
       THEN   deposit(v is D_1)
       R_2 :   **IF** $(x$ is $A_1)$ & $(y$ is $B_3)$
       THEN   delete(x is A_1), deposit(v is D_2)
       R_3 :   **IF** $(y$ is $B_3)$
       THEN   delete(y is B_3), deposit(v is D_3)
       R_4 :   **IF** $(v$ is $D_2)$
       THEN   deposit(w is E_1), stop
       R_5 :   **IF** $(v$ is $D_3)$
       THEN   deposit(w is E_2), stop

Figure 3–2   An Example of a Production System

cycle	conflict set	selected rule	DB after the execution
0			x is A_1, y is B_3
1	R_2, R_3	R_2	y is B_3, v is D_2
2	R_3, R_4	R_3	v is D_2, v is D_3
3	R_4, R_5	R_4	v is D_2, v is D_3, w is E_1

Figure 3–3   Execution Profile for the Production
System in Figure 3–2

R_1 :	**IF**	the engine does not turn & the battery is not flat
	THEN	ask the user to test the starter motor
R_2 :	**IF**	there is no spark
	THEN	ask the user to check the points
R_3 :	**IF**	the engine turns & does not start
	THEN	ask the user check the spark
R_4 :	**IF**	the engine does not turn
	THEN	ask the user to check the battery
R_5 :	**IF**	the battery is flat
	THEN	ask the user to charge the battery and exit

$\vdots$

R_n :

Suppose that the interpreter cycles through the rules looking for one whose condition part is satisfied by the database. When it finds such a rule, it executes the action part. If the action part conditions a statement of the form "ask the user to check ...", then the interpreter causes an appropriate message to be displayed to the user requesting the check to be carried out and the results to be entered into the database.

As an example of the use of the system, suppose that the database contains the following single statement relevant to a particular problem:

"the engine does not turn"

The interpreter cycles through the rules, recognises that the condition part of rule R_4 is satisfied by the database and executes the action part of R_4 by requesting the operator to check the battery. Suppose that the battery is not flat and a statement of this fact is entered into the database. The database will now condition the statements:

the engine does not turn
the battery is not flat

Suppose that the interpreter continues by looking at rules R_5 to R_n and finds no rule whose condition part is satisfied by the database. It returns to R_1 to begin a new cycle through the rules. R_1 is satisfied, therefore the user is asked to test the starter motor and to enter the results of the test into the database.

The process continues until either (i) a rule with an "exit" is executed or (ii) the database remains unchanged throughout one complete cycle.

Note that the production rules are usually judgmental, that is, they make approximate reasoning on a confidence scale. The conclusions, therefore, are evaluated by certainty factors. Standard statistical measures were rejected in favour of certainty factors because experience with human experts shows that experts do not use information in a way compatible with standard statistical methods.

Certainty factor is a measure of the association between the premise and action clauses in each rule, and indicates how strongly each clause is believed. When a production rule succeeds because its premise clauses are true, the certainty factors of the component clauses are combined. The resulting certainty factor is specified in the action clauses. Thus, if the premise is believed only weakly, conclusions derived from the rule reflect this weak belief.

There is, however, another type of fuzziness in word meaning. For examples, "It is a *small* animal" and "If the animal is *more or less small* then it is a dog", where the words *small* and *more or less small* have fuzzy meanings. It seems to be difficult for a conventional production system to handle this type of fuzzy knowledge. We will propose an approach to represent and process this type of fuzzy knowledge using fuzzy sets and possibility distributions in the later chapters.

3.2 Logic Programming

Logic studies the relationship of implication between conditions and conclusions. It was originally devised as a way of representing the form of arguments, so that it would be possible to check in a formal way whether or not they were valid. Thus we can use logic to express propositions, the relation between propositions and how one can validly infer some propositions from others. From the logic point of view, a generalized DBMS is just a general-purpose question-answering system in which the set of facts necessary for question-answering (or problem-solving) can be viewed as the conclusion of the theorem. Therefore, the emphasis of such a database management system is on its deductive power. This is why logic plays such an important role in DBMSs. Recent development in automated deduction has led to the increasing use of logic as a very high level programming language and as a language for database description.

3.2.1 The First Order Predicate Calculus

A particular form of mathematical logic is called first order predicate calculus or simply predicate logic [Chang and Lee, 1973]. In predicate logic objects are represented by terms. In order to express the relationship between objects, formulae are used. We give brief definitions of these concepts below:

Definition 3.1

Terms are defined recursively:

(a)   A constant is a term.

(b)   A variable is a term.

(c)   If f is an n-ary function symbol, and $t_1, t_2, \ldots, t_n$ are terms, then $f(t_1, t_2, \ldots, t_n)$ is a term.

(d)   All terms are generated by applying (a), (b), and (c).

Definition 3.2

If P is an n-ary predicate symbol, and $t_1, t_2, \ldots, t_n$ are terms, then $P(t_1, t_2, \ldots, t_n)$ is an atomic formula. No other expressions can be atomic formulae.

Definition 3.3

Well formed formulae (WFF) are defined recursively:

(a)   An atomic formula is a WFF.

(b)   If F and G are WFFs, then $\neg F$, $F \wedge G$, $F \vee G$, $G \leftarrow F$, and $F \leftrightarrow G$ are WFFs, where $\neg$, $\wedge$, $\vee$, $\leftarrow$, and $\leftrightarrow$ are 'negation', 'conjunction', 'disjunction', 'implication', and 'equivalence' connectives respectively.

(c)   If F is a WFF, x is a free-variable, then $(\forall x)F$ and $(\exists x)F$ are WFFs, where $\forall x$ and $\exists x$ are universal and existential quantifiers respectively.

(d)   WFFs are generated only by a finite number of applications of (a), (b) and (c).

Example 3.3

Smith is a man.

man(smith)

Example 3.4

All men are mortal.

$(\forall x)(\text{mortal}(x) \leftarrow \text{man}(x))$

Example 3.5

Every man is mortal, Smith is a man,
therefore Smith is mortal.

$\text{mortal}(\text{smith}) \leftarrow (\forall x)(\text{mortal}(x) \leftarrow \text{man}(x)) \wedge \text{man}(\text{smith})$

Example 3.6

Susan sits between Albert and David.

between(albert,susan,david)

Example 3.7

Some men are clever.

$(\exists x)(\text{man}(x) \wedge \text{clever}(x))$

Example 3.8

All people eat food.

$(\forall x)((\forall y)(\text{eat}(x,y) \leftarrow \text{food}(y)) \leftarrow \text{people}(x))$

or

$(\forall x)(\forall y)(\text{people}(x) \wedge \text{food}(y) \wedge \text{eat}(x,y))$

3.2.2 Clausal Form

In a WFF, a connective can be expressed in terms of the other connectives. For instance:

$$G \leftrightarrow F \quad \Longleftrightarrow \quad (G \leftarrow F) \wedge (F \leftarrow G)$$
$$G \leftarrow F \quad \Longleftrightarrow \quad \neg F \vee G$$
$$\neg \neg P \quad \Longleftrightarrow \quad P$$
$$\neg (F \wedge G) \quad \Longleftrightarrow \quad \neg F \vee \neg G$$
$$\neg (F \vee G) \quad \Longleftrightarrow \quad \neg F \wedge \neg G$$
$$(\exists x)P \quad \Longleftrightarrow \quad \neg((\forall x)(\neg P))$$
$$(\forall x)P \quad \Longleftrightarrow \quad \neg((\exists x)(\neg P))$$

A functionally complete set of connectives in predicate calculus, which is sufficient to express any formula in an equivalent form, could be $\{\wedge, \neg, \forall x\}$ or $\{F, \leftarrow, \forall x\}$. As a result of the redundancy, there are many ways to express the same formula in an equivalent form. (The same situation exists in database query languages: different queries can express the same request.) If we wish to carry out formal manipulations on predicate calculus formulae, this turns out to be most inconvenient. It would be much nicer if everything we wanted to say could be expressed only in one way. So let us consider a special form, clausal form, where there are fewer ways of saying the same thing.

Definition 3.4

A clause is an expression of the form

$$B_1, B_2, \ldots, B_m \leftarrow A_1, A_2, \ldots, A_n \tag{3.1}$$

where B_1, B_2, ..., B_m, A_1, A_2, ..., A_n are atomic formulae, $n \geq 0$ and $m \geq 0$. The atomic formulae A_1, A_2, ..., A_n are joint conditions of the clause; and B_1, B_2, ..., B_m are the alternative conclusions. If the clause contains the variables x_1, x_2, ..., x_k, then interpret it as stating that for all x_1, x_2, ..., x_k, B_1 or B_2 or $\cdots$ or B_m holds if A_1 and A_2 and $\cdots$ and A_n hold.

There are three special cases:

(a)   If $n = 0$, that is,

$$B_1, B_2, \cdots, B_m \;\leftarrow$$

then B_1 **or** B_2 **or** $\cdots$ **or** B_m is unconditionally true
for all $x_1, x_2, \ldots, x_k$.

(b)   If $m = 0$, that is,

$$\leftarrow\; A_1, A_2, \ldots, A_n$$

then, for all $x_1, x_2, \ldots, x_k$, it is not the case that
A_1 **and** A_2 **and** $\cdots$ **and** A_n.

(c)   If $m = n = 0$, that is the empty clause:

$$\leftarrow$$

then this is a formula which is always false.

Example 3.9

For every X, Y and Z, X is grandparent of Y
if X is parent of Z and Z is parent of Y.

grandparent(X,Y) $\leftarrow$ parent(X,Z), parent(Z,Y)

Example 3.10

For every X, X is male or X is female
if X is human.

male(X), female(X) $\leftarrow$ human(X)

Example 3.11

Nothing is both good and bad.

$\leftarrow$ good(X), bad(X)

3.2.3   Horn Clauses

Clauses containing at most one conclusion are called Horn clauses, first investigated by the logician Alfred Horn [Horn, 1951]. For many applications of logic,
it is sufficient to restrict the form of clauses to Horn clauses. There are obviously
two kinds of Horn clauses:

(i)   Headed Horn Clauses

$$B \leftarrow A_1, A_2, \ldots, A_n$$

   or

$$B \leftarrow$$

(ii)   Headless Horn Clauses

$$\leftarrow A_1, A_2, \ldots, A_n$$

   or

$$\leftarrow$$

Any soluble problem which can be expressed in Horn clauses can be expressed in such a way that: there is one headless clause, and all the rest of the clauses are headed [Kowalski, 1979].

Thus, we can decide to view the headless clause as the goal which must be present for a problem to be soluble and the other clauses as the hypotheses (axioms). Because resolution with Horn clauses is relatively simple, they are an obvious choice as the basis of a theorem prover which provides a practical programming system.

Example 3.12

   The factorial of 0 is 1. The factorial of X+1 is X+1
   times the factorial of X.

   fact(0,1) $\leftarrow$
   fact(add_1(X),Y) $\leftarrow$ fact(X,A), times(add_1(X),A,Y)

   where "add_1(X)" is a function indicating the X+1
   function; "times(M,N,R)" is a predicate formula
   showing that M multiplied by N is R.

Example 3.13

   Write Horn clauses describing the Fibonacci function.

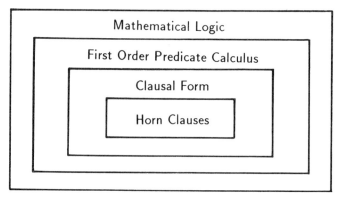

Figure 3–4 The Onion-Layer of Logic Programming

fib(0,1) ←
fib(1,1) ←
fib(add_1(add_1(X)),R) ←
      fib(X,R1), fib(add_1(X),R2), plus(R1,R2,R)

where "add_1(X)" is the same as that in Example 3.12;
"plus(R1,R2,R)" indicates the sum of R1 and R2 is
R. This is instantly recognizable as a definition of
the Fibonacci series.

As a conclusion of this section, Figure 3–4 gives a clear concept of logic programming.

3.3 PROLOG as a Logic Programming Language

Over the past ten years, there has been a great deal of research work in logic programming. The language PROLOG based on Horn clause logic was developed and is quickly gaining popularity throughout the world. It has been used in many areas of database systems and artificial intelligence.

3.3.1 A Brief View of PROLOG

PROLOG is by now available in many different versions. In the present section only the bare essentials are given.

(a)   **Term**

The data objects of the language PROLOG are called terms. A term is a constant, variable or structure.

(i)   Constants

A constant is thought of as the name of a specific object or a specific relationship. The constants include integers such as: 0, 45, 533, and atoms which normally begin with a lower-case letter, such as: john, flower. Those made up from only symbols are also atoms, such as: ?-, :-, ←, *etc.* The special underline character '_' may be inserted in the middle of an atom to improve legibility, for instance, alice_smith.

(ii)   Variables

Variables look like atoms except they begin with a capital letter or an underline sign '_'. For example: X, Var, _value. There is a special variable named *anonymous variable* '_' which never shares with any other. A variable should be thought of as standing for some definite but unspecified object.

(iii)   Structures

The structured data objects of PROLOG are the structures. A structure comprises a functor and a sequence of one or more terms called arguments. A functor is characterized by its name, which is an atom, and its arity or number of arguments. For instance, the structure whose functor is named 'point' of arity 3, with arguments A, B, and C is written:

        point(A,B,C)

Structures are usefully pictured as trees. For example, the term:

        line(point(X,Y,Z), point(A,B,C))

would be pictured as the structure (see Figure 3–5).

Sometimes it is convenient to write a compound term using an optional infix notation. For instance, X+Y+Z is equivalent to +(+(X,Y),Z), and instead of $;(P,Q)$ we may write $P;Q$. Finally, note that an atom is treated as a functor of arity 0.

(b)   Headed Clauses

There are two kinds of headed clauses: facts and rules.

(i)   Facts

A fact is an assertion which is an axiom, such as: likes(john,mary) stating that

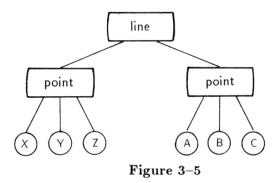

Figure 3-5

John likes Mary. When defining the relationship between objects using facts, the order of objects is arbitrary, but must be consistent. So the fact likes(john,mary) is not the same thing as likes(mary,john).

(ii)   Rules

A rule is a conditional assertion which consists of a head and a body. The head and the body are connected by the symbol ":–" which can be pronounced "if". For instance: to state John likes anyone who likes wine in PROLOG becomes:

likes(john,X) :– likes(X,wine).

The head of this rule describes what fact the rule is intended to define. The body, in this case likes(X,wine), describes the conjunction of goals that must be satisfied, one after the other, for the head to be true. Suppose John likes any person who likes sports, we have:

likes(john,X) :– person(X), likes(X,sports).

(c)   **Headless Clauses**

Headless clauses in PROLOG are questions. A special symbol "?–" is always put before the question. When a question is asked of PROLOG, it will search through the database, and look for facts or rules that match the question. Two facts match if their predicates are the same and if their corresponding arguments are each the same.

3.3.2   Resolution Proof Procedures of PROLOG

Any collection of Horn clauses can be run directly as a PROLOG program. In PROLOG, a simple depth-first backtracking strategy is used to explore the search tree (see Figure 3–6)—the resolution process chooses the first sub-goal in the query and the first matching clause in the database. The matching process (unification) ensures, by appropriate substitutions, that the clause head and sub-goal are identical. A new goal is obtained by replacing the matched literal with the body of the clause, and applying any substitutions generated by the unification process. Thus, from the goal statement

$$\leftarrow A_1, A_2, \ldots, A_n.$$

and a database containing the clause

$$A_1' \leftarrow B_1, B_2, \ldots, B_m.$$

the new goal statement

$$\leftarrow \{B_1, B_2, \ldots, B_m, A_2, \ldots, A_n\}\theta$$

is obtained, where θ is the most general unifier of the sub-goal A_1 and the clause head A_1'.

A solution to the original query is found when there are no further sub-goals to be solved. If, on the other hand, a sub-goal is found for which no unifiable clause exists in the database, the sub-goal is unsolvable, and the system backtracks. This is accomplished by discarding any substitutions created by the most recent unification, and resatisfying the corresponding sub-goal. If an unsolvable sub-goal is found and the system is unable to backtrack, the original goal fails.

The most important features in PROLOG are recursion and backtracking.

(a)   Recursion

In PROLOG, recursion is the normal and natural way of viewing data structures and programs. Consider for example the PROLOG program:

    member(X,[X | _]).   /* clause P */

    member(X,[_ | Y]) :– member(X,Y).   /* clause Q */

The clause P is to be understood as: "X is a member of the list if X is the head of the list". The clause Q is to be understood as: "X is a member of the list if X is a member of the tail of the list". Here the "[X | _]" or "[_ | Y]" is the notation of a list in PROLOG, in which the head and the tail of the list are separated by the vertical bar " | ".

The proof that clauses P and Q imply member(d,[a,b,c,d,e]) works as follows: each time the clause Q attempts to satisfy itself, the goal is given a shorter list.

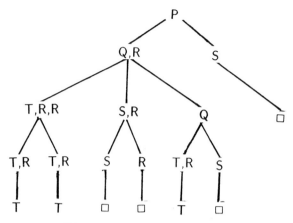

Figure 3–6 The Search Tree for a Goal Statement P
and a Database Containing the Clauses:
P:–Q,R. P:–S. Q:–T,R. Q:–S. R. S.

Eventually the clause P, which is a fact and does not cause any further sub-goal to be considered, will match. The "recurrence" of the clause Q will come to an end (see Figure 3–7).

(b)   Backtracking

PROLOG uses a depth-first backtracking search strategy to explore alternative branches of the search space. The order in which clauses are written determines the order in which they are tried. Thus it interprets a clause

$$A :- B, C, D.$$

as a procedure which attempts to solve A by first solving B then solving C then solving D. C is solved in the context created by having solved B, and so on. If a goal, say C, has failed, PROLOG then attempts to resatisfy the next goal on the left, in this case B, by returning to the uninstantiated state any variables that became instantiated when this goal B was previously satisfied. PROLOG resumes searching the database, but begins the search from where the goal's place-marker was previously put. As before, this new "backtracked" goal may either succeed or fail, which will decide whether or not to have another backtracking. For example, given clauses P and Q above, the problem of finding a common element in two lists

90

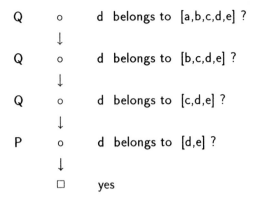

Figure 3-7 Recursion in Proving 'member(d,[a,b,c,d,e])'

?–member(X,[d,a,t,a]), member(X,[n,s,a,w,e,r]).

will generate a double nested loop.

This method of solving a query can be regarded as the construction of a proof tree [van Emden, 1984; Bruynooghe, 1982], corresponding to a branch of the search tree. A convenient representation of proof tree growth is provided by Ferguson diagrams [van Emden, 1984]. Each clause is written as a single lower semi-circle, together with 0 or more upper semi-circles. The lower semi-circle corresponds to the head of the clause, and the upper semi-circles to its body. The head of a clause also contains slots to record the binding of variables. An example is shown in Figure 3-8.

3.3.3 Extralogical Facilities of PROLOG

PROLOG incorporates only a simple proof procedure. In order to be able to compensate for this limitation and simulate programming styles more appropriate to conventional programming languages it provides various extralogical primitives, which can be used to extend the power of the language while retaining its logic foundations.

These extralogical primitives can be regarded as ways of expressing control information about how the proof is to be carried out. For instance, the built-in predicate write(N) does not have any interesting logical properties, but presupposes that the proof will have reached a certain state (with N instantiated)

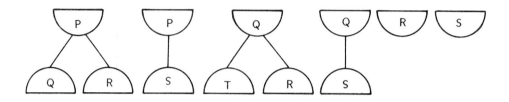

(a)   The Ferguson diagrams for the simple database
      and query used in Figure 3–6

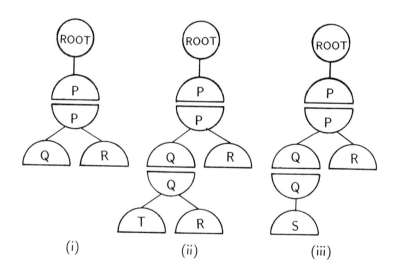

(i)   (ii)   (iii)

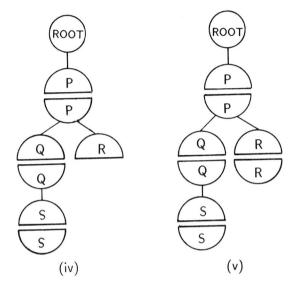

(iv)   (v)

(b)   The development of a solution:

(i)   The goal P is matched by the first clause in the databse, yielding a new goal, Q, R.

(ii)   The first clause for Q is tried, but is rejected as the sub-goal T is not satisfiable.

(iii)   The second clause for Q is used. The new goal is S, R.

(iv) S is solved, leaving only R.

(v)   The completed proof tree.

Figure 3–8   Execution of a Simple PROLOG Program

and initiates a communication with the programmer. The built-in predicate name(N,L) is saying something about the internal structure of what, in predicate calculus, would be an indivisible symbol. A set of built-in predicates supported by the PROLOG system has been collected in Appendix 1. The reader may find it valuable to refer to the Appendix from time to time in order to supplement his understanding of the precise meaning of the concepts. Here there is space to discuss only the distinctive extralogical primitive cut (written "!").

The cut is used to control backtracking. As a goal, the cut "!" succeeds immediately and cannot be resatisfied. However, it also has side-effects which alter the way backtracking works afterwards. It removes the place markers for certain goals so that they cannot be resatisfied. For instance, to compute the maximum of two numbers, instead of writing

max(X,Y,X) :- X >= Y.
max(X,Y,Y) :- X < Y.

a more efficient program is obtained by using "!":

max(X,Y,X) :- X >= Y, !.   /* clause *A* */
max(X,Y,Y).   /* clause *B* */

Thus, the clause *B* will be used only if the clause *A* (before "!") fails. It avoids the redundant computation of X < Y; but it results in individual clauses which cannot be understood correctly in isolation.

In PROLOG we can convert symbols to character strings, convert structures to lists and convert structures to clauses. A logical variable can be allowed to stand for a proposition appearing in an axiom. If the built-in predicate asserta is used to set up a new clause, there may be a different set of axioms at different times of proof! These operations violate the simple self-contained nature of predicate calculus propositions. There are no safeguards against using PROLOG in a manner which obscures and even conflicts with its logical foundations.

The ultimate goal of a logic programming language has not, then, been achieved with PROLOG. One day, the extralogical facilities of PROLOG will no longer be necessary. In the meanwhile they provide a valuable safety valve which allows logic programming to be practical today. For the sake of efficiency, the extralogical features of PROLOG can always be confined within high-level predicates which extend either the level of the logic or the power of the control facilities.

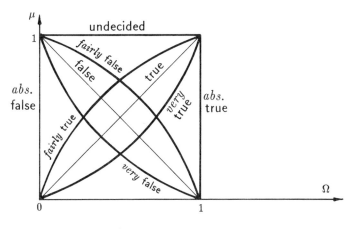

Figure 3–9

3.4 Fuzzy Linguistic Logic

The axiomatic approach described above suffers from one drawback. That is, all traditional logic habitually assumes that the information stored as axioms is absolutely correct and precise symbols are being employed. It is therefore not applicable to this terrestrial life but only to an imagined celestial existence.

In 1970's, L. A. Zadeh proposed the concepts of fuzzy restriction, linguistic variable, linguistic truth value and approximate reasoning, respectively. Fuzzy linguistic logic was then suggested by Zadeh and others [Zadeh, 1975(a)(b); Baldwin, 1979; Giles, 1979], in which *"Truth"* was treated as a linguistic variable.

3.4.1 Fuzzy Linguistic Truth Values

In our daily life, *"very true"*, *"fairly true"*, *"more or less true"*, *"false"* or *"absolutely false"* are often used to characterize the degree of truth. Therefore, it might be appropriate to treat *"Truth"* as a linguistic variable.

The term set of the linguistic variable *Truth* has been defined in different ways by different authors. Baldwin defines some of the terms, as shown in Figure 3–9.

Here

$$\mu_{very\ true}(x) = \mu_{true}^2(x), \qquad \forall x \in [0,1];$$
$$\mu_{fairly\ true}(x) = \mu_{true}^{\frac{1}{2}}(x), \qquad \forall x \in [0,1];$$

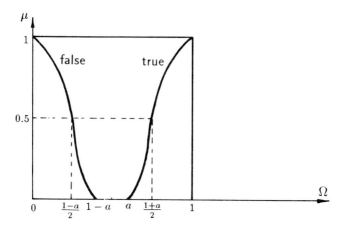

Figure 3–10 Terms *true* and *false*

and so on. Zadeh [Zadeh, 1975(a)(b)] suggests for the term *true* the membership function

$$\mu_{true}(x) = \begin{cases} 0, & 0 \le x \le \alpha; \\ 2\left(\frac{x-\alpha}{1-\alpha}\right)^2, & \alpha < x \le \frac{\alpha+1}{2}; \\ 1 - 2\left(\frac{x-1}{1-\alpha}\right)^2, & \frac{\alpha+1}{2} < x \le 1. \end{cases}$$

where $x = \frac{\alpha+1}{2}$ is called the crossover point, and $\alpha \in [0,1]$ is a parameter which indicates the subjective judgment about the minimum value of x in order to consider a statement as "*true*" at all.

Correspondingly, the membership function of *false* is considered as

$$\mu_{false}(x) = \mu_{true}(1-x), \qquad \forall x \in [0,1].$$

Figure 3–10 shows the terms *true* and *false*.

3.4.2 Connectives in Fuzzy Linguistic Logic

Fuzzy linguistic logic can be seen as the extension of set theoretic multi-valued logic in which the truth values are linguistic ones.

Since operators, like **and** ($\wedge$), **or** ($\vee$), **not** ($\neg$) and **implies** ($\rightarrow$) in fuzzy linguistic logic are also defined by using truth tables, the extension principle can be applied to derive definitions of the operators. In this book we limit consideration to possibilistic interpretations of linguistic values and adhere to Zadeh's original proposals [Zadeh, 1975(a)(b)].

Definition 3.5

If $t(\tilde{A})$ is a point in $[0,1]$, representing the truth value of the proposition "u is $\tilde{A}$" or simply $\tilde{A}$ then the truth value of **not** $\tilde{A}$ is given by

$$t(\textbf{not } \tilde{A}) \; = \; 1 - t(\tilde{A}). \tag{3.2}$$

Definition 3.6

If $t(\tilde{A})$ is a fuzzy subset in $[0,1]$, *i.e.*,

$$t(\tilde{A}) \; = \; \mu_1/t_1 + \mu_2/t_2 + \cdots + \mu_n/t_n, \tag{3.3}$$

then by applying the extension principle, the truth value of $t(\textbf{not } \tilde{A})$ is defined as

$$t(\textbf{not } \tilde{A}) \; = \; \mu_1/(1 - t_1) + \mu_2/(1 - t_2) + \cdots + \mu_n/(1 - t_n). \tag{3.4}$$

In particular, let $t(\tilde{A}) = true$, then "$false$" is interpreted as "**not** $true$", that is, for instance,

$$true \; = \; 0.6/0.5 + 0.7/0.6 + 0.8/0.7 + 0.9/0.8 + 1/0.9 + 1/1,$$

then

$$false \; = \; t(\textbf{not } true) \; = \; 0.6/0.5 + 0.7/0.4 + 0.8/0.3 + 0.9/0.2 + 1/0.1 + 1/0.$$

Definition 3.7

For numerical truth values $t(\tilde{A})$ and $t(\tilde{B})$ the connectives **and, or, implies** are defined as

$$\begin{aligned} t(\tilde{A} \textbf{ and } \tilde{B}) \; &= \; t(\tilde{A}) \wedge t(\tilde{B}) \\ &= \; \min\{\mu_{\tilde{A}}(t_1), \mu_{\tilde{B}}(t_1)\}/t_1 + \cdots + \min\{\mu_{\tilde{A}}(t_n), \mu_{\tilde{B}}(t_n)\}/t_n. \end{aligned} \tag{3.5}$$

$$\begin{aligned} t(\tilde{A} \textbf{ or } \tilde{B}) \; &= \; t(\tilde{A}) \vee t(\tilde{B}) \\ &= \; \max\{\mu_{\tilde{A}}(t_1), \mu_{\tilde{B}}(t_1)\}/t_1 + \cdots + \max\{\mu_{\tilde{A}}(t_n), \mu_{\tilde{B}}(t_n)\}/t_n. \end{aligned} \tag{3.6}$$

$$\begin{aligned} t(\textbf{not } \tilde{A}) \; &= \; t(\neg \tilde{A}) \\ &= \; (1 - \mu_{\tilde{A}}(t_1))/t_1 + \cdots + (1 - \mu_{\tilde{A}}(t_n))/t_n. \end{aligned} \tag{3.7}$$

$$t(\tilde{A} \text{ implies } \tilde{B}) = t(\tilde{A}) \rightarrow t(\tilde{B}) =$$

$$\max\{(1 - \mu_{\tilde{A}}(t_1)), \mu_{\tilde{B}}(t_1)\}/t_1 + \cdots + \max\{(1 - \mu_{\tilde{A}}(t_n)), \mu_{\tilde{B}}(t_n)\}/t_n. \quad (3.8)$$

Example 3.14

Let

$$t(\tilde{A}) = \textit{true}$$
$$= 0.7/0.5 + 0.7/0.7 + 0.8/0.8 + 0.9/0.9 + 1/1$$

and

$$t(\tilde{B}) = \textbf{not } \textit{true}$$
$$= 1/0 + 0.9/0.1 + 0.8/0.2 + 0.7/0.3 + 0.3/0.5 + 0.2/0.6 + 0.1/0.7$$

then

$$t(\tilde{A} \textbf{ and } \tilde{B}) = \textit{true} \textbf{ and not } \textit{true}$$
$$= 1/0 + 0.9/0.1 + 0.8/0.2 + 0.7/0.3 + 0.3/0.5 + 0.1/0.7$$
$$= \textbf{not } \textit{true}$$

Definition 3.8

For linguistic truth values

$$t(\tilde{A}) = a_1/t_1 + \cdots + a_n/t_n \qquad (3.9)$$
$$t(\tilde{B}) = b_1/s_1 + \cdots + b_m/s_m \qquad (3.10)$$

By applying the extension principle, the conjunctions **and**, **or** and **implies** are defined as follows:

$$t(\tilde{A} \textbf{ and } \tilde{B}) = t(\tilde{A}) \wedge t(\tilde{B})$$
$$= (a_1/t1 + \cdots + a_n/t_n) \wedge (b_1/s_1 + \cdots + b_m/s_m)$$
$$= \sum_{i,j}(a_i \wedge b_j)/(t_i \wedge s_j). \qquad (3.11)$$

$$t(\tilde{A} \textbf{ or } \tilde{B}) = t(\tilde{A}) \vee t(\tilde{B})$$
$$= (a_1/t1 + \cdots + a_n/t_n) \vee (b_1/s_1 + \cdots + b_m/s_m)$$
$$= \sum_{i,j}(a_i \wedge b_j)/(t_i \vee s_j). \qquad (3.12)$$

and	T	F	T+F
T	T	F	T+F
F	F	F	F
T+F	T+F	F	T+F

(a) Truth Table for **and**

or	T	F	T+F
T	T	T	T
F	T	F	T+F
T+F	T	T+F	T+F

(b) Truth Table for **or**

Figure 3–11

$$
\begin{aligned}
t(\tilde{A} \text{ implies } \tilde{B}) &= t(\tilde{A} \rightarrow \tilde{B}) \\
&= (a_1/t_1 + \cdots + a_n/t_n) \rightarrow (b_1/s_1 + \cdots + b_m/s_m) \\
&= \sum_{i,j}(a_i \wedge b_j)/(1 - t_i) \wedge (t_i \wedge s_j).
\end{aligned}
\tag{3.13}
$$

3.4.3 Truth Tables and Linguistic Approximation

In classical logic, binary conjunctions are usually defined by the tabulation of truth values in truth tables. In fuzzy logic, however, the number of truth values is, in general, infinite. Therefore tabulation of all truth values for logic operators is impossible. Nevertheless, we can tabulate truth values, that is, terms of the linguistic variable *"Truth"* for a finite number of terms, such as *true*, **not** *true*, *very true*, *false*, *fairly false*, *more or less true*, *absolutely true*, and so on.

Zadeh has suggested truth tables for the determination of truth values *true*, *false*, *unknown* and *undefined*, where *"unknown"* was interpreted as *"true or false"* (T+F) and *"undefined"* was denoted by θ [Zadeh, 1975(a)(b)].

Extending the classical two-valued logic with truth values *true* and *false* to a three-valued logic with a universe of truth values being two-valued (*true* and *false*) we obtain the truth tables as shown in Figure 3–11. If the number of truth values increases one can still "tabulate" the truth table for operators by using Definition 3.7 as follows:

Let us assume that the i-th row of the table represents **"not** *true"* and the j-th column *"more or less true"*. The (i,j)-th entry in the truth table for **"and"** would then contain the entry for **"not** *true* **and** *more or less true"*. The resulting fuzzy set would, however, most likely not correspond to any fuzzy set assigned to the terms of the term set of *"Truth"*. In this case one could try to find the fuzzy set of the term which is most similar to the fuzzy set resulting from the computations. Such a term would then be called linguistic approximation. This is an analogy to statistics, where empirical distribution functions are often approximated by well-known standard distribution functions.

Baldwin has suggested an alternative version of fuzzy linguistic logic, fuzzy truth tables, and their determination [Baldwin, 1979]: The truth values on which he bases his suggestions we have already shown in Figure 3–9. They were defined as:

$$\mu_{true}(x) = x; \qquad \qquad \mu_{false}(x) = 1 - x;$$

$$\mu_{very\ true}(x) = \mu_{true}^2(x); \qquad \mu_{very\ false}(x) = \mu_{false}^2(x);$$

$$\mu_{fairly\ true}(x) = \mu_{true}^{\frac{1}{2}}(x); \qquad \mu_{fairly\ false}(x) = \mu_{false}^{\frac{1}{2}}(x);$$

$$\mu_{abs.true}(x) = \begin{cases} 1, & x = 1; \\ 0, & \text{otherwise.} \end{cases} \qquad \mu_{abs.false}(x) = \begin{cases} 1, & x = 0; \\ 0, & \text{otherwise.} \end{cases}$$

where $x \in [0,1]$. Hence

$$(very)^k true \longrightarrow absolutely\ true \quad \text{as} \quad k \longrightarrow \infty$$
$$(very)^k true \longrightarrow absolutely\ false \quad \text{as} \quad k \longrightarrow \infty$$
$$(fairly)^k true \longrightarrow undecided \quad \text{as} \quad k \longrightarrow \infty$$
$$(fairly)^k false \longrightarrow undecided \quad \text{as} \quad k \longrightarrow \infty$$

Finally, using the possibilistic interpretation of **"and"** and **"or"** respectively, we have the truth table shown in Figure 3–12 [Baldwin, 1979].

3.5 The Syntax and Semantics of f-Horn Clause Rules

Based on first order predicate logic, from now on, we will present a new approach to generalizing the syntax and semantics of ordinary Horn clause rules to establish the fuzzy proof theory [Liu and Li, 1989(a), 1990]. First of all, each Horn clause rule is associated with a numerical implication strength f; therefore, we obtain f-Horn clause rules. Secondly, Herbrand interpretations can be generalized to fuzzy subsets of the Herbrand base. We show that as a result, the procedural interpretation for Horn clause rules presented by R. A. Kowalski [Kowalski, 1974] can be developed in much the same way for f-Horn clause rules. Hence, we obtain the fuzzy logic programming system.

$t(\tilde{P})$	$t(\tilde{Q})$	$t(\tilde{P}$ and $\tilde{Q})$	$t(\tilde{P}$ or $\tilde{Q})$
false	false	false	false
true	false	false	true
true	true	true	true
undecided	false	false	undecided
undecided	undecided	undecided	undecided
true	very true	true	very true
true	fairly true	fairly true	true

Figure 3–12

3.5.1 Syntax of Finite Sets of f-Horn Clause Rules

The implication of a Horn clause is called a Horn clause rule. In the quantitative case, an f-Horn clause rule also has a conclusion and a condition, it is similar to a Horn clause rule in form, and the difference is that each f-Horn clause rule has a numerical implication strength f, where $f \in (0,1]$. The formal specification of an f-Horn clause rule is

$$A \leftarrow (f) - B_1 \wedge B_2 \wedge \cdots \wedge B_n, \qquad n \geq 0. \qquad (3.14)$$

Suppose the truth value of B_i is $tv(B_i)$, $i = 1, 2, \ldots, n$, and the truth value of the condition is t. When $n > 0$,

$$t = \min\{tv(B_i)|i = 1, 2, \ldots, n\};$$

when $n = 0$, we define $t = 1$. The truth value of conclusion $tv(A) = f \times t$.

When $f = 1$, quantitative f-Horn clause rules correspond to qualitative Horn clause rules in form. However, in both the quantitative case and the qualitative case, the concepts of truth value are essentially distinct. To emphasize this distinction, we use S_f to denote the set of f-Horn clause rules.

To facilitate generalization of the procedural interpretation, we distinguish four kinds of f-Horn clause rules [Liu and Li, 1988(a), 1989(b)]:

(a) $A \leftarrow (f) -$.

A rule consisting of only one conclusion, is interpreted as an **f-Assertion** or an **f-Fact**.

(b) $A \leftarrow (f) - B_1 \wedge B_2 \wedge \cdots \wedge B_n.$

A rule consisting of exactly one conclusion and $n (\geq 0)$ conditions, is interpreted as an **f-Procedure**. The A is the name of the f-Procedure, and $\{B_1, B_2, \ldots, B_n\}$ $(n \geq 0)$ is its body. Each B_i $(i = 1, 2, \ldots, n)$ is interpreted as an **f-Procedural call**. When $n = 0$, it is an f-Assertion or an f-Fact. So (a) is a special case of (b).

(c) $\leftarrow (f) - B_1 \wedge B_2 \wedge \cdots \wedge B_n.$

A rule consisting of no conclusions and $n (\geq 1)$ conditions, is interpreted as an f-Goal.

(d) $\square$.

Empty rule, containing no atomic formulae, is interpreted as a halt statement.

Now we have the formalization of f-Horn clause rules. Though quantitative f-Horn clause rules are similar to qualitative Horn clause rules in form, their procedural interpretation becomes more complex because of the distinct notions of the truth value and the occurrence of implication strength f.

3.5.2   Semantics of Finite Sets of f-Horn Clause Rules

In this section, the semantics of Horn clause rules will be generalized, for the purpose of presenting the semantics of finite sets of f-Horn clause rules. We first extend some basic concepts of Horn clause logic.

Definition 3.9

Let S_f be a set of f-Horn claues rules, the Herbrand base $H(S_f)$ of the S_f is the set of all basic atomic formulae that can be formed with the symbols contained in S_f.

Definition 3.10

Let S_f be a set of f-Horn clause rules, $H(S_f)$ denote the Herbrand base of S_f. The Herbrand interpretation I of S_f is defined as a mapping $H(S_f) \rightarrow [0, 1]$.

In this case, a Herbrand interpretation is regarded as a fuzzy subset of $H(S_f)$. The mapping $H(S_f) \rightarrow [0, 1]$ can be thought of as the membership function characterizing a fuzzy subset I of S_f. All Herbrand interpretations of a given set S_f can be specified by a function μ taking as arguments a variable-free atomic formula A, and an interpretation I, and having as result $\mu_I(A)$, the value of the membership function for I at the argument A.

In the quantitative case, when is set of f-Horn clause rules true in a given interpretation I?

Definition 3.11

For a set S_f of f-Horn clause rules and its interpretation I,

(i) S_f is true in I **iff**
      every one of its f-Horn clause rules is true in I.

(ii) An f-Horn clause rule R in S_f is true in I **iff**
      every one of its basic instances is true in I.

(iii) A basic instance $A \leftarrow (f) - B_1 \wedge B_2 \wedge \cdots \wedge B_n$
      of the R is true in I **iff**

$$\mu_I(A) \geq f \times \min\{\mu_I(B_i)|i = 1, 2, \ldots, n\} \tag{3.15}$$

(iv) A basic instance $A \leftarrow (f) -$ is true in I **iff**

$$\mu_I(A) \geq f \tag{3.16}$$

Here, we define $\min \emptyset = 1$. In this definition, parts (i) and (ii) are the same as in the qualitative case. When $f = 1$ and $\mu_I(B_i) = 0$ or $\mu_I(B_i) = 1$ $(i = 1, 2, \ldots, n)$, (iii) and (iv) are also the same as in the qualitative case. So the qualitative case can be seen as the special case of the quantitative case.

Definition 3.12

A Herbrand interpretation I such that a set S_f of f-Horn clause rules is true in I is called a Herbrand model of S_f.

Definition 3.13

For any set S_f of f-Horn clause rules (let its Herbrand base be $H(S_f)$), any $A \in H(S_f)$, and any $f \in (0, 1]$, $S_f \models \{A \leftarrow (f) -\}$ iff the right-hand side is true in every Herbrand model of S_f.

Note that the symbol "$\models$" means truth in all Herbrand models rather than in all models.

For a set S_f of f-Horn clause rules, it is clear that

$$S_f \models \{A \leftarrow (f) -\} \textbf{ implies } S_f \models \{A \leftarrow (f') -\},$$
$$\forall f, f' \in [0, 1], \textbf{ and } f \geq f'. \tag{3.17}$$

103

Let S_f be a set of f-Horn clause rules, and $M(S_f)$ denote the set of Herbrand models of S_f. $\cap M(S_f)$ is defined in the quantitative case by adopting

$$\mu_{\cap S_I}(A) = \inf\{\mu_I(A) \mid I \in S_I\}, \tag{3.18}$$

where S_I is a set of Herbrand interpretations and inf is the greatest lower bound.

Theorem 3.1

Let S_f be a set of f-Horn clause rules, and $\cap M(S_f)$ denote the intersection of all Herbrand models of S_f. Therefore

$$\mu_{\cap M(S_f)}(A) = \sup\{f \mid S_f \models \{A \leftarrow(f)\!\!-\}\}, \tag{3.19}$$

where sup is the least upper bound.

PROOF. If S_f is a set of f-Horn clause rules, I is a Herbrand model of S_f, $A \in H(S_f)$, and $S_f \models \{A \leftarrow (f)\!\!-\}$, then $\{A \leftarrow (f)\!\!-\}$ is true in I, and $\mu_I(A) \geq f$, by Definition 3.11. Therefore

$$\mu_I(A) \geq \sup\{f_1 \mid S_f \models \{A \leftarrow(f_1)\!\!-\}\}, \tag{3.20}$$

for any Herbrand model $I \in M(S_f)$, and

$$\mu_{\cap M(S_f)}(A) \geq \sup\{f_1 \mid S_f \models \{A \leftarrow(f_1)\!\!-\}\}. \tag{3.21}$$

However, we have $S_f \models A \leftarrow(f_2)\!\!-$, where $f_2 = \mu_{\cap M(S_f)}(A)$, for any S_f and all $A \in H(S_f)$. So the relation

$$\mu_{\cap M(S_f)}(A) > \sup\{f \mid S_f \models \{A \leftarrow(f)\!\!-\}\}$$

is impossible. So far, the theorem has been proved.

For the qualitative case, fixed point theory associates each set S of Horn clause rules with a mapping T_S from interpretation to interpretation, and it shows that fixed points of T_S are models of S.

Now we follow the same way to establish the fixed point semantics for a set S_f of f-Horn clause rules.

Definition 3.14

Let S_f be a set of f-Horn clause rules. For every $A \in H(S_f)$,

$$\begin{aligned}
\mu_{T_{S_f}(I)}(A) = {}& \sup\{f \times \min\{\mu_I(B_i) \mid i = 1, 2, \ldots, n\} \mid \\
& A \leftarrow(f)- \; B_1 \wedge B_2 \wedge \cdots \wedge B_n \text{ is a basic instance} \\
& \text{of a f-Horn clause rule in } S_f\}.
\end{aligned} \tag{3.22}$$

Definition 3.15

Let S_f be a set of f-Horn clause rules, and $H(S_f)$ denote the Herbrand base of S_f. For two interpretations I_1, I_2 of S_f,

$$I_1 \subseteq I_2 \text{ iff } \mu_{I_1}(A) \le \mu_{I_2}(A) \qquad \forall A \in H(S_f). \tag{3.23}$$

Theorem 3.2

For any set S_f of f-Horn clause rules, T_{S_f} is a monotone function.

PROOF. Let $I_1 \subseteq H(S_f)$, $I_2 \subseteq H(S_f)$, and $I_1 \subseteq I_2$. By Definition 3.15, if

$$A \leftarrow (f) - B_1 \wedge B_2 \wedge \cdots \wedge B_n$$

is the basic instance of a f-Horn clause rule in S_f, then

$$\mu_{I_1}(Bi) \le \mu_{I_2}(Bi), \qquad i = 1, 2, \ldots, n.$$

For any $A \in H(S_f)$,

$$\mu_{I_1}(A) \le \mu_{I_2}(A),$$

by Definition 3.14. Therefore $T_{S_f}(I_1) \subseteq TS_f(I_2)$. It is said that T_{S_f} is a monotone function.

The following theorem will associate models with fixed points in the quantitative case.

Inference 3.1

For the set of f-Horn clause rules, the monotonicity of S_f implies that the least fixed point $lfp(T_{S_f})$ of T_{S_f}, namely

$$\cap \{I | T_{S_f}(I) = I\}$$

exists and is equal to

$$\cap \{I | T_{S_f}(I) \subseteq I\}.$$

Theorem 3.3

For any set S_f of f-Horn clause rules, and any $I \subseteq H(S_f)$,

$$I \in M(S_f) \text{ iff } T_{S_f}(I) \subseteq I. \tag{3.24}$$

PROOF. ($\Longrightarrow$)
If $I \in M(S_f)$, then S_f is true in I. For any basic instance

$$A \leftarrow (f) - B_1 \wedge B_2 \wedge \cdots \wedge B_n$$

of an f-Horn clause rule in S_f we have

$$\mu_I(A) \geq f \times \min\{\mu_I(B_i)|i = 1, 2, \ldots, n\}. \tag{3.25}$$

by Definition 3.11. Hence

$$\begin{aligned}
\mu_I(A) \geq\ & \sup\{f \times \min\{\mu_I(B_i)|i = 1, 2, \ldots, n\}| \\
& A \leftarrow(f)-\ B_1 \wedge B_2 \wedge \cdots \wedge B_n \text{ is a basic instance} \\
& \text{of a f-Horn clause rule in } S_f\}. \tag{3.26}
\end{aligned}$$

and $\mu_I(A) \geq \mu_{T_{S_f}(I)}(A)$ by Definition 3.14. Therefore

$$T_{S_f}(I) \subseteq I.$$

$(\Longleftarrow)$

If $T_{S_f}(I) \subseteq I$, then $\mu_I(A) \geq \mu_{T_{S_f}(I)}(A)$, for any $A \in H(S_f)$, by Definition 3.15. In addition, for any basic instance

$$A \leftarrow(f)-\ B_1 \wedge B_2 \wedge \cdots \wedge B_n$$

of a f-Horn clause rule in S_f we have

$$\mu_{T_{S_f}(I)}(A) \geq f \times \min\{\mu_I(B_i)|i = 1, 2, \ldots, n\}, \tag{3.27}$$

by Definition 3.14. Hence

$$\mu_I(A) \geq f \times \min\{\mu_I(B_i)|i = 1, 2, \ldots, n\},$$

and this implies that S_f is true in I by Definition 3.11. It is said that $I \in M(S_f)$.

Theorem 3.3 enables us to discover properties of Herbrand models by studying fixed points of T_{S_f}.

Theorem 3.4

For any set S_f of f-Horn clause rules

$$\cap M(S_f) = lfp(T_{S_f}). \tag{3.28}$$

PROOF. We know that

$$lfp(T_{S_f}) = \cap\{I|T_{S_f}(I) = I\},$$

by Inference 3.1. By Theorem 3.3,

$$T_{S_f}(I) = I \quad \textbf{iff} \quad I \in M(S_f).$$

Hence

$$lfp(T_{S_f}) = \cap\{I \mid T_{S_f}(I) = I\}$$
$$= \cap\{I \mid I \in M(S_f)\}$$
$$= \cap M(S_f).$$

Theorem 3.5

For any set S_f of f-Horn clause rules, mapping T_{S_f} is continuous, *i.e.*

$$\cup\{T_{S_f}(I_j) \mid j \in N\} = T_{S_f}(\cup\{I_j \mid j \in N\})$$

for all chains $I_1 \subseteq I_2 \subseteq \cdots$ of Herbrand interpretations.

PROOF. For any atomic formula $A \in H(S_f)$, we have

$$\mu_{T_{S_f}(\cup\{I_j|j\in N\})}(A) = \sup\{f \times \min\{\mu_{\cup\{I_j|j\in N\}}(B_k) \mid k = 1, 2, \ldots, n\} \mid$$
$$A \leftarrow(f)- B_1 \wedge B_2 \wedge \cdots \wedge B_n \text{ is a basic instance}$$
$$\text{of a f-Horn clause rule in } S_f\}.$$

Suppose

$$A \leftarrow(f_\alpha)- B_{\alpha 1} \wedge B_{\alpha 2} \wedge \cdots \wedge B_{\alpha n_\alpha}$$

is the α-th basic instance of f-Horn clause rules in S_f having A as conclusion. The above expression can be shortened to

$$\mu_{T_{S_f}(\cup\{I_j|j\in N\})}(A) =$$
$$\sup_\alpha(f_\alpha \times \min_k \mu_{\cup\{I_j|j\in N\}}(B_{\alpha k})).$$

However,

$$\mu_{\cup\{I_j|j\in N\}}(B_{\alpha k}) = \sup_j \mu_{I_j}(B_{\alpha k}),$$

where j indexes the monotone chain $I_1 \subseteq I_2 \subseteq \cdots$ of Herbrand interpretations, therefore

$$\mu_{T_{S_f}(\cup\{I_j|j\in N\})}(A) = \sup_\alpha \sup_j f_\alpha \times \min_k \mu_{I_j}(B_{\alpha k})$$
$$= \sup_\alpha \sup_j v_{\alpha j},$$

where $v_{\alpha j} = f_\alpha \times \min_k \mu_{I_j}(B_{\alpha k})$. Using the same method we find

$$\mu_{\cup\{T_{S_f}(I_j)|j\in N\}}(A) = \sup_j \sup_\alpha v_{\alpha j}.$$

Now

$$\sup_{\alpha} \sup_{j} v_{\alpha j} \;=\; \sup_{j} \sup_{\alpha} v_{\alpha j}$$

needs to be proved. The set consisting of all $v_{\alpha j}$ is bounded above; therefore, it has a least upper bound, say v. Hence,

$$\sup_{\alpha} \sup_{j} v_{\alpha j} \;>\; v.$$

On the other hand, for all $\alpha \in N$, we have

$$\sup_{j} v_{\alpha j} \;<\; v;$$

therefore

$$\sup_{\alpha} \sup_{j} v_{\alpha j} \;<\; v.$$

Hence,

$$\sup_{\alpha} \sup_{j} v_{\alpha j} \;=\; v.$$

Similarly, we show that

$$\sup_{j} \sup_{\alpha} v_{\alpha j} \;=\; v.$$

Therefore

$$\cup \{ T_{S_f}(I_j) | j \in N \} \;=\; T_{S_f}(\cup \{ I_j | j \in N \}).$$

It is easy to prove the important property of T_{S_f} by the above Theorem 3.5.

Theorem 3.6

For any set S_f of f-Horn clause rules,

$$lfp(T_{S_f}) \;=\; \cup \{ T_{S_f}^n(\emptyset) | n \in N \},$$

where $\emptyset$ is a special interpretation such that

$$\mu_{\emptyset}(A) \;=\; 0, \qquad \forall A \in H(S_f).$$

Now we present a theorem that can serve as a foundation for the completeness result on the quantitative proof theory. A completeness result for a proof method is of the form: if an assertion is true, then it can be proved according to the method.

We assume $\mu_{M(S_f)}(A) \;=\; c$, and want to show that $A \leftarrow (c) \vdash$ can be derived from S_f. By Theorem 3.4 and Theorem 3.6, we have

$$\cap M(S_f) \;=\; \cup \{ T_{S_f}^n(\emptyset) | n \in N \}.$$

But we try to draw the stronger conclusion from $\mu_{M(S_f)}(A) = c$ that there exists an $n \in N$ such that $\mu_{T_{S_f}^n(\emptyset)}(A) = c$. Here is one of the methods.

Lemma 3.1

For any finite set S_f of f-Horn clause rules, any $A \in H(S_f)$, and any real number $\varepsilon > 0$,

$$\{\mu_{T_{S_f}^n(\emptyset)}(A) \mid n \in N \text{ and } \mu_{T_{S_f}^n(\emptyset)}(A) \geq \varepsilon\}$$

is finite.

PROOF. Let $F(S_f)$ be the set of implications of f-Horn clause rules in S_f. Note that S_f is finite, therefore $F(S_f)$ is a finite set. Let m be the greatest element of $F(S_f)$ such that $m < 1$. The real number $\mu_{T_{S_f}^n(\emptyset)}(A)$ is a product of a sequence of elements of $F(S_f)$. In this sequence, if q is the smallest integer such that $m^q < \varepsilon$, then at most q elements can be less than 1. The sequence can have any length, because 1 can occur in the sequence any number of times. So we conclude that the number of different products $(> \varepsilon)$ of the sequences of elements of $F(S_f)$ is not greater than $|F(S_f)|^q$.

Theorem 3.7

For any finite set S_f of f-Horn clause rules, and any $A \in H(S_f)$, there exists an $n \in N$ such that

$$\mu_{\cap M(S_f)}(A) = \mu_{T_{S_f}^n(\emptyset)}(A). \tag{3.29}$$

PROOF. If $v = \mu_{\cap M(S_f)}(A) = 0$, then there exists $n = 0 \in N$ such that the expression holds. Suppose $v > 0$, then

$$\cap M(S_f) = lfp(T_{S_f}) = \cup\{T_{S_f}^n(\emptyset) \mid n \in N\},$$

by Theorem 3.4 and Theorem 3.6. Hence

$$
\begin{aligned}
\mu_{\cap M(S_f)}(A) &= \sup\{\mu_{T_{S_f}^n(\emptyset)}(A) \mid n \in N\} \\
&= \sup\{\mu_{T_{S_f}^n(\emptyset)}(A) \mid n \in N \text{ and } \mu_{T_{S_f}(\emptyset)}(A) \geq \varepsilon\}. \tag{3.30}
\end{aligned}
$$

for any $\varepsilon < \mu$. If we choose such an ε positive, according to $\mu > 0$, then (3.25) is finite by Lemma 3.1. Hence the least upper bound is attained for an $n \in N$.

Note that the sets of f-Horn clause rules discussed in this section are finite; it is not a superfluous condition.

3.6 Proof Theory Based on f-Horn Clause Rules

In this section we describe a fuzzy proof procedure precisely for f-Horn clause rules, and justify its results using the semantics results presented in the previous section.

As in the qualitative case, the quantitative proof procedure for f-Horn clause rules is also a search of an **and/or** tree. This tree is determined by a set S_f of f-Horn clause rules and an initial atom G is defined as follows:

Definition 3.16

(1) There are two kinds of nodes: and-nodes and or-nodes.

(2) Each or-node is labelled by a single atomic formula.

(3) Each and-node is labelled by an f-Horn clause rule in S_f and a substitution.

(4) The descendants of each or-node are all and-nodes, and the descendants of each and-node are all or-nodes.

(5) The root is an or-node labelled G.

(6) For each f-Horn clause rule R in S_f with a left-hand side unifying with the atomic formula A (with the most general substitution θ) in an or-node, there is an and-node descendant of the or-node labelled with R and θ. An and-node with no descendants is called a failure node.

(7) For each atomic formula B in the right-hand side of the f-Horn clause rule labelling an and-node, there is a descendant or-node labelled with B. An and-node with no descendants is called a success node.

(8) Each node is associated with a real number which is called the value of the node. The value of a success node is the implication of its associated f-Horn clause rule. The value of a nonterminal and-node is $f \times t$, where f is the implication strength of the f-Horn clause rule labelling the and-node and t is the minimum of the values of its descendants. The value of a failure node is 0. The value of a nonterminal or-node is the maximum of the values of its descendants.

In the quantitative case, a proof tree is a subtree of an and/or tree defined

110

as follows: the root of the proof tree is the root of the and/or tree. An or-node of the proof tree which also occurs in the and/or tree has one descendant in the proof tree which is one of the descendants of that node in the and/or tree. An and-node in the proof tree which also occurs in the and/or tree has as descendants in the proof tree all of the descendants of that node in the and/or tree. Furthermore, all terminal nodes in a proof tree are success nodes. We assign values to proof tree nodes in the same way as we do to nodes in an and/or tree.

In the qualitative case, correctness of the (SLD-resolution) proof procedure says, in the most elementary form: if $A \in H(S_f)$ is proved, then $A \in M(S_f)$. We can express correctness like this: results of the proof procedure are not more true than they are in the minimal model $\cap M(S_f)$.

In the quantitative case limited to finite and/or trees, the form of the corresponding correctness is suggested.

Theorem 3.8

For any set S_f of f-Horn clause rules with a finite and/or tree and any $A \in H(S_f)$, the value of the root in the and/or tree with A as root is not greater than $\mu_{\cap M(S_f)}(A)$.

PROOF. Note first that the value of the root in the and/or tree is the maximum of the values of the roots of its constituent proof trees. It can easily be verified that the value of the root of a proof tree with A as root is not greater than $T_{S_f}^{n+1}(\emptyset)$, where n is the length of a longest path from the root to a terminal node. Here one unit of path length is from or-node to or-node along the path. It is proved by Theorem 3.7.

The following is the completeness of the proof procedure.

Theorem 3.9

For any set S_f of f-Horn clause rules with a finite and/or tree and any $A \in H(S_f)$, the value μ of the root in the and/or tree with A as root is at least $\mu_{\cap M(S_f)}(A)$.

PROOF. By induction on n, we prove that $\mu_{S_f}^n(\emptyset)(A)$, for all $n \in N$. Then we conclude that

$$
\begin{aligned}
\mu &\geq \sup\{\mu_{T_{S_f}^n(\emptyset)}(A)|n \in N\} \\
&= \mu_{\cup\{T_{S_f}^n(\emptyset)|n \in N\}}(A)
\end{aligned}
$$

$$= \mu_{\cap M(S_f)}(A).$$

Now we start the inductive proof of $\mu \geq \mu_{T^n_{S_f}(\emptyset)}(A)$.

(1) for $n = 0$, it is true.

(2) suppose it holds for $n = n_0$, then

$$\mu_{T^{n_0+1}_{S_f}(\emptyset)}(A) = \sup\{f \times \min\{\mu_{T^{n_0}_{S_f}(\emptyset)}(B_k) \mid k \in N\} \mid$$
$$A \leftarrow (f)- B_1 \wedge B_2 \wedge \cdots \wedge B_n \text{ is a basic instance}$$
$$\text{of a f-Horn clause rule in } S_f\}.$$

The set over which the supremum is taken is finite by Lemma 3.1. Therefore the supremum must be attained for basic instance

$$A \leftarrow (f)- B_1 \wedge B_2 \wedge \cdots \wedge B_n$$

of an f-Horn clause rule R:

$$A' \leftarrow (f)- B'_1 \wedge B'_2 \wedge \cdots \wedge B'_n$$

in S_f. Hence

$$\mu_{T^{n_0+1}_{S_f}(\emptyset)}(A) = f \times \min\{\mu_{T^{n_0}_{S_f}(\emptyset)}(B_k) \mid k \in N\}. \tag{3.31}$$

Let us consider the and/or tree for S_f having A as root. One of the descendants of the root must be the f-Horn clause rule. Because its left-hand side A' has A as basic instance, there is a most general substitution of A' and A. Hence one of the descendants of the root is the node (R, θ) labelled with R and θ. Its descendants are B'_1, B'_2, ..., B'_k with values μ'_1, μ'_2, ..., μ'_k and having B_1, B_2, ..., B_k respectively as basic instances.

By the induction hypothesis, B_1, B_2, ..., B_k are roots of the and/or tree having values μ_1, μ_2, ..., μ_k such that $\mu_i \geq \mu_{T^{n_0}_{S_f}(\emptyset)}(B_i)$, $i = 1, 2, \ldots, k$. Because B'_i has B_i as an instance, we must have $\mu'_i > \mu_i$. For the value μ of the entire and/or tree, with A as root, we have

$$\mu = f \times \min\{\mu'_i \mid i = 1, 2, \ldots, k\}$$

and hence

$$\mu \geq f \times \min\{\mu_{T^{n_0}_{S_f}(\emptyset)}(B_i) \mid i = 1, 2, \ldots, k\}.$$

We conclude

$$\mu \geq \mu_{T_{S_f}^{n_0+1}(\emptyset)}(A)$$

by (3.26), which completes the induction proof.

3.7 The Fuzzy Procedural Interpretation

In the logic programming system presented by R. A. Kowalski [Kowalski, 1974], each Horn clause rule is interpreted as a procedure. More clearly, all kinds of Horn clause rules in the set of S are referred to as follows:

1. Goal statement $\leftarrow A_1 \wedge A_2 \wedge \cdots \wedge A_n$ $(n \geq 1)$, in which atoms are goals or questions needed to be answered. In the logic programming system presented by Kowalski, the sub-goal $\leftarrow A_1$ is the first to be answered, then the $\leftarrow A_2$ is answered, ..., until finally the $\leftarrow A_n$ is answered.

2. Procedure declaration $A \leftarrow B_1 \wedge B_2 \wedge \cdots \wedge B_n$ $(n \geq 0)$ is interpreted as a method or a rule for question answering. For answering question $\leftarrow A$, the subquestions $\leftarrow B_i$ $(i = 1, 2, \ldots, n)$ need to be answered first. The question answering procedure is also according to the sequence from left to right.

3. Assertion $A \leftarrow$ (*i.e.* fact) can be regarded as a special rule of question answering; however it answers the question $\leftarrow A$ directly with no subquestion derivation.

A fuzzy logic program can be interpreted procedurally also. The procedural interpretation is similar to the nonfuzzy case, except that a truth value is also computed from the truth values of the fuzzy procedures used. Here, f-Horn clause rules in the set of S_f are interpreted in a similar way [Liu and Li, 1988(a)]:

1. f-Goal $\leftarrow (f) - A_1 \wedge A_2 \wedge \cdots \wedge A_n$ $(n \geq 1)$, in which atoms are goals or questions related to the f needed to be answered. In the fuzzy logic programming system, the f-Goal will not be satisfied until the n sub-goals are all satisfied.

2. f-Procedure $A \leftarrow (f) - B_1 \wedge B_2 \wedge \cdots \wedge B_n$ $(n \geq 0)$ is interpreted as a fuzzy rule of question answering. For a given question $\leftarrow (g) - A$, when $g > f$, this rule for A goes nowhere; when $g \leq f$, the subquestions $\leftarrow (f') - B_1$,

$\leftarrow(f')- B_2, \ldots$, and $\leftarrow(f')- B_n \ (n > 0)$ need to be answered first, where $f' = \frac{g}{f}$. The question answering procedure is according to the sequence from left to right.

3. f-Assertion $A \leftarrow(f)\vdash$ (*i.e.* f-Fact) can be regarded as a special rule of fuzzy question answering. For question $\leftarrow(g)- A$, if $g \leq f$, then it is satisfied; if $g > f$, then it is not satisfied. The question is answered directly with no subquestion derivation.

A set S_f of f-Horn clause rules can be seen as a fuzzy logic program. It is initiated by an initial f-Goal, similar to the case of ordinary Horn clause rules. By using f-Procedures constantly, new f-Goals can be derived from old ones, so as to advance the computation procedure. Finally, it terminates with the derivation of the halt statement $\square$ (it is derived from $\leftarrow(f_1)- A$ and $A \leftarrow(f_2)\vdash$, where $f_1 \leq f_2$).

Suppose we have f-Goal

$$\leftarrow(f_1)- A_1 \wedge A_2 \wedge \cdots \wedge A_n, \qquad n \geq 1 \qquad (3.32)$$

corresponding to the n sub-goals

$$\begin{cases} \leftarrow(f_1)- A_1, \\ \leftarrow(f_1)- A_2, \\ \quad\vdots \\ \leftarrow(f_1)- A_n. \end{cases} \qquad (3.33)$$

We may well select f-Procedural call A_1, to prove the subquestion $\leftarrow(f_1)- A_1$. Now suppose f-Procedure

$$A \leftarrow(f_2)- B_1 \wedge B_2 \wedge \cdots \wedge B_m, \qquad m \geq 0 \qquad (3.34)$$

exists in S_f. If A_1 matches A, namely $f_1 \leq f_2$ and the most general substitution exists between A_1 and A, then it derives the new f-Goal:

$$\begin{cases} \leftarrow(f_1')- (B_1 \wedge B_2 \wedge \cdots \wedge B_n)\theta, \\ \leftarrow(f_1)- A_2\theta, \\ \quad\vdots \\ \leftarrow(f_1)- A_n\theta. \end{cases} \qquad (3.35)$$

where $f_1' = \frac{f_1}{f_2}$, i.e.,

$$\left\{ \begin{array}{l} \leftarrow (f_1') - B_1\theta, \\ \leftarrow (f_1') - B_2\theta, \\ \quad\vdots \\ \leftarrow (f_1') - B_m\theta, \\ \leftarrow (f_1) - A_2\theta, \\ \quad\vdots \\ \leftarrow (f_1) - A_n\theta. \end{array} \right. \tag{3.36}$$

where $f_1' = \frac{f_1}{f_2}$.

The derivation method is reiterated for the present f-Goal, until the computation is terminated by the derivation of the halt statement $\square$.

Such an f-Goal oriented derivation from an initial set S_f of f-Horn clause rules and an initial f-Goal $\tilde{G}_1$ ($\tilde{G}_1 \in S_f$) is a sequence of f-Goals

$$\tilde{G}_1, \tilde{G}_2, \ldots, \tilde{G}_n.$$

where $\tilde{G}_i$ contains a single selected f-Procedural call according to the given strategy, and $\tilde{G}_{i+1}$ is obtained from $\tilde{G}_i$ by procedure invocation. For instance, if the initial f-Goal $\tilde{G}_1$ is (3.28):

$$\left\{ \begin{array}{l} \leftarrow (f_1) - A_1, \\ \leftarrow (f_1) - A_2, \\ \quad\vdots \\ \leftarrow (f_1) - A_n. \end{array} \right.$$

then the corresponding G_2 is (3.32):

$$\left\{ \begin{array}{l} \leftarrow (f_1') - B_1\theta, \\ \leftarrow (f_1') - B_2\theta, \\ \quad\vdots \\ \leftarrow (f_1') - B_m\theta, \\ \leftarrow (f_1) - A_2\theta, \\ \quad\vdots \\ \leftarrow (f_1) - A_n\theta. \end{array} \right.$$

where $f_1' = f_1/f_2$.

The set of all f-Horn clause rules can be seen as a nondeterministic programming language, because: given a single f-Goal, several f-Procedures may have a name which matches the selected f-Procedural call at the same time. Each f-Procedure gives rise to a new f-Goal. We have mentioned that a proof procedure which sequences the generation of derivations in the search for a refutation is a search of an and/or tree. In the proof procedure, each value of f is given according to the **min–max** rule.

The fuzzy logic program system based on f-Horn clause rules can be regarded as a quantitative generalization of the pure-PROLOG subset—a set of Horn clause rules.

Now we are going to illustrate the characteristics of fuzzy logic programs and their question answering procedures. The following is a simple example.

Example 3.15

There is a set of f-Horn clause rules, where m and n are constants.

$$\text{aa}(X,Y) \leftarrow (0.9) - \text{bb}(X) \wedge \text{cc}(Y). \qquad R_1$$
$$\text{aa}(X,Y) \leftarrow (0.5) - \text{bb}(X) \wedge \text{dd}(Y). \qquad R_2$$
$$\text{bb}(m) \leftarrow (0.3) - . \qquad R_3$$
$$\text{cc}(X) \leftarrow (0.7) - \text{ee}(X). \qquad R_4$$
$$\text{dd}(n) \leftarrow (1.0) - . \qquad R_5$$
$$\text{ee}(n) \leftarrow (0.4) - . \qquad R_6$$

Let us now examine how the fuzzy logic program system satisfies the f-Goal1:

$$\leftarrow (0.3) - \text{aa}(m,n).$$

First it tries to find any f-Rule (with the implication strength f) or f-Assertion (with the truth value f) whose head matches $\text{aa}(m,n)$ and $f \geq 0.3$.

According to the rule ordered strategy, R_1 is the first matching f-Rule of f-Goal1. The system marks it and instantiates X and Y to m and n respectively, and derives the sub-goals as follows:

$$(1) \qquad \leftarrow (0.33) - \text{bb}(m).$$
$$(2) \qquad \leftarrow (0.33) - \text{cc}(n).$$

Sub-goal (1) fails in matching R_3 because $0.33 > 0.3$, and there is no other f-Rule or f-Assertion whose head matches $\text{bb}(m)$; that is, the sub-goal (1) is unsolvable, hence backtracking returns it to f-Goal1.

R_2 is the second and also the last matching f-Rule of the f-Goal1. It fails similarly, and now the system is unable to backtrack. So the f-Goal1 fails and it gives the answer: NO.

However, if we examine f-Goal2:

$$\leftarrow (0.2)- \ aa(m,n).$$

instead of the f-Goal1:

$$\leftarrow (0.3)- \ aa(m,n).$$

then it will be satisfied.

Specifically, R_1 is the first matching f-Rule. The system marks it and instantiates X and Y to m and n respectively, and derives the sub-goals as follows:

(1) $\qquad \leftarrow (0.22)- \ bb(m).$

(2) $\qquad \leftarrow (0.22)- \ cc(n).$

Sub-goal (1) succeeds in matching R_3, because the head of R_3 matches $bb(m)$, and $0.22 < 0.3$. Sub-goal (2) succeeds in matching R_4 in a similar way, and X is instantiated by n, and it derives the sub-goal

(1') $\qquad \leftarrow (0.31)- \ ee(n).$

This is satisfied because R_6 is in the database.

There are no further sub-goals to be solved, so the solution YES to the f-Goal2 is found.

Consider the f-Goal3:

$$\leftarrow (f)- \ aa(m,n).$$

R_1 is the first matching f-Rule. The system marks it and instantiates X and Y to m and n respectively, and it derives the sub-goals as follows:

(1) $\qquad \leftarrow (f/0.9)- \ bb(m).$

(2) $\qquad \leftarrow (f/0.9)- \ cc(n).$

R_3 is the only one which matches the sub-goal (1), therefore $f/0.9 = 0.3$, hence $f_1 = 0.27$. R_4 is the only matching one which matches the sub-goal (2), and X is instantiated by n, and it derives the sub-goal

(1') $\qquad \leftarrow (f/0.63)- \ ee(n).$

117

R_6 is the only one which matches sub-goal (1'), therefore $f/0.63 = 0.4$, hence $f_2 = 0.25$. An intermediate solution to the f-Goal3 is found by the min-operation: $f_{min}^{(1)} = \min\{f_1, f_2\} = \min\{0.27, 0.25\} = 0.25$, since there are no further sub-goals to be solved. Backtracking returns it to f-Goal3.

R_2 is the second matching f-Rule. The system marks it and instantiates X and Y to m and n respectively, and it derives the sub-goals as follows:

$$(1) \qquad \leftarrow (f/0.5) - \text{bb}(m).$$
$$(2) \qquad \leftarrow (f/0.5) - \text{dd}(n).$$

R_3 is the only one which matches the sub-goal (1), therefore $f/0.5 = 0.3$, hence $f_1 = 0.15$. R_5 is the only one which matches the sub-goal (2), therefore $f/0.5 = 1$, hence $f_2 = 0.5$. Another intermediate solution to the f-Goal3 is found by the min-operation: $f_{min}^{(2)} = \min\{f_1, f_2\} = \min\{0.15, 0.5\} = 0.15$, since there are no further sub-goals to be solved.

Now the system is unable to backtrack, the final solution to the original f-Goal3 is found according to the max-operation: $f = \max\{f_{min}^{(1)}, f_{min}^{(2)}\} = \max\{0.25, 0.15\} = 0.25$.

3.8 f-PROLOG as a Fuzzy Logic Programming Language

As a logic programming language, PROLOG has become increasingly popular in recent years, and is widely used in artificial intelligence research, such as natural language processing, database systems, expert systems, pattern recognition, and many other areas. Unfortunately, one of its shortcomings is the lack of a natural mechanism to deal with uncertain or fuzzy information and knowledge in such applications. A possible way to solve this problem, is to base PROLOG on fuzzy logic rather than on classical binary logic. This leads to a more general system, of which conventional PROLOG is a special case of fuzzy PROLOG.

The f-PROLOG system described in this section is a fuzzy PROLOG interpreter implemented on VAX-11/780 under the operating system VAX/VMS, and MicroVAX II under the operating system MicroVMS respectively.

3.8.1 Syntax of the f-PROLOG Language

The syntax of the f-PROLOG language is as simple as conventional PROLOG. An f-PROLOG program can be regarded as a sequence of f-Horn clause rules, starting on separate lines [Liu and Li, 1988(b), 1989(a)]. Definitions and grammar rules in the sequence are grouped in procedures. There are quite a few principles that govern "consulting"/"reconsulting", and dynamically "asserting"/"retracting" clauses. Therefore a formal definition of procedures would be unnecessarily involved: it should account for the fact that procedures change in time.

The following extended BNF notation is used to define the f-PROLOG syntax:

⟨**term**⟩	Names of language constructs are surrounded by "⟨" and "⟩".
{ **X** }*	Represents zero or more repetitions of **X**.
{ **X** }	Means that **X** is optional.
X | **Y**	Indicates that **X** and **Y** are alternatives and that either **X** or **Y** must be used.

$$
\begin{array}{lll}
\langle\text{statement}\rangle & ::= & \langle\text{clause}\rangle \quad | \\
 & & \langle\text{function}\rangle \quad | \\
 & & \langle\text{comment}\rangle \\[4pt]
\langle\text{clause}\rangle & ::= & \langle\text{fact}\rangle. \quad | \\
 & & \langle\text{rule}\rangle. \quad | \\
 & & \langle\text{goal}\rangle. \\[4pt]
\langle\text{fact}\rangle & ::= & \langle\text{head}\rangle{:}{-}[\langle\text{truth-value}\rangle]{-}. \\[4pt]
\langle\text{rule}\rangle & ::= & \langle\text{head}\rangle{:}{-}[\langle\text{implication-strength}\rangle]{-}\langle\text{body}\rangle. \\[4pt]
\langle\text{goal}\rangle & ::= & ?{-}[\langle\text{f}\rangle]{-}\langle\text{body}\rangle. \\[4pt]
\langle\text{truth-value}\rangle & ::= & 1 \quad | \\
 & & \langle\text{decimal}\rangle \quad | \\
 & & \langle\text{linguistic-values}\rangle
\end{array}
$$

⟨implication-strength⟩ ::= { } |
                           1 |
                           ⟨decimal⟩ |
                           ⟨function⟩ |
                           ⟨linguistic-values⟩

⟨f⟩   ::= 1 |
                    ⟨decimal⟩ |
                    ⟨variable⟩ |
                    ⟨linguistic-values⟩

⟨decimal⟩   ::= 0.⟨digits⟩

⟨function⟩ ::= ⟨fname⟩(⟨variable-list⟩) = ⟨arith⟩

⟨fname⟩   ::= ⟨name⟩

⟨comment⟩ ::= /* ⟨symbol-string⟩ */

⟨head⟩   ::= ⟨atom⟩

⟨body⟩   ::= ⟨subgoal-list⟩ { ⟨or⟩ ⟨subgoal-list⟩ }

⟨subgoal-list⟩ ::= ⟨subgoal⟩ |
                    ⟨subgoal⟩ ⟨and⟩ ⟨subgoal-list⟩

⟨subgoal⟩   ::= ⟨atom⟩ |
                    ⟨comparison⟩ |
                    ⟨findall-literal⟩ |
                    ⟨database-literal⟩ |
                    not (⟨atom⟩) |
                    !

⟨atom⟩   ::= ⟨predicate⟩ { ({ ⟨term-list⟩ }) }

⟨predicate⟩   ::= ⟨name⟩

⟨findall-literal⟩ ::= findall(⟨variable⟩,⟨atom⟩,⟨variable⟩)

$\langle\text{database-literal}\rangle \quad ::= \quad \text{asserta}(\ \langle\text{fact}\rangle\ ) \quad | $
$\qquad\qquad\qquad\qquad\qquad \text{assertz}(\ \langle\text{fact}\rangle\ ) \quad | $
$\qquad\qquad\qquad\qquad\qquad \text{retract}(\ \langle\text{fact}\rangle\ )$

$\langle\text{and}\rangle \qquad\quad ::= \quad \text{and} \quad | \quad ,$

$\langle\text{or}\rangle \qquad\qquad ::= \quad \text{or} \quad | \quad ;$

$\langle\text{term-list}\rangle \quad ::= \quad \langle\text{term}\rangle \quad | \quad \langle\text{term}\rangle\ ,\ \langle\text{term-list}\rangle$

$\langle\text{term}\rangle \qquad\quad ::= \quad \{\ \langle\text{sign}\rangle\ \}\ \langle\text{number}\rangle \quad |$
$\qquad\qquad\qquad\qquad \langle\text{char}\rangle \qquad\qquad\qquad |$
$\qquad\qquad\qquad\qquad \langle\text{list}\rangle \qquad\qquad\qquad\ |$
$\qquad\qquad\qquad\qquad \langle\text{string}\rangle \qquad\qquad\quad |$
$\qquad\qquad\qquad\qquad \langle\text{variable}\rangle \qquad\qquad |$
$\qquad\qquad\qquad\qquad \langle\text{compound term}\rangle$

$\langle\text{number}\rangle \quad\ ::= \quad \langle\text{digits}\rangle\ \{\ .\ \langle\text{digits}\rangle\ \{\ \langle\text{exponent}\rangle\ \}\ \}$

$\langle\text{digits}\rangle \qquad ::= \quad \langle\text{digit}\rangle \quad | \quad \langle\text{digit}\rangle\ \langle\text{digits}\rangle$

$\langle\text{exponent}\rangle \quad ::= \quad \text{e}\ \langle\text{sign}\rangle\ \langle\text{digits}\rangle$

$\langle\text{sign}\rangle \qquad\quad ::= \quad + \quad | \quad -$

$\langle\text{char}\rangle \qquad\quad ::= \quad \text{‘}\langle\text{character}\rangle\text{’} \quad | \quad \text{‘}\backslash\langle\text{character}\rangle\text{’}$

$\langle\text{symbol-string}\rangle \quad ::= \quad \{\ \langle\text{character}\rangle\ \}*$

$\langle\text{string}\rangle \qquad\qquad ::= \quad \text{“}\{\ \langle\text{character}\rangle\ \}*\text{”}$

$\langle\text{list}\rangle \qquad\qquad\quad ::= \quad \{\ \} \quad |$
$\qquad\qquad\qquad\qquad\quad \{\ \langle\text{element-list}\rangle\ \}$

$\langle\text{element-list}\rangle \quad ::= \quad \langle\text{term}\rangle[\quad |$
$\qquad\qquad\qquad\qquad\ \ \langle\text{term}\rangle] \quad |$
$\qquad\qquad\qquad\qquad\ \ \langle\text{term}\rangle\ ,\ \langle\text{element-list}\rangle$

$\langle\text{compound-term}\rangle \quad ::= \quad \langle\text{functor}\rangle\ \{\ (\ \{\ \langle\text{term-list}\rangle\ \}\ )\ \}$

$\langle\text{comparison}\rangle \qquad ::= \quad \langle\text{ascii}\rangle\ \langle\text{operator}\rangle\ \langle\text{ascii}\rangle\ \langle\text{arith}\rangle \quad |$
$\qquad\qquad\qquad\qquad\quad \langle\text{compare}\rangle\ \langle\text{arith}\rangle$

⟨ascii⟩	::=	⟨functor⟩ |
		⟨string⟩ |
		⟨char⟩ |
		⟨variable⟩

⟨arith⟩   ::=   ⟨multexp⟩ ⟨adding⟩ ⟨arith⟩   \|
                           ⟨multexp⟩

⟨multexp⟩   ::=   ⟨factor⟩ ⟨multiplying⟩ ⟨arith⟩   \|
                           ⟨factor⟩

⟨factor⟩   ::=   ⟨variable⟩   \|
                           ⟨number⟩   \|
                           (⟨arith⟩)   \|
                           ⟨built-in-function⟩ (⟨arith⟩)

⟨compare⟩   ::=   == \| /== \| =:= \| =/= \| ⟨ \|
                           ⟩ \| =⟨ \| ⟩= \| = \| /=

⟨adding⟩   ::=   + \| -

⟨multiplying⟩ ::=   * \| / \| div \| mod

⟨built-in-function⟩ ::=   abs \| acos \| asin \| atan \| ceil \|
                                cos \| cosh \| exp \| float \| floor \|
                                ln \| log \| sign \| sin \| sinh \|
                                sqrt \| tan \| tanh \| trunc

⟨name⟩   ::=   (⟨letter⟩ \| _) { ⟨letter⟩ \| ⟨digit⟩ \| _ }*

⟨name-list⟩   ::=   ⟨name⟩ \| ⟨name-list⟩

⟨variable-list⟩ ::=   ⟨variable⟩ \|
                     ⟨variable⟩ , ⟨variable-list⟩

⟨variable⟩   ::=   (⟨capital-letter⟩ \| _) { ⟨name⟩ }

⟨functor⟩   ::=   ⟨small-letter⟩ { ⟨name⟩ }

⟨letter⟩   ::=   ⟨small-letter⟩ \| ⟨capital-letter⟩

⟨small-letter⟩ ::=   a \| b \| c \| ⋯ x \| y \| z

$$\langle \text{capital-letter} \rangle \quad ::= \quad A \mid B \mid C \mid \cdots X \mid Y \mid Z$$

$$\langle \text{digit} \rangle \quad\quad\quad ::= \quad 0 \mid 1 \mid 2 \mid \cdots 8 \mid 9$$

As in conventional versions of PROLOG, in the f-PROLOG language constants start with a digit or a lower-case letter, while variables start with either an upper-case letter or an underscore symbol. Variables used in f-Horn clause rules are usually quantified. As a convenience, it provides a facility to use "logic or", by typing "or" or a semi-colon ";", and "logic and" by "and" or a comma ",", even if it is not strictly necessary.

3.8.2 Semantics of the f-PROLOG Language

An f-PROLOG program is similar to a conventional PROLOG program except that some facts have associated truth values, and some rules contain implication strength, showing their grade of membership in the set of true assertions (the database) or true rules (the rulebase). It is not necessary to store truth values for nonfuzzy facts and implication strength for nonfuzzy rules, since these have full membership of the database and rulebase, respectively.

Specifically, a program in f-PROLOG mainly consists of three parts:

(1) f-Assertion $P(t_1, t_2, \ldots, t_n) :-[f]- \ .$

This means that, $P(t_1, t_2, \ldots, t_n)$ is true with the truth value of f, or there exists a relationship P, among t_1, t_2, $\ldots$, t_n, with the degree of belief f.

(2) f-Rule $P :-[f]- Q_1, Q_2, \ldots, Q_n.$

Suppose the truth value of Q_i is $tv(Q_i)$, $i = 1, 2, \ldots, n$, and the truth value of all conditions is α. When $n > 0$,

$$\alpha \ = \ \min\{tv(Q_i) \mid i = 1, 2, \ldots, n\};$$

when $n = 0$, we define $\alpha = 1$. Therefore the truth value $tv(P) = f \times \alpha$.

(3) f-Goal
$$?-[f]- Q_1, Q_2, \ldots, Q_n. \quad\quad (f \text{ is a constant})$$

or

$$?-[F]- Q_1, Q_2, \ldots, Q_n. \quad\quad (F \text{ is a variable})$$

The former means "can the n sub-goals $Q_1, Q_2, \ldots, Q_n$ all be satisfied when the threshold is f?" while the latter is a question for answering the truth value of $Q_1 \wedge Q_2 \wedge \cdots \wedge Q_n$.

3.8.3 Fuzzy Goals

Some important fields of application of fuzzy PROLOG are question answering, decision making, and so on. Imprecise information and vague questions are typical for complex realistic problems. Even if a problem is rather well structured, a crisp inference model is frequently too inflexible with its hard goals and its strict discrimination between admissible and inadmissible solutions. A fuzzy approach, representing information and questions by fuzzy logic, often is much more applicable to real situations. In a fuzzy inference model, multiple objectives and flexible regions of feasible solutions can be dealt with as we have shown above.

Three kinds of f-PROLOG clause have been demonstrated in the preceding subsection. To further illustrate our fuzzy PROLOG language, we introduce fuzzy goals in f-PROLOG in detail by means of a simple example.

Example 3.16

The following f-PROLOG program represents: anyone who is tall wears large shoes to a high degree of confidence.

$$\text{wear\_large\_shoes}(X) :-[0.9]- \text{ tall}(X).$$
$$\text{tall}(\text{smith}) :-[1]- \; .$$
$$\text{tall}(\text{john}) :-[0.8]- \; .$$
$$\text{tall}(\text{tom}) :-[0.9]- \; .$$
$$\text{tall}(\text{barry}) :-[0.6]- \; .$$

After the f-Goal is input, the f-PROLOG system will search for corresponding answers and print them out. f-Goals are not remembered in the knowledge base. For convenience, we are concerned with fuzzy goals in which only one sub-goal is involved.

In f-PROLOG, fuzzy goals can be flexibly used in several situations. As examples, the following f-Goals are considered, and the actual answers to these fuzzy goals are illustrated, respectively.

(1)   ?–[0.8]–wear_large_shoes(tom).

YES

(2)   ?–[0.8]–wear_large_shoes(barry).

NO

(3)   ?–[0.8]–wear_large_shoes(X).

X = smith

X = tom

(4)   ?–[F]–wear_large_shoes(smith).

F = 0.90

(5)   ?–[F]–wear_large_shoes(X).

X = smith   F = 0.90

X = john   F = 0.72

X = tom   F = 0.81

X = barry   F = 0.54

We can say that the conclusion reached by f-PROLOG is no longer the alternatives of true or false. The answer may be a fuzzy solution with a degree of truth. This is the main advantage of the generalization from conventional PROLOG to f-PROLOG [Liu and Li, 1988(b), 1989(a)].

3.8.4   Implementation Aspects of the f-PROLOG Language

IF/PROLOG was chosen as the primary implementation language for the f-PROLOG interpreter. IF/PROLOG is a convenient language for such applications, since its syntax is scarcely different from the common Edinburgh syntax similar to the syntax of f-Horn clause rules mentioned in Section 3.5, and it provides ready-made facilities for matching, backtracking, *etc.* By using its meta-variable feature, which allows variable predicate symbols to be employed in the defintion of rules but insists that they will be instantiated before evaluation, these facilities can be embedded naturally in the f-PROLOG interpreter. Thus IF/PROLOG can be seen as a special case of the f-PROLOG language. In addition, PROLOG has become a universally accepted tool for systems programming, since the PROLOG environment is well suited to program development, and yields portable code. Furthermore, IF/PROLOG provides a complete SQL interface to the relational database system ORACLE, simplifying the task of linking f-PROLOG to ORACLE databases.

The implementation of f-PROLOG is fairly standard, and follows conventional approaches [van Emden, 1984; Bruynooghe, 1982] with necessary variations based on the theory of f-Horn clause logic [Liu and Li, 1988(a)] and its linguistic extension discussed later. Simply speaking, the f-PROLOG interpreter also uses a stack to keep a record of the fuzzy proof tree as it is created, and represents complex terms by structure sharing [Boyer, Moore, 1972]. It also utilizes some techniques to optimize the tail recursion, the detection of deterministic subtrees, and so on.

In the f-PROLOG system, fuzziness can be handled automatically, that is, it is able to treat fuzzy assertions (*i.e.* f-Assertions) and fuzzy rules (*i.e.* f-Rules), and process the truth values to produce an overall truth value for each solution.

As a consequence of holding a cumulative truth value, backtracking may be triggered by "generalized failure" of a query. This means that if only solutions with a truth value greater than some threshold are required, the system can backtrack as soon as it uses a fact with a truth value lower than the threshold, rather than solving the query and then finding that the truth value is lower than the threshold. A simple example illustrates this as follows.

Example 3.17

A simple f-PROLOG program contains

>   beautiful(X) :–[0.9]– flower(X), fragrant(X), bright_coloured(X).
>   flower(rose) :–[1]– .
>   fragrant(rose) :–[0.95]– .
>   bright_coloured(rose) :–[0.9]– .

The solution to the f-Goal:

$$?–[F]–beautiful(rose).$$

is illustrated in Figure 3–13.

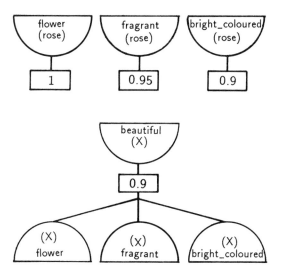

(a) The diagrams for the knowledge base

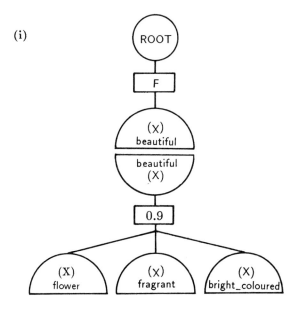

(i)

(ii)

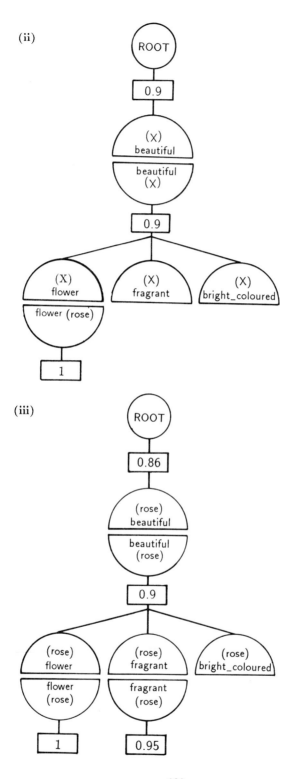

(iii)

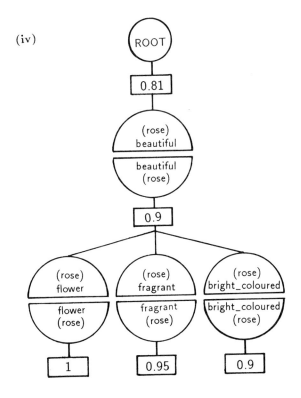

(iv)

(b)   The development of a solution

Figure 3–13   Execution of a Simple f-PROLOG Program

129

3.8.5 Linguistic Extension of the f-PROLOG Language

The fuzziness in practical applications can be expressed in possibility terms but there may still be doubt about the actual value of the numerical possibilities concerned. It may be more convenient and suitable to express a possibility in linguistic terms such as definite, possible, _very_ possible, _fairly_ possible, _etc._ rather than attempt to give a point value, which would fall into the trap of approximating via forced precision.

In order to provide a user friendly interface to the f-PROLOG language, we suggest, in this subsection, the notion of an f-Rule whose implication strength or truth value can be a linguistic value which is defined on the possibility space $[0, 1]$, instead of a point value. If we call point-valued f-Rules, such as those considered so far, as **Type I** f-Rules, then linguistic-valued f-Rules are called **Type II** f-Rules.

A **Type II** f-Rule is also of the form

$$A : -[f] - B_1, B_2, \ldots, B_n.$$

where A, B_1, B_2, $\ldots$, B_n are atoms, provided that we use the linguistic-valued implication strength f defined by the possibility distribution, in place of, or in addition to, the numerical point-valued implication strength.

"A" is known as the head of the rule and $\{B_1, B_2, \ldots, B_n\}$ as the body of the rule. Similarly, if the body of the rule is empty we have an f-Assertion, represented as

$$A : -[f] - .$$

To facilitate the implementation of the extended f-PROLOG, we adopt a finite collection of linguistic values of "Possibility" for the implication strength in f-Rules (_i.e._ the 'degree of belief' of the f-Rule), and the truth value in f-Assertions (_i.e._ the 'degree of belief' of the f-Assertion).

$$T(\text{Possibility}) = \{ \text{ definite}, \textit{very} \text{ possible}, \text{ possible}, \\ \textit{fairly} \text{ possible}, \ldots \}$$

In short, we use

$$T(\text{Possibility}) = \{ \text{ d, VERY p, p, FAIRLY p}, \ldots \}$$

Each such implication strength and truth value represents a fuzzy set of the unit interval $[0,1]$. In this approach,

$$\mu_d(x) = \begin{cases} 1, & x = 1; \\ 0, & x \neq 1. \end{cases}$$

$$\mu_p(x) = \begin{cases} 0, & 0 \leq x \leq 0.5; \\ 2\left(\frac{x-0.5}{0.2}\right)^2, & 0.5 < x \leq 0.6; \\ 1 - 2\left(\frac{x-0.7}{0.2}\right)^2, & 0.6 < x \leq 0.8; \\ 2\left(\frac{0.9-x}{0.2}\right)^2, & 0.8 < x \leq 0.9; \\ 0, & 0.9 < x \leq 1. \end{cases}$$

are defined. By using the fuzzifiers, such as VERY, FAIRLY, and so on, we have

$$\mu_{VERY\ p}(x) = \begin{cases} 0, & 0 \leq x \leq 0.6; \\ 4\left(\frac{x-0.6}{0.2}\right)^4, & 0.6 < x \leq 0.7; \\ \left[1 - 2\left(\frac{x-0.8}{0.2}\right)^2\right]^{0.2}, & ; 0.7 < x \leq 0.9; \\ 4\left(\frac{1-x}{0.2}\right)^4, & 0.9 < x \leq 1. \end{cases}$$

$$\mu_{FAIRLY\ p}(x) = \begin{cases} 0, & 0 \leq x \leq 0.4; \\ \sqrt{2}\left(\frac{x-0.4}{0.2}\right), & 0.4 < x \leq 0.5; \\ \sqrt{1 - 2\left(\frac{x-0.6}{0.2}\right)^2}, & 0.5 < x \leq 0.7; \\ \sqrt{2}\left(\frac{0.8-x}{0.2}\right), & 0.7 < x \leq 0.8; \\ 0, & 0.8 < x \leq 1. \end{cases}$$

Hence the set $T(Possibility)$ is defined (see Figure 3–14).

In such an extension, **Type I** is a special case of **Type II**. A knowledge base of the f-PROLOG language consists of f-Rules and f-Assertions, some of which may be modified to take into account the fuzziness of possibility distributions. This modification takes the form of a linguistic value associated with each f-Rule and f-Assertion. A query asked of the system is answered with almost no changes, as a set of **Type I** f-Rules and f-Assertions, but a linguistic value is computed by using a possibility distribution and associated with the final answer.

Example 3.18

The following simple program
        drives(X,large-car) :–[VERY p]– american(X).
        american(robert) :–[1]– .

131

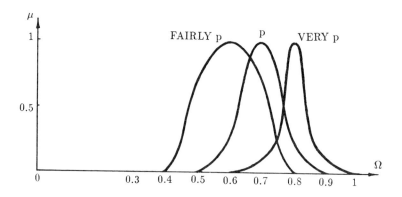

Figure 3–14 Linguistic Values of *"Possibility"*

indicates "If X is an American, then it is very possible that, he/she drives a large car." and "Robert is an American with the 'degree of belief' of 1." We can now ask the queries of the system in the f-PROLOG style and obtain the corresponding replies. For example

?-[F]-drives(X,large-car).

X = robert   F = VERY possible

The last line is returned by the f-PROLOG system.

?-[F]-drives(robert,large-car).

YES   F = VERY possible

This illustrates another form of query, and we have

?-[p]-drives(robert,large-car).

YES

In this subsection, we have shown how the fuzzy linguistic value [Zadeh, 1975(a)(b)] and the f-PROLOG [Liu and Li, 1988(b), 1989(a)] can be combined to form a suitable framework for an English-like language style of fuzzy inference. This inference mechanism must include recognition that f-Rules are possibilistic rather than probabilistic in nature.

This is not the only way for linguistic extension of the f-PROLOG language. Other operations of holding cumulative truth values may be suggested.

3.9 Built-in Fuzzy Comparison Operators: ~=, >> and <<

f-PROLOG's arithmetic capabilities are similar to those provided in conventional PROLOG, and other programming languages such as PASCAL, FORTRAN, C and BASIC. It includes a full range of arithmetic functions and standard predicates. All of these are illustrated in Appendix 1.

In this section, we will introduce a group of fuzzy comparison predicates: ~=, >> and <<, which is another important advantage of the f-PROLOG language. Nevertheless, here we are only concerned about their function, not their mathematical definitions, because they will be defined in detail in Chapter 6 as fuzzy comparison operators.

In the following statement:

$$X + 3 \mathrel{\tilde=} ABOUT\ 10$$

which is the f-PROLOG equivalent of: The total of X and 3 is approximately equal to ABOUT 10, the comparison operator ~= (approximately equal) indicates the fuzzy relation between the two expressions, X + 3 and ABOUT 10. If Value_1 and Value_2 represent the values of the two expressions, we could write this fuzzy relation in a "normal" f-PROLOG statement format as:

fuzzy_eq(Value_1,Value_2).

We could also write the f-PROLOG clause

add(X,3,Value_1).

to describe how X + 3 is evaluated to Value_1. The entire comparison

$$X + 3 \mathrel{\tilde=} ABOUT\ 10$$

could thus be formulated as:

add(X,3,Value_1).
fuzzy_eq(Value_1,ABOUT 10).

f-PROLOG allows the more familiar formulation we began with, but be aware that a single comparison such as X + 3 ~= ABOUT 10 (this is called infix notation) corresponds to as many f-PROLOG clauses as there are operators in the original sentence.

X ˜= Y	approximately equal
X >> Y	much greater than
X << Y	much less than

Figure 3–15 Fuzzy Comparison Operators

Besides the operator ˜=, other fuzzy comparison operators can also be defined, such as >> (much_gt) and << (much_ls) which stand for 'much greater than' and 'much less than', respectively. The complete range of fuzzy comparison operations allowed in f-PROLOG is shown in Figure 3–15.

To describe how to use these fuzzy comparison operators in approximate reasoning, the following f-PROLOG examples are presented.

Example 3.19

Suppose we have an f-PROLOG program as follows:

$$small(0.01) :-[0.9]- .$$
$$small(Y) :-[0.99]- X \text{ ˜}= Y, small(X).$$
$$Y \text{ ˜}= X :-[1]- X \text{ ˜}= Y.$$
$$0.02 \text{ ˜}= 0.01 :-[0.9]- .$$
$$0.03 \text{ ˜}= 0.01 :-[0.7]- .$$

A possible interpretation of the inference may be the following

> X is small
> X and Y are approximately equal
> ――――――――――――――――――――――
> Y is almost definitely small

After typing the f-Goal:

$$?-[F]-small(0.02).$$

We proved that

$$F = 0.89.$$

It is that 0.02 is small with the confidence degree of 0.89. Consequently, we may say that 0.02 is quite small, because 0.01 is very small and 0.02 is very approximately equal to 0.01.

134

Example 3.20

We have the following f-PROLOG program:

$$Y << X :-[1]- X >> Y. \qquad\qquad R_1$$
$$X >> Z :-[0.8]- X >> Y, Y \mathbin{\tilde{}} = Z. \qquad R_2$$
$$a >> b :-[0.95]- . \qquad\qquad R_3$$
$$b \mathbin{\tilde{}} = c :-[0.8]- . \qquad\qquad R_4$$

It may be interpreted as

$$\frac{\text{X is much greater than Y}}{\text{Y is much less than X}}$$

and

$$\frac{\begin{array}{c}\text{X is much greater than Y}\\ \text{Y is approximately equal to Z}\end{array}}{\text{X is very possibly much greater than Z}}$$

If the f-Goal

$$?-[F]- c << a.$$

is input, the f-PROLOG system will run, searching for the corresponding answer. The inference procedure is illustrated as follows:

First of all, it tries to find any f-Rule or f-Assertion whose head matches c << a. According to the rule ordered strategy, R1 is the first matching f-Rule of the f-Goal. The system marks it and instantiates Y and X to c and a respectively, and derives the following sub-goal:

$$?-[F]- a >> c.$$

R_2 is the only matching f-Rule of this sub-goal. The system marks it and instantiates X and Z to a and c, and it derives the sub-goals as follows:

$$(1) \qquad ?-[F/0.8]- a >> Y.$$
$$(2) \qquad ?-[F/0.8]- Y \mathbin{\tilde{}} = c.$$

Sub-goal (1) succeeds in matching R_3; in such a case, we have

$$F/0.8 = 0.95$$

hence,

$$F_1 = 0.76.$$

Sub-goal (2) succeeds in matching R_4; similarly, we obtain

$$F_2 = 0.64.$$

As a result, an intermediate solution to the f-Goal is found by the min-operation: $F_{min} = \min\{F_1, F_2\} = 0.64$. Now there are no further sub-goals to be solved, backtracking returns it to the f-Goal. Since R_1 is the only f-Rule matching this f-Goal, the final answer to the original f-Goal is found according to the max-operation:

$$F = \max\{F_{min}\} = 0.64.$$

Chapter 4

FUZZY RELATIONAL DATABASES

A fuzzy representation of data for fuzzy relational databases is defined and discussed in this chapter. A fuzzy relational model in the FPDB system is defined as a collection of fuzzy relations which allow possibility distributions as attribute values for representing fuzzy and even incomplete data. This model can be considered as an extension of Codd's relational model of data.

To pave the way for later discussion, the following section reviews some of the basic definitions and concepts of the classical relational model [Codd, 1970; Date, 1981, 1986].

4.1 The Relational Model

The relational model of data, first introduced by Codd [Codd, 1970], has undergone a certain amount of revision and refinement since its original formulation. Like any other data model, it consists of three components:

(1)   a set of objects;

(2)   a set of operators;

(3)   a set of general integrity rules.

The intention of this section is to examine each of these components in turn, and provide some preliminary definitions and concepts on relational database

CANDIDATES			
Name	**Sex**	**Age**	**Address**
Smith	Male	30	Newcastle
John	Male	28	Carlisle
Anna	Female	22	Penrith
Mary	Female	40	Carlisle
Jill	Female	30	Penrith

Figure 4–1   The Relation CANDIDATES

models.

4.1.1   Relations

Definition 4.1

Given a collection of sets D_1, D_2, ..., D_n (not necessarily distinct), R is a relation on those n sets if there is a set of ordered n-ary tuples $\langle d_1, d_2, \ldots, d_n \rangle$ such that $d_1 \in D_1$, $d_2 \in D_2$, ..., $d_n \in D_n$. Sets D_1, D_2, ..., D_n are the domains of R. The value n is the degree of R. Relations of degree one are usually said to be unary; simiarly, relations of degree two are binary, ..., and relations of degree n are n-ary.

A relation has a description. The description includes a description of each of its domains.

Example 4.1

Figure 4–1 illustrates a 4-ary relation called CANDIDATES. The four domains are sets of values representing, respectively, names, sexes, ages, and addresses. The "sex" domain, for example, contains male and female; the "address" domain is the set of all valid addresses; note that there may be addresses included in this domain that do not actually appear in the CANDIDATES relation at this particular time.

As Figure 4–1 illustrates, it is convenient to display a relation as a table. Each row of the table represents one n-ary tuple (or simply one tuple) of the relation, while each column of the table is headed by an attribute of the relation.

In other words, a table is a multi-set of rows. A row is a non-empty sequence of values. Every row of the same table contains a value of every column of that table. The n-th value in every row of a table is a value of the nth column of that table. The row is the smallest unit of data that can be inserted into a table and deleted from a table. The degree of a table is the number of columns of the table. Hence table and relation are used interchangeably in this book. The number of tuples in a relation is called the cardinality of the relation; for instance, the cardinality of the CANDIDATES relation is five.

Equivalently, we give another definition of relation that is sometimes useful. First we define a Cartesian product. Given a collection of sets D_1, D_2, ..., D_n (not necessarily distinct), the Cartesian Product of these n sets, written $D_1 \times D_2 \times \cdots \times D_n$, is the set of all possible ordered n-ary tuples $\langle d_1, d_2, \ldots, d_n \rangle$ such that $d_1 \in D_1$, $d_2 \in D_2$, ..., $d_n \in D_n$.

Example 4.2

Figure 4–2 shows the Cartesian Product of two sets A and B.

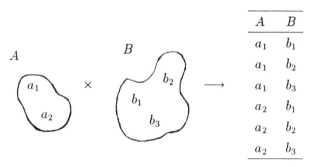

A	B
a_1	b_1
a_1	b_2
a_1	b_3
a_2	b_1
a_2	b_2
a_2	b_3

Figure 4–2   An Example of a Cartesian Product

Now we define R to be a relation on the sets D_1, D_2, ..., D_n if it is a subset of the Cartesian Product $D_1 \times D_2 \times \cdots \times D_n$.

Strictly speaking, there is no ordering defined among the tuples of a relation, since a relation is a set, and sets are not ordered. In Figure 4–1, for example, the tuples of the relation CANDIDATES could just as well have been shown in the reverse sequence—it would still have been the same relation. However, there are situations where it is very convenient to be able to guarantee some particular ordering, so that we know, for example, that the "get next" operator will fetch CANDIDATES tuples in ascending alphabetical sequence of names.

In a database context, therefore, we do frequently consider relations to have an ordering—in fact, we must do so if "get next" is to have a meaning—but either (a) the ordering is system-defined, *i.e.* the user does not care what the ordering is (just so long as it remains stable), or (b) it is defined in terms of the values appearing within the relation, *e.g.* as ascending sequence by name (*alphabetical* ordering). All other types of ordering, *e.g.*, first-in/first-out or program-controlled, are specifically excluded.

Referring back to the original definition, we can see that, by contrast, the domains of a relation do have an ordering defined among them (a relation is a set of ordered n-ary tuples, with the j-th element in each n-ary tuple being drawn from the j-th domain). If we were to rearrange the four columns of the CANDIDATES relation (Figure 4–1) into some different order, the resulting table would be a different relation, mathematically speaking. However, since users normally refer to columns by name rather than by their relative position, many systems relax this restriction and treat column order as if it were just as irrelevant as row order. In this book we shall generally assume that column ordering is insignificant unless explicitly stated otherwise.

4.1.2   Domains and Attributes

It is important to appreciate the difference between a domain, on the one hand, and columns (or attributes) which are drawn from that domain, on the other.

Attributes are symbols taken from a finite set $\{A_1, A_2, \ldots, A_n\}$. With each attribute A_i is associated a domain, denoted by D_i, which is the set of possible values for that attribute. For a set of attributes X, an X-value is an assignment of values to the attributes of X from their domains. That is, an attribute represents the use of a domain within a relation. To emphasize the distinction, we may give attributes names that are distinct from those of the underlying domains; for example, see Figure 4–3.

Example 4.3

In Figure 4–3, we have part of a relational schema, in which four domains (NAME, SEX, AGE and CITY) and one relation (CANDIDATES) have been declared. The relation is defined with four attributes (Name, Sex, Age and Address), and each attribute is specified as being drawn from a corresponding

```
DOMAIN     NAME     CHARACTER   (6)
DOMAIN     SEX      CHARACTER   (6)
DOMAIN     AGE      NUMERIC     (4)
DOMAIN     CITY     CHARACTER   (15)
RELATION     CANDIDATES
                     ( Name    :   DOMAIN   NAME,
                        Sex    :   DOMAIN   SEX,
                        Age    :   DOMAIN   AGE,
                    Address    :   DOMAIN   CITY )
```

Figure 4–3   Domains *vs.* Attributes

domain. The schema is written in a hypothetical data definition language.

We shall very often make use of a convention that allows us to omit the specification of the domain from an attribute declaration if the attribute bears the same name. However, it is not always possible to do this, as the example in Figure 4–4 shows.

Example 4.4

LOCATION		
City1	**City2**	**Distance**
Newcastle	Carlisle	58
Newcastle	Penrith	45
Newcastle	Darlington	40
Carlisle	Penrith	23
Carlisle	Darlington	10
Penrith	Darlington	52

Figure 4–4   The Relation LOCATION

In this example we have a relation with three attributes but only two distinct domains. A tuple of the relation LOCATION shows that the distance between the city1 and the city2. The two distinct domains are CITY and DISTANCE. The example illustrates a common domain name with distinct attribute names

141

by prefixing a common domain name with distinct role names to indicate the distinct roles being played by that domain in each of its appearances.

4.1.3 Keys and Integrity

1. Keys

It is frequently the case that within a given relation there is one attribute with values that are unique within the relation and thus can be used to identify the tuples of that relation. For example, attribute Name of the CANDIDATES relation has this property—each CANDIDATES tuple contains a distinct Name value, and this value may be used to distinguish that tuple from all others in the relation. Name is said to be the key for CANDIDATES.

Not every relation will have a single-attribute primary key. However, every relation will have some combination of attributes that, when taken together, have the unique identification property; a "combination" consisting of a single attribute is merely a special case. In the relation LOCATION of Figure 4-4, for example, the combination (City1,City2) has this property. The existence of such a combination is guaranteed by the fact that a relation is a set: since sets do not contain duplicate elements, each tuple of a given relation is unique with respect to that relation, and hence at least the combination of all attributes has the unique identification property. In practice it is not usually necessary to involve all the attributes—some lesser combination is normally sufficient. Thus every relation does have a (possibly composite) primary key. We shall assume that the primary key is nonredundant, in the sense that none of its constituent attributes is superfluous for the purpose of unique identification; for example, the combination (Name,Age) is not a primary key for CANDIDATES.

Occasionally we may encounter a relation in which there is more than one attribute combination possessing the unique identification property, and hence more than one candidate key.

Example 4.5

Figure 4-5 illustrates such a relation named COMPANY. Here the situation is that each company has a unique company name and a unique president. In such a case we may arbitrarily choose one of the candidates, say Cname, as the primary key for the relation. A candidate key that is not the primary key, such

COMPANY				
Cname	Location	President	Employees	Profit
C1	Newcastle	David	400	300,000
C2	Carlistle	Edward	100	100,000
C3	Penrith	Felix	2000	1,000,000

Figure 4–5   The COMPANY Relation

as President in the example, is called an alternate key.

So far we have considered the primary key from a purely formal point of view, that is, purely as an identifier for tuples in a relation, without paying any heed to how those tuples are interpreted. Typically, however, those tuples represent entities in the real world, and the primary key really serves as a unique identifier for those entities. For example, the tuples in the COMPANY relation represent individual companies, and values of the Cname attribute actually identify those companies, not just the tuples that represent them. This interpretation leads us to impose the following integrity rules.

2.   Integrity

It is now possible to state the two integrity rules of the relational model. Note that these rules are general, in the sense that any database that conforms to the model is required to satisfy them. However, any specific database will have a set of additional specific rules that apply to it alone. But such specific rules are outside the scope of the relational model .

(1)   Entity integrity:

No attribute participating in the primary key of a base relation[1] is allowed to accept null values.

(2)   Referential integrity:

Let D be a primary domain[2], and let R_1 be a relation with an attribute X that is defined on D. Then, at any given time, each value of X in R_1

---

[1] A base relation is an independent, named relation. It is represented in the physical database by a stored file.
[2] A given domain may optionally be designed as primary if and only if there exists some single-attribute primary key defined on that domain.

143

must be either (a) null, or (b) equal to V, say, where V is the primary key value of some tuple in some relation R_2 with primary key defined on D. R_1 and R_2 are not necessarily distinct.

The justification for the entity integrity rule is as follows:

(i)   Base relations correspond to entities in the real world.

(ii)   By definition, entities in the real world are distinguishable; that is, they have a unique identification of some kind.

(iii) Primary keys perform the unique identification function in the relational model.

(iv)   Thus, a primary key value that was null would be a contradiction in terms–in effect, it would be saying that there was some entity that had no identity (*i.e.* did not exist). Hence the name "entity integrity".

As for the rule of referential integrity, it is clear that a given value of the attribute X (which is sometimes called a foreign key) must have a matching primary key value in some tuple of the referenced relation if that foreign key value is non-null. Sometimes, however, it is necessary to permit the foreign key to accept null values.

4.1.4 Normalization

Normalization theory is built around the concept of normal forms. A relation is said to be in a particular normal form if it satisfies a certain specified set of constraints. In such a theory, Codd has identified certain structural features in relations which create retrieval and update problems. These undesirable features can be removed by breaking a relation into other relations of desirable structures.

Numerous normal forms have been defined (see Figure 4–6). Originally Codd defined three types of undesirable properties—data aggregates, partial key dependency and indirect key dependency, which can be removed in three stages of normalization known as first, second, and third normal form (1NF, 2NF, 3NF) [Codd, 1972]. Briefly, as Figure 4–6 suggests, all normalized relations are in 1NF; some 1NF relations are also in 2NF; and some 2NF relations are also in 3NF. The motivation behind the definitions was that 2NF was "more desirable" than 1NF, in a sense to be explained, and 3NF in turn was more desirable than

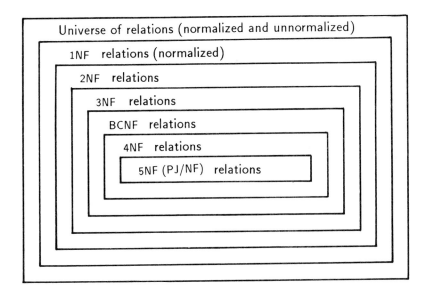

Figure 4–6 Normal Forms

2NF. That is, the designer should generally choose 3NF relations in designing a database, rather than 2NF or 1NF relations.

A relation is unnormalized if it contains data aggregates. In the first normal form, data aggregates are removed, by breaking the unnormalized relation, if necessary, into several other relations. The second and third normal forms remove partial and indirect dependencies of attributes on candidate keys.

1. Functional Dependence

We begin by introducing the fundamental notion of functional dependence (fd).

Definition 4.2

Given a relation R, attribute Y of R is functionally dependent on attribute X of R if and only if each X-value in R has associated with it precisely one Y-value in R (at any time).

For example, in the relation CANDIDATE (see Figure 4–1), attributes Sex, Age and Address are each functionally dependent on attribute Name because, given a particular value of Name in CANDIDATES, there exists precisely one corresponding value for each of Sex, Age and Address. In symbols, we have

$$\text{Name} \longrightarrow \text{Sex} \tag{4.1}$$

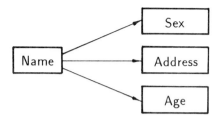

Figure 4–7   Functional Dependencies in Relation CANDIDATES

$$\text{Name} \longrightarrow \text{Age} \qquad (4.2)$$

$$\text{Name} \longrightarrow \text{Address} \qquad (4.3)$$

As an example, (4.3) means that attribute Address is functionally dependent on attribute Name, or equivalently, attribute Name functionally determines attribute Address.

Note that there is no requirement in the definition of functional dependence that a given X-value appear in only one tuple of R. We now give an alternative definition that makes this point explicitly.

Definition 4.3

Given a relation R, attribute Y of R is functionally dependent on attribute X of R if and only if, whenever two tuples of R agree on their X-value, they also agree on their Y-value.

Obviously, the definition above is equivalent to Definition 4.2. In fact, functional dependence is a special form of integrity constraint. When we say, for example, that relation CANDIDATES satisfies the fd : Name $\longrightarrow$ Address, we mean that every tabulation of the relation satisfies that constraint.

It is convenient to represent the fds in a given relation in terms of a functional dependency diagram. An example is shown in Figure 4–7.

We also introduce the concept of full functional dependence.

Definition 4.4

Attribute Y is fully functionally dependent on attribute X if it is functionally dependent on X and not functionally dependent on any proper subset of X.

For example, in the relation CANDIDATES, the attribute Address is functionally dependent on the composite attribute (Name,Age); however, it is not fully functionally dependent on this composite attribute because, of course, it is also functionally dependent on Name alone.

Recognizing functional dependencies is an essential part of understanding the semantics of the data. The fact that Address is functionally dependent on Name, for example, means that each candidate lives in precisely one city. In other words, we have a constraint in the real world that the database represents, namely, that each candidate lives in precisely one city. Later we will see that the concepts of normalization lead to a simple means of declaring such functional dependencies.

2.   First, Second, and Third Normal Forms

We are now in a position to describe the first, second, and third normal forms (1NF, 2NF, and 3NF). And we will pay most attention to the 3NF.

The purpose of the first normal form is to simplify the structure of a relation by ensuring that it contains only data items and no aggregates. More formally, we have

Definition 4.5

A relation R is in first normal form (1NF) if and only if every component in it is an atomic value.

In other words, a relation is said to be in 1NF if and only if it satisfies the constraint that it contains atomic values only. This definition merely states that any normalized relation is in 1NF. A relation that is only in 1NF, rather than 2NF or 3NF, has a structure that is undesirable for a number of reasons.

Now we give a definition of second normal form.

Definition 4.6

A relation R is in second normal form (2NF) if and only if it is in 1NF and every non-key attribute is fully dependent on the primary key.

An attribute is non-key if it does not participate in the primary key. A relation that is in first normal form and not in second can always be reduced to an equivalent collection of 2NF relations. The reduction consists of replacing the relations by suitable projection; the collection of these projections is equivalent to the original relation, in the sense that the original relation can always be recovered by taking the natural join of these projections, so no information is lost in the process.

However, 2NF relations still cause problems. We now present a definition of 3NF in order to give some idea of the point we are aiming for.

Definition 4.7

A relation R is in third normal form (3NF) if and only if it is in 2NF and every non-key attribute is nontransitively dependent on the primary key.

Intuitively speaking, a relation R is in 3NF if and only if, for all time, each tuple of R consists of a primary key value that identifies some entity, together with a set of mutually independent attribute values that describe that entity in some way.

A relation is said to be in third normal form if each non-key domain is functionally dependent on the (entire) key in a nontransitive manner. In the following discussion, it will be assumed that all relations are in third normal form.

For example, relation CANDIDATES is in 3NF: Each CANDIDATES tuple consists of a Name value, identifying some particular candidate, together with three pieces of descriptive information concerning that candidate—sex, age, and address. Moreover, each of the three descriptive items is independent of the other three. Relation COMPANY is also in 3NF; the entities in this case are companies. In general, the entities identified by the primary key values are the fundamental entities about which data are recorded in the database.

A relation that is in second normal form and not in third can always be reduced to an equivalent collection of 3NF relations. We have already mentioned that the process is reversible, and hence that no information is lost in the reduction.

We conclude that the level of normalization of a given relation is a matter of semantics, not a matter of the idea values that happen to appear in that relation at some particular time. It is not possible just to look at the tabulation of a given relation at a given time and to say whether or not that relation is 3NF—it is necessary to know the meaning of the data, *i.e.* the dependencies involved, before such a judgment can be made.

To sum up, a relational database is a collection $R = \{R_i\}$ describing certain objects in the world having certain attributes D, and the relationship among

Terms	Corresponding Names	Examples
relation	table/file	CANDIDATES
relational schema	table heading	⟨Name,Sex,Age,Address⟩
attribute	column name/field type	Name
attribute values	underlying domain	Smith,John
component	value	30
arity	degree	4
tuple	row/entity/record	⟨Smith,Male,30,Newcastle⟩
cardinality	—	5
fd	—	Name $\longrightarrow$ Address

Figure 4–8   Terminology

D, for instance, a set of dependencies F. Each relation R_i is characterized by a set of attributes $S_i = \{D_j | D_j \in D\}$ called its schema, and consists of a set of tuples. Each tuple is a map from the attributes of the relation schema to their domains that satisfies all the dependencies of F.

Corresponding to Figure 4–1, each term involved in relation CANDIDATES is given in Figure 4–8.

A relational database is accessed by a set of jobs submitted by users in order to retrieve, delete, insert or modify any subset of the data. In general, retrieval is an essential part of these processes. Users submit their requests for information in the form of queries, specifying the set of desired data. The task of query processing is to determine the set of data, the proper order in which the data should be accessed and the types of manipulation that must be performed on the data. This processing is referred to by different authors as query translation, access path finding, or optimization.

4.1.5   Relational Operations

The operations of relational algebra are an integral component of the relational model. Each operation of relational algebra takes either one or two relations as its operand(s) and produces a new relation as its result. Originally Codd defined eight such operations [Codd, 1972], two groups of four each: (1) the classical

R_1		
U	V	W
a	b	c
d	a	f
c	b	d

S_1		
U	V	W
b	g	a
d	a	f

R_2			
U	V	W	X
a	b	c	d
a	b	e	f
b	c	e	f
e	d	c	d
e	d	e	f
a	b	d	e

S_2	
W	X
c	d
e	f

R3		
U	V	W
1	2	3
4	5	6
7	8	9

S_3	
X	Y
3	1
6	2

R_4		
U	V	W
a	b	c
b	b	f
c	a	d

S_4		
V	W	X
b	c	d
b	c	e
a	d	b

Figure 4–9   The Mathematical Database

set operations **Union, Intersection, Difference,** and **Extended Cartesian Product**; (2) the special relational operations **Selection, Projection, Join** and **Division**.

For the purpose of discussing them, we assume R_1, R_2, R_3, R_4, S_1, S_2, S_3, and S_4 are relations in a mathematical database (see Figure 4–9).

1. Classical Set Operations

Each of the classical set operations takes two operands. For all except Cartesian Product, the two operand relations must be union-compatible; that is, they must be of the same degree, say n, and the i-th attribute of each must be based on the same domain, where $i = 1, 2, \ldots, n$.

Definition 4.8

The **union** of two (union-compatible) relations R and S, $R \cup S$, is the set of all tuples t belonging to either R or S (or both).

Example 4.6

The union of R_1 and S_1, $R_1 \cup S_1$, is illustrated in Figure 4–10.

$R_1 \cup S_1$		
U	V	W
a	d	c
d	a	f
c	b	d
b	g	a

Figure 4–10   A Sample Union

Definition 4.9

The **intersection** of two relations R and S, $R \cap S$, is the set of all tuples t belonging to both R and S.

Example 4.7

The intersection of R_1 and S_1, $R_1 \cap S_1$, is shown in Figure 4–11.

$R_1 \cap S_1$		
U	V	W
d	a	f

Figure 4–11   A Sample Intersection

Definition 4.10

The **difference** between two relations R and S, $R - S$, is the set of all tuples t belonging to R and not to S.

Example 4.8

The difference between R_1 and S_1, $R_1 - S_1$, is illustrated in Figure 4–12.

$R_1 - S_1$		
U	V	W
a	b	c
c	b	d

Figure 4–12   A Sample Difference

Definition 4.11

The **Extended Cartesian Product** of two relations R and S, $R \times S$, is the set of all tuples t such that t is the concatenation of a tuple t_1 belonging to R and a tuple t_2 belonging to S.

Example 4.9

The Extended Cartesian Product of R_1 and S_1, $R_1 \times S_1$, is shown in Figure 4–13.

2.   Special Relational Operations

Let ϑ represent any valid scalar comparison operator, such as, $=, / =, >, >=,$ *etc.*; we have

Definition 4.12(1)

The ϑ-**selection** of relation R on attributes X and Y is the set of all tuples t of R such that the predicate "$t.X \vartheta t.Y$" evaluates to true. (Attributes X and Y should be defined on the same domain, and the operation ϑ must make sense for that domain). A constant value may be specified instead of attribute Y. Thus,

152

$R_1 \times S_1$					
U_1	V_1	W_1	U_2	V_2	W_2
a	b	c	b	g	a
a	b	c	d	a	f
d	a	f	b	g	a
d	a	f	d	a	f
c	b	d	b	g	a
c	b	d	d	a	f

Figure 4–13   A Sample Extended Cartesian Product

the ϑ-selection operation yields a "horizontal" subset of a given relation, that is, that subset of the tuples of the given relation for which a specified predicate is satisfied.

We can define the selection operation in another way.

Definition 4.12(2)

Let R be a given relation and E a formula involving

(1)   operands that are constants or attributes;

(2)   the arithmetic comparison: $=, /=, <, >, =<, >=$;

(3)   the arithmetic operators: $+, -, *, /$.

then $R : E$, is the set of tuples t in R such that when all attributes occurring in E are substituted by the corresponding components of t, the formula E becomes true.

Example 4.10

Figure 4–14 shows the result of selecting tuples from relation R_3 where $V > 2$.

$R_3 : V > 2$		
U	V	W
4	5	6
7	8	9

Figure 4–14   A Sample Selection

Definition 4.13

The **projection** of relation R on attributes $X_1, X_2, \ldots, X_m$, $R[X_1, X_2, \ldots, X_m]$, yields a "vertical" subset of a given relation, that is, that subset obtained by selecting specified attributes and then eliminating redundant duplicate tuples within the attributes selected, if necessary.

Example 4.11

Project relation R_1 on attributes W and U, denoted $R_1[W, U]$, is formed by taking each tuple in R_1 and forming a new tuple from the third and first components of R_1 in that order. Figure 4–15 shows the result.

$R_1[W, U]$	
W	U
c	a
f	d
d	c

Figure 4–15 A Sample Projection

Definition 4.14

The ϑ-**join** of relation R on attribute X with relation S on attribute Y is the set of all tuples t such that t is the concatenation of a tuple t_1 belonging to R and a tuple t_2 belonging to S and the predicate "$t_1.X \vartheta t_2.Y$" evaluates to true, where attributes $R.X$ and $S.Y$ should be defined on the same domain, and the operation ϑ must make sense for that domain.

If ϑ is equality (=), the join is called an **equi-join**. It follows from the definition that the result of an equi-join must include two identical attributes. If one of those two attributes is eliminated, the result is called the **natural join**. The unqualified term "join" is usually taken to mean the natural join.

It should be clear, however, that such joins are not essential; by definition, they are equivalent to taking the Extended Cartesian Product of the two given relations and then performing a suitable selection on that product.

Example 4.12

The greater-than join of R_3 and S_3, written R_3 **JOIN** S_3 : $X > V$, produces the same result as the expression $R_3 \times S_3$: $X > V$. The result is illustrated in

Figure 4–16.

R_3 **JOIN** S_3 : $X > V$				
U	V	W	X	Y
1	2	3	3	1
1	2	3	6	2
4	5	6	6	2

Figure 4–16 A Sample ϑ-Join

Example 4.13

The natural join of R_4 and S_4 is shown in Figure 4–17.

R_4 **JOIN** S_4			
U	V	W	X
a	b	c	d
a	b	c	e
c	a	d	b

Figure 4–17 A Sample Natural Join

Definition 4.15

The **division** operation divides a dividend relation R of degree $m + n$ by a divisor relation S of degree n, and produces a result relation of degree m. The $(m + i)$-th attribute of R and the i-th attribute of S ($i = 1, 2, \ldots, n$) must be defined on the same domain. Consider the first m attributes of R as a single composite attribute X, and the last n as another, Y; R may then be thought of as a set of pairs of values $\langle x, y \rangle$. Similarly, S may be thought of as a set of single values, $\langle y \rangle$. Then the result of dividing R by S, namely, R DIVIDE_BY S, is the set of values x such that the pair $\langle x, y \rangle$ appears in R for all the y values appearing in S. The attributes of the result have the same qualified names as the first m attributes of R.

Example 4.14

Figure 4–18 illustrates the result of R_2 DIVIDE_BY S_2.

155

R_2 **DIVIDE_BY** S_2	
U	V
a	b
e	d

Figure 4–18 A Sample Division

4.2 Fuzzy Relations

We have mentioned that, for various reasons, the information contained in a real-world database is usually imprecise, uncertain, and even incomplete. This creates a need for developing methods to handle situations where a database does not contain all the precise information a user would like to know.

For this reason, we attempt to present such an approach, in which the theory of fuzzy sets and fuzzy logic are used as fundamental tools in designing and implementing the FPDB system. Fuzzy data, especially fuzzy linguistic data, can be captured and stored in this manner.

4.2.1 Fuzzy Domains and Fuzzy Attributes

The data we have to manage in a real database system are far from being always precise and certain.

The idea of representing fuzzy and incomplete information for the purposes of question-answering has been studied for many years. As previously noted, Grant and Lipski have investigated the impact of NULL and multi-valued attribute values [Grant, 1977, 1980; Lipski, 1981]. They generally attempt to formulate consistent schemes to permit the interpretation of queries in which such incomplete data exist.

However, the concept of fuzzy data was not really used because they simply considered that while data could be missing (incomplete), the existing data were exact (non-fuzzy). Fuzzy data structures were studied more recently by Mizumoto, Umano, Baldwin, Buckles, Petry and others. They have defined and implemented a collection of set operations and data structures in order to deal with fuzzy information in a database system.

156

In this book, we propose a general model based on possibility theory; our approach embodies the relational approach to databases.

A key aspect of fuzzy relations, in the FPDB, is that attribute values need not be atomic, precise. Fuzzy attributes are symbols taken from a finite set $\{A_1, A_2, \ldots, A_n\}$. With each attribute A_i is associated a fuzzy domain, denoted by $D_f(A_i)$, which is the set of possible values for the fuzzy attribute. That is, fuzzy attribute values are elements of a fuzzy domain which consist of fuzzy linguistic values or fuzzy numbers represented by means of possibility distributions. In such a system, it enables us to represent precisely, partially, or fuzzily known, or even totally unknown, attribute values in a common framework.

The treatment of incomplete attribute values in FPDB will be discussed in detail in Chapter 8. Here we discuss the representation of uncertain information by means of $[0, 1]$-valued possibility distributions.

Let A be an attribute and D be a universe of discourse of A, i.e. the set of all possible values which can be taken by A. The available knowledge concerning the value of the attribute A for an object x will be represented by a possibility distribution $\pi_{A(x)}$ on D. In other words, the possibility distribution function $\pi_{A(x)}$ associated with an attribute A of an object x is a mapping:

$$\pi_{A(x)} : D \to [0, 1]$$

where D is a universe of discourse of $A(x)$ and $\pi_{A(x)}(d)$ represents the possibility that $A(x)$ assumes the value d in D.

Let us consider an example where we have to represent our knowledge concerning the age of Smith. We may have the following situations, where π is short for $\pi_{Age}(Smith)$:

(1)   We are completely sure that Smith is 30 years old:

$$\pi(d) = \begin{cases} 1, & d = 30; \\ 0, & \text{otherwise.} \end{cases}$$

(2)   We are sure that Smith is young:

$\pi(d) = \mu_{young}(d), \quad \forall d \in D.$

where μ_{young} is a membership function which represents the fuzzy predicate 'young'.

4.2.2 Fuzzy Relations on Data and Fuzzy Data

It was mentioned that the relational model introduced by Codd is a convenient tool for describing data and their relationship. However, available implementations of relational databases are in terms of relations whose definition assumes only a two-valued logic. We show that the definition of the relation can be generalized to the fuzzy case.

A conventional relational database consists of one or more two-dimensional tables called relations. The columns of relations are called attributes and the rows are called tuples. For each attribute, A_i, in a relation, a domain, D_i, is understood. A tuple t either satisfies a relation R, or not. If instead of two-valued logic, we use fuzzy logic, then the tuple $t \in R$ at the grade μ if R is satisfied with a truth value μ, where $0 \leq \mu \leq 1$. Thus we define fuzzy relations on data as follows.

Definition 4.16

A fuzzy relation R in $D_1, D_2, \ldots, D_n$ is characterized by an n-variate membership function

$$\mu_R : \ D_1 \times D_2 \times \cdots \times D_n \to [0,1] \tag{4.4}$$

where $D_1 \times D_2 \times \cdots \times D_n$ is the Cartesian Product of $D_1, D_2, \ldots, D_n$.

A fuzzy relation R in $D_1 \times D_2 \times \cdots \times D_n$ is expressed as

$$R = \int \mu_R(d_{i1}, d_{i2}, \ldots, d_{in})/(d_{i1}, d_{i2}, \ldots, d_{in})$$

where $d_{ij} \in D_j$, $j = 1, 2, \ldots, n$.

Figure 4–19 illustrates a fuzzy relation **resemblance**, as a simple example

Example 4.15

resemblance		
Name1	**Name2**	
Tom	Kelley	0.8
Joan	Jim	0.6
Laurie	Grace	1.0
Funk	Hart	0.9
Emily	Flynn	0.8

Figure 4–19 An Example of Fuzzy Relations on Data

This is a most direct and simple way of generalizing the concept of relation to fuzzy relation [Zadeh, 1978(b)]. In such a case, however, the attribute values are still precise. Now the fuzzy relation on fuzzy data is defined for the FPDB system.

Definition 4.17

Let D_1, D_2, ..., D_n be n universal sets, $\tilde{\mathcal{P}}(D_i)$ collections of all possibility distributions on D_i, $i = 1, 2, \ldots, n$. Then a fuzzy relation R of a relation scheme $(A_1, A_2, \ldots, A_n)$ is defined by an n-variate membership function

$$\mu_R : D_f(A_1) \times D_f(A_2) \times \cdots \times D_f(A_n) \to [0,1] \qquad (4.5)$$

where $D_f(A_i) = \tilde{\mathcal{P}}(D_i) \cup \{NULL\}$ is called a fuzzy domain, whereas D_i is a base set.

In the relational model proposed by Codd [Codd, 1970], any member of an n-ary relation is called a n-tuple or, more simply, a tuple. As a particular form of fuzzy data, fuzzy tuples are used in the FPDB system. In such a case, a fuzzy tuple t of fuzzy relation R is an element $(d_1, d_2, \ldots, d_n)$ of $D_f(A_1) \times D_f(A_2) \times \cdots \times D_f(A_n)$ with a grade of membership μ obtained by (4.5), where $d_i \in D_f(A_i)$.

We have mentioned that in conventional relational databases, it is normal to display relations as two-dimensional tables, where attributes head the columns and rows are tuples. It is also helpful to view a fuzzy relation as a table. We may display a fuzzy relation in a similar way to a conventional relation, adding a special column which is used to express the membership function. However, the reader should keep in mind that in such a case, a fuzzy relation is actually a three-dimensional table, in the sense that it is defined by a membership function from a (two-dimensional) Cartesian Product to the interval $[0,1]$.

Example 4.16

Let us consider the fuzzy relation **candidates** whose attributes are Name, Sex, Age, and Address. Let the base set D_1 of attribute Name be a set of individuals' names, *e.g.* practically a set of character strings, D_2 of attribute Sex be {male,female}, D_3 of Age be a set of numerical ages, *e.g.* the integer interval $[0, 200]$, and D_4 of Address be a set of valid addresses. Then the fuzzy relation

candidates is defined by

$$D_f(Name) \times D_f(Sex) \times D_f(Age) \times D_f(Address) \rightarrow [0,1]$$

where $D_f(Name) = \tilde{\mathcal{P}}(D_1)$, $D_f(Sex) = \tilde{\mathcal{P}}(D_2)$, $D_f(Age) = \tilde{\mathcal{P}}(D_3)$, and $D_f(Address) = \tilde{\mathcal{P}}(D_4)$. For example, one of its occurrences is shown in Figure 4–20.

candidates			
Name	**Sex**	**Age**	**Address**
Smith	Male	30	Newcastle
John	Male	ABOUT 28	Carlisle
Anna	Female	22	Penrith
Mary	Female	\$Middle-aged	Carlisle
Martin	Male	\$Young	Newcastle

Figure 4–20   An Example of Fuzzy Relations on Fuzzy Data

This fuzzy relation **candidates** represents the following meaning. We know that Smith is a male, he is 30 years old, and he lives in Newcastle; John is a male also, his age is a possibility distribution '*about* 28' and he lives in Carlisle; Anna is a female, she is 22 years old and lives in Penrith; Mary is also a female, her age is a possibility distribution '*middle-aged*' and she lives in Carlisle; Lastly, Martin is a young male who lives in Newcastle.

4.2.3   Similarity Relations

An implied identity relation over a given domain D_i used in conventional relational databases induces equivalence classes which affect the result of certain operations and the removal of redundant tuples. The identity relation is replaced in the fuzzy relational database by an explicitly declared similarity relation [Zadeh, 1970] of which the identity relation is a special case.

Definition 4.18

A similarity relation, $s(x, y)$, for given domain, D_i, is a mapping of every pair of elements in the domain into the unit interval $[0, 1]$:

$$s : D_i \times D_i \rightarrow [0, 1].$$

A similarity relation is a generalization of equivalence relations in that if $a, b, c \in D_i$, then s is:

$$\textbf{reflexive :} \qquad s(a, a) \;=\; 1 \qquad\qquad (4.6)$$

$$\textbf{symmetric :} \qquad s(a, b) \;=\; s(b, a) \qquad\qquad (4.7)$$

$$\textbf{transitive :} \quad s(a, c) \;\geq\; \max_{\forall b \in D_i} \{\min [s(a, b), s(b, c)]\} \qquad\qquad (4.8)$$

Example 4.17

An example of a similarity relation for a finite scalar domain satisfying (4.6), (4.7), and (4.8) is:

	w	x	y	z
w	1	0	0	0
x	0	1	0.5	0.3
y	0	0.5	1	0.3
z	0	0.3	0.3	1

where $D_i = \{w, x, y, z\}$.

In an athletics team there are usually a number of specialized positions. Various similarities and dissimilarities exist between pairs of positions. In a baseball team, for example, a manager needing a right fielder might select a centre fielder to fill that position.

Example 4.18

A similarity relation for baseball team positions is illustrated in Figure 4-21 (see [Buckles and Petry, 1982(a)]). It reflects the beliefs that outfielders are completely interchangeable while pitchers and catchers are unique with respect to the skills required; with respect to the infielders, there are varying degrees of interchangeability; first basemen are the least interchangeable, shortstops are very interchangeable with the second basemen, and third basemen slightly less interchangeable.

It is clear that the identity relation is a special case of the definition for similarity relations. Here, we will asume that domain sets consist either of a finite set of scalars with a similarity relation or an infinite set of scalars with a similarity relation.

	P	C	LF	CF	RF	FB	SB	TB	SS
P	1	0	0	0	0	0	0	0	0
C	0	1	0	0	0	0	0	0	0
LF	0	0	1	1	1	0	0	0	0
CF	0	0	1	1	1	0	0	0	0
RF	0	0	1	1	1	0	0	0	0
FB	0	0	0	0	0	1	0.6	0.6	0.6
SB	0	0	0	0	0	0.6	1	0.8	0.9
TB	0	0	0	0	0	0.6	0.8	1	0.8
SS	0	0	0	0	0	0.6	0.9	0.8	1

P	Pitcher	CF	Centerfielder	SB	Secondbaseman
C	Catcher	RF	Rightfielder	TB	Thirdbaseman
LF	Leftfielder	FB	Firstbaseman	SS	Shortstop

Figure 4–21   Similarity Relation for Baseball Team Positions

4.3   Satisfactory Solutions Based on Fuzzy Relations

In conventional databases, a query model is frequently too inflexible with its one query expression and its strict discrimination between admissible and inadmissible solutions. The FPDB system provides an interactive fuzzy querying approach based on fuzzy relations. It is much more applicable to real situations, because the fuzzy query no longer requires that the solution completely satisfies the conditions, but requires that the solution satisfies the conditions with a certain degree. This is consistent with the ideas of replacing 'precise solution' by 'approximate solution' and replacing 'optimum solution' by 'satisfactory solution' in real life.

The difference between crisp and fuzzy retrieval conditions is that in the case of crisp conditions the database user can strictly differentiate between feasibility and infeasibility; in the case of fuzzy conditions he wants to consider a certain degree of feasibility in the interval $[0, 1]$. Thus a flexible modelling tool is needed.

The treatment of relational database queries under fuzzy conditions requires the concept 'satisfactory solution' instead of 'optimum solution'. The system

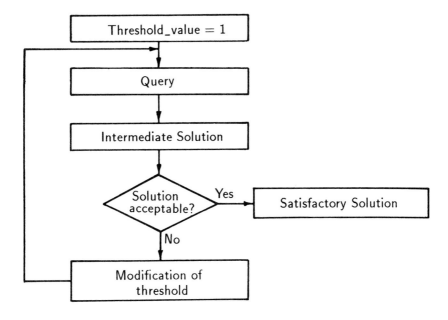

Figure 4–22 Interactive Fuzzy Querying Model in FPDB

determines intermediate solutions. They are judged by the database user and he decides whether one of them is subjectively the satisfactory one or whether modifications of threshold values are necessary. At the beginning, the database user may adopt 1 as the threshold for the query expressions. The rough flowchart shown in Figure 4–22 sketches the interactive fuzzy querying model.

In fact, the database user does not always have a clear idea of his goals but takes account of what he can achieve at most under the given circumstances. When he uses the conventional query model, he considers a solution as completely satisfying his conditions. He has not yet got a precise conception of which value the goal will reach. The additional information obtained from the intermediate solutions during the interactive procedure thus causes the database user to transform his previous idea into one which satisfies him. Usually, the degree of feasibility considered by the database user is greater than 0.5. As a result, those solutions with a degree of truth less than 0.5 will be always ignored in the FPDB system, unless we explicitly state otherwise.

During the interactive procedure the database user has the opportunity to modify the threshold values for the goals. The substitution model is changed accordingly and another intermediate solution is proposed to the database user. In fact, this is a heuristic approach of question-answering.

4.4 Fuzzy Constraints and Fuzzy Functional Dependency

Integrity constraints play a crucial role in the logical design of a relational database, because database consistency is enforced by them. Integrity constraints define the valid states of the database by constraining the values in the base tables. Data dependencies are special cases of integrity constraints. Various types of data dependencies, such as functional, multi-valued, and join dependencies, *etc.* have been discussed in the literature [Codd, 1970, 1972; Fagin, 1977; Rissanen, 1977].

For fuzzy relations, the concept of particularization proposed by Zadeh can be used to deal with fuzzy data constraints [Zadeh, 1978(a)]. Some authors are strongly influenced by Zadeh's "Possibility Theory". Following [Zadeh, 1978(a); Raju and Majumdar, 1987], in this section, we have a brief discussion on the functional dependency of fuzzy relational databases. The implementation of fuzzy constraints in FPDB will be introduced in Chapter 8.

Suppose the possibility distribution of $X = (X_1, X_2, \ldots, X_n)$ is conditioned on the values assigned to a specified subset $X_{(s)} = (X_{i_1}, X_{i_2}, \ldots, X_{i_m})$ of the constituent variables of X. Thus, we say that Π_X is particularized by specifying that $\Pi_{X_{(s)}} = G$ where G is a given m-ary possibility distribution. In general, we have

Definition 4.19

Let the possibility distributions induced by the propositions "X is F" and "$X_{(s)}$ is G" are $\Pi_X = \Pi_{(x_1, x_2, \ldots, x_n)} = F$ and $\Pi_{X_{(s)}} = \Pi_{(x_{i_1}, x_{i_2}, \ldots, x_{i_m})} = G$, respectively. Then, the particularization of Π_X by $\Pi_{X_{(s)}} = G$ is defined by

$$\Pi_X \left[\Pi_{X_{(s)}} = G \right] = F \cap \overline{G} \tag{4.9}$$

where $\overline{G}$ is the cylindrical extension of G [Zadeh, 1978(a)].

Example 4.19

The fuzzy relation shown in Figure 4–23 (a) corresponds to the proposition "X is F" where F = candidate, which induces the possibility assignment equation

164

$\Pi_X = F$ where $X = (X_1, X_2, \ldots, X_n)$. The proposition "candidate is young" may be expressed equivalently as "AGE(candidate) is young", which is of the form "Y is G" where $Y =$ candidate's age and $G =$ young. Let the fuzzy relation defined by G be as shown in Figure 4–23 (b), then the particularization "candidate's age is young", when applied to the given fuzzy relation F, gives the fuzzy relation of "young-candidate" shown in Figure 4–23 (c).

We show that the functional dependency (fd) of classical relational databases can be generalized to fuzzy relational databases by using the concept of particularization.

Consider the fd $X \longrightarrow Y$, where X and Y are sets of attributes of relation schema R. Then the fd can be treated as a particularization of R, such that Π_R is conditioned on the values assigned to a specified subset (XY) of the constituent variables of any instant r of R. That is, we say that $\pi_R = \mu_r$ is particularized by specifying that $\pi_{R(XY)} = \mu_{fd}$, where μ_{fd} is a mapping

$$\mu_{fd} : \Omega_X \times \Omega_Y \longrightarrow [0, 1]$$

and it must satisfy the following

$$\forall t_1, t_2 \in \text{Supp}\mu_{fd}\{(t_1[X] \neq t_2[X]) \vee (t_1 = t_2)\} \tag{4.10}$$

where $\text{Supp}\mu_{fd} = \{t | \mu_{fd}(t) > 0, t \in \Omega_X \times \Omega_Y\}$, and π is the possibility distribution function associated with Π.

Now, according to the "Possibility Theory" proposed by Zadeh [Zadeh, 1978(a)], we may express the functional dependency (fd) $X \longrightarrow Y$ in a fuzzy relation r by the proposition "R is r and XY is an fd" where R is the relation schema corresponding to r and $XY \subseteq R$. It means that Π_R is conditioned by $\pi_{R(XY)} = \mu_{fd}$. In such a case, using (4.9) the possibility distribution $\pi_R \left[\pi_{R(XY)} = \mu_{fd}\right]$ defines a fuzzy relation $\hat{r}$ such that

$$\mu_{\hat{r}}(t) = \min\{\mu_r(t), \overline{\mu}_{fd}(t)\} \tag{4.11}$$

where $\overline{\mu}_{fd}(t)$ is the cylindrical extension of $\mu_{fd}(t)$.

Applying (4.10) and the definition of cylindrical extension to (4.11), it can be readily seen that for any two tuples of $\hat{r}$ for which $\mu_{\hat{r}}(t_i) > 0$, $i = 1, 2, \ldots$, we must have

$$\forall t_1, t_2 \in \text{Supp}(\mu_{\hat{r}})\{(t_1[X] \neq t_2[X]) \vee [(t_1[X] = t_2[X]) \wedge (t_1[Y] = t_2[Y])]\} \tag{4.12}$$

candidate

Name	Sex	Age	Address
Smith	Male	30	Newcastle
John	Male	ABOUT 28	Carlisle
Anna	Female	22	Penrith
Mary	Female	$Middle-aged	Carlisle
Jill	Female	30	Penrith

(a)

young

Name	Age	
Smith	30	0.5
John	ABOUT 28	0.7
Anna	22	1.0
Mary	$Middle-aged	0.1
Jill	30	0.5

(b)

young-candidate

Name	Sex	Age	Address	
Smith	Male	30	Newcastle	0.5
John	Male	ABOUT 28	Carlisle	0.7
Anna	Female	22	Penrith	1.0
Jill	Female	30	Penrith	0.5

(c)

Figure 4–23

where $\text{Supp}(\mu_{\tilde{r}}) = \{t \mid \mu_{\tilde{r}}(t) > 0\}$.

Example 4.20

Suppose that the attributes are Name, Health, Height, and Looks. Figure 4–24 shows a fuzzy relation of height candidate of relation schema R(Name,Health,Height, Looks) where the particularization induced by an fd : Name $\longrightarrow$ Height holds.

Name	Health	Height	Looks	
Smith	Good	\$Tall	Good	1.0
John	Good	ABOUT 175	Good	0.5
Jill	Good	174	Moderate	0.5
Tom	VERY Good	180	Moderate	0.8
Harry	Moderate	185	Good	0.9
Fred	Good	178	FAIRLY Good	0.7

Figure 4–24

The inference rules of classical relations, namely reflexivity, augmentation and transitivity can be easily extended for particularization induced by fds in fuzzy relations.

Theorem 4.1   (Reflexivity property)

If $Y \subseteq X \subseteq \Omega$, then XY is an fd.

PROOF.   Let R be a fuzzy relation. For any two tuples t_1, t_2, having $t_1[\mu] > 0$ and $t_2[\mu] > 0$, if they agree on X, i.e., $t_1[X] = t_2[X]$, then they should agree on any subset of X. We know $Y \subseteq X$, therefore the reflexivity property is true.

Theorem 4.2   (Augmentation property)

If XY is an fd and $Z \subseteq \Omega$ then $XZYZ$ is an fd.

PROOF.   Let R be a fuzzy relation that satisfies particularization XY is an fd. Suppose any two tuples, say t_1 and t_2, with $t_1[\mu] > 0$ and $t_2[\mu] > 0$, agree on the attributes of XZ but disagree on YZ. It is that $t_1[XZ] = t_2[XZ]$ but $t_1[YZ] \neq t_2[YZ]$. Since there is no possibility to disagree on any attributes in Z, t_1 and t_2 must disagree on some attributes in Y. However, since R satisfies XY is an fd and, by (4.10) and (4.12), these two tuples should agree on Y, i.e.

167

$t_1[Y] = t_2[Y]$, therefore R satisfies the particularization $XZYZ$ is an fd.

Theorem 4.3   (Transitivity property)

If XY is an fd and YZ is an fd then XZ is an fd.

PROOF.   Let R be a fuzzy relation. Suppose it satisfies the particularizations XY is an fd and YZ is an fd. If there exist two tuples t_1 and t_2 ($t_1[\mu] > 0$ and $t_2[\mu] > 0$), such that $t_1[X] = t_2[X]$ but $t_1[Z] \neq t_2[Z]$, by assumption R satisfies that XY is an fd and YZ is an fd. But by (4.10) and (4.12) $t_1[Y] = t_2[Y]$ and hence $t_1[Z] = t_2[Z]$. Otherwise either XY is an fd or YZ is an fd would be violated, thereby contradicting our assumption.

4.5   A Sample Database

For future discussion throughout this book, we present a sample fuzzy relational database. Suppose that the database contains all the data for some large component of the organization at a job information centre. It is used by people to select their jobs. Every person has conditions for selecting what job is most interesting for him. There are some companies with their several conditions and requirements in the database. The candidates' background and abilities are also given in order to be able to make bidirectional selection. The databse system consists of three major parts. These include:

(a)   Information about candidates

(b)   Information about companies

(c)   Information about the environment

There are many careers open to each of the candidates and choosing the right career is very important. Most of us spend a great part of our lives at our jobs. For that reason we should try to find out what the candidates' talents are and how companies can use them. Sometimes we say that someone is "a square peg in a round hole". This simply means that the person is not suited for the job he is doing. Unfortunately, many people in the world are "square pegs". The data are organized into eight relations: candidates, background, ability, body, company, job, relationship and location. The relationship between these relations together with their keys are given in Figure 4–25.

1. Information about candidates

candidates

Name	Sex	Age	Address

background

Name	Education	Profession	Experience	Hobby

ability

Name	Intelligence	Initiative	SocialMaturity	Skill

body

Name	Health	Height	Looks

2. Information about companies

company

Cname	Location	President	Employees	Profit

job

Position	Cname	Salary	Benefits

3. Environment

relationship

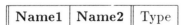

Name1	Name2	Type

location

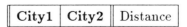

City1	City2	Distance

Figure 4–25 Job Information Centre

169

The **candidates** table contains, for each candidate, a candidate name, sex, age, and address; the **background** table contains, for each candidate, a name, education, profession, the length of service (Experience) and a hobby; the **ability** table describes each candidate's intelligence, initiative, social maturity (Social-Maturity), and skill; the **body** table shows, for each candidate, a name, health, height and looks; the **company** table describes company name (Cname), location, company president, number of employees (Employees), and gross profit (Profit) for each company; the **job** table, for each pair of position and company, contains position, company name (Cname), salary, and benefits; the **relationship** table shows, for each two of candidates, name1, name2, and their relationship (Type); the **location** table lists, for each pair of cities, city1, city2, and their distance. All these relations are illustrated in Figure 4–26.

candidates			
Name	**Sex**	**Age**	**Address**
Smith	Male	30	Newcastle
John	Male	ABOUT 28	Carlisle
Anna	Female	22	Penrith
Mary	Female	$Middle-aged	Carlisle
Jill	Female	30	Penrith
Susan	Female	ABOUT 28	Darlington
Tom	Male	24	Carlisle
Harry	Male	36	Darlington
Fred	Male	ABOUT 25	Darlington
Margaret	Female	20	Penrith
Andrew	Male	24	Carlisle
Barry	Male	33	Newcastle
Thomas	Male	31	Darlington
Martin	Male	$Young	Newcastle
Henry	Male	29	Penrith

background				
Name	**Education**	**Profession**	**Experience**	**Hobby**
Smith	University	Manager	2	Travelling
John	High-school	Assistant	6	Sports
Anna	High-school	Secretary	3	Singing
Mary	University	Technician	$Long	Cooking
Jill	Post-graduate	Manager	4	Travelling
Susan	University	Manager	1	Painting
Tom	University	Engineer	1	Singing
Harry	University	Manager	7	Reading
Fred	University	Technician	5	Sports
Margaret	High-school	Secretary	1	Dancing
Andrew	University	Engineer	2	Singing
Barry	Post-graduate	Engineer	6	Sports
Thomas	Post-graduate	Manager	3	Fishing
Martin	University	Engineer	2	Dancing
Henry	University	Clerk	8	Fishing

ability

Name	Intelligence	Initiative	SocialMaturity	Skill
Smith	VERY Good	Excellent	Excellent	VERY Good
John	FAIRLY Good	Good	VERY Good	Good
Anna	Good	VERY Good	Excellent	Good
Mary	VERY Good	Good	Good	Moderate
Jill	Excellent	Moderate	VERY Good	VERY Good
Susan	Good	VERY Good	VERY Good	Good
Tom	Moderate	Bad	Moderate	VERY Good
Harry	VERY Good	Moderate	Good	Good
Fred	Moderate	FAIRLY Good	Excellent	Bad
Margaret	Good	Moderate	Good	Bad
Andrew	Good	VERY Good	Moderate	Moderate
Barry	Good	Good	FAIRLY Good	Good
Thomas	Excellent	Good	Excellent	Moderate
Martin	Good	Moderate	Good	VERY Good
Henry	Moderate	Good	Good	Moderate

body			
Name	**Health**	**Height**	**Looks**
Smith	Good	$Tall	Good
John	Good	ABOUT 175	Good
Anna	Good	ABOUT 170	Good
Mary	Good	165	VERY Good
Jill	Good	174	Moderate
Susan	Moderate	$Short	Moderate
Tom	VERY Good	180	Moderate
Harry	Moderate	185	Good
Fred	Good	178	FAIRLY Good
Margaret	Good	170	Good
Andrew	VERY Good	$Short	Good
Barry	Good	169	FAIRLY Good
Thomas	Moderate	190	Moderate
Martin	VERY Good	171	Good
Henry	Good	173	Moderate

(1) Information about Candidates

company				
Cname	**Location**	**President**	**Employees**	**Profit**
C1	Newcastle	David	400	300,000
C2	Carlistle	Edward	100	100,000
C3	Penrith	Felix	2000	1,000,000
C4	Darlington	Alice	800	600,000

job			
Position	**Cname**	**Salary**	**Benefits**
Manager	C1	12000	Good
Manager	C2	10000	VERY Good
Manager	C3	8000	Moderate
Manager	C4	10000	Bad
Engineer	C1	9000	Good
Engineer	C2	9000	Good
Engineer	C3	8000	Moderate
Engineer	C4	9000	Bad
Secretary	C1	7000	VERY Good
Secretary	C2	7000	Good
Secretary	C3	6000	Good
Secretary	C4	5000	Moderate
Technician	C1	6000	Moderate
Technician	C2	5000	Good
Technician	C3	4500	Moderate
Technician	C4	7000	Bad
Clerk	C1	7000	Moderate
Clerk	C2	7000	Moderate
Clerk	C3	6000	Moderate
Clerk	C4	5000	Bad
Assistant	C1	6000	Good
Assistant	C2	5000	FAIRLY Good
Assistant	C3	3000	Moderate
Assistant	C4	5000	Moderate

(2)   Information about Companies

relationship		
Name1	**Name2**	**Type**
Smith	Anna	Couple
Smith	Susan	Friend
Smith	Fred	Friend
Smith	Henry	Friend
Andrew	Smith	Friend
Barry	Smith	Friend
John	Smith	Friend
Anna	Mary	Friend
Tom	Susan	Couple
Jill	Harry	Friend
Thomas	Henry	Friend
Tom	Martin	Friend
Henry	Margaret	Friend
Harry	Anna	Friend
David	John	Relative
David	Margaret	Relative
Felix	Anna	Relative
Alice	Martin	Relative

location		
City1	**City2**	**Distance**
Newcastle	Carlisle	ABOUT 60
Newcastle	Penrith	45
Newcastle	Darlington	40
Carlisle	Penrith	23
Carlisle	Darlington	$Near
Penrith	Darlington	52

(3)   Environment

Figure 4-26   A Sample Database

175

Base sets of the attributes Name, Name1, Name2 and President are sets of individuals' names, *i.e.* practically sets of character strings, *e.g.*

{ Smith, John, Richard, ... }.

The base set of the attribute Sex is

{ Male, Female }.

The base set of the attribute Age is a set of numerical ages, *e.g.*

$$\{0, 1, 2, \ldots, 200\},$$

where the possibility distributions on it are as follows: $Young, $Old, $Middle-aged, and ABOUT n (see Appendix 2).

The base set of the attribute Education is

{ High-school, University, Post-graduate },

where the possibility distribution

$HE = { 1/University, 1/Post-graduate }

indicates "higher-education".

Base sets of the attributes Address, Location, City1 and City2 are sets of valid place names, **i.e.** practically a set of character strings,

{ Newcastle, Carlisle, Penrith, Darlington, ... }.

Base sets of the attributes Profession and Position are sets of names of jobs, *e.g.*

{ Manager, Engineer, Secretary, Clerk, Technician, Assistant, ... }.

Base sets of the attributes Salary, Height, Experience, Employees, Profit and Distance are sets of numerical values, while base sets of the attributes Intelligence, Initiative, SocialMaturity, Skill, Health, Looks, Benefits and Type are sets of fuzzy linguistic values, namely,

{ Excellent, VERY Good, Good, FAIRLY Good, Moderate, Bad, ... },

{ VERY Good, Good, FAIRLY Good, Moderate, Bad, ... },

and

{ Friend, Couple, Relative, ... },

The base set of the attribute Cname is a set of names of companies, *e.g.*

{ C1, C2, C3, C4, ... }.

Chapter 5

A FUZZY RELATIONAL
QUERY LANGUAGE—FSQL

The aim of this chapter is to present an introduction to some of the major facilities of the FSQL (Fuzzy Relational Query Language). FSQL is a fuzzy SQL language which can be regarded as an extention of the standard SQL. By means of FSQL, fuzzy and even incomplete data can be handled appropriately; whereas the standard SQL is a special case of FSQL.

5.1 SQL as a Standard Relational Query Language

In order to understand why the SQL language has become so widespread and so generally important, it is helpful to review the development history of database technology, especially relational query languages, during the past fifteen or so years.

The entire field of the relational database technology originated following Codd publishing his well-known paper "A Relational Model of Data for Large shared Data Banks" [Codd, 1970]. One particular aspect of the research just referred to was the design and prototype implementation of a variety of relational query languages.

A number of relational query languages were designed and implemented to serve as practical tools for casual users of relational databases in the early 1970s. Queries in such languages have clear structure and meaning, and are expressed in a way which is much closer to the way one would ask such queries in natural language, particularly in English.

One such language in particular was the SEQUEL (Structured English Query Language, defined by D. D. Chamberlin and others at the IBM San Jose Research Laboratory [Chamberlin and Boyce, 1974] and first implemented in an IBM prototype called SEQUEL-XRM [Astrahan and Lorie, 1975].

Partly as a result of experience with SEQUEL-XRM, a revised version of SEQUEL called SEQUEL/2 was defined in 1977 and its name was subsequently changed to SQL meaning Structured Query Language, when the acronym SEQUEL was found to have been used previously by someone else. Work began on another, more ambitious, IBM prototype called System R. System R, an implementation of a large subset of the SEQUEL/2 (or SQL) language, became operational in 1977 and was subsequently installed in a number of user sites.

Thanks in large part to the success of System R, it became apparent in the late 1970s that IBM would probably develop one or more products based on the System R technology, specifically, products that implemented the SQL language. At the same time, other vendors also began to construct their own SQL-based products. In particular, ORACLE, a relational database system based on the SQL language, from Oracle Corporation, was introduced to the market prior to IBM's own products. Nowadays, ORACLE is becoming more and more popular.

There are now more than fifty products in the marketplace that support some dialect of SQL, running on all kinds of machines. SQL has become the de facto standard in the relational database world.

The fundamental operation in SQL is a SELECT–FROM–WHERE block formed as:

SELECT	⟨target attributes⟩
FROM	⟨relations⟩
WHERE	⟨condition⟩

The SELECT clause specifies the attributes of the target result, or SQL built-in functions involving one or more attributes or permitted arithmetical expressions with one or more attributes. The permitted arithmetical expressions include +, -, * and /. The FROM clause specifies the names of relations which are involved in forming the result, both in conditioning selection and in actually supplying result values. The WHERE clause specifies the condition on which the result is to be obtained. The condition is a Boolean logic expression which allows

(1)   logical operators: NOT, AND, OR;

(2)   standard comparison operators: =, / =, >, <, =<, and >=;

(3)   IN, ALL and some other operators.

The WHERE statement can be omitted if there is no specific condition required.

In general, a SELECT–FROM–WHERE block returns a collection of SELECTED attribute values of tuples FROM the specified relation(s), optionally subject to the condition stated in the WHERE clause.

To increase the retrieval power, standard SQL supports the following five statistical functions:

COUNT (Col)	to count the values in column Col
SUM (Col)	to sum the values in column Col
AVG (Col)	to find the average value in column Col
MAX (Col)	to find the maximum value in column Col
MIN (Col)	to find the minimum value in column Col

In addition, there are also an ORDER_BY, a GROUP_BY and a HAVING clause in the SQL language.

SQL was originally an abbreviation, standing for the Structured Query Language. However, it does not mean that SQL is only a language for querying. In fact, the SQL language consists of a set of facilities for defining, querying, updating, operating, and controlling data in a relational database. Besides querying, the most important types of facility are insertion (INSERT), deletion (DELETE) and modification (UPDATE).

SQL "data operation" statements, **i.e.**, SQL statements that perform data retrieval or updating functions can be invoked either interactively or from within an application program. In general, interactive invocation means that the statement in question is executed from an interactive terminal and the result is displayed at that terminal. Invocation from within an application program means that the statement is executed as part of the process of executing that program and the result is fetched into an input area within that program.

The SQL language is simple enough in its basic structure so that casual users, without prior experience, are able to learn a usable subset on their first sitting.

From the user's standpoint, SQL is probably the most important relational sublanguage at present.

Since 1986, SQL has been adopted as an official standard by the American National Standards Institute (ANSI), and now it has also been adopted as an international standard by the International Standards Organization (ISO).

5.2 Basic Concepts of the Fuzzy SQL Language

As we have shown, SQL is the most important relational query language in the database world. However, it only provides facilities to deal with well-defined and precise data. In other words, it is not oriented towards the representation and operation of fuzzy data. For this reason, a fuzzy SQL language named FSQL has been designed and implemented in f-PROLOG [Liu and Li, 1989(a)] by the authors. FSQL can be thought of as an extension of the standard SQL language, whereas SQL standard is a special case of the FSQL language.

The characteristic style and structure of standard SQL are preserved in the FSQL language. In addition, in the structure of FSQL language, fuzzy linguistic values defined by means of possibility distributions are permitted. Moreover, some necessary operators for fuzzy comparision are defined (see Chapter 6). Therefore, fuzzy queries can be answered appropriately.

Like the standard SQL language, the function of the fuzzy SQL language is to support the definition, operation, and control of data (fuzzy or nonfuzzy) in the FPDB system.

The most basic operation in the FSQL language is so-called mapping, which implies transformation of values from the database to user requirements. This operation is syntactically represented by a

SELECT	⟨list of attributes⟩
FROM	⟨list of relations⟩
WHERE	⟨condition⟩
WITH	⟨degree⟩

block called a fuzzy query block.

In general, a mapping returns a relation which consists of a collection of SELECTED attribute values of tuples FROM the specified relation(s), optionally subject to the condition stated in the WHERE clause, WITH the given degree. More specifically, the result of the execution of a fuzzy query block is a fuzzy relation whose structure and contents are determined by that block. Attributes of that relation are specified in the list of attributes. The attribute values listed are selected from the fuzzy relations in the list of relations. SELECT and FROM clauses in the query block define the operation of projection. The condition in the WHERE clause is a fuzzy logic expression. It contains attributes of the relations listed in the FROM clause. The degree in the WITH clause is a threshold value. WHERE and WITH clauses in the query block determine what tuples of those relations qualify for the operation of projection. This means that only the attribute values of those tuples for which the condition, fuzzy logic expression, is true with the given degree will appear in the result of the query block. WHERE and WITH clauses in the query block thus contain the specification of the fuzzy selection and the fuzzy join operations. As a special case, the WITH statement can be omitted if the threshold value ⟨degree⟩ is 1.

To summarize, the basic fuzzy query block as a whole represents a composition of the operations of projection, selection, and join of fuzzy relational algebra.

Example 5.1

Get the names of all candidates who are young with the confidence degree of 0.9.

$$
\begin{array}{ll}
\text{SELECT} & \text{Name} \\
\text{FROM} & \text{candidates} \\
\text{WHERE} & \text{Age} = \$\text{Young} \\
\text{WITH} & 0.9 \ ;
\end{array}
\qquad \text{(Q5.1)}
$$

Similar to SQL standard, the FSQL language permits nested query blocks to an arbitrary depth. The attributes in a WHERE clause of an inner block can come from relations specified in the FROM clause of any outer block.

Example 5.2

Retrieve the names of all candidates who have been secretaries and are young girls, with the confidence degree of 0.8.

181

```
SELECT     Name
FROM       background
WHERE      Profession = secretary
AND        Name  IN
                (SELECT    Name                           (Q5.2)
                 FROM      candidates
                 WHERE     Sex = female
                 AND       Age = $Young
                 WITH      0.8) ;
```

5.3   Fuzzy Queries

5.3.1   Translation of Fuzzy Queries for Relational Database Systems

To understand the potential power of fuzzy queries, let us consider an example. Suppose you wish to find the subset of jobs that have attractive salaries. Using a conventional or precise search criterion set, you might search for jobs with salary equal to or greater than $9000. With fuzzy queries you could, alternatively, phrase your request as "Find those jobs with high salaries." The fuzzy linguistic value "*high* salary" is defined as a possibility distribution (see Appendix 2).

Figure 5–1 shows the responses of the precise and the fuzzy query.

The precise query response identifies six jobs. All others in the table **job** are passed over, since their salaries are not high enough. By contrast, the fuzzy query returns thirteen candidate jobs. However, the key difference is that the fuzzy query finds more new jobs that meet the user's needs more fully than the precise response. By any standard, the fuzzy query is more productive in finding candidate jobs as the user would perceive candidate jobs.

Two ideas led us to introduce fuzzy linguistic values in database retrieval in order to translate fuzzy queries posed by the database user into standard query language—the rejection of the opinion that human reasoning can be specified and refined to binary formal logic, and the assumption that the power of human reasoning lies, by contrast, in its ability to handle fuzzy concepts. The model's linguistic values represent the fundamentally imprecise human perception of physical reality.

Queries of the database may be expressed in essentially standard query lan-

Position	Cname	Salary
Manager	C1	12000
Manager	C2	10000
Manager	C4	10000
Engineer	C1	9000
Engineer	C2	9000
Engineer	C4	9000

(a)   The Precise Query Response

Position	Cname	Salary	
Manager	C1	12000	0.92
Manager	C2	10000	0.86
Manager	C3	8000	0.70
Manager	C4	10000	0.86
Engineer	C1	9000	0.80
Engineer	C2	9000	0.80
Engineer	C3	8000	0.70
Engineer	C4	9000	0.80
Secretary	C1	7000	0.50
Secretary	C2	7000	0.50
Technician	C4	7000	0.50
Clerk	C1	7000	0.50
Clerk	C2	7000	0.50

(b)   The Fuzzy Query Response

Figure 5–1

guage. A classical data retrieval specification returns a sharply defined set from the database.

Suppose the user asks the database to retrieve a set of jobs for the purpose of evaluating candidates for building a *"high* salary" list. The standard deterministic rules of computer language insist that we employ arbitrary cutoff points. These cutoffs may not reflect the purpose of the user adequately. That user hardly means that at salary of 8999 the candidate job is of no interest whatsoever, whereas at salary of 9000 it is suddenly as interesting as it possibly can be. More likely, the user means that he/she starts to become interested in a job when its salary approaches that value; only the limitation of the retrieval language forces the user into spurious precision.

Artificial intelligence emphasizes natural language processing. Because fuzziness is a property of natural language, fuzzy set technology seems useful for understanding and expressing the problems in fuzzy situations a database designer or user faces.

With FSQL one can rephrase database queries to take advantage of linguistic values. The linguistic approach permits the users to express themselves more nearly in natural language, and also generates additional information concerning the data retrieval. Section 5.4 gives the detail.

5.3.2 The Formulation and Evaluation of Fuzzy Queries

To see how to add the concept of linguistic values to the facilities at the user's disposal in formulating and evaluating retrieval queries across a database, we need to explore the mechanism of the fuzzy query further.

Up to now, natural language cannot be used directly in database systems, so formal query languages are still necessary. The FSQL language which has been developed in the FPDB system enables the user to formulate queries according to an English-like syntax. For instance, the query mentioned in the preceding subsection should be written as follows:

$$
\begin{array}{ll}
\text{SELECT} & \text{Position, Cname, Salary} \\
\text{FROM} & \text{job} \\
\text{WHERE} & \text{Salary} = \text{\$High} \\
\text{WITH} & \text{F ;}
\end{array}
\qquad (Q5.3)
$$

where $High is a fuzzy linguistic value represented by the possibility distribution, and **F** is a variable denoting the threshold for which the grade of membership of each tuple in the result table will be received.

Although many problems can be solved by keying in the appropriate numbers and symbols, the greatest benefits of writing queries in FSQL become evident when we use linguistic values. Because a single linguistic value may refer to a large collection of information, we can simply key in the single word rather than all of its members. FSQL syntax was designed to be similar to that of English, an elegant feature those implementing approximate reasoning techniques in knowledge engineering can exploit.

In the FPDB system, there is no limit to the complexity of the fuzzy query, since the FSQL syntax permits a query block to be nested within an outer query block. In the vast majority of FSQL retrievals we construct one or more fuzzy query blocks, and such a block specifies a set of fuzzy tuples, that is a fuzzy relation. In such cases, a fuzzy query expression may contain one or more variables **F** in the WITH statements. They need not be distinguished, because each of them is locally bounded in the subquery involved. As a result, the intermediate values of the membership degree arising from the fuzzy conditions involved in the WHERE statements can be received respectively. The final value of the membership degree will be accumulated based on the fuzzy relational algebra or fuzzy relational calculus which will be presented in Chapter 6.

5.4   Linguistic Values in Fuzzy SQL

We have already stated that a word in a natural language is usually a summary of a complex, multifaced concept which is incapable of precise characterization. For this reason, the denotation of a word is generally a fuzzy rather than nonfuzzy set of a universe of discourse. For example, if Ω is a collection of individuals, the denotation of the term *young-man* in Ω is a fuzzy subset of Ω which is characterized by a membership function $\mu_{young-man} : \Omega \to [0,1]$, which associates with each individual i in Ω the degree from 0 to 1, to which i is a young man. When necessary or expedient, this degree may be expressed in linguistic values such as possible, impossible, very possible, not very possible, more or less possible, very impossible, *etc.*, with each such term representing a fuzzy subset of the unit interval. In this case, the denotation of young man is a fuzzy set of

Type 2.

The FSQL language is closer to natural English than the standard SQL, since it permits fuzzy linguistic values; especially, the threshold value stated in the WITH clause can be a fuzzy linguistic truth value. Let us examine the basic query block again.

Example 5.3

Show all candidates with respect to the condition: their ages are very possibly about 25.

$$
\begin{array}{ll}
\text{SELECT} & \text{Name} \\
\text{FROM} & \text{candidates} \\
\text{WHERE} & \text{Age} = \text{ABOUT } 25 \\
\text{WITH} & \text{VERY possible ;}
\end{array}
\qquad (\text{Q5.4})
$$

In this fuzzy query block, the WHERE clause contains a fuzzy linguistic value ABOUT 25, defined by means of the possibility distribution

$$
\begin{aligned}
&\text{Poss}\{X{=}25\} = 1; \\
&\text{Poss}\{X{=}24\} = \text{Poss}\{X{=}26\} = 0.8; \\
&\text{Poss}\{X{=}23\} = \text{Poss}\{X{=}27\} = 0.5.
\end{aligned}
$$

The WITH clause in the query block contains a fuzzy linguistic truth value of very possible as a threshold, which is a possibility distribution on $[0,1]$. Such a query block is quite similar to the query expressed in a natural language.

We conclude that the logic underlying the fuzzy SQL language is not a two-valued logic, but a fuzzy logic, in which the truth values are both numerical values in the unit interval $[0,1]$, and linguistic values, such as true, false, very true, not very true, more or less true, very false, *etc.*, with each such truth value representing a fuzzy subset of the unit interval. Since we have shown that the truth value of a statement is equivalent to its degree of belief, we often use possible, impossible, very possible, not very possible, more or less possible, very impossible, *etc.* instead of true, false, very true, not very true, more or less true, very false, *etc.* It thus provides a mechanism for the association of fuzzy truth values with fuzzy query statements expressed in a natural language, and thereby endows the FSQL language with a capability for modelling the type of fuzzy query which humans employ in fuzzy environments, and returns a fuzzy answer to satisfy the vague requirements of the query.

5.5   Retrieval Statements

We now proceed to illustrate the basic retrieval operations of the FSQL language by means of a collection of examples, based on the sample fuzzy relational database given in Section 4.5.

We have argued that the most fundamental operation in FSQL language is the basic fuzzy query block:

$$
\begin{array}{ll}
\text{SELECT} & \langle \textit{list of attributes} \rangle \\
\text{FROM} & \langle \textit{list of relations} \rangle \\
\text{WHERE} & \langle \textit{condition} \rangle \\
\text{WITH} & \langle \textit{degree} \rangle
\end{array}
$$

and the fuzzy query block as a whole represents a composition of the operations of projection, restriction, and join of fuzzy relational algebra. In the FSQL language, a fuzzy query could have been written within one line:

SELECT $\langle \textit{attributes} \rangle$ FROM $\langle \textit{relations} \rangle$ WHERE $\langle \textit{condition} \rangle$ WITH $\langle \textit{degree} \rangle$

FSQL does not require a query in a fixed format; it does not care about more spaces between words. Both upper and lower case letters are all acceptable. The only thing the user must remember is to avoid spelling mistakes. If a mistake is made in entering a query, the system will respond with an error message.

To illustrate the use of the fuzzy query block of the FSQL language, let us see some special cases.

(1)   Projection

Example 5.4

The following query block (Q5.5) constructs a table which consists of all positions shown in the relation **job**:

$$
\begin{array}{ll}
\text{SELECT} & \text{Position} \\
\text{FROM} & \text{job ;}
\end{array}
\qquad (Q5.5)
$$

Since the WHERE and WITH clauses are missing, it appears that the query block (Q5.5) represents the operation of projection. Nevertheless, that is not quite true, since elimination of redundant tuples which appear after selection of the attribute Position will not be performed. The elimination process which is usually necessary and sometimes very expensive must be explicitly specified, as in query block (Q5.6)

$$\begin{aligned}&\text{SELECT} \quad \text{DISTINCT(Position)}\\&\text{FROM} \qquad \text{job ;}\end{aligned} \qquad\qquad (Q5.6)$$

Query block (Q5.6) defines precisely the operation of projection of the relation **job** over its attribute Position.

The word "redundant" here is somewhat fuzzy; it may be treated in different ways. Most simply, we may directly adopt the definition of redundant tuples for conventional databases, provided we consider the column of membership function μ as a special attribute of the relation. The lack of redundant tuples in a conventional database is tantamount to the absence of multiple occurrences of equal tuples. In the FPDB system, we define the concept of redundant tuples as follows.

Definition 5.1

Let $t_i = (d_{i1}, \ldots, d_{in})$ with the membership degree $\mu(t_i)$ and $t_j = (d_{j1}, \ldots, d_{jn})$ with the membership degree $\mu(t_j)$ be two tuples of a relation R, where $i \neq j$. t_i and t_j are redundant tuples if

$$d_{ik} = d_{jk}, \qquad k = 1, 2, \ldots, n.$$

In the FPDB system, if $\mu(t_i) > \mu(t_j)$, then t_j will be removed and *vice versa*, when the elimination of redundant tuples is performed.

This is one of the important concepts in fuzzy relational databases. When the operations Projection, Union, Intersection, *etc.* of fuzzy relational algebra are executed, elimination of redundant tuples will always be performed. Thus the unique results will be given in a fuzzy environment.

It is possible to order the table which represents the result of a query block.

Example 5.5

We obtain an alphabetical listing of candidates, each one with his/her sex, by typing query block (Q5.7).

$$\begin{aligned}&\text{SELECT} \qquad \text{Name, Sex}\\&\text{FROM} \qquad\;\; \text{candidates}\\&\text{ORDER\_BY} \quad \text{Name ;}\end{aligned} \qquad\qquad (Q5.7)$$

Note that fuzzy ordering can be also treated by the ORDER_BY clause (see Chapter 6).

188

(2) Selection

Example 5.6

Get full details of all companies from the table **company**.

$$\begin{array}{ll} \text{SELECT} & * \\ \text{FROM} & \text{company ;} \end{array} \qquad \text{(Q5.8)}$$

The asterisk * is a shorthand for an ordered list of all attributes in the FROM table. The query shown is thus equivalent to (Q5.9)

$$\begin{array}{ll} \text{SELECT} & \text{Cname, Address, President, Employees, Profit} \\ \text{FROM} & \text{company ;} \end{array} \qquad \text{(Q5.9)}$$

Example 5.7

Select those tuples from the table **candidates** which possibly represent young persons.

$$\begin{array}{ll} \text{SELECT} & * \\ \text{FROM} & \text{candidates} \\ \text{WHERE} & \text{Age} = \$\text{Young} \\ \text{WITH} & \text{possible ;} \end{array} \qquad \text{(Q5.10)}$$

This is precisely the operation of selection of the fuzzy relation **candidates** with respect to the condition Age = $Young.

The composition of operations of projection, selection and ordering is specified by the fuzzy query block (Q5.11).

Example 5.8

Get a table of names of candidates who are very possibly young, ordered by names.

$$\begin{array}{ll} \text{SELECT} & \text{Name} \\ \text{FROM} & \text{candidates} \\ \text{WHERE} & \text{Age} = \$\text{Young} \\ \text{WITH} & \text{VERY possible} \\ \text{ORDER\_BY} & \text{Name ;} \end{array} \qquad \text{(Q5.11)}$$

So far, the condition has the simplest form possible; it is only a comparison of the value of an attribute with a constant (fuzzy or nonfuzzy data). FSQL permits much more complex forms of the logic expressions as conditions. The most frequently used form is probably a fuzzy conjunction of several simple

189

comparisons. In such a case, the condition following WHERE may include the conventional arithmetic comparison operators $=$, $/ =$, $>$, $<$, $=<$, $>=$, which are extended to the fuzzy cases, and fuzzy comparison operators $>>$, $<<$, $\tilde{} =$ (see Chapter 6). The AND and OR appearing in the condition expression represent fuzzy conjunction and disjunction.

Example 5.9

The fuzzy query block (Q5.12) constructs a table of names of all candidates who are young men with the degree of 0.9.

SELECT	Name	
FROM	candidates	
WHERE	Sex = male	(Q5.12)
AND	Age = $Young	
WITH	0.9 ;	

In the following example, the condition expression has the form of a disjunction of a simple comparison.

Example 5.10

Get a table of candidates who are young or middle-aged with the degree of 0.8.

SELECT	Name	
FROM	candidates	
WHERE	Age = $Young	(Q5.13)
OR	Age = $Middle-aged	
WITH	0.8 ;	

All the examples given so far represent queries on single relations. The final example of a one-relation query shows how embedding a query on one relation into a query on another permits implicit specification of the natural join operation.

Example 5.11

Fuzzy query block (Q5.14) constructs a table of young candidates (with the degree of 0.9) who are assistants or technicians.

```
SELECT   Name
FROM     candidates
WHERE    Age = $Young
AND      Name IN
              (SELECT  Name                              (Q5.14)
               FROM     background
               WHERE    Profession = assistant
               OR       Profession = technician)
WITH     0.9 ;
```

For optimizing the fuzzy query, it would be better to type the query block
(Q4.15) instead of (Q5.14).

```
SELECT   Name
FROM     background
WHERE    Profession IN  (assistant,technician)
AND      Name IN
              (SELECT   Name                             (Q5.15)
               FROM     candidates
               WHERE    Age = $Young
               WITH     0.9);
```

(3)   Join

The join operation of FSQL is described by placing attributes from more than
one relation in the SELECT clause, placing the multiple relation names in the
FROM clause, and including a join criterion in the WHERE clause.

Example 5.12

Query block (Q5.16) constructs a table of candidate names, ages, and looks.

```
SELECT   Name, Age, Looks
FROM     candidates, body                               (Q5.16)
WHERE    candidates.Name = body.Name ;
```

It is our first example of a query on two fuzzy relations: **candidates** and **body**.
Query block (Q5.16) is a composition of two operations of the fuzzy relational
algebra: projection and join. The attributes over which the join of the relations
candidates and **body** is performed are Name in the first relation and Name in

the second. A more complex example follows.

Example 5.13

Retrieve the name, sex, education and address of all candidates who have been managers and are young with the degree of 0.8.

SELECT	Name, Sex, Education, Address
FROM	candidates, background
WHERE	candidates.Name = background.Name
AND	candidates.Age = $Young
AND	background.Profession = manager
WITH	0.8 ;

(Q5.17)

Apart from the operations of projection and join, fuzzy query block (Q5.17) also contains the operation of selection of the relations **candidates** and **background**. As such, it is not only the most general type of fuzzy query we have had so far, but it is typical of fuzzy queries on two relations.

In addition, the user may name several relations in the FROM clause, and use the relation names as qualifiers in the SELECT clause to resolve ambiguities if necessary (or for clarity). The SELECT clause in the fuzzy query block (Q5.16) could have been written

SELECT   candidates.Name, candidates.Age, body.Looks

if desired. The criterion following WHERE can be any expression involving arithmetic comparisons (=, / =, >, <, =<, and >=) on attributes.

Of particular interest is retrieval using equijoin in a fuzzy environment.

Example 5.14

Retrieve the companies in which the candidate Smith may very possibly get a high salary.

SELECT	Cname
FROM	background, job
WHERE	candidates.Name = smith
AND	background.Profession = job.Position
AND	job.Salary = $High
WITH	VERY possible ;

(Q5.18)

FSQL actually provides several ways of handling equijoin. Equivalently, it is possible to express the fuzzy query (Q5.18) in the form:

SELECT	Cname	
FROM	job	
WHERE	Salary = $High	
AND	Position =	(Q5.19)
	(SELECT Profession	
	FROM background	
	WHERE Name = smith	
	WITH VERY possible) ;	

The expression in parentheses is a subquery. In general, the condition

$$f \ = \ (\ \text{SELECT Sth FROM} \ \ldots)$$

evaluates to true if and only if the value f is equal to at least one value in the result of evaluating the "SELECT Sth FROM ..." with the degree which is stated in the WITH clause. Similarly, the condition

$$f \ < \ (\ \text{SELECT Sth FROM} \ \ldots)$$

evaluates to true if and only if f is less than at least one value in the result of evaluating the "SELECT Sth FROM ..." with the degree which is stated in the WITH clause. The operators $/ =, >, =<,$ and $>=$ are analogously defined. Of the various comparison conditions, easily the most useful is

$$f \ = \ (\ \text{SELECT Sth FROM} \ \ldots)$$

This form may equivalently (and more clearly) be written as

$$f \ \text{IN} \ (\ \text{SELECT Sth FROM} \ \ldots).$$

(4)   Intersection, Union, and Difference

The FSQL language uses the usual set operations, Intersection, Union, and Difference, to combine the results of independent fuzzy query blocks. The result of execution of a query block on fuzzy relations (a set of tuples) is still a fuzzy relation. Because of that, query blocks may appear as operands of the set operations: Intersection, Union, and Difference. That way, we obtain FSQL query expressions, query blocks being their particular and most frequently occurring form. What we should keep in mind is that operands of the operations of Intersection, Union and Difference must be compatible. This means that the tuples must have the same number of attributes and the domains of the corresponding attributes must be the same.

An example of a fuzzy query expression is (Q5.18).

Example 5.15

Retrieve the names of all candidates who have very good looks and excellent intelligence.

SELECT	Name
FROM	body
WHERE	Looks = VERY good
WITH	F
INTERSECT	(Q5.20)
SELECT	Name
FROM	ability
WHERE	Intelligence = excellent
WITH	F ;

Query expression (Q5.21) is an example of the set operation: Difference.

Example 5.16

Show all young candidates, with the confidence degree of 0.9, who have never been engineers.

SELECT	Name
FROM	candidates
WHERE	Age = $Young
WITH	0.9
DIFFERENCE	(Q5.21)
SELECT	Name
FROM	background
WHERE	Profession = engineer

A more complex example of Union is given below.

Example 5.17

Fuzzy query expression (Q5.22) will find all candidates, for each one who is very possibly a friend of a beautiful young girl.

SELECT	Name1		
FROM	relationship		
WHERE	Type = friend		
AND	Name2 IN		
	(SELECT	Name	
	FROM	candidates	
	WHERE	Sex = female	
	AND	Age = $Young	
	WITH	VERY possible)	
AND	Name2 IN		
	(SELECT	Name	
	FROM	body	
	WHERE	Looks = good	
	WITH	VERY possible)	
UNION			(Q5.22)
SELECT	Name2		
FROM	relationship		
WHERE	Type = friend		
AND	Name1 IN		
	(SELECT	Name	
	FROM	candidates	
	WHERE	Sex = female	
	AND	Age = $Young	
	WITH	VERY possible)	
AND	Name1 IN		
	(SELECT	Name	
	FROM	body	
	WHERE	Looks = good	
	WITH	VERY possible)	

5.6 Storage Statements

FSQL is not just a query language. It permits specification of other actions on
the fuzzy relational database. The most important types of action are insertion,

deletion and modification of tuples. These actions may refer to a set of tuples or to a particular tuple.

(1) Insertion

An example that illustrates the action of insertion of a particular tuple is as follows.

Example 5.18

(Q5.23) insert two new tuples into the relation **candidates**.

> INSERT_INTO   candidates(Name,Sex,Age,Address):
>
> ⟨richard,male,ABOUT 28,carlisle⟩   (Q5.23)
> ⟨david,male,30,penrith⟩ ;

In (Q5.23), since the values of all attributes are specified, it is not necessary to specify their names. Thus we can type (Q5.24) instead of (Q5.23):

> INSERT_INTO   candidates :
>
> ⟨richard,male,ABOUT 28,carlisle⟩   (Q5.24)
> ⟨david,male,30,penrith⟩ ;

Now suppose that in addition to the relations specified in the sample database (see Section 4.5), the database also contains (at least temporarily) the relation

> employee(Name,Sex,Age,Health,Height)

Then we have

Example 5.19

Statement (Q5.25) inserts into the relation **employee** selected tuples from the relations **candidates** and **body**.

> INSERT_INTO   employee
> SELECT   Name, Sex, Age, Health, Height
> FROM   candidates, body   (Q5.25)
> WHERE   candidates.Name = body.Name ;

(2) Deletion

Deletion of a particular tuple from a relation is illustrated by the following example.

Example 5.20

Statement (Q5.26) deletes the candidate Smith from the relation **candidates**.

$$
\begin{array}{ll}
\text{DELETE} & \text{candidates} \\
\text{WHERE} & \text{Name = smith ;}
\end{array}
\qquad (Q5.26)
$$

Example 5.21

Statement (Q5.27) deletes all young candidates who live in Newcastle or Darlington with the degree of VERY possible.

$$
\begin{array}{ll}
\text{DELETE} & \text{candidates} \\
\text{WHERE} & \text{Age = \$Young} \\
\text{AND} & \text{Address IN (newcastle,darlington)} \\
\text{WITH} & \text{VERY possible ;}
\end{array}
\qquad (Q5.27)
$$

(3)   Modification

Example 5.22

Statement (Q5.28) changes the president of C1 company to Taylor.

$$
\begin{array}{ll}
\text{MODIFY} & \text{company} \\
\text{SET} & \text{President = taylor} \\
\text{WHERE} & \text{Cname = c1 ;}
\end{array}
\qquad (Q5.28)
$$

Within a SET clause, any reference to an attribute on the right-hand side of an equal sign refers to the value of that attribute before the modification has been done. Hence we have

Example 5.23

Statement (Q5.29) illustrates how to double the salaries of all engineers and managers working in big companies with the degree of 0.9.

$$
\begin{array}{ll}
\text{MODIFY} & \text{job} \\
\text{SET} & \text{Salary = Salary * 2} \\
\text{WHERE} & \text{Position IN (engineer,manager)} \\
\text{AND} & \text{Cname IN} \\
& \quad \text{(SELECT} \quad \text{Cname} \\
& \quad \text{FROM} \quad \text{company} \\
& \quad \text{WHERE} \quad \text{Employees = \$Big} \\
& \quad \text{WITH} \quad \text{0.9) ;}
\end{array}
\qquad (Q5.29)
$$

(4)   Creation of a Fuzzy Relation

Specification of our sample fuzzy relational database has not yet been given in the FSQL language. As an example, we now present such a specification for the fuzzy relation **candidates**. Statement (Q5.30) creates this table and specifies its attributes and their domain base sets. It also states which attributes (keywords) may never assume the NULL value.

CREATE_TABLE   candidates

(Name (CHAR(10),NONULL),
Sex (CHAR(6)VAR),   (Q5.30)
Age (INTEGER),
Address (CHAR(10)VAR)) ;

The domain base set of the attribute Name is the set of sequences of characters (CHAR). The length of those sequences is variable (VAR) but it does not exceed 10. NULL values of this attribute are not permitted (NONULL). Base sets of the attributes Sex and Address are likewise specified, except that NULL values of these attributes are permitted. The base set of the attribute Age is the set of integers (INTEGER).

Fuzzy relations which the user creates in this way may be permanent or temporary. The existence of temporary relations in the fuzzy relational database is limited to the period of interaction of the user of the database who created them. In addition, the membership function of a fuzzy relation is always specified implicitly. In the special case of an extended relation, the grades of membership of all tuples are 1 (usually omitted).

From the discussion above, it can be seen that FSQL is a self-contained structured English-like language. The form SELECT ...FROM ...WHERE ...WITH ...is an expression which, as far as the user is concerned, produces a set of objects. The use of such expressions greatly simplifies the process of constructing a fuzzy query. Many problems which humans employ in fuzzy environments can be expressed in FSQL easily and concisely.

Chapter 6

THE OPERATIONS ON FUZZY RELATIONAL DATABASES

In this chapter, we begin by introducing the concepts of base relations and virtual relations in order to show that the fuzzy relational model, and especially fuzzy relational operations, are necessary in the FPDB system. Then we present three types of fuzzy relational operations (fuzzy relational algebra, fuzzy tuple calculus and fuzzy domain calculus), and some other useful facilities of FPDB system.

6.1 Base Relations and Virtual Relations

6.1.1 The Architecture of the FPDB System

We now illustrate the architecture of the FPDB system. Figure 6-1 is an attempt to show the FPDB system as perceived by an individual user.

We explain Figure 6-1 at a simple level as follows.

1. A base relation is a relation that has independent existence. Each base relation is represented in storage by a distinct stored file.

2. A table that is seen by the user may be a base relation or it may be a virtual relation. A virtual relation is a table that does not have any existence

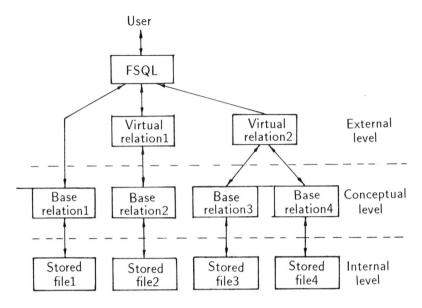

Figure 6-1 The FPDB System as Seen by an Individual User

in its own right but is instead derived from one or more base relations. For example, if the database includes a base relation **candidates**, with attributes Name, Sex, Age, and Address, then we may define a virtual relation called **young-candidates**, say, with attributes Name, Sex, and Age, derived from **candidates** by selecting those tuples satisfying Age = $Young (with a degree of truth) and then projecting out the attribute Address.

3. At the internal level, as stated earlier, each base relation is represented in storage by a distinct stored file, *i.e.* by a named set of stored record occurrences, all of the same type. One row (tuple) in the base relation corresponds to one stored record occurrence in the stored file. A given stored file may have any number of indexes associated with it. Users above the internal level may be aware of the existence of such indexes but they cannot refer to them directly in data access requests. Indexes can be created and destroyed at any time without affecting users.

4. FSQL is the data sublanguage of the FPDB system. As such, it includes both a fuzzy data definition language (FDDL) and a fuzzy data manipula-

200

tion language (FDML). The FDML can operate at both the external and the conceptual level. Similarly, the FDDL can be used to define objects at the external level (virtual relations), the conceptual level (base relations), and even the internal level (indexes). Moreover, FSQL also provides "data control" facilities, that is, facilities that cannot really be classified as belonging to either the FDDL or the FDML. An example of such a facility is a statement to GRANT certain access rights to another user.

5. One particular interactive application, supplied with the system, is the user-friendly interface. It allows the on-line user to access the database using FSQL as an interactive query language. That is, the user-friendly interface accepts FSQL statements from the terminal, passes them to FPDB system for execution, and then returns the result to the terminal if appropriate. It also provides various special commands to control the output display, to modify and reexecute previously entered FSQL statements, and so on.

6.1.2 Base Relations

The primary data structure in the FPDB system is the base relation. As explained above, a base relation is a table that has its own independent existence. It is represented in the physical database by a stored file. A base relation can be created at any time by executing the FSQL statement CREATE_TABLE (see Section 5.6).

Successful execution of a CREATE_TABLE statement causes a new, empty base relation to be created in the specified segment with the specified base-relation-name and specified attribute-definitions (see below). The user may now proceed to enter data into that relation using the INSERT statement of FSQL.

The FPDB system is partitioned into a set of disjoint segments. Segments provide a mechanism for controlling the allocation of storage and the sharing of data among users. Any given base relation is wholly contained within a single segment; any indexes on that base relation are also contained in that same segment. However, a given segment may contain several base relations (plus their indexes).

A public segment contains shared data that can be simultaneously accessed by multiple users. A private segment contains data that can be used by only one user at a time. The CREATE_TABLE statement optionally specifies the segment that is to contain the new base relation; if no segment is specified, the base table will go in a private segment belonging to the user who issued the CREATE_TABLE.

Each attribute-definition in the CREATE_TABLE statement includes four items: an attribute-name, a basic data-type for the attribute, (optionally) a NOFUZZY clause, and (optionally) a NONULL specification. The attribute-name must, of course, be unique within the base relation. The permissible basic data-types are as follows:

INTEGER	integer	CHAR(n)	fixed-length character string
FLOAT	floating-point number	CHAR(n)VAR	variable-length character string

To support fuzzy attribute values, there must be a mechanism to indicate which columns can contain fuzzy values and which cannot. In FPDB, this is accomplished through the clause NOFUZZY. FPDB also supports the concept of NULL attribute values. In fact, any attribute can accept fuzzy and even NULL values unless the definition of that attribute in CREATE_TABLE explicitly includes the specification NOFUZZY or NONULL.

It should understood that any tuple which is shown in a fuzzy relation has a grade of membership. An issue of difficulty for FPDB users is that the grade of membership of each tuple in a fuzzy relation often cannot be given by the user directly, easily and reliably. On the contrary, users are used to expressing fuzzy data in terms of fuzzy linguistic values adopted from natural language directly, whereas a fuzzy linguistic value can be represented by means of a possibility distribution, as we stated previously.

For this reason, the concept of an extended relation is introduced in the FPDB system. An extended relation R is a subset of the Cartesian Product of a collection of possibility distributions, i.e. $R \subseteq \widetilde{\mathcal{P}}(\Omega_1) \times \widetilde{\mathcal{P}}(\Omega_2) \times \cdots \times \widetilde{\mathcal{P}}(\Omega_n)$, where the signs $\times$ and $\subseteq$ denote the classical set operations; $\widetilde{\mathcal{P}}(\Omega_i)$, $i = 1, 2, \ldots, n$, are collections of all possibility distributions on a universe of discourse Ω_i.

Obviously, conventional relations can be seen as a special case of these extended relations, whereas extended relations can be regarded as a special case of fuzzy relations. When the tuples shown in a fuzzy relation are all assumed to

202

have 1 as their grades of membership, it becomes an extended relation, even a conventional relation.

Fortunately, all the base relations in the FPDB can be expressed by means of extended relations. For the original base relations which are general fuzzy relations, they could be transformed to equivalent extended relations in which fuzzy attributes are permitted. Thus the difficulty we have stated above is avoided. Therefore, in our sample database of "job-information-centre", presented in Section 4.5, all the base relations are extended relations.

6.1.3   Virtual Relations

Unlike base relations, virtual relations are defined within the FPDB system. A virtual relation is a table that does not really exist in its own right but is instead derived from one or more underlying base relations. In other words, there is no stored file that directly represents the virtual relation *per se*. Instead, a definition of the virtual relation is stored in the dictionary. This definition shows how the virtual relation is derived from the underlying base relations.

In principle, any derivable table can be defined as a virtual relation. The derivation process might involve projecting a base relation over certain attributes, or joining two or more base relations together, or indeed performing any sequence of projections, joins, and similar operations on any collection of base relations. A virtual relation is created by executing the statement DEFINE_VIRTUAL_TABLE, which takes the form

DEFINE_VIRTUAL_TABLE	virtual-table-name
	[(attribute [, attribute] ...)]
AS	fuzzy-query-block ;

Example 6.1

The following statement defines a virtual relation that is a projection of a fuzzy horizontal subset of the base relation **candidates**.

DEFINE_VIRTUAL_TABLE	young-candidates	
AS	SELECT	Name, Sex, Address
	FROM	candidates
	WHERE	Age = $Young
	WITH	F ;

203

The virtual relation is called **young-candidates**, and has three attributes, with names Name, Sex, and Address inherited from the names in the base relation candidates. We could, if we liked, have given the attributes new names by specifying (NewName, NewSex, NewAddress), say, after the virtual-table-name **young-candidates** in the DEFINE_VIRTUAL_TABLE statement.

Once a virtual relation is defined, the user can go on to use it just as if it were a real base relation, subject to certain constraints.

Example 6.2

The following fuzzy query block shows a query on the virtual relation **young-candidates**.

SELECT	Name,Address
FROM	young-candidates
WHERE	Sex = female
ORDER_BY	Name ;

Successful execution of a DEFINE_VIRTUAL_TABLE statement causes the virtual relation to be stored always in the dictionary of the FPDB system. The fuzzy query block within that definition is not executed at this time. Instead, when the user does a retrieval or update operation against the virtual relation, that operation and the fuzzy query block in the DEFINE_VIRTUAL_TABLE statement are combined to form a modified statement that operates on the underlying data.

Example 6.3

The fuzzy query block in Example 6.2 will be combined with the definition of "young-candidates" to produce

SELECT	Name, Address
FROM	candidates
WHERE	Sex = female
AND	Age = $Young
WITH	F
ORDER_BY	Name ;

The modified statement is then processed in the normal way.

Note that, in Example 6.1, the fuzzy–query–block in the virtual relation definition permits variable **F** following the WITH clause, as the threshold, for which a general fuzzy relation will be derived, because different attribute values of Age will satisfy the condition Age = \$Young in different degrees.

In general, we have concluded that all the real base relations can be represented in terms of extended relations. For those base relations which were originally general fuzzy relations, we transform them to be equivalent extended relations which contain fuzzy attributes. Hence all the tuples in a real base relation having a grade of membership of 1 (which is usually omitted) means that the tuples fully satisfy the relation or are compatible with the relation. However, owing to fuzzy conditions being permitted in fuzzy query blocks, different attribute values of tuples usually satisfy the fuzzy logic expression (the condition) in different degrees; therefore virtual relations derived from real base relations are usually general fuzzy relations. The grade of membership of each tuple is obtained automatically, by using the fuzzy logic in f-PROLOG.

We conclude Section 6.1 by noting that all the real base relations in the FPDB system are extended relations (a special case of fuzzy relations), which contain fuzzy attributes, but even so, the fuzzy relational model, and especially fuzzy relational operations, are essential in the FPDB system, since the virtual relations derived from the base relations are usually fuzzy relations, in which each tuple t has a grade of membership $\mu(t) \in [0,1]$, denoting the degree to which t satisfies the relation or is compatible with the relation.

6.2   Fuzzy Relational Algebra

As the basis for FSQL, a fuzzy relational algebra is described in this section, for which ordinary relational algebra is a special case.

In Chapter 5, we pointed out that a high-level fuzzy relational query language FSQL has been designed and developed by the authors, and the FPDB system supports such a language rather than fuzzy relational algebra. But the algebra is still important, nevertheless, and in this section we will describe it in some detail.

Fuzzy relational algebra used in a fuzzy relational database is a collection of operations on fuzzy relations. Each operation takes one or more fuzzy relations as its operand(s) and produces a new fuzzy relation as its result. Basic operations in the FPDB system, which consist of Union, Intersection, Difference, Cross Product, Projection and Join are defined as follows:

Definition 6.1

The **union** of two compatible fuzzy relations R and S with membership functions $\mu_R(t)$ and $\mu_S(t)$ respectively, denoted by $R \cup S$, is a set of all tuples t where each tuple t satisfies the following relation:

$$\mu_{R \cup S}(t) = \max\{\mu_R(t), \mu_S(t)\}. \tag{6.1}$$

Definition 6.2

The **intersection** of two compatible fuzzy relations R and S with membership functions $\mu_R(t)$ and $\mu_S(t)$ respectively, denoted by $R \cap S$, is a set of all tuples t where tuple t satisfies the following relation:

$$\mu_{R \cap S}(t) = \min\{\mu_R(t), \mu_S(t)\}. \tag{6.2}$$

Definition 6.3

The **difference** of two compatible fuzzy relations R and S with membership functions $\mu_R(t)$ and $\mu_S(t)$ respectively, denoted by $R - S$, is a set of all tuples t where each tuple t satisfies the following relation:

$$\mu_{R - S}(t) = \min\{\mu_R(t), (1 - \mu_S(t))\}. \tag{6.3}$$

The word "compatible" means that two relations R and S must have the same arity, say n, and the i-th attribute of them ($i = 1, 2, \ldots, n$) must be drawn from the same domain.

Definition 6.4

The **Cartesian Product (Cross Product)** of n fuzzy relations R_1, R_2, ..., R_n with membership functions $\mu_{R_i}(t_i)$ ($i = 1, 2, \ldots, n$) respectively, denoted by $R_1 \times R_2 \times \cdots \times R_n$, is a set of all tuples t with the grade of membership $\mu_{R_1 \times R_2 \times \cdots \times R_n}(t)$ defined by

$$\mu_{R_1 \times R_2 \cdots \times R_n}(t) = \min\{\mu_{R_1}(t_1), \mu_{R_2}(t_2), \ldots, \mu_{R_n}(t_n)\} \tag{6.4}$$

where $t = (t_1, t_2, \ldots, t_n)$.

Definition 6.5

Let $R(A_1, A_2, \ldots, A_n)$ be an n-ary fuzzy relation, if $X = (A_{i_1}, A_{i_2}, \ldots, A_{i_k})$ is a subset of $(A_1, A_2, \ldots, A_n)$, then the projection of R onto X, denoted by $R[X]$, is a k-ary fuzzy relation, and its membership function is defined by

$$\mu_{R[X]}(d_{i_1}, d_{i_2}, \ldots, d_{i_k}) = \max_{d_j \in D_f(A_j), j \in (i_1, i_2, \ldots, i_k)} \{\mu_R(d_1, d_2, \ldots, d_n)\} \tag{6.5}$$

where $d_l \in D_f(A_l)$.

It is clear that different fuzzy relations in $D_f(A_1) \times D_f(A_2) \times \cdots \times D_f(A_n)$ can have identical projections on $D_f(A_{i_1}) \times D_f(A_{i_2}) \times \cdots \times D_f(A_{i_k})$, where $D_f(A_{i_j}) \in \{D_f(A_1), D_f(A_2), \ldots, D_f(A_n)\}$ for $j = 1, 2, \ldots, k$. However, given a fuzzy relation R_i in $D_f(A_{i_1}) \times D_f(A_{i_2}) \times \cdots \times D_f(A_{i_k})$, there exists a unique fuzzy relation $\overline{R_i}$ in $D_f(A_1) \times D_f(A_2) \times \cdots \times D_f(A_n)$ whose projection on $D_f(A_{i_1}) \times D_f(A_{i_2}) \times \cdots \times D_f(A_{i_k})$ is R_i. The membership function of $\overline{R_i}$ is given by

$$\mu_{\overline{R_i}}(a_1, a_2, \ldots, a_n) = \mu_{R_i}(b_{i_1}, b_{i_2}, \ldots, b_{i_k}) \tag{6.6}$$

where $a_{i_j} = b_{i_j}$ for $j = 1, 2, \ldots, k$.

This implies that the value of μ_{R_i} at the point $(a_1, a_2, \ldots, a_n)$ is the same as that at the point $(b_1, b_2, \ldots, b_n)$ provided that $a_{i_1} = b_{i_1}$, $a_{i_2} = b_{i_2}$, $\ldots$, $a_{i_n} = b_{i_n}$. For this reason, $\overline{R_i}$ is referred to as the cylindrical extension of R_i, with R_i constituting the base of $\overline{R_i}$ [Zadeh, 1978(a)].

Definition 6.6

Let R_1, R_2, $\ldots$, R_s be s fuzzy relations, and $\cup_{i=1}^s R_i = R(A_1, A_2, \ldots, A_n)$. The join of fuzzy relations R_1, R_2, $\ldots$, R_s denoted by $\bowtie_{i=1}^s R_i$ is a fuzzy relation over $D_f(A_1)$, $D_f(A_2)$, $\ldots$, $D_f(A_n)$. Its membership function is defined by

$$\mu_{\bowtie_{i=1}^s R_i}(a_1, a_2, \ldots, a_n) = \min\{\mu_{\overline{R_1}}(a_1, a_2, \ldots, a_n), \ldots, \mu_{\overline{R_s}}(a_1, a_2, \ldots, a_n)\}. \tag{6.7}$$

where $\mu_{\overline{R_i}}(a_1, a_2, \ldots, a_n)$ is the cylindrical extension of $\mu_{R_i}(a_{i_1}, a_{i_2}, \ldots, a_{i_k})$.

Definition 6.7

Let R be a fuzzy relation, E a fuzzy conditional expression involving

(i)   operands that are constants (fuzzy or nonfuzzy data) or attributes

(ii)   the logic operators: AND, OR, NOT

(iii) the arithmetic operators: $+, -, *, /$

(iv)   the arithmetic comparison operators: $=, / =, <, >, =<, >=$ (which are extended to fuzzy cases)

(v)   the special fuzzy comparison operators: $>>, <<, \tilde{} =$

then the **selection** $R : E(f)$ is the set of tuples t in R such that when all attributes occurring in E are substituted by the corresponding components of t, the truth value of the fuzzy logic expression E, $T(E) \geq f$, where $0 \leq f \leq 1$.

We have stated that fuzzy relational algebra is still important, even though it is less "user-friendly" than FSQL. The basic reason for its importance is that it provides a yardstick against which other languages can be measured. Fuzzy relational algebra also lays a foundation for research into several other aspects of fuzzy relational database management, such as database design, virtual relation definition, and so on. In Chapter 5, we showed that most of the FSQL operations have direct algebraic equivalents.

At the beginning of this chapter we argued that the fuzzy relational model is necessary for the FPDB system. Now we are in a position to define simply the fuzzy relational database model. It consists of two principal components:

(1)   the fuzzy relational data structure defined in Chapter 4;

(2)   fuzzy relational algebra.

A fuzzy database system may be called fully relational if it supports a relational database including the concepts of fuzzy domain, key and the two integrity rules, and a language that is at least as powerful as fuzzy relational algebra. A system that supports a fuzzy relational database but only has a language that is less powerful than fuzzy relational algebra may be called semi-relational.

6.3   Fuzzy Relational Calculus

The data sublanguages for fuzzy relational database systems can be broadly categorized as procedural (fuzzy relational algebra) and nonprocedural (fuzzy relational calculus). A complete fuzzy relational algebra for the fuzzy relational model exists and has been described in the previous section. Fuzzy relational calculus can be subdivided into two classes, depending on whether the primary relational objectives are tuples or are elements of the domain of some attribute. The former is called **Fuzzy Tuple Calculus**, the latter is **Fuzzy Domain Calculus**. The difference between fuzzy tuple calculus and fuzzy domain calculus lies basically in how the user perceives the database.

The idea of using predicate calculus as the basis for a query language is not new, and the concept of a relational calculus, namely, an applied predicate calculus specifically tailored to relational databases, was first proposed by Codd [Codd, 1972]. In this section, the principal ideas are generalized for dealing with fuzzy relational databases.

6.3.1 Fuzzy Tuple Relational Calculus

A fundamental aspect of fuzzy relational calculus is the notion of the tuple variable. A tuple variable is a variable that ranges over some named table. Specifically, if tuple variable t ranges over table R, then, at any given time, t represents some individual tuple of R.

In fuzzy tuple relational calculus (fuzzy tuple calculus for short), relations are represented by means of fuzzy tuple calculus expressions. A fuzzy tuple calculus expression is essentially a nonprocedural definition of some fuzzy relation in terms of some given set of base relations. Such an expression can thus clearly be used to define the result of a query, or the target of an update, or a virtual relation, and so on. More specifically, a fuzzy relation R, in fuzzy tuple calculus, is defined by the expression $\varphi(t)$, namely, $\mu_R(t) = \varphi(t)$, where t is the only free tuple variable which ranges over the fuzzy relation R. Note that, $\varphi(t)$ is a fuzzy logic expression; when it is evaluated it returns a fuzzy truth value which is from 0 to 1. As a special case, sometimes a λ-level-relation (as an extention of the notion of λ-level-set) should be returned. This is a conventional relation denoted by

$$R_{(\lambda)} = \{t | \mu_R(t) \geq \lambda\}. \tag{6.8}$$

Similar to the expressions of fuzzy predicate calculus, the expressions of fuzzy tuple calculus are defined recursively as follows.

Definition 6.8

(1)   Every atomic formula is a fuzzy tuple calculus formula. An atomic formula is of three forms.

(a) $\mu_R(t)$

R is a fuzzy relation name, t is a tuple variable which ranges over the fuzzy relation R. $\mu_R(t)$ denotes the degree to which t satisfies the relation or is compatible with the relation.

(b) $t[i] \vartheta C$ or $C \vartheta t[i]$

The expression $t[i]$ represents the i-th component of t (at that time), C is a constant (fuzzy or nonfuzzy data), and ϑ is any one of the conventional arithmetic comparison operators: $=, /=, <,$ $=<, >,$ or $>=$, and special fuzzy comparison operators: $>>, <<,$ $\tilde{}=$. $t[i] \vartheta C$ or $C \vartheta t[i]$ represents a fuzzy proposition that the i-th component of t and C (constant) satisfy the ϑ operation with a certain degree which is from 0 to 1 (The fuzzy comparison will be discussed in detail in Section 6.4.) When the fuzzy comparison expression is evaluated, it will return a fuzzy truth value.

(c) $t[i] \vartheta u[j]$

t and u are two tuple variables; similar to (b), $t[i] \vartheta u[j]$ represents a fuzzy proposition that the i-th component of t and the j-th component of u satisfy the ϑ operation with a certain degree which is from 0 to 1. When the fuzzy comparison expression is evaluated, it will return a fuzzy truth value.

(2)   If φ_1 is a fuzzy tuple calculus formula, then so are (φ_1) and $\neg(\varphi_1)$, where $\neg$ is the fuzzy logic operator NOT.

(3)   If φ_1 and φ_2 are fuzzy tuple calculus formulae, then so are $(\varphi_1 \wedge \varphi_2)$ and $(\varphi_1 \vee \varphi_2)$, where $\wedge$ and $\vee$ are fuzzy logic operators AND and OR respectively.

(4)   Nothing else is a fuzzy tuple calculus formula.

Example 6.4

Consider the "job-information-centre" database given in Section 4.5 and the following queries expressed in fuzzy tuple calculus:

(a) Retrieve the name, sex, education and health of all candidates who are young with the degree of ABOUT 0.8.

$$R = R_{1(ABOUT0.8)} = \{t | \mu_{R_1}(t) >= \text{ABOUT } 0.8\},$$

where

$$\mu_{R_1}(t) = \mu_{candidates}(u) \wedge \mu_{body}(v) \wedge \mu_{background}(w)$$
$$\wedge u[1] = v[1] \wedge v[1] = w[1] \wedge t[1] = u[1] \wedge t[2] = u[2]$$
$$\wedge t[3] = w[2] \wedge t[4] = v[4] \wedge u[3] = \$\text{Young}.$$

(b) Find the salaries of all candidates who are young female secretaries or clerks, if they are employed by company C1.

$$\mu_{R_2}(t) = \mu_{candidates}(u) \wedge \mu_{background}(v) \wedge \mu_{job}(w)$$
$$\wedge u[1] = v[1] \wedge v[1] = w[1] \wedge t[1] = u[1]$$
$$\wedge t[2] = w[3] \wedge u[3] = \$\text{Young} \wedge u[2] = \text{female}$$
$$\wedge (v[3] = \text{secretary} \vee v[3] = \text{clerk}) \wedge w[2] = \text{c1}.$$

(c) Retrieve the names and addresses of all candidates, who are relatives of company C1's president and who are fairly intelligent.

$$\mu_{R_3}(t) = \mu_{candidates}(u) \wedge \mu_{ability}(v) \wedge \mu_{relationship}(w)$$
$$\wedge \mu_{company}(x) \wedge u[1] = v[1] \wedge t[1] = u[1] \wedge t2[2] = u[4]$$
$$\wedge [(u[1] = w[1] \wedge w[2] = x[3]) \vee (u[1] = w[2] \wedge w[1] = x[3])]$$
$$\wedge w[3] = \text{relative} \wedge v[2] = \text{FAIRLY good}.$$

(d) Retrieve the names, intelligence, initiative and social maturity of all candidates who have been managers for a long time and whose addresses are different from company C1's address.

$$\mu_{R_4}(t) = \mu_{candidates}(u) \wedge \mu_{background}(v) \wedge \mu_{ability}(w)$$
$$\wedge \mu_{company}(x) \wedge u[1] = v[1] \wedge v[1] = w[1] \wedge t[1] = u[1]$$

211

$$\wedge t[2] = w[2] \wedge t[3] = w[3] \wedge t[4] = w[4] \wedge v[3] = \text{manager}$$
$$\wedge v[4] = \$\text{Long} \wedge x[1] = \text{c1} \wedge u[4]/ = x[2].$$

The advantages of fuzzy tuple calculus are as follows.

Firstly, once familiar with fuzzy tuple calculus, the FPDB user will find that even complex fuzzy queries can be expressed simply and concisely.

Secondly, fuzzy tuple calculus is nonprocedural and statements expressed in it simply define what the user requires. This simplifies its use and enables the system to determine the most efficient method of obtaining the answer.

Thirdly, fuzzy tuple calculus is relationally complete. That is, any fuzzy relation which can be derived from any set of fuzzy relations can be defined, using fuzzy tuple calculus, in terms of those relations. Also, any expression of fuzzy relational algebra can be converted into an expression in tuple calculus, so the two languages are formally equivalent. These go beyond the scope of this book.

Various high level fuzzy query languages may be developed, based on fuzzy tuple calculus. One of them, FSQL, has been designed and developed by the authors. We show that, as an example, all of the queries illustrated in Example 6.4 by using fuzzy tuple calculus can be converted into fuzzy query blocks in FSQL.

Example 6.5

(a) Retrieve the name, sex, education and health of all candidates who are young with the degree of ABOUT 0.8.

    SELECT   Name, Sex, Education, Health
    FROM   candidates, background, body
    WHERE   Age = $Young
    WITH   ABOUT 0.8 ;

(b) Find the salaries of all candidates who are young female secretaries or clerks, if they are employed by company C1.

```
SELECT   Name, Salary
FROM     candidates, background, job
WHERE    Age = $Young
AND      Sex = female
AND      Profession IN  (secretary,clerk)
AND      Cname = c1
WITH     F ;
```

(c)   Retrieve the names and addresses of all candidates who
      are relatives of company C1's president and who are fairly
      intelligent.

```
SELECT   Name, Address
FROM     candidates, ability
WHERE    Intelligence = FAIRLY good
AND      Name IN
                 (SELECT   Name1
                  FROM     relationship
                  WHERE    Type = relative
                  AND      Name2 IN
                                   (SELECT   President
                                    FROM     company
                                    WHERE    Cname = c1))
         UNION
                 (SELECT   Name2
                  FROM     relationship
                  WHERE    Type = relative
                  AND      Name1 IN
                                   (SELECT   President
                                    FROM     company
                                    WHERE    Cname = c1)) ;
```

(d)   Retrieve the names, intelligence, initiative and social
      maturity of all candidates who have been managers for
      a long time and whose addresses are different from
      company C1's address.

213

```
SELECT    Name, Intelligence, Initiative, SocialMaturity
FROM      candidates, ability
WHERE     candidates.Name  IN
              (SELECT   Name
               FROM     background
               WHERE    Profession = manager
               AND      Experience = $Long
               WITH     F)
AND       candidates.Address /=
              (SELECT   Location
               FROM     company
               WHERE    Name = c1)
WITH      F ;
```

As an aside, we remind the reader that the FSQL formulation does not require the explicit introduction of a tuple variable, but instead allows the name of relation to play the role implicitly. The underlying concept is the same. To understand how the FSQL query is evaluated, it is necessary to imagine a tuple variable ranging over a relation. In effect, FSQL simply has a default rule for the automatic definition of tuple variables that is adequate in simple cases. In more complex cases the user still has to introduce tuple variables explicitly; see, for instance, Example 6.5.

6.3.2   Fuzzy Domain Relational Calculus

As we indicated, the fuzzy domain relational calculus (fuzzy domain calculus for short) differs from the fuzzy tuples in that its variables range over domains rather than relations. However, it can be seen as a nonprocedural query language based on the fuzzy predicate logic as well. In fuzzy domain calculus, queries are presented as expressions of the type

$$\mu_R(\langle t_1 t_2 \cdots t_k \rangle) \;=\; \varphi(t_1, t_2, \ldots, t_k),$$

where $t_1, t_2, \ldots, t_k$ are components of a tuple variable, called domain variables; $\varphi(t_1, t_2, \ldots, t_k)$ is a fuzzy logic expression. Similar to fuzzy tuple calculus, expressions of fuzzy domain calculus are constructed recursively.

Definition 6.9

(1) Every atomic formula is a fuzzy domain calculus formula. An atomic formula is in one of three forms:

(a) $\mu_R(\langle t_1 t_2 \cdots t_k \rangle)$

R is a k-ary fuzzy relation, t_i is either a domain variable or a constant. $\mu_R(\langle t_1 t_2 \cdots t_k \rangle)$ denotes the degree to which the tuple $\langle t_1 t_2 \cdots t_k \rangle$ satisfies the relation or is compatible with the relation.

(b) $t_i \vartheta C$ or $C \vartheta t_i$

t_i represents the i-th component of tuple variable t, C is a constant (fuzzy or nonfuzzy data), and ϑ is any one of the conventional arithmetic comparison operators: $=$, $/=$, $<$, $=<$, $>$, or $>=$, and special fuzzy comparison operators: $>>$, $<<$, or $\tilde{}=$.

(c) $t_i \vartheta u_j$

t_i and u_j are two domain variables, t_i is the i-th component of tuple variable t, while u_j is the j-th component of tuple variable u. ϑ is the same as in (b).

(2) If φ_1 is a fuzzy domain calculus formula, then so is $\neg(\varphi_1)$, where $\neg$ is the fuzzy logic operator NOT.

(3) If φ_1 and φ_2 are fuzzy domain calculus formulae, then so are $(\varphi_1 \wedge \varphi_2)$ and $(\varphi_1 \vee \varphi_2)$, where $\wedge$ and $\vee$ are fuzzy logic operators AND and OR respectively.

(4) Nothing else is a fuzzy domain calculus formula.

Example 6.6

(a) Retrieve the name, sex, education and health of all candidates who are young with the degree of ABOUT 0.8.

$$R = R_{1_{(ABOUT0.8)}} = \{X_1 X_2 X_3 X_4 | \mu_{R_1}(X_1 X_2 X_3 X_4) >= \text{ABOUT } 0.8\},$$

where

$$\mu_{R_1}(X_1 X_2 X_3 X_4) = \mu_{candidates}(X_1 X_2 U_1 U_2) \wedge \mu_{body}(X_1 X_4 V_1 V_2)$$

$$\wedge \mu_{background}(X_1 X_3 W_1 W_2) \wedge U_1 = \$\text{Young}.$$

(b) Find the salaries of all candidates who are young female secretaries or clerks, if they are employed by company C1.

$$\mu_{R_2}(XY) = \mu_{candidates}(X U_1 U_2 U_3) \wedge \mu_{background}(X V_1 V_2 V_3)$$
$$\wedge \mu_{job}(W_1 W_2 Y W_3) \wedge U_2 = \$\text{Young} \wedge U_1 = \text{female}$$
$$\wedge (V_2 = \text{secretary} \vee V_2 = \text{clerk}) \wedge W_2 = \text{c1}.$$

(c) Retrieve the names and addresses of all candidates who are relatives of company C1's president and who are fairly intelligent.

$$\mu_{R_3}(XY) = \mu_{candidates}(X U_1 U_2 Y) \wedge \mu_{ability}(X U_1 U_2 U_3 U_4)$$
$$\wedge \mu_{relationship}(W_1 W_2 W_3) \wedge \mu_{company}(P_1 P_2 P_3 P_4 P_5)$$
$$\wedge [(X = W_1 \wedge W_2 = P_3) \vee (X = W_2 \wedge W_1 = P_3)] \wedge P_1 = \text{c1}$$
$$\wedge W_3 = \text{relative} \wedge U_1 = \text{FAIRLY good}.$$

(d) Retrieve the names, intelligence, initiative and social maturity of all candidates who have been managers for a long time and whose addresses are different from company C1's address.

$$\mu_{R_4}(X_1 X_2 X_3 X_4) = \mu_{candidates}(X_1 U_1 U_2 U_3) \wedge \mu_{background}(X_1 V_1 V_2 V_3)$$
$$\wedge \mu_{ability}(X_1 X_2 X_3 X_4 W) \wedge \mu_{company}(P_1 P_2 P_3 P_4 P_5)$$
$$\wedge V_2 = \text{manager} \wedge V_3 = \$\text{Long} \wedge P_1 = \text{c1} \wedge U_3/ = P_2.$$

As we have stated, the differece between fuzzy tuple calculus and fuzzy domain calculus lies basically in how the user preceives the database. For the "job-information-centre" database, fuzzy tuple calculus encourages the user to think in terms of eight entity types (candidates, standing, ability, body, company, job, relationship, and location), each having various fuzzy or nonfuzzy properties. By contrast, fuzzy domain calculus encourages the user to think in terms of rather more entity types (Name, Sex, Age, Address, Education, Profession, Experience, ...), and to see the eight relations (shown above) as representing association among these entity types. The fuzzy domain calculus formulation of a given query tends to be closer to natural language. This is because if a given entity, say Name, occurs several times in the English statement of the query, then the fuzzy domain calculus formulation will contain several occurrences of a corresponding domain variable. The tuple calculus formulation, on the other hand, will contain occurrences of several distinct tuple variables with "join conditions" connecting those occurrences together.

Summarizing, fuzzy tuple calculus is an extension of ordinary tuple calculus, while fuzzy domain calculus is an extension of ordinary domain calculus, such that binary predicate logic is replaced by using fuzzy predicate logic. As a nonprocedural query language, fuzzy relational calculus is powerful enough to handle much of the origin of fuzziness modelled in the FPDB system. Finally, any fuzzy tuple calculus expression can be converted to an equivalent fuzzy domain calculus expression, and any fuzzy domain calculus expression can be converted to an equivalent fuzzy algebraic expression. The three languages are thus all equivalent to each other in their selective power. However, this goes beyond the scope of the present book.

6.4 Fuzzy Comparison and Fuzzy Sorting

We have known that fuzzy comparison operations play an very important role in fuzzy relational algebra and fuzzy relational calculus, particularly in FSQL. In this section, we are in a position to summarize some ideas and notions of fuzzy comparison proposed by Zadeh and others, and then to present the approach involved in the FPDB system by means of some FSQL examples.

To pave the way for discussion later in this section, we first introduce some basic concepts.

6.4.1 Inclusions and Equalities of Fuzzy Sets

In the sense of Zadeh [Zadeh, 1965], the concept of inclusion is defined as follows.

Definition 6.10

Let $\tilde{A}$ and $\tilde{B}$ be two fuzzy sets on the universe of discourse Ω, then $\tilde{A}$ is said to be included in $\tilde{B}$, denoted $\tilde{A} \subseteq \tilde{B}$, if and only if

$$\forall x \in \Omega, \quad \mu_{\tilde{A}}(x) \leq \mu_{\tilde{B}}(x).$$

When the inequality is strict, the inclusion is said to be strict and is denoted $\tilde{A} \subset \tilde{B}$. $\subseteq$ and $\subset$ are transitive. $\subseteq$ is an order relation on $\tilde{\mathcal{P}}(\Omega)$ (the set of fuzzy subsets of Ω); however, it is not a linear ordering. Obviously,

$$\tilde{A} = \tilde{B} \quad \text{iff} \quad \tilde{A} \subseteq \tilde{B} \quad \text{and} \quad \tilde{B} \subseteq \tilde{A}.$$

In fact, we may define the notion of equality in another equivalent way.

Definition 6.11

Let $\tilde{A}$ and $\tilde{B}$ be the two fuzzy sets on the universe of discourse Ω, then $\tilde{A}$ and $\tilde{B}$ are said to be equal (denoted $\tilde{A} = \tilde{B}$) if and only if

$$\forall x \in \Omega, \quad \mu_{\tilde{A}}(x) = \mu_{\tilde{B}}(x).$$

Zadeh's definitions of inclusion and equality may appear very strict, especially because precise membership values are by essence out of reach. The first way to relax fuzzy set inclusion is by defining the concepts of weak inclusion and weak equality.

Definition 6.12

(1) x λ-*belongs to* $\tilde{A}$ if and only if $x \in \tilde{A}_\lambda$;

(2) $\tilde{A}$ is weakly included in $\tilde{B}$, denoted $\tilde{A} \prec_\lambda \tilde{B}$, as soon as all the elements of Ω λ-*belong to* $\neg \tilde{A}$ or to $\tilde{B}$; mathematically,

$$\tilde{A} \prec_\lambda \tilde{B} \quad \text{iff} \quad x \in (\neg \tilde{A} \cup \tilde{B})_\lambda, \quad \forall x \in \Omega, \tag{6.9}$$

(6.9) is equivalent to

$$\forall x \in \Omega, \quad \max\{1 - \mu_{\tilde{A}}(x), \mu_{\tilde{B}}(x)\} \geq \lambda.$$

Practically, $\tilde{A} \prec_\lambda \tilde{B}$ is not true as soon as

$$\exists x \in \Omega, \quad \mu_{\tilde{A}}(x) > 1 - \lambda \quad \text{and} \quad \mu_{\tilde{B}}(x) < \lambda.$$

As such $\prec_\lambda$ is transitive only for $\lambda > \frac{1}{2}$. Transitivity for $\lambda = \frac{1}{2}$ can be recovered by slightly modifying the above condition and stating

$$\tilde{A} \prec_{\frac{1}{2}} \tilde{B} \quad \text{iff} \quad \forall x \in \Omega, \mu_{\tilde{A}}(x) \leq \frac{1}{2} \text{ or } \mu_{\tilde{B}}(x) > \frac{1}{2}. \tag{6.10}$$

We may want to impose the condition that Zadeh's inclusion ($\subseteq$) be a particular case of $\prec_\lambda$, *i.e.*

$$\text{if} \quad \tilde{A} \subseteq \tilde{B}, \quad \text{then} \quad \tilde{A} \prec_{\lambda} \tilde{B}.$$

This holds only for $\lambda \leq \frac{1}{2}$. Hence, the only transitive $\prec_{\lambda}$ consistent with $\subseteq$ is $\prec_{\frac{1}{2}}$ (abbreviated $\prec$), provided that we adopt the slight modification.

The set equality $\bowtie$ associated with $\prec$ is defined as

$$\tilde{A} \bowtie \tilde{B} \quad \text{iff} \quad \tilde{A} \prec \tilde{B} \quad \text{and} \quad \tilde{B} \prec \tilde{A}.$$

Equivalently, we have

Definition 6.13

$\tilde{A} \bowtie \tilde{B}$ iff $\forall x \in \Omega$,

$$\min\{\max\{1 - \mu_{\tilde{A}}(x), \mu_{\tilde{B}}(x)\}, \max\{\mu_{\tilde{A}}(x), 1 - \mu_{\tilde{B}}(x)\}\} \geq \frac{1}{2}. \tag{6.11}$$

(6.11) is equivalent to

$\forall x \in \Omega$,

$$\max\{\min\{\mu_{\tilde{A}}(x), \mu_{\tilde{B}}(x)\}, \min\{1 - \mu_{\tilde{A}}(x), 1 - \mu_{\tilde{B}}(x)\}\} \geq \frac{1}{2}. \tag{6.12}$$

The weak equality $\tilde{A} \bowtie \tilde{B}$ is thus interpreted as follows. Both membership values $\mu_{\tilde{A}}(x)$ and $\mu_{\tilde{B}}(x)$ are either greater than or equal to $\frac{1}{2}$ or both smaller than or equal to $\frac{1}{2}$. This weak equality is not transitive. Lack of transitivity does not contradict our intuition concerning weak inclusion or equality. However, to recover the transitivity of $\bowtie$, we could use Equation (6.10) to define equality.

Another way of defining less strong inclusions or equalities is to use some scalar measures S of similarity or "inclusion grades" I between two fuzzy sets $\tilde{A}$ and $\tilde{B}$. A threshold ε is chosen such that

Definition 6.14

(1) $\tilde{A} \subset_{\varepsilon} \tilde{B}$ iff $I(\tilde{A}, \tilde{B}) \geq \varepsilon$
(2) $\tilde{A} =_{\varepsilon} \tilde{B}$ iff $S(\tilde{A}, \tilde{B}) \geq \varepsilon$

where $\subset_{\varepsilon}$ and $=_{\varepsilon}$ denote respectively ε-inclusion and ε-equality.

According to the definitions of I and S, $\subset_1$ and $=_1$ may coincide with $\subseteq$ and $=$, respectively. We must state at least the following conditions. If $\tilde{A} \subseteq \tilde{B}$, then $\tilde{A} \subset_1 \tilde{B}$; if $\tilde{A} = \tilde{B}$, then $\tilde{A} =_1 \tilde{B}$. Moreover, S must be symmetrical.

Inclusion grades and similarity measures are very numerous in the literature. Based on intersection, union and cardinality, inclusion grade I and similarity measure S are defined as follows.

Definition 6.15   (see [Sanchez, 1977])

$$I(\tilde{A}, \tilde{B}) = \frac{\| \tilde{A} \cap \tilde{B} \|}{\| \tilde{A} \|} \tag{6.13}$$

Obviously, when $\tilde{A} \subseteq \tilde{B}$, then $I(\tilde{A}, \tilde{B}) = 1$.

Definition 6.16

$$S(\tilde{A}, \tilde{B}) = \frac{\| \tilde{A} \cap \tilde{B} \|}{\| \tilde{A} \cup \tilde{B} \|} \tag{6.14}$$

When $\tilde{A} = \tilde{B}$, then $S(\tilde{A}, \tilde{B}) = 1$.

The cardinality of a finite fuzzy set $\tilde{A}$ has been defined [Zadeh, 1981].

Definition 6.17

For a finite fuzzy set $\tilde{A}$ on the universe of discourse Ω, the cardinality $|\tilde{A}|$ is defined as

$$|\tilde{A}| = \sum_{x \in \Omega} \mu_{\tilde{A}}(x) \tag{6.15}$$

whereas

$$\| \tilde{A} \| = \frac{|A|}{|\Omega|} \tag{6.16}$$

is called the relative cardinality of $\tilde{A}$.

The cardinality $|\tilde{A}|$ is sometimes called the power of $\tilde{A}$ [De Luca and Termini, 1972]. The relative cardinality can be interpreted as the fraction of elements of Ω that are in $\tilde{A}$, weighted by their degrees of membership in $\tilde{A}$.

For infinite Ω, $|\tilde{A}|$ does not always exist. However, if $\tilde{A}$ has a finite support, then

$$|\tilde{A}| = \sum_{x \in \sup \tilde{A}} \mu_{\tilde{A}}(x). \tag{6.17}$$

Otherwise, if Ω is a measurable set and P is a measure on Ω ($\int_\Omega dP(x) = 1$), $\| \tilde{A} \|$ can be the **weighted sum**

$$\int_\Omega \mu_{\tilde{A}}(x) dP(x). \tag{6.18}$$

Other important concepts such as semantic distance, compatibility, *etc.* will be investigated in the next subsection.

6.4.2 Semantic Distance and Compatibility of Two Fuzzy Sets

1. Semantic Distance of Two Fuzzy Sets

A semantic distance S_d between fuzzy sets $\tilde{A}$ and $\tilde{B}$ on the universe of discourse Ω, denoted $S_d(\tilde{A}, \tilde{B})$, models a possibility degree of equality between two fuzzy sets $\tilde{A}$ and $\tilde{B}$, or a similarity degree between them. The larger the distance is, the smaller the possibility degree of equality is. For convenience, we may normalize the semantic distances and restrict:

$$0 \leq S_d(\tilde{A}, \tilde{B}) \leq 1 \tag{6.19}$$

According to the actual situation, $S_d(\tilde{A}, \tilde{B})$ may be computed by using

(1) **Hamming Distance**

$$S_d(\tilde{A}, \tilde{B}) = \sum_{i=1}^{n} |\mu_{\tilde{A}}(x_i) - \mu_{\tilde{B}}(x_i)| \tag{6.20}$$

or

$$S_d(\tilde{A}, \tilde{B}) = \int_{a}^{b} |\mu_{\tilde{A}}(x) - \mu_{\tilde{B}}(x)| dx \tag{6.21}$$

(2) **Weighted Hamming Distance**

$$S_d(\tilde{A}, \tilde{B}) = \sum_{i=1}^{n} w(x_i) |\mu_{\tilde{A}}(x_i) - \mu_{\tilde{B}}(x_i)| \tag{6.22}$$

or

$$S_d(\tilde{A}, \tilde{B}) = \int_{a}^{b} w(x) |\mu_{\tilde{A}}(x) - \mu_{\tilde{B}}(x)| dx \tag{6.23}$$

where $w(x_i)$ $(i = 1, 2, \ldots, n)$ is the weight of x_i, and $w(x_i)/2 = 1$; $w(x)$ is the continuous weight function in $[a, b]$, and $\frac{1}{a-b} \int_{a}^{b} w(x) dx = 1$.

(3) **Euclidean Distance**

$$S_d(\tilde{A}, \tilde{B}) = \sum_{i=1}^{n} \left[\mu_{\tilde{A}}(x_i) - \mu_{\tilde{B}}(x_i)\right]^2 \tag{6.24}$$

(4) **Chebyshev's Distance**

$$S_d(\tilde{A}, \tilde{B}) = \max_{1 \leq i \leq n} |\mu_{\tilde{A}}(x_i) - \mu_{\tilde{B}}(x_i)| \tag{6.25}$$

and so on. However, if we use such formulae directly without any additional restrictions, the results are often not in keeping with the actual situations. For example, we have

$$\tilde{A} = \{0.9/a_1, 0.2/a_2\},$$

and

$$\tilde{B} = \{0.9/b_1, 0.2/b_2\}.$$

Obviously, when $\{a_1, a_2\} \cap \{b_1, b_2\} = \emptyset$, then $S_d(\tilde{A}, \tilde{B}) = 1$, because $\tilde{A}$ will never be equal to $\tilde{B}$. Using any one of the formulae shown above, however,

$$S_d(\tilde{A}, \tilde{B}) < 1$$

holds. Hence we have to add the additional restriction

If $\{a_1, a_2, \ldots, a_n\} \cap \{b_1, b_2, \ldots, b_n\} = \emptyset$
Then $S_d(\tilde{A}, \tilde{B}) = 1$

to the semantic distance.

2. Compatibility of Two Fuzzy Sets

Given a fuzzy set $\tilde{A}$ on the universe of discourse Ω, $\mu_{\tilde{A}}(x)$ is the grade of membership of x in $\tilde{A}$. We may also call it the degree of compatibility of the fuzzy value $\tilde{A}$ with the nonfuzzy value x. The extension principle allows us to evaluate the compatibility of the fuzzy value $\tilde{A}$ with another fuzzy value $\tilde{B}$, taken as a reference.

Let τ be this compatibility. τ is a fuzzy set on $[0,1]$ since it is $\mu_{\tilde{A}}(\tilde{B})$. Using the extension principle [Zadeh, 1975(a)(b)],

$$\mu_\tau(u) = \sup_{x:u=\mu_{\tilde{A}}(x)} \mu_{\tilde{B}}(x) \qquad \forall u \in [0,1], \qquad (6.26)$$

or, using Zadeh's notation [Zadeh, 1977(b)],

$$\tau = \mu_{\tilde{A}}(\tilde{B}) = \int_\Omega \mu_{\tilde{B}}(x)/\mu_{\tilde{A}}(x). \qquad (6.27)$$

An example of the computation of $\mu_\tau(u)$ is shown in Figure 6–2. When $\mu_{\tilde{A}}$ is one to one, $\mu_\tau = \mu_{\tilde{B}} \circ \mu_{\tilde{A}^{-1}}$, where $\circ$ is the composition of functions. When $\tilde{A} = \tilde{B}$, μ_τ is the identity function, $\mu_\tau(u) = u$. Remember that the converse proposition does not hold: $\tilde{A}$ and $\tilde{B}$ can be very different while $\mu_\tau(u) = u$.

τ is a normalized fuzzy set if $\tilde{B}$ is. To prove this, observe that if b is such that $\mu_{\tilde{B}}(b) = 1$, $\mu_\tau(\mu_{\tilde{A}}(b)) = 1$ also. The converse proposition is obvious provided that the **sup** is reached in Equation (6.23).

If $\mu_{\tilde{B}}$ has only one relative maximum b, $\mu_{\tilde{B}}(b) = hgt(\tilde{B})$, then μ_τ has only one relative maximum.

This is obvious from Zadeh's form of the extension principle.

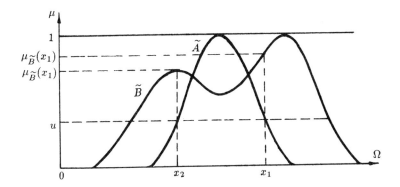

Figure 6–2

From now on $\tilde{B}$ is assumed to have only one global maximum b. $\mu_{\tilde{A}}(b)$ is the mean value of τ, *i.e.* the compatibility degree of $\tilde{A}$ with respect to $\tilde{B}$ is "approximately $\mu_{\tilde{A}}(b)$". $\mu_{\tilde{A}}(b)$ can be considered as a scalar inclusion index somewhat like consistency; instead of choosing $hgt(\tilde{A} \cap \tilde{B})$, we prefer here the membership value in $\tilde{A}$ of the element that mostly belongs to $\tilde{B}$. Note that the mean value of τ is always less than $hgt(\tilde{A})$.

More generally, the compatibility of $\tilde{A}$ with respect to $\tilde{B}$ is a fuzzy inclusion index.

6.4.3 Fuzzy Comparison By Using Conventional Arithmetic Comparison Operators

1. The Definitions Based on the Semantic Distances

To compare two fuzzy values represented by means of fuzzy sets, it is necessary to present new interpretations for the comparison operators. Now we re-define the comparison operators $=, \neq, >, \leq, <$, and $\geq$ based on the concept of semantic distance.

Let $\widetilde{A_1}$ and $\widetilde{A_2}$ be two fuzzy sets on the universe of discourse Ω. The semantic distance of $\widetilde{A_1}$ and $\widetilde{A_2}$ is $S_d(\widetilde{A_1}, \widetilde{A_2})$, where $0 \leq S_d(\widetilde{A_1}, \widetilde{A_2}) \leq 1$. Now the comparison operator $=$ is defined by using $S_d(\widetilde{A_1}, \widetilde{A_2})$:

$$\widetilde{A_1} = \widetilde{A_2}: \quad T = 1 - S_d(\widetilde{A_1}, \widetilde{A_2}) \tag{6.28}$$

where T is the degree of truth of the expression $\widetilde{A_1} = \widetilde{A_2}$. Correspondingly, $\neq$

is defined as:

$$\widetilde{A}_1 \neq \widetilde{A}_2 : \quad T = S_d(\widetilde{A}_1, \widetilde{A}_2) \tag{6.29}$$

Let $\widetilde{A}_1 = \{\mu(x_1)/x_1, \mu(x_2)/x_2, \ldots, \mu(x_k)/x_k\}$
$\widetilde{A}_2 = \{\mu(y_1)/y_1, \mu(y_2)/y_2, \ldots, \mu(y_s)/y_s\}$

where $x_1, x_2, \ldots, x_k, y_1, y_2, \ldots, y_s$ are real numbers in Ω.

The Cartesian product of $\{x_1, x_2, \ldots, x_k\}$ and $\{y_1, y_2, \ldots, y_s\}$ is that

$$P = \{(x_i, y_j) | i = 1, 2, \ldots, k; \ j = 1, 2, \ldots, s\}.$$

Thus the comparison operators $<, \leq, >$, and $\geq$ are defined as follows.

(a) $\quad \widetilde{A}_1 < \widetilde{A}_2$

The set P above can be classified by two subsets:

$$P_1 = \{(x_i, y_j) | x_i < y_j\}$$
$$P_2 = \{(x_i, y_j) | x_i \geq y_j\}$$

If we define

$$\sigma_1 = \begin{cases} \sum_{(x_i, y_j) \in P_1} \min\{\mu(x_i), \mu(y_j)\}, & P_1 \neq \emptyset; \\ 0, & P_1 = \emptyset. \end{cases} \tag{6.30}$$

$$\sigma_2 = \begin{cases} \sum_{(x_i, y_j) \in P_2} \min\{\mu(x_i), \mu(y_j)\}, & P_2 \neq \emptyset; \\ 0, & P_2 = \emptyset. \end{cases} \tag{6.31}$$

then

$$T = \sigma_1/(\sigma_1 + \sigma_2). \tag{6.32}$$

where T is the degree of truth of the expression $\widetilde{A}_1 < \widetilde{A}_2$. Note that, if $\widetilde{A}_1 = \{1/x\}$, $\widetilde{A}_2 = \{1/y\}$, the definition is equivalent to the ordinary comparison between two real numbers $x_1 < y_1$. So this definition is consistent with the conventional comparison operator "$<$".

(b) $\quad \widetilde{A}_1 \leq \widetilde{A}_2$

Similarly, the set P can be classified by two subsets:

$$P_1 = \{(x_i, y_j) | x_i \leq y_j\}$$
$$P_2 = \{(x_i, y_j) | x_i > y_j\}$$

According to (6.30), (6.31) and (6.32), the degree of truth of the expression $\widetilde{A}_1 \leq \widetilde{A}_2$ is concluded.

(c) $\quad \widetilde{A_1} > \widetilde{A_2}$

The set P can be classified by

$$
\begin{aligned}
P_1 &= \{(x_i, y_j)|x_i > y_j\} \\
P_2 &= \{(x_i, y_j)|x_i \leq y_j\}
\end{aligned}
$$

According to (6.30), (6.31) and (6.32), the degree of truth of the expression $\widetilde{A_1} > \widetilde{A_2}$ is concluded.

(d) $\quad \widetilde{A_1} \geq \widetilde{A_2}$

The set P can be classified by

$$
\begin{aligned}
P_1 &= \{(x_i, y_j)|x_i \geq y_j\} \\
P_2 &= \{(x_i, y_j)|x_i < y_j\}
\end{aligned}
$$

According to (6.32), (6.33) and (6.34), the degree of truth of the expression $\widetilde{A_1} \geq \widetilde{A_2}$ is concluded.

2. The Definitions Involved in the FPDB System

Besides precise values, fuzzy values, even fuzzy linguistic values, which are represented by means of possibility distributions, are permitted in the FPDB system. In other words, it enables us to represent and deal with precisely or fuzzily known attribute values in a common framework.

As we have mentioned, the fuzzy selection operation consists in retrieving the tuples whose components satisfy a given fuzzy condition. This operation plays a central role in fuzzy relational algebra, even the high-level language FSQL. A selection applied to a fuzzy relation R with a condition expression $E(f)$ could be denoted by the expression $R : E(f)$. A compound condition E is built from atomic conditions using fuzzy logic connectives (NOT, AND, and OR). Atomic conditions can be classified into two kinds: (1) conditions of the form '$Atr_{(1)} \vartheta Atr_{(2)}$' involving two attributes $Atr_{(1)}$ and $Atr_{(2)}$ and a comparison operator ϑ; (2) conditions of the form '$Atr \vartheta C$' or '$C \vartheta Atr$' involving one attribute Atr and a constant (fuzzy or nonfuzzy data) C. In our approach, crisp comparison operators $=, / =, >, >=, <$, and $=<$ involved in conventional relational algebra are extended to fuzzy cases based on the theory of possibility. To facilitate later discussion, we distinguish between three kinds of atomic conditions:

(a) conditions of the form '$p_1 \; \vartheta \; p_2$' involving two precise values p_1 and p_2, and a comparison operator ϑ;

(b) conditions of the form '$p \; \vartheta \; \widetilde{fv}$' (or '$\widetilde{fv} \; \vartheta \; p$') involving a precise value p and a fuzzy value $\widetilde{fv}$, and a comparison operator ϑ;

(c) conditions of the form '$\widetilde{fv_1} \; \vartheta \; \widetilde{fv_2}$' involving two fuzzy values $\widetilde{fv_1}$ and $\widetilde{fv_2}$, and a comparison operator ϑ.

In the case of (a), the operation ϑ is the same as the ordinary comparison operation, since the operands p_1 and p_2 involved in the expression '$p_1 \; \vartheta \; p_2$' are all precise values. Hence the degree of truth of '$p_1 \; \vartheta \; p_2$' is either 1 or 0.

To the case (b) and (c), we first consider the operators $=$ and $/=$.

We have stated that, given a fuzzy set $\tilde{A}$ on Ω, $\mu_{\tilde{A}}(x)$ is the grade of membership of x in A. We may also call it the degree of compatibility of the fuzzy value $\tilde{A}$ with the nonfuzzy value x. As a result, in the case of (b), we define

$$p \;=\; \widetilde{fv} \;(\text{or } \widetilde{fv} = p) \;:\; T \;=\; \mu_{\widetilde{fv}}(p) \qquad (6.33)$$

$$p \;/=\; \widetilde{fv} \;(\text{or } \widetilde{fv}/ = p) \;:\; T \;=\; 1 - \mu_{\widetilde{fv}}(p) \qquad (6.34)$$

in the light of the concept—the compatibility between a fuzzy value and a precise value [Zadeh, 1977; Dubois and Prade, 1980].

Example 6.7

Given a fuzzy set *about* 25 on $\{0,1,2,\ldots,200\}$ expressed as

$$about\; 25 = 0.5/23 + 0.8/24 + 1/25 + 0.8/26 + 0.5/27.$$

We have
$$\text{ABOUT } 25 = 23 \;:\; T \;=\; \mu_{about\;25}(23) = 0.5;$$
$$\text{ABOUT } 25 = 24 \;:\; T \;=\; \mu_{about\;25}(24) = 0.8;$$
$$\text{ABOUT } 25 = 25 \;:\; T \;=\; \mu_{about\;25}(25) = 1.0;$$
$$\text{ABOUT } 25 = 26 \;:\; T \;=\; \mu_{about\;25}(26) = 0.8;$$
$$\text{ABOUT } 25 = 27 \;:\; T \;=\; \mu_{about\;25}(27) = 0.5;$$
$$\text{ABOUT } 25 = 28 \;:\; T \;=\; \mu_{about\;25}(28) = 0$$

where ABOUT 25 is a fuzzy attribute value defined by the possibility distribution $\Pi_{ABOUT\;25}(x)$ which is equal to the fuzzy set *about* 25, i.e.

$$\Pi_{ABOUT\;25}(x) \;=\; about\; 25$$

implying that

$$Poss\{ABOUT\ 25 = x\} \ = \ \mu_{about\ 25}(x), \qquad x \in \{0, 1, 2, \dots, 200\}.$$

Similarly, we have also

Example 6.8

Given a fuzzy set *young* on the set of $[0, 200]$ expressed as

$$young \ = \ \int_0^{200} \mu_{young}(x)/x$$

where

$$\mu_{young}(x) \ = \ \begin{cases} 1, & 0 \le x \le 25; \\ \left[1 + \left(\frac{x-25}{5}\right)^2\right]^{-1}, & 25 < x \le 200. \end{cases}$$

Then

$$\begin{aligned} \$\text{Young} \ /= 25: \ & T \ = \ 1 - \mu_{young}(25) = 1 - 1 = 0; \\ \$\text{Young} \ /= 28: \ & T \ = \ 1 - \mu_{young}(28) = 1 - 0.74 = 0.26; \\ \$\text{Young} \ /= 30: \ & T \ = \ 1 - \mu_{young}(30) = 1 - 0.50 = 0.50 \end{aligned}$$

where $Young is a fuzzy attribute value defined by the possibility distribution $\Pi_{\$Young}(x)$ which is equal to the fuzzy set *young*, i.e.

$$\Pi_{\$Young}(x) \ = \ young$$

implying that

$$Poss\{\$Young = x\} \ = \ \mu_{young}(x), \qquad x \in [0, 200].$$

Note that, in such a case, = and /= are symmetric.

In the case of (c), to compare two fuzzy values, the compatibility of two fuzzy sets has been investigated by Zadeh [Zadeh, 1977] (see Section 6.4.2). Now, we propose an alternative approach by defining the concept of the degree of coincidence.

Definition 6.18

Let $\tilde{A}$ and $\tilde{B}$ be two fuzzy sets on the universe of discourse Ω, denoted by

$$\tilde{A} \ = \ \int_\Omega \mu_{\tilde{A}}(x)/x$$

and

$$\tilde{B} \ = \ \int_\Omega \mu_{\tilde{B}}(x)/x$$

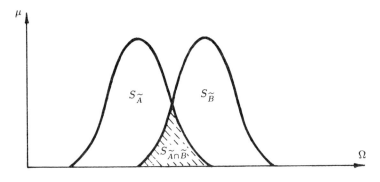

Figure 6–3

then the **degree of coincidence** of $\tilde{A}$ with respect to $\tilde{B}$ is

$$\bar{w}(\tilde{A}, \tilde{B}) = \frac{\int_\Omega \min\{\mu_{\tilde{A}}(x), \mu_{\tilde{B}}(x)\}dx}{\int_\Omega \mu_{\tilde{B}}(x)dx}.$$

$\bar{w}(\tilde{A}, \tilde{B})$ can be interpreted as the 'proportion' of $\tilde{A}$ in $\tilde{B}$.

See Figure 6–3, Let $S_{\tilde{A}}$, $S_{\tilde{B}}$ and $S_{\tilde{A} \cap \tilde{B}}$ represent the areas covered by the functions $\mu_{\tilde{A}}(x)$, $\mu_{\tilde{B}}(x)$ and $\mu_{\tilde{A} \cap \tilde{B}}(x)$ respectively, then the $\bar{w}(\tilde{A}, \tilde{B})$ can be defined also as

$$\bar{w}(\tilde{A}, \tilde{B}) = \frac{S_{\tilde{A} \cap \tilde{B}}}{S_{\tilde{B}}}.$$

As a result, we define

$$\widetilde{fv_1} = \widetilde{fv_2} : T = \bar{w}(\widetilde{fv_1}, \widetilde{fv_2}) \tag{6.35}$$

$$\widetilde{fv_1} /= \widetilde{fv_2} : T = 1 - \bar{w}(\widetilde{fv_1}, \widetilde{fv_2}) \tag{6.36}$$

where

$$\bar{w}(\widetilde{fv_1}, \widetilde{fv_2}) = \frac{\int_\Omega \min\{\mu_{\widetilde{fv_1}}(x), \mu_{\widetilde{fv_2}}(x)\}dx}{\int_\Omega \mu_{\widetilde{fv_2}}(x)dx.}$$

Note that, in this case, $=$ and $/=$ are not symmetric, because $\bar{w}(\widetilde{fv_1}, \widetilde{fv_2})$ is usually not equal to $\bar{w}(\widetilde{fv_1}, \widetilde{fv_2})$.

Example 6.9

Given fuzzy sets *young* and *middle-aged* on the set of $[0, 200]$ expressed as

$$young = \int_1^{200} \mu_{young}(x)/x$$
$$middle\text{-}aged = \int_0^{200} \mu_{middle-aged}(x)/x$$

228

where

$$\mu_{young}(x) = \begin{cases} 1, & 0 \le x \le 25; \\ \left[1 + \left(\frac{x-25}{5}\right)^2\right]^{-1}, & 25 < x \le 200. \end{cases}$$

$$\mu_{middle-aged}(x) = \begin{cases} 0, & 0 \le x \le 25; \\ \frac{1}{2} + \frac{1}{2}\sin\frac{\pi}{10}(x - 50), & 25 < x \le 35; \\ 1, & 35 < x \le 45; \\ \frac{1}{2} - \frac{1}{2}\sin\frac{\pi}{10}(x - 50), & 45 < x \le 55; \\ 0, & 55 < x \le 200. \end{cases}$$

Then we have

$$\$\text{Middle-aged} = \$\text{Young} \quad : \quad T = \bar{w}(\$\text{Middle-aged}, \$\text{Young})$$

where $\$$Young and $\$$Middle-aged are two fuzzy attribute values defined by the possibility distributions $\Pi_{\$Young}(x)$ and $\Pi_{\$Middle-aged}(x)$ which are equal to the fuzzy sets *young* and *middle-aged* respectively, *i.e.*

$$\begin{aligned} \Pi_{\$Young} &= young, \\ \Pi_{\$Middle-aged} &= middle - aged. \end{aligned}$$

Now we begin to consider the operators $>$, $>=$, $<$, and $=<$.

In the case of (b), we define the four operators based on partial integrals. As an example, we first examine the operators $>=$ and $>$. We define

$$\widetilde{fv} \;>=\; pv \quad : \quad T = \frac{\int_{pv}^{\infty} \mu_{\widetilde{fv}}(x)dx}{\int_{\Omega} \mu_{\widetilde{fv}}(x)dx} \tag{6.37}$$

$$\widetilde{fv} \;>\; pv \quad : \quad T = \frac{\int_{pv+1}^{\infty} \mu_{\widetilde{fv}}(x)dx}{\int_{\Omega} \mu_{\widetilde{fv}}(x)dx} \tag{6.38}$$

Obviously, (6.37) and (6.38) are consistent with (6.35), since, as special cases, "$>= pv$" and "$> pv$" could be seen as possibility distributions, and hence they could be regarded as special fuzzy values. On the other hand, we will see that the degree of truth of the expression $\widetilde{fv} >= pv$ is equal to the degree of truth of the expression $\widetilde{fv} >= pv + 1$.

Consider (6.37) again, see Figure 6–4, for example,

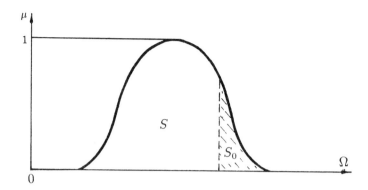

Figure 6–4

Let $S_0 = \int_{pv}^{\infty} \mu_{\widetilde{fv}}(x)dx$, $S = \int_{\Omega} \mu_{\widetilde{fv}}(x)dx$, then $T = \frac{S_0}{S}$.

Similarly, we define

$$\widetilde{fv} =< pv \; : \; T = \frac{\int_{-\infty}^{pv} \mu_{\widetilde{fv}}(x)dx}{\int_{\Omega} \mu_{\widetilde{fv(x)}}dx} \tag{6.39}$$

$$\widetilde{fv} < pv \; : \; T = \frac{\int_{-\infty}^{pv-1} \mu_{\widetilde{fv}}(x)dx}{\int_{\Omega} \mu_{\widetilde{fv(x)}}dx} \tag{6.40}$$

We see that (6.40) is equivalent to

$$\widetilde{fv} =< pv - 1 \; : \; T = \frac{\int_{-\infty}^{pv-1} \mu_{\widetilde{fv}}(x)dx}{\int_{\Omega} \mu_{\widetilde{fv(x)}}dx}$$

Thus, such comparison operators involved in fuzzy query blocks of FSQL can be executed and the final answers can be obtained.

Example 6.10

Select all candidates whose age is greater than or equal to 25.

[In FSQL]

> SELECT   Name
> FROM   candidates
> WHERE   Age >= 25
> WITH   F ;

[In f-PROLOG]

> ?–[F]–answer(Name ,
>   (candidates(Name,_,Age,_),
>   Age >= 25)).

[Analyses]

(1)   Smith   30 >= 25 :   **F** = 1 ;

(2)   John   ABOUT 28 >= 25 :   **F** = 1 ;

              (See Figure 6–5, $S_0 = S$)

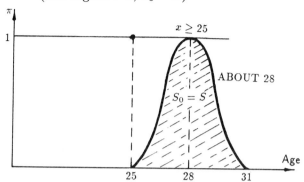

Figure 6–5

(3)   Anna   22 >= 25 :   **F** = 0 ;

(4)   Mary $Middle-aged >= 25 :   **F** = 1 ;

              (See Figure 6–6, $S_0 = S$)

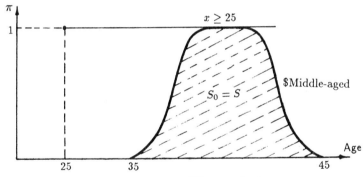

Figure 6–6

(5)   Jill   30 >= 25 :   **F** = 1 ;

(6)   Susan   ABOUT 28 >= 25 :   **F** = 1 ;

              (See Figure 6–5, $S_0 = S$)

(7)   Tom   24 >= 25 :   **F** = 0 ;

(8)   Harry   36 >= 25 :   **F** = 1 ;

(9)   Fred   ABOUT 25 >= 25 :   **F** = 0.5 ;

              (See Figure 6–7, $S_0 = \dfrac{S}{2}$)

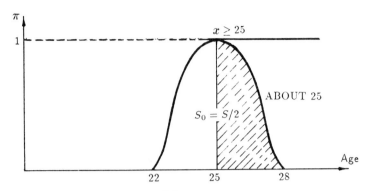

Figure 6–7

(10)   Margaret   20 >= 25 :   F = 0 ;

(11)   Andrew   24 >= 25 :   F = 0 ;

(12)   Barry   33 >= 25 :   F = 1 ;

(13)   Thomas   31 >= 25 :   F = 1 ;

(14)   Martin $Young >= 25 :   F = 0.33 ;

(See Figure 6–8, $S_0 = \dfrac{S}{3}$)

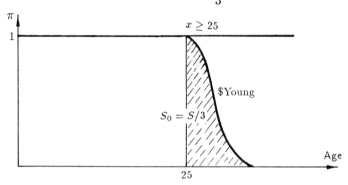

Figure 6–8

(15)   Henry   29 >= 25 :   F = 1 .

[Result]

232

Name	
Smith	1.0
John	1.0
Mary	1.0
Jill	1.0
Susan	1.0
Harry	1.0
Fred	0.5
Barry	1.0
Thomas	1.0
Henry	1.0

If we use a threshold value 0.9 instead of the threshold variable F, we have

Example 6.11

Select all candidates whose age is greater than or equal to 25 with the confidence degree of 0.9.

[In FSQL]

$$
\begin{aligned}
&\text{SELECT} \quad \text{Name} \\
&\text{FROM} \quad \text{candidates} \\
&\text{WHERE} \quad \text{Age} >= 25 \\
&\text{WITH} \quad 0.9 \; ;
\end{aligned}
$$

[In f-PROLOG]

```
?-[0.9]-answer( Name ,
          (candidates(Name,_,Age,_),
          Age >= 25)).
```

[Result]

Name
Smith
John
Mary
Jill
Susan
Harry
Barry
Thomas
Henry

6.4.4 Fuzzy Comparison Operators

In the FPDB system, fuzzy comparison operators such as 'approximately equal to', 'much greater than' and 'much less than' denoted by $\tilde{=}$, $>>$ and $<<$, are modelled. In our approach, fuzzy comparison can be made by using binary possibility distributions taking values in $[0, 1]$.

To define $\tilde{=}$, we consider three kinds of atomic conditions:

(1)   conditions of the form '$pv_1 \tilde{=} pv_2$' involving two precise values pv_1 and pv_2;

(2)   conditions of the form '$\widetilde{fv} \tilde{=} pv$' involving a fuzzy value $\widetilde{fv}$ and a precise value pv;

(3)   conditions of the form '$\widetilde{fv_1} \tilde{=} \widetilde{fv_2}$' involving two fuzzy values $\widetilde{fv_1}$ and $\widetilde{fv_2}$.

We first consider the case of (1). As a soft comparison operator, $\tilde{=}$ is represented by its possibility distribution $\Pi\text{-}_{=}$ which is equal to the fuzzy set 'approximately equal to' ($\widetilde{AE}$ for short), i.e.

$$\Pi\text{-}_{=}(x, y) = \widetilde{AE}$$

where $\mu_{\widetilde{AE}}(x, y) = e^{-c|x-y|}$, c is a parameter.

As a result, we define

$$pv_1 \tilde{=} pv_2 : T = \mu_{\widetilde{AE}}(pv_1, pv_2) \tag{6.41}$$

We have argued that Fuzziology did not seek excessive accuracy. Therefore,

234

in the case of (2) and (3), we define $\tilde{=}$ following (6.33) and (6.28) respectively:

$$\widetilde{fv} \; \tilde{=} \; pv \; : \; T \; = \; \mu_{\widetilde{fv}}(pv) \tag{6.42}$$

$$\widetilde{fv_1} \; \tilde{=} \; \widetilde{fv_2} \; : \; T \; = \; 1 - S_d(\widetilde{fv_1}, \widetilde{fv_2}) \tag{6.43}$$

Obviously, $\tilde{=}$ is symmetric in the three cases.

To define $>>$ we also consider three kinds of atomic conditions:

(a)   conditions of the form '$pv_1 >> pv_2$' involving two precise values pv_1 and pv_2;

(b)   conditions of the form '$\widetilde{fv} >> pv$' involving a fuzzy value $\widetilde{fv}$ and a precise value pv;

(c)   conditions of the form '$\widetilde{fv_1} >> \widetilde{fv_2}$' involving two fuzzy values $\widetilde{fv_1}$ and $\widetilde{fv_2}$.

Consider the case of (a); the fuzzy comparison operator $>>$ is represented by its possibility distribution $\Pi_{>>}$ which is equal to the fuzzy set 'much greater than' ($\widetilde{MGT}$ for short), $i.e.$

$$\Pi_{>>}(x, y) \; = \; \widetilde{MG}$$

where

$$\mu_{\widetilde{MGT}}(x, y) \; = \; \begin{cases} 0, & x \le y; \\ \left[1 + c(y - x)^{-2}\right]^{-1}, & x > y. \end{cases} \quad (c > 0)$$

Consequently, we define

$$pv_1 >> pv_2 \; : \; T \; = \; \mu_{\widetilde{MGT}}(pv_1, pv_2) \tag{6.44}$$

In the case of (b) and (c), we use the expected value E instead of the fuzzy value itself. Thus we obtain

$$\widetilde{fv} >> pv \; : \; T \; = \; \mu_{\widetilde{MGT}}(E(\widetilde{fv}), pv) \tag{6.45}$$

and

$$\widetilde{fv_1} >> \widetilde{fv_2} \; : \; T \; = \; \mu_{\widetilde{MGT}}(E(\widetilde{fv_1}), E(\widetilde{fv_2})) \tag{6.46}$$

The fuzzy comparison operator $<<$ could be defined by using the possibility distribution $\Pi_{<<}$ in the same way as the operator $>>$. However, we prefer to simply define it still by using $\Pi_{>>}$ shown above:

$$pv_1 << pv_2 \; : \; T \; = \; \mu_{\widetilde{MGT}}(pv_2, pv_1) \tag{6.47}$$

$$\widetilde{fv} << pv \ : \ T \ = \ \mu_{\widetilde{MGT}}(pv, E(\widetilde{fv})) \tag{6.48}$$

$$\widetilde{fv_1} << \widetilde{fv_2} \ : \ T \ = \ \mu_{\widetilde{MGT}}(E(\widetilde{fv_2}), E(\widetilde{fv_1})) \tag{6.49}$$

Based on this approach, FSQL language provides a facility to deal with condition expressions involving such fuzzy comparison operators. As an example, FSQL permits the following fuzzy query.

Example 6.12

Show all pairs of candidates who are friends with each other, and are approximately the same age with the confidence degree of 0.8.

```
SELECT    Name1, Name2
FROM      relationship
WHERE     Type = friend
AND       Name1  IN
              (SELECT   Name
               FROM     candidates
               WHERE    Age ~=
                            (SELECT   Age
                             FROM     candidates
                             WHERE    Name = Name2)
               WITH      0.8)
UNION
SELECT    Name1, Name2
FROM      relationship
WHERE     Type = friend
AND       Name2  IN
              (SELECT   Name
               FROM     candidates
               WHERE    Age ~=
                            (SELECT   Age
                             FROM     candidates
                             WHERE    Name = Name1)
               WITH      0.8) ;
```

6.4.5 Fuzzy Sorting

Before we present the approach which enables us to sort precise and fuzzy values in a common framework, we first introduce the concept of hard comparison between fuzzy values represented by means of possibility distributions.

When comparing fuzzy values, two kinds of question may arise:

(1)   What is the value of the least or the greatest one from a family of fuzzy values ?

(2)   Which is the greatest or the least among several fuzzy values ?

The answer to the first question is given by the use of the operations **min** and **max** [Dubois and Prade, 1980]. However, the above two questions are not simultaneously answered because, given a family $\widetilde{fv}_1, \widetilde{fv}_2, \ldots, \widetilde{fv}_n$ of fuzzy values, $\min\{\widetilde{fv}_1, \widetilde{fv}_2, \ldots, \widetilde{fv}_n\}$ or $\max\{\widetilde{fv}_1, \widetilde{fv}_2, \ldots, \widetilde{fv}_n\}$ is not necessarily one of the $\widetilde{fv}_i$, $i = 1, 2, \ldots, n$.

In fact, the second question is more important to fuzzy sorting. We must evaluate the degree of possibility for $x \in \Omega$, fuzzily restricted to belong to $\widetilde{fv}_1 \in \tilde{\mathcal{P}}(\Omega)$, to be greater than $y \in \Omega$, fuzzily restricted to belong to $\widetilde{fv}_2 \in \tilde{\mathcal{P}}(\Omega)$. Hence another method is required.

The degree of possibility of $\widetilde{fv}_1 \geq \widetilde{fv}_2$ is defined as

$$\pi_{\geq}(\widetilde{fv}_1, \widetilde{fv}_2) \;=\; \sup_{x,y \in \Omega, x \geq y} \min\{\pi_{\widetilde{fv}_1}(x), \pi_{\widetilde{fv}_2}(y)\}. \qquad (6.50)$$

where $\pi_{\widetilde{fv}_1}(x)$ represents the possibility that $\widetilde{fv}_1$ assumes the value $x \in \Omega$, and $\pi_{\widetilde{fv}_2}(y)$ the possibility that $\widetilde{fv}_2$ assumes the value $y \in \Omega$.

This formula is an extension of the inequality $x \geq y$ according to the extension principle. It is a degree of possibility in the sense that when a pair (x, y) exists such that, $x \geq y$ and $\pi_{\widetilde{fv}_1}(x) = \pi_{\widetilde{fv}_2}(y) = 1$, then $\pi_{\geq}(\widetilde{fv}_1, \widetilde{fv}_2) = 1$.

Suppose $\widetilde{fv}_1$ and $\widetilde{fv}_2$ are convex fuzzy values, it can be seen on Figure 6–9 that

$$\pi_{\geq}(\widetilde{fv}_1, \widetilde{fv}_2) \;=\; 1 \;\textbf{ iff }\; b \geq a,$$

$$\pi_{\geq}(\widetilde{fv}_2, \widetilde{fv}_1) \;=\; hgt(\widetilde{fv}_1 \cap \widetilde{fv}_2) \;=\; \pi_{\widetilde{fv}_1}(d)$$

where d is the abscissa of the highest intersection point D between $\pi_{\widetilde{fv}_1}$ and $\pi_{\widetilde{fv}_2}$. Note that $hgt(\widetilde{fv}_1 \cap \widetilde{fv}_2)$ is a good separation index for two fuzzy values— the closer $hgt(\widetilde{fv}_1 \cap \widetilde{fv}_2)$ is to 1, the harder it is to know whether $\widetilde{fv}$ is either greater or less than $\widetilde{fv}_2$. To compare $\widetilde{fv}_1$ and $\widetilde{fv}_2$, we need both $\pi_{\geq}(\widetilde{fv}_1, \widetilde{fv}_2)$ and

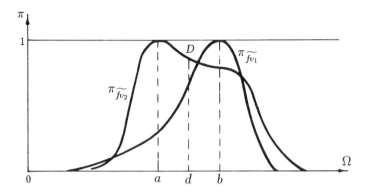

Figure 6–9

$\pi_{\geq}(\widetilde{fv_2}, \widetilde{fv_1})$. If, for instance, $\pi_{\geq}(\widetilde{fv_1}, \widetilde{fv_2}) = 1$, we know that either $\widetilde{fv_1} \geq \widetilde{fv_2}$, or $\widetilde{fv_1}$ and $\widetilde{fv_2}$ are too close to be separated. We may then choose a threshold λ and admit that $\widetilde{fv_1} \geq_\lambda \widetilde{fv_2}$ as soon as $\pi_{\geq}(\widetilde{fv_2}, \widetilde{fv_1}) < \lambda$.

Obviously, all results above hold for flat fuzzy values as well. Now we are ready to define hard comparison between fuzzy values represented by means of possibility distributions.

Definition 6.19

Let $\widetilde{fv_1}$ and $\widetilde{fv_2}$ be two fuzzy values (convex or flat) represented by the possibility distributions $\pi_{\widetilde{fv_1}}$ and $\pi_{\widetilde{fv_2}}$ on the universe of discourse Ω, respectively. Let

$$x = \frac{x_{min} + x_{max}}{2}, \qquad y = \frac{y_{min} + y_{max}}{2},$$

where

$$
\begin{aligned}
x_{min} &= \min\{x_i | x_i \in \Omega \text{ and } \pi_{\widetilde{fv_1}}(x_i) = 1\} \\
x_{max} &= \max\{x_i | x_i \in \Omega \text{ and } \pi_{\widetilde{fv_1}}(x_i) = 1\} \\
y_{min} &= \min\{y_j | y_j \in \Omega \text{ and } \pi_{\widetilde{fv_2}}(y_j) = 1\} \\
y_{max} &= \max\{y_j | y_j \in \Omega \text{ and } \pi_{\widetilde{fv_2}}(y_j) = 1\}
\end{aligned}
$$

(1) $\widetilde{fv_1}$ is **hard greater than** $\widetilde{fv_2}$, denoted $\widetilde{fv_1} \, \| > \| \, \widetilde{fv_2}$, **iff** $x > y$.
(2) $\widetilde{fv_1}$ is **hard less than** $\widetilde{fv_2}$, denoted $\widetilde{fv_1} \, \| < \| \, \widetilde{fv_2}$, **iff** $x < y$.
(3) $\widetilde{fv_1}$ is **hard equal to** $\widetilde{fv_2}$, denoted $\widetilde{fv_1} \, \| = \| \, \widetilde{fv_1}$, **iff** $x = y$.
(4) $\widetilde{fv_1} \, \| \geq \| \, \widetilde{fv_2}$ **iff** $\widetilde{fv_1} \, \| > \| \, \widetilde{fv_2}$ **or** $\widetilde{fv_1} \, \| = \| \, \widetilde{fv_2}$.
(5) $\widetilde{fv_1} \, \| \leq \| \, \widetilde{fv_2}$ **iff** $\widetilde{fv_1} \, \| < \| \, \widetilde{fv_2}$ **or** $\widetilde{fv_1} \, \| = \| \, \widetilde{fv_2}$.

As an example, (1), (2) and (3) are shown in Figure 6–10. Remember that

238

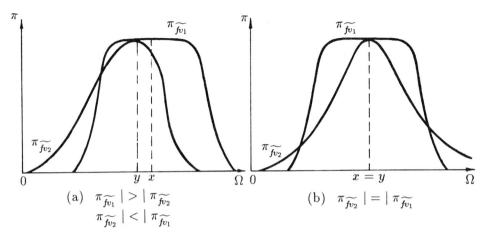

$$(a) \quad \pi_{\widetilde{fv_1}} \mid > \mid \pi_{\widetilde{fv_2}}$$
$$\pi_{\widetilde{fv_2}} \mid < \mid \pi_{\widetilde{fv_1}}$$

$$(b) \quad \pi_{\widetilde{fv_2}} \mid = \mid \pi_{\widetilde{fv_1}}$$

Figure 6–10

the notion of hard comparison is quite different from the fuzzy comparison discussed above. In the FPDB system hard comparisons are not only used to determine the relative positions between fuzzy values when sorting them, but also to answer "which is the greatest or the least among several fuzzy values?" (see the next section).

In fact, precise values can be thought of as special convex possibility distributions. As a result, precise and fuzzy values can be sorted in a common framework. To improve the power of FSQL, the ORDER_BY statement can be embedded in the fuzzy query block of the language. Thus crisp as well as fuzzy sorting can be performed by using the ORDER_BY statement.

Example 6.13

Get a list of candidates who have a university education, ordered by their ages, each one with his/her age and address.

[**In FSQL**]

```
SELECT      Name, Age, Address
FROM        candidates, background
WHERE       Education = university
ORDER_BY    Age ;
```

[**Result**]

239

Name	Age	Address
Martin	$Young	Newcastle
Tom	24	Carlisle
Andrew	24	Carlisle
Fred	ABOUT 25	Darlington
Susan	ABOUT 28	Darlington
Henry	29	Penrith
Smith	30	Newcastle
Harry	36	Darlington
Mary	$Middle-aged	Carlisle

6.5 Fuzzy Aggregate Functions in FPDB

One of the important functions in real-life DBMSs is the application of aggregate or statistical functions. The functions currently supported in FPDB are CNT, SUM, AVG, MAX and MIN. Apart from the special case of CNT(*), each of these functions operates on the collection of scalar values in one column of some table (base relation or virtual relation) and produces a single scalar value, defined as follows, as its result:

CNT	number of scalars in the column
SUM	sum of scalars in the column
AVG	average of scalars in the column
MAX	greatest scalar in the column
MIN	least scalar in the column

6.5.1 Formal Definition

While relational database theory proposed by Codd has provided a sound mathematical basis for studying many database systems, the use of aggregate functions in existing conventional query languages is not well understood. In particular, precise and general definitions are lacking, and their embedding into query languages is not well defined. Two examples are SQL and QBE, in which the definitions of aggregate functions rely unnecessarily on "sets" of tuples having duplicate members. This goes completely outside the set-theoretic definition of the relational model. For this reason, we have given a general definition for aggregate functions in the fuzzy relational model.

Definition 6.20

A fuzzy aggregate function takes a set of fuzzy tuples (a fuzzy relation) as an argument and produces a single simple value as a result.

The definition does not require that aggregate functions be able to accept arguments with duplicates. Formally, we hypothesize:

$$\text{Aggregate Function} = \text{AGG } Atr \ (R)$$

where AGG is an aggregate function name, Atr is an attribute within the fuzzy relation R. For instance, we could have:

$$\text{CNT Name (candidates)} \longrightarrow \alpha$$
$$\text{AVG Age (candidates)} \longrightarrow \alpha$$
$$\text{MAX Employees (company)} \longrightarrow \alpha$$
$$\text{MIN Height (body)} \longrightarrow \alpha$$

where α, as a result, is a single value. For SUM and AVG the argument must be of type numeric.

6.5.2 Single Value Simulation of Fuzzy Attribute Values

To extend the aggregate functions such as SUM, AVG from conventional databases to the fuzzy relational database system, FPDB, in this subsection, we introduce an approach called "Fuzzy-Numerical Simulation" (see [Chanas and Nowakowski, 1988], which allows for ascribing a precise numerical value to a fuzzy value by generating a value of a random variable according to the associated possibility distribution.

Suppose that we have the following proposition:

$$g : \quad V \text{ is } \tilde{G}$$

where $\tilde{G}$ is a normal, convex and bounded fuzzy set in the real domain, with a continuous membership function $\mu_{\tilde{G}}: \Omega \to [0,1]$, where Ω is the set R of real numbers. Such a proposition induces the possibility distribution of the fuzzy variable $\tilde{V}$ according to the possibility assignment equation, *i.e.*

$$\pi_{\tilde{V}}(x) = \mu_{\tilde{G}}(x) \qquad \forall x \in \Omega,$$

where $\pi_{\tilde{V}}(x)$ is the possibility that the variable $\tilde{V}$ takes on a value $x \in \Omega$. Chanas and Nowakowski suggest the following procedure for generating a single value of the fuzzy variable $\tilde{V}$:

(1)   Generate a value t of the uniform random variable T over $(0,1]$.

(2)   Generate a value x of the uniform random variable U over the t-level-set $G_t = \{x | \mu_{\tilde{G}}(x) \geq t\}$ of the fuzzy set $\tilde{G}$.

(3)   Assume that $\tilde{V} = x$, i.e. that x is a single value of the fuzzy variable $\tilde{V}$.

The procedure is also correct for discrete fuzzy variables, i.e. the case when $\tilde{G}$ is a fuzzy set in the space of integers. Then in (2), $\tilde{G}_t$ is a finite discrete set and x should be generated according to the probability distribution $\pi_U = \frac{1}{card(\tilde{G}_t)}$.

It is clear that the assumptions accepted for $\tilde{G}$ are essential in (2) of the procedure. Due to these, $\tilde{G}_t$ is a non-empty, bounded set. In the continuous case $\tilde{G}_t$ becomes a bounded interval. Discussion at this point will be confined to the continuous case, i.e. the case when $\tilde{V}$ takes on values from the set R of real numbers.

With the given assumptions concerning $\tilde{G}$, the procedure is the same as generating a value of the random variable $U_{\tilde{G}}(T,S)$ defined in the following way:

$$U_{\tilde{G}}(T,S) = g^-(T) + S(g^+(T) - g-(T)) = (1-S)g^-(T) + Sg^+(T), \quad (6.51)$$

where T and S are independent uniform random variables over $(0,1]$ and $[0,1]$, respectively, and the functions g^- and g^+ are defined as follows: $g^-(t) = \inf \tilde{G}_t$ and $g^+(t) = \sup \tilde{G}_t$, $t \in (0,1]$. Further on we will often use the shortened notation $U_{\tilde{G}}$ instead of $U_{\tilde{G}}(T,S)$.

For some cases of the fuzzy set $\tilde{G}$ one may easily deduce an analytical form of the probability distribution of the random variable $U_{\tilde{G}}$. For instance, let $\tilde{G}$ be defined by a 'triangular' membership function (see Figure 6–11), i.e.

$$\mu_{\tilde{G}}(x) = \begin{cases} 0, & x \leq a - d_1; \\ \frac{x-a+d_1}{d_1}, & a - d_1 \leq x \leq a; \\ \frac{a+d_2-x}{d_2}, & a \leq x \leq a + d_2; \\ 0, & x \geq a + d_2. \end{cases} \quad (6.52)$$

The cumulative distribution function F_U of the random variable $U_{\tilde{G}}$ now has

242

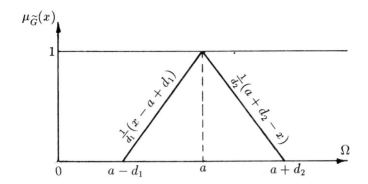

Figure 6-11 Triangular Membership Function of
a Fuzzy Set $\tilde{G}$.

the form

$$
F_U(x) \;=\; \begin{cases}
0, & x \le a - d_1; \\[4pt]
\dfrac{(a-x)\ln(\frac{a-x}{d_1\cdot e})+d_1}{d_1+d_2}, & a - d_1 < x < a; \\[8pt]
\dfrac{d_1}{d_1+d_2}, & x = a; \\[8pt]
\dfrac{(x-a)\ln(\frac{e\cdot d_2}{x-a})+d_1}{d_1+d_2}, & a < x < a + d_2; \\[8pt]
1, & x > a + d_2.
\end{cases}
\tag{6.53}
$$

Indeed, in the case of a triangular fuzzy set $\tilde{G}$ we obtain

$$
g^-(t) \;=\; a - (1-t)d_1, \qquad g^+(t) \;=\; a + (1-t)d_2, \qquad t \in (0,1]
\tag{6.54}
$$

and that is why

$$
U_{\tilde{G}}(T,S) \;=\; a - (1-T)d_1 + S(1-T)(d_1 + d_2).
\tag{6.55}
$$

It is obvious that $F_U(x) = 0$ for $x \le a - d_1$ and $F_U(x) = 1$ for $x > a + d_2$ because
$U_{\tilde{G}}(T,S)$ takes on values from the interval $[a - d_1, a + d_2]$. To determine $F_U(x)$
for the other x, one can use the theorem of total probability [Papoulis, 1965]:

$$
\begin{aligned}
F_U(x) &= P\left[a - (1-T)d_1 + S(1-T)(d_1 + d_2) < x\right] \\[4pt]
&= \int_0^1 P\left[a - (1-T)d_1 + S(1-T)(d_1 + d_2) < x/T = t\right] dF_T(t) \\[4pt]
&= \int_0^1 P\left[a - (1-t)d_1 + S(1-t)(d_1 + d_2) < x\right] dt \\[4pt]
&= \int_0^1 P\!\left(S < \frac{x - a + (1-t)d_1}{(1-t)(d_1 + d_2)}\right) dt.
\end{aligned}
$$

243

Calculating the last integral we obtain $F_U(x)$ for the other intervals of x (the three middle cases in (6.53)). Using the random variable $U_{\widetilde{G}}$ associated with fuzzy variable $\widetilde{V}$, one may suggest some useful number characteristics of $\widetilde{V}$, called generative characteristics of $\widetilde{V}$. It is natural to use the classic characteristics of a random variable. So the **generative expected value**, $GE(\widetilde{V})$, and the **generative variance**, $Gvar(\widetilde{V})$, of a fuzzy variable $\widetilde{V}$ are defined in the following way:

$$GE(\widetilde{V}) \stackrel{\mathrm{df}}{=} E(U_{\widetilde{G}}) \tag{6.56}$$

$$Gvar(\widetilde{V}) \stackrel{\mathrm{df}}{=} var(U_{\widetilde{G}}) \tag{6.57}$$

where $E(U_{\widetilde{G}})$ is the **mathematical expected value** of the random variable $U_{\widetilde{G}}$ and $var(U_{\widetilde{G}})$ is its **variance**.

The introduced characteristics reflect the way of 'realizing' or taking on a value by the fuzzy variable $\widetilde{V}$.

Using (6.51), the properties of the expected value and the properties of the variance of a random variable, we obtain the following formula:

$$
\begin{aligned}
GE(\widetilde{V}) &= E(U_{\widetilde{G}}) \\
&= \frac{1}{2}\{E\left[g^-(T)\right] + E\left[g^+(T)\right]\} \\
&= \frac{1}{2}\int_0^1 \left[g^-(t) + g^+(t)\right] dt
\end{aligned}
\tag{6.58}
$$

$$
\begin{aligned}
Gvar(\widetilde{V}) &= E(U_{\widetilde{G}}^2) - E^2(U_{\widetilde{G}}) \\
&= \frac{1}{3}\{E\left[g^-(T)^2\right] + E\left[g^-(T)g^+(T)\right] + E\left[g^+(T)^2\right]\} \\
&\quad -\frac{1}{4}\{E\left[g^-(T)\right] + E\left[g^+(T)\right]\}^2 \\
&= \frac{1}{3}\int_0^1 \left[g^-(t)^2 + g^-(t)g^+(t) + g^-(t)^2\right] dt \\
&\quad -\frac{1}{4}\{\int_0^1 [g(t) + g(t)]\, dt\}^2
\end{aligned}
\tag{6.59}
$$

where T is the uniform random variable over $(0,1]$.

For the triangular fuzzy set $\widetilde{G}$ illustrated in Figure 6–11, we have

$$GE(\widetilde{V}) = \frac{a + (d_2 - d_1)}{4}, \tag{6.60}$$

$$Gvar(\widetilde{V}) = \frac{(7d_1^2 + 7d_2^2 + 2d_1 d_2)}{144} \tag{6.61}$$

244

This approach supplies a way to determine a probability distribution consistent with the given possibility distribution which is normal, convex and bounded. In our opinion, all the results above hold for a flat fuzzy possibility distribution also. In fact, a fuzzy attribute value within a fuzzy relation could be seen as a fuzzy variable (usually fuzzy linguistic variable) associated with a possibility distribution. As we have stated in the FPDB system, attribute values were mostly precise, whereas fuzzy values were in the minority. Thus aggregate functions SUM, AVG can be used in the FPDB system, provided that fuzzy attribute values are replaced by the corresponding simulated precise values.

6.5.3 Fuzzy Aggregations as Built-in Functions in FSQL

The language FSQL described so far is still not adequate for many practical problems. For example, even a query as simple as "How many candidates are there?" cannot be expressed using only the constructs given in Chapter 5. Such retrieval power can be easily improved by provision of built-in functions. So the built-in functions CNT, SUM, AVG, MAX and MIN supported by the standard SQL have been extended to FSQL. In addition, there are also a GROUP_BY statement and a HAVING statement, as will be explained with examples later.

The extension of SUM and AVG were accomplished as soon as we finished the introduction of so called "Fuzzy-Numerical Simulation". As for MAX and MIN, we still take the concept of hard comparison as a similar way to fuzzy sorting. As a matter of fact, for an attribute within the fuzzy relation, once fuzzy sorting of its values has been achieved, the greatest or least one among these values has been found. Finally, CNT can be simply used in FSQL as well as in the standard SQL, only the key-word DISTINCT will never be allowed.

In the standard SQL language, the argument may optionally be preceded by the key-word DISTINCT, to indicate that redundant duplicate values are to be eliminated before the function is applied; other than that, it is unnecessary in FSQL for the reason which has been stated in Section 6.5.1.

Below we give a number of examples of the use of functions. Each of the following examples could form the basis of a singleton SELECT statement or could be nested within some more complex expression.

1.   Functions in the SELECT statement

Example 6.14

Get the total number of candidates.

$$\text{SELECT} \quad \text{CNT(*)}$$
$$\text{FROM} \quad \text{candidates ;}$$

Example 6.15

How many different addresses are shown in the table **candidates**?

$$\text{SELECT} \quad \text{CNT(Address)}$$
$$\text{FROM} \quad \text{candidates ;}$$

Example 6.16

How many girls who are young with the degree of 0.9 are in the **candidates** table?

$$\text{SELECT} \quad \text{CNT(Name)}$$
$$\text{FROM} \quad \text{candidates}$$
$$\text{WHERE} \quad \text{Age} = \$\text{Young}$$
$$\text{AND} \quad \text{Sex} = \text{female}$$
$$\text{WITH} \quad 0.9 \text{ ;}$$

Example 6.17

Get numbers of those candidates, for each candidate whose age is greater than or equal to 25 with the confidence degree of 0.9.

$$\text{SELECT} \quad \text{CNT(Name)}$$
$$\text{FROM} \quad \text{candidates}$$
$$\text{WHERE} \quad \text{Age} >= 25$$
$$\text{WITH} \quad 0.9 \text{ ;}$$

Example 6.18

Get the greatest and the least value of candidate ages.

$$\text{SELECT} \quad \text{MAX(Age), MIN(Age)}$$
$$\text{FROM} \quad \text{candidates ;}$$

Example 6.19

Get the average age of female candidates.

```
SELECT    AVG(Age)
FROM      candidates
WHERE     Sex = female ;
```

2.   Functions in Subquery

Example 6.20

Get candidate names for each candidate whose age is less than the average of all candidates who live in Carlisle.

```
SELECT    Name
FROM      candidates
WHERE     Age <
              (SELECT    AVG(Age)
               FROM      candidates
               WHERE     Address = carlisle) ;
```

Example 6.21

Who is the tallest among young male candidates with the confidence degree of 0.8?

```
SELECT    Name
FROM      candidates, body
WHERE     Sex = male
AND       Height =
              (SELECT    MAX(Height)
               FROM      candidates, body
               WHERE     Sex = male
               AND       Age = $Young
               WITH      0.8)
AND       Age = $Young
WITH      0.8 ;
```

3.   Use of GROUP_BY

Example 6.22

Get the total numbers and average ages of male candidates and female candidates respectively.

```
SELECT      Sex, CNT(Name), AVG(Age)
FROM        candidates
GROUP_BY    Sex ;
```

Example 6.23

For each profession, get the profession name and the total number of candidates who have that profession.

```
SELECT      Profession, CNT(Profession)
FROM        background
GROUP_BY    Profession ;
```

The GROUP_BY operator conceptually rearranges the FROM relation into partitions or groups, such that within any one group all tuples have the same value for the GROUP_BY attribute.

4.   Use of GROUP_BY with HAVING

Example 6.24

Get profession names for all professions in which more than two candidates have that profession.

```
SELECT      Profession
FROM        background
GROUP_BY    Profession
HAVING      CNT(Profession) > 2 ;
```

The HAVING statement is only used to restrict a partitioned relation. So HAVING is always used with GROUP_BY. The expression in a HAVING statement must be single-valued for each group.

5.   A Comprehensive Example

Example 6.25

How many positions will pay much more than $5000 with the degree of 0.8 in each company?

SELECT	Cname, CNT(Position)
FROM	job
GROUP_BY	Cname
WHERE	Salary >> 5000
WITH	0.8 ;

It is important to make the distinction between HAVING and WHERE statements. In comparison with Example 6.24, both the WHERE statement and the HAVING statement are followed by GROUP_BY, but they differ in that an expression in a HAVING statement involves a built-in function showing the property of each group, whereas a WHERE statement (and WITH statement) only specifies a fuzzy condition in a grouped relation.

Chapter 7

ON FUZZY RELATIONAL DATABASE SYSTEMS THROUGH FUZZY LOGIC

In this chapter we begin with the introduction of the relationships between fuzzy logic and fuzzy relational databases. Various approaches to incorporating deductive capability into fuzzy relational database systems through the use of fuzzy logic have been examined. The discussion introduces the use of the inference mechanism of f-PROLOG, the fuzzy logic programming language, in fuzzy deductive databases and even knowledge bases. The emphasis will be on how well the transformation of an FSQL query into the f-PROLOG form can be made by using a parser—a set of deductive axioms—therefore, how well the fuzzy relational query language can be supported by the FPDB system. An implementation of the FSQL parser is given in particular.

7.1 Deductive Power in Fuzzy Relational Databases

The idea of using fuzzy logic as a programming language has been applied in many different areas, such as expert systems, knowledge engineering, decision making, fuzzy control, and natural language processing. In recent years, fuzzy logic and fuzzy PROLOG have been more extensively studied, and fuzzy logic has been found to be a highly useful tool both for representing the structure of fuzzy relational databases and for processing fuzzy information involved in the database. On the other hand, the evolution in fuzzy relational database technology has drifted more and more towards the use of fuzzy logic.

As far as fuzzy relational query languages and user-interfaces are concerned, there are many problems that can be conveniently transformed into fuzzy logic. In the present section, we focus on the application of fuzzy logic programming to fuzzy relational databases, for the purpose of introducing fuzzy deductive databases and knowledge bases.

7.1.1 Fuzzy Relational Databases and Fuzzy Deductive Databases

From the viewpoint of theorem proving, a fuzzy relational database can be regarded as a question-answering system which consists of a collection of axioms of a theorem expressed in fuzzy logic formulae, instead of a fuzzy relational structure. A fuzzy query of the database is regarded as a theorem to be proved from the axioms. The inference mechanism provided with fuzzy logic can be used to deduce the fuzzy query on the basis of the set of fuzzy assertions and rules. In other words, answering a question from the axioms may be considered as proving that a formula corresponding to the answer is derivable from the formulae representing the facts. This approach is different from the ordinary fuzzy relational database approach in regarding a database as a theory, in which it is natural to describe data both by means of explicit assertions and by means of general rules. The inclusion of recursive definitions can be accommodated without leaving fuzzy predicate logic. Hence, deductive searches become important.

As mentioned earlier, a fuzzy relational database consists of a real database and a virtual database. The real database contains base relations stored explicitly in secondary storage. Virtual relations represent information not required to be stored explicitly, but able to be derived from the real database. Definitions of virtual relations are stored in the virtual database (data dictionary). The represention of information as explicit tables that might otherwise be derived from base relations would incur storage redundancy and lead to update and consistency problems.

In a fuzzy relational database system, virtual relations are usually defined by data definition statements (such as the FSQL DDL statement DEFINE_VIRTUAL TABLE). In a fuzzy deductive database system, virtual relations are defined as fuzzy logic rules, and extensions of virtual relations are derived from base relations using the intrinsic inference mechanism provided with fuzzy logic. The definition of virtual relations can be considered procedural in the fuzzy relational database but declarative in the fuzzy deductive database.

Queries in a fuzzy relational database are based mostly on fuzzy relational calculus (or equivalently fuzzy relational algebra). However, expressing queries with fuzzy relational calculus has two drawbacks. Firstly, fuzzy relational calculus may be difficult to use for expressing some complex queries. Secondly, and perhaps more important, as a simple extension of binary relational calculus proposed by Codd [Codd, 1972], fuzzy relational calculus (see Section 6.3) does not allow recursion. Fuzzy logic has been regarded as a promising solution for these problems because the fuzzy relational data model can be formulated in fuzzy logic, particularly, f-Horn clause logic, or the f-PROLOG language [Liu and Li, 1988(a)(b), 1989(a)]; and the intrinsic inference mechanism in fuzzy logic provides a natural way to extend the power of the fuzzy relational data model beyond the definition in Chapter 4.

To develop a fuzzy deductive database system, the ideas of fuzzy logic programming and fuzzy relational database systems can be combined in two ways. The first is to construct a single integrated system combining an inference mechanism and a database system. Such a system would involve generalizing some fuzzy database system components and adding them to a fuzzy logic programming system. The second way uses two components: (1) a fuzzy relational database to manage the real database; (2) a fuzzy logic programming system (or fuzzy logic system) to perform fuzzy deductive reasoning using the virtual database. Either way, fuzzy logic plays a crucial role in a fuzzy deductive database.

As a fuzzy logic programming language, f-PROLOG (introduced in Chapter 3) can be used widely in such applications as database systems, expert systems, natural language processing, fuzzy control and many other areas of artificial intelligence. From the following discussion, we can see the advantages of applying fuzzy logic programming, particularly f-PROLOG, in fuzzy relational databases.

The following example illustrates the mechanism f-PROLOG uses to perform

252

fuzzy deductive inferencing over a database of f-Assertions and f-Rules. Consider the **relationship** table shown in Figure 4–26.

Given a name, we can easily find that person's friends with a simple fuzzy relational calculus (or an FSQL) expression. However, it would not be possible to list all close-friends of a person with fuzzy relational calculus (or FSQL) expressions alone. For one reason, the system as presented does not have a priori knowledge about the meaning of "close-friends". For another, answering this query requires recursion or iteration on the base relation, which is not available in fuzzy relational calculus or FSQL.

A fuzzy tuple in a base relation is represented as an f-Assertion in f-PROLOG. For instance,

relationship(smith,barry,friend) :–[1]– .

or

relationship(smith,barry,friend).

for short, is an assertion meaning smith and barry are definitely friends with each other. f-Assertions with the same predicate symbol, *e.g.* "relationship", and number of arguments define the extension of a base relation, *e.g.* "relationship" with attributes Name1, Name2 and Type.

Virtual relations in fuzzy relational databases can be represented by f-Rules in f-PROLOG programs. For instance,

close_friends(Name1,Name2) :–[0.8]–
            relationship(Name1,Name2,friend),
            candidates(Name1,_,Age1,_),
            candidates(Name2,_,Age2,_),
            background(Name1,_,_,_,Hobby1),
            background(Name2,_,_,_,Hobby2),
            Age1 ~= Age2, Hobby1 == Hobby2.

is an f-Rule meaning that for all Name1 and Name2, if candidates Name1 and Name2 are friends, their ages Age1 and Age2 are approximately equal to each other, and their hobbies Hobby1 and Hobby2 are the same, then Name1 and Name2 are 'very possible' to be close-friends. f-Rules having the same predicate symbol, *e.g.* "close-friends", and number of arguments define a virtual relation

253

which is usually a typical fuzzy relation (see Section 4.2.3), *e.g.* "close-friends" with attributes Name1 and Name2. As a result, we have

Example 7.1

The "close-friends" example above can be expressed with the following f-PROLOG program:

```
relationship(smith,susan,friend).
relationship(smith,fred,friend).
relationship(smith,mary,friend).
relationship(andrew,smith,friend).
relationship(barry,smith,friend).
relationship(john,smith,friend).
relationship(anna,mary,friend).
relationship(jill,harry,friend).
relationship(thomas,henry,friend).
relationship(tom,martin,friend).
close_friends(Name1,Name2) :-[0.8]-
        relationship(Name1,Name2,friend),
        candidates(Name1,_,Age1,_),
        candidates(Name2,_,Age2,_),
        background(Name1,_,_,_,Hobby1),
        background(Name2,_,_,_,Hobby2),
        Age1 ~= Age2, Hobby1 == Hobby2.
```

A query in f-PROLOG is represented by an f-Goal. For instance, the fuzzy query

$$?-[F]-relationship(smith,X,friend);$$
$$relationship(X,smith,friend).$$

means "Who is a possible friend of Smith?" and indeed will return all possible friends of Smith (each solution with a confidence degree). A query without variable arguments may produce a yes or no answer. For instance, the query

$$?-[0.9]-relationship(smith,barry,friend);$$
$$relationship(barry,smith,friend).$$

254

means "Is it true (with the degree of 0.9) that Smith and Barry are friends?"

Beyond fuzzy relational calculus or FSQL, the fuzzy query

$$?-[F]-close\_friends(Name1,Name2).$$

can be answered with f-PROLOG. f-PROLOG tries to replace a fuzzy query with subqueries by unifying the fuzzy query to the head of an f-Rule. Chapter 3 had the detail.

As this example illustrates, uniformity in expressing f-Assertions, f-Rules, programs, and queries (f-Goals) is achieved in f-PROLOG by using the same syntax in all cases. Most important, the unification mechanism can deduce additional f-Assertions from a given set of f-Assertions and f-Rules.

7.1.2 From Fuzzy Relational Databases to Knowledge Bases

A fuzzy relational database system, in some sense, can be also thought of as a knowledge base system, in which a fuzzy query is written in a very high level non-procedural query language, and the execution of such a query is to perform tasks that could be called intelligent. Starting with an initial state, one tries to find a sequence of operations that will transform the initial state into the desired state—that is, knowledge information processing. In this case, we can describe states and the state transition rules by fuzzy logic formulae. In other words, a fuzzy logic program system, such as f-PROLOG, can be applied to the task of writing compilers for high level fuzzy query languages. The major advantage of f-PROLOG as a language for writing compilers is that it specifies algorithms in a human-oriented way. Such specification can be interpreted as a uniform resolution theorem-prover.

Now the basic concepts of fuzzy relational databases and knowledge bases are compared and the analogies are shown in Figure 7–1.

As we have discussed, fuzzy relational database systems can only be used to handle fuzzy assertions in the form of fuzzy relations and fuzzy tuples. The main characteristics of applications well-suited to these systems are applications with a huge amount of data having the same structure, described in a schema. The number of data types is very limited. However, new application areas require fuzzy relational databases fulfilling other characteristics. The number of data types is now enormous; the knowledge to be represented, therefore cannot now

Fuzzy Relational Database System	Knowledge Base System
data	knowledge
input	knowledge acquisition
storage structure	knowledge representation
data processing	inference
data item	knowledge unit
database system	knowledge base system

Figure 7–1

be described only with assertions, and inference rules become more and more important. Eventually, traditional fuzzy relational databases will be replaced by knowledge bases in such application areas.

We see, from the discussion above, that fuzzy logic also plays a crucial role in the knowledge base system as well as in the fuzzy deductive database system. As the sister to ILEX [Li, 1984], FPDB system transforms the fuzzy logic form of FSQL queries into the fuzzy logic programming language—f-PROLOG through IF/PROLOG, a binary logic programming language. The resulting f-PROLOG form is directly executed to yield the answer to the original question. This approach will be discussed later in detail.

7.2   Fuzzy Logic as a Database Query Language

As a matter of fact, a great deal of fuzzy logic programming theory can be transferred to databases. In a logic-programmed fuzzy relational database system, such as FPDB, fuzzy logic is used not only as the programming tool, but also as the internal query language. Such a fuzzy relational database is viewed as a fuzzy logic program, in which retrieval is automatically taken care of through fuzzy resolution (or equivalently fuzzy procedural interpretation). The use of fuzzy logic for data description abolishes the distinction between databases and programs. Strategies which apply to the execution of programs apply also to the retrieval of answers to fuzzy queries. In other words, the program serving to define the data serves at the same time to compute it, while in traditional (nonlogical) fuzzy relational database systems, these two functions (description and retrieval of fuzzy relations) are performed by separate components, generally based on different formalisms. For instance, several fuzzy queries within f-PROLOG have been shown in Example 7.1.

In general, given a predicate definition for an n-ary predicate p, the retrieval of the i-th argument corresponding to specific values of the others is simply obtained by posing the query

$$?-[f]-p(v_1, \ldots, v_{i-1}, X, v_{i+1}, \ldots, v_n).$$

where v_i $(i = 1, 2, \ldots, n)$ are those specific values and X is a variable, and f is a threshold value. Because of nondeterminism, more than one value for X may be retrieved. Because of the nondistinction between input and output, any argument or combination of arguments can be chosen for retrieval. Thus basic operations on fuzzy relational databases (e.g., for the above example, projection and selection) become very simple within fuzzy logic programming.

Relational completeness is a basic measure of the selective power of a language. A language is said to be relationally complete if any relation derivable from the given base relations by means of an expression of the relational algebra can be retrieved using that language [Codd, 1972].

What fuzzy relational completeness means to the user is that, very loosely speaking, if the information required is in the fuzzy relational database, then it can be retrieved by means of a single self-contained request. Of course, most queries will be fairly simple in practice; but from the underlying theory the user can ask arbitrarily complex questions if he wishes.

We will show that as a fuzzy logic programming language, f-PROLOG itself, with necessary **meta-predicate** "answer" for generating multiple solutions, is a fuzzy relationally complete query language, *i.e.* it can express all fuzzy query operations expressed in fuzzy relational algebra, the common base language to all fuzzy relational database systems with operators such as union, projection, selection, and join, *etc.*

(1)   For fuzzy set operations:

The concepts of intersection, union, difference, and Cartesian product respectively can be implemented in f-PROLOG as follows:

(a)   Intersection

$$?\text{-}[F]\text{-answer}((X_1, X_2, \ldots, X_n),$$
$$(p(X_1, X_2, \ldots, X_n), q(X_1, X_2, \ldots, X_n)))).$$

(b)   Union

$$?\text{-}[F]\text{-answer}((X_1, X_2, \ldots, X_n),$$
$$(p(X_1, X_2, \ldots, X_n); q(X_1, X_2, \ldots, X_n)))).$$

(c)   Difference

$$?\text{-}[F]\text{-answer}((X_1, X_2, \ldots, X_n),$$
$$(p(X_1, X_2, \ldots, X_n), not(q(X_1, X_2, \ldots, X_n))))).$$

(d)   Cartesian Product

$$?\text{-}[F]\text{-answer}((X_1, X_2, \ldots, X_n, Y_1, Y_2, \ldots, Y_m),$$
$$(p(X_1, X_2, \ldots, X_n), q(Y_1, Y_2, \ldots, Y_m)))).$$

(2)   For fuzzy relational algebra operations:

The concepts of projection, ϑ-join, and ϑ-selection respectively can be implemented in f-PROLOG as follows:

(a)   Projection

$$?\text{-}[F]\text{-answer}((X_i, X_j, \ldots, X_k),$$
$$(p(X_1, \ldots, X_i, \ldots, X_j, \ldots, X_k, \ldots, X_n)))).$$

(b) ϑ-join

$$?\text{-}[F]\text{-answer}((X_1, \ldots, X_n, Y_1, \ldots, Y_m),$$
$$(X_i \vartheta Y_j, p(X_1, X_2, \ldots, X_n), q(Y_1, Y_2, \ldots, Y_m)))).$$

(c) ϑ-selection

$$?\text{-}[F]\text{-answer}((X_1, \ldots, X_i, \ldots, X_j, \ldots, X_n),$$
$$(X_i \vartheta X_j, p(X_1, \ldots, X_j, \ldots, X_j, \ldots, X_n)))).$$

From (1) and (2), the fuzzy relational completeness of f-PROLOG with the meta-predicate "answer" is shown.

f-PROLOG representation is not only sufficient for relational completeness; many other functions, including updating and deleting of tuples, the ability to group together certain tuples and fuzzy aggregate functions such as CNT, SUM, MAX, MIN, AVG, *etc.* can also be converted to the uniform (see Appendix 1). We show that, as a result, fuzzy logic can be used as a uniform language for expressing base relations, virtual relations, programs, queries, and integrity constraints of fuzzy relational databases.

The link with fuzzy logic was not only found at the language level and query evaluaton. For instance, it is rather straightforward for fuzzy dependency statements to be expressed as fuzzy logic formulae, but it goes beyond the scope of this book.

It is our belief that a wider use of fuzzy logic would have a positive effect on fuzzy relational databases, since it provides not only a conceptual framework for formalizing various concepts in the fuzzy relational model, but also a tool for implementing them.

These considerations led us to develop FPDB—the fuzzy relational database system implemented in f-PROLOG—fuzzy logic programming language.

7.3   A Canonical Logic Form for Fuzzy Query Languages

As a formal basis for translating FSQL queries into f-PROLOG representation and other related researches, the formal definition of the canonical logic form [Li, 1984] is simply extended in this section. We use the following notation to form the canonical logic expression.

Q An entire fuzzy query.

\#   The Boolean logic operator OR, by which subqueries are linked together. We have

$$Q = SUB_1 \ \# \ SUB_2 \ \# \ \cdots \ \# \ SUB_k.$$

H_i A set of required variables in a retrieval subquery. We have

$$H_i = [X_1, X_2, \ldots, X_j]$$

!   An "end" notation of a subquery.

\&   The Boolean logic operator AND, linking different parts within a subquery. We may have

$$SUB_i = H_i \ \& \ BODY_i \ \& \ !$$

$BODY_i$ The body of a subquery which is a set of fuzzy query tuples T_i linked together by the operator "&". We have

$$BODY_i = T_1 \ \& \ T_2 \ \& \ \cdots \ \& \ T_n$$

T_i A fuzzy query tuple. We define it as follows

$$T_i = sub\_q(N_i, A_i, F_i, FF_i, V_i, FUN_i, D_i)$$

where:

N_i A relation name in the fuzzy query tuple T_i.

A_i A set of attributes of the relation N_i.

V_i A set of free variables in A_i.

F_i A set of independent formulae in the fuzzy query tuple T_i. A formula is said to be independent if it is a comparison with a constant.

FF_i A set of relevant formulae in a fuzzy query tuple T_i. A formula is said to be relevant if it contains variables involving other base relations.

FUN_i Functional description in a fuzzy query tuple Q_i. It may be

!	A basic query tuple involving no aggregation.
not	A negation involved in the query tuple.
asserta	An insert operation.
retract	A delete operation.
[cnt,X,Sum]	CNT function: count number of values.
[sum,X,Sum]	SUM function: sum the values.
[max,X,Max]	MAX function: pick up the largest value.
[min,X,Min]	MIN function: pick up the smallest value.
[avg,X,Avg]	AVG function: average the values.
[all,X,Set]	All function: collect values.

[group,X,X] partition function: group values.

[u,X,E]   An update function: update values.

D_i A threshold level in the fuzzy query tuple T_i.

VJ_i A set of relevant variables belonging to several relations; these variables will be called join variables.

VI_i A set of independent variables, standing for nonjoin variables.

As far as a retrieval operation is concerned, a complete fuzzy query expression in the canonical logic form is:

$$H_1 \ \& \ BODY_1 \ \& \ ! \ \# \ H_2 \ \& \ BODY_2 \ \& \ ! \ \# \ \cdots \ \# \ H_n \ \& \ BODY_n \ \& \ !.$$

As for a storage operation, the general canonical logic expression is:

$$BODY_1 \ \& \ ! \ \# \ BODY_2 \ \& \ ! \ \# \ \cdots \ \# \ BODY_n \ \& \ !.$$

Note that the canonical logic form is of classical binary logic rather than fuzzy logic. However, every fuzzy relational algebraic operator can be expressed in these terms, and hence all FSQL queries can be transformed into canonical logic representation, but this goes beyond the scope of this book. In addition, the symbol '!' in the canonical logic form is nothing to do with the cut in PROLOG.

7.4 Implementation of the FSQL Parser

This section is devoted to an implementation technique for the fuzzy relational query language FSQL. As a matter of fact, the technique is general and may be used for other structured fuzzy or nonfuzzy query languages. The emphasis is on those aspects which have been put to practical use in IF/PROLOG, a popular logic programming language which is indeed a subset of f-PROLOG. It shows how a structured fuzzy query is understood by logic-program solving and then is transformed into the canonical logic form, and eventually into f-PROLOG (see Figure 7–2). There is the additional purpose of demonstrating the particular advantages of PROLOG for compiler writing.

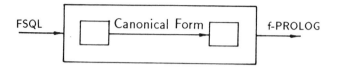

Figure 7–2 The Parser of FSQL

7.4.1 Considering Keywords as Operators

One of important strategies in writing the parser of FSQL is that each structured keyword in FSQL is considered as an operator in PROLOG by declaring it in advance. These operators not only provide syntactic convenience when reading or writing, but also allow the use of simple expressions for what would otherwise have to be implemented through more complicated code containing explicit control structures such as iteration. Each operator in IF/PROLOG has three attributes: position, precedence, and associativity.

POSITION of an operator defines where the operator is relative to the argument(s), and can be:

Prefix	**op** Term	before its single argument
Infix	Term **op** Term	between its two arguments
Postfix	Term **op**	after its single argument

PRECEDENCE (or priority) of operators is an integer **0–1200** used to choose between interpretations of a term with operators of different precedence, *i.e.* it makes expressions unambiguous where the use of syntax of the terms is not made explicit through the use of parentheses. For instance, "$a + b * c$":

$$a + (b * c) \quad \text{or} \quad (a + b) * c$$

Terms of lowest precedence bind most strongly. The precedence of a bracketed or unstructured term is 0. Normally the first interpretation above is chosen because "*" has a lower predecence than "+". However, the second would be chosen if "+" had a lower precedence than "*".

262

ASSOCIATIVITY of operators is used to choose between interpretations of a term with operators of equal precedence, *i.e.* it makes expression unambiguous where there are two operators with the same precedence. For instance, "$a + b - c$" :

$$a + (b - c) \quad \text{or} \quad (a + b) - c$$

The position/associativity attribute **OpType** is specified by the following mnemonics, where "f" represents the operator and "x" and "y" represent the argument(s). "x" means an argument of lower precedence than the operator, "y" means an argument of equal or lower precedence:

yfx	infix,	left associative
xfy	infix,	right associative
xfx	infix,	not associative
fx,fy	prefix	
xf,yf	postfix	

ORDER of EVALUATION of an expression is dependent on both the associativity and the precedence of the operators in the expression. Terms of lowest precedence are bound first. The precedence of an unstructured term or a term in brackets is 0.

A left associative operator (*e.g.* +, −) requires a right argument of lower precedence than its own. The expression "$a + b - c$" is interpreted as "$(a + b) - c$" because "+" and "−" are defined as left associative (yfx).

A right associative operator requires that the main operator of the left argument must be of lower precedence. If "+" and "−" were right associative (xfy), then "$a + b - c$" would be interpreted as "$a + (b - c)$".

xfx defines the operator to be not associative, *i.e.* both operators appearing in the two arguments must be of a lower precedence than the top operator.

Brackets can be used to circumvent defined precedence rules. Although "+" has a higher precedence than "*", the term "$(a + b) * c$" is understood because the brackets hide the "+" operator behind a precedence of 0.

Prefix and **postfix** operators behave in similar ways.

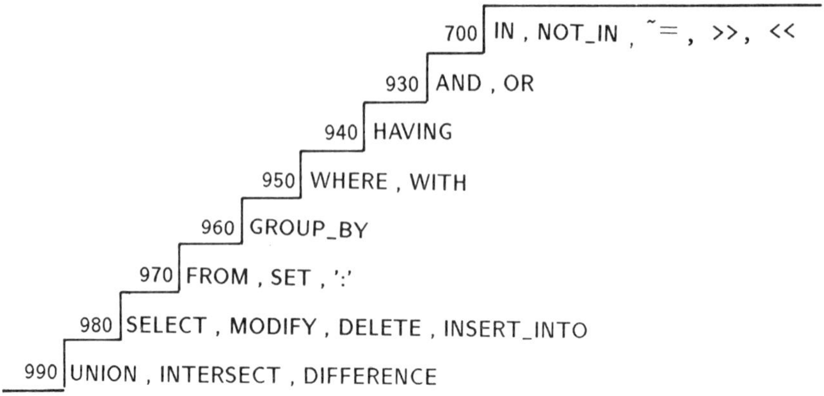

```
700 | IN , NOT_IN , ~= , >>, <<
   930 | AND , OR
     940 | HAVING
       950 | WHERE , WITH
         960 | GROUP_BY
           970 | FROM , SET , ':'
             980 | SELECT , MODIFY , DELETE , INSERT_INTO
               990 | UNION , INTERSECT , DIFFERENCE
```

Figure 7–3   The Comparison of Operators in FSQL

If we wish to declare that an operator with a given position, precedence, and associativity is to be recognised when terms are read and written, we use the IF/PROLOG built-in predicate **op(Precedence,OpType,Operator)**, where **Precedence** must be an integer between 0 and 1200. The higher the number, the lower the precedence; **OpType** must be one of the atoms xf, yf, fy, fx, yfx, xfx, xfy; **Operator** is the symbol for the operator itself.

Here we give the declaration of operators involved in FSQL.

> declare :– op(700,xfx,in), op(700,xfx,not_in),
> op(700,xfx,~=), op(700,xfx,>>), op(700,xfx,<<),
> op(930,xfy,and), op(930,xfy,or), op(940,yfx,having),
> op(950,yfx,where), op(950,yfx,with),
> op(960,yfx,group_by), op(970,yfx,from),
> op(970,yfx,set), op(970,yfx,':'), op(980,fx,select),
> op(980,fx,modify), op(980,fx,insert_into),
> op(980,fx,delete), op(990,xfy,union),
> op(990,xfy,intersect), op(990,xfy,difference).

It is important to note how these operators have been defined, since in declarations a little bit of syntactic sugar makes a big difference. All particular query structures will be based on the definition. The precedence comparison of operators with one another is given in Figure 7–3.

It is this declaration that permits the nesting of operators and such nesting may be carried to any depth, so that queries in FSQL could be constructed with arbitrary complexity. By means of the declaration, an FSQL query is internally represented as a function or function form. We shall use "E" to denote the internal representation of an FSQL query "Q". The rules for the translation are illustrated as follows:

Q_1: modify N set Attr = Exp

E_1: modify(set(N,=(Attr,Exp)))

Q_2: modify N set Attr = Exp where Conds

E_2: modify(set(N,where(=(Attr,Exp),Conds)))

Q_3: modify N set Attr = Exp where Conds with Degr

E_3: modify(set(N,where(=(Attr,Exp),with(Conds,Degr))))

Q_4: insert_into N: NewTu

E_4: insert_into(:(N,NewTu))

Q_5: delete N

E_5: delete(N)

Q_6: delete N where Conds

E_6: delete(where(N,Conds))

Q_7: delete N where Conds with Degr

E_7: delete(where(N,with(Conds,Degr)))

Q_8: select Attrs from N

E_8: select(from(Attrs,N))

Q_9: select Attrs from N where Conds

E_9: select(from(Attrs,where(N,Conds)))

Q_{10}: select Attrs from N where Conds with Degr

E_{10}: select(from(Attrs,where(N,with(Conds,Degr))))

Q_{11}: select Attrs from M, N

E_{11}: select(from(Attrs,and(M,N)))

Q_{12}: select Attrs from M, N where Conds

E_{12}: select(from(Attrs,where(and(M,N),Conds)))

Q_{13}: select Attrs from M, N where Conds with Degr

E_{13}: select(from(Attrs,where(and(M,N),with(Conds,Degr))))

Q_{14}:   select Fun(Attr) from N

E_{14}:   select(from(Fun(Attr),N))

Q_{15}:   select Fun(Attr) from N where Conds

E_{15}:   select(from(Fun(Attr),where(N,Conds)))

Q_{16}:   select Fun(Attr) from N where Conds with Degr

E_{16}:   select(from(Fun(Attr),where(N,with(Conds,Degr))))

Q_{17}:   select Attr, Fun from N group_by Attr where Conds

E_{17}:   select(from(and(Attr,Fun),group_by(N,where(Attr,Conds))))

Q_{18}:   select Attr, Fun from N group_by Attr where Conds with Degr

E_{18}:   select(from(AND(Attr,Fun),

               group_by(N,where(Attr,with(Conds,Degr)))))

Q_{19}:   select Attrs from N group_by Attr

E_{19}:   select(from(Attrs,group_by(N,Attr)))

Q_{20}:   select Attrs from N group_by Attr having Fun

E_{20}:   select(from(Attrs,group_by(N,having(Attr,Fun))))

Q_{21}:   select A from M where C1 union select B from N where C2

E_{21}:   union(select(from(A,where(M,C1))),select(from(B,where(N,C2))))

Q_{22}:   select A from M where C1 with D1 union

       select B from N where C2 with D2

E_{22}:   union(select(from(A,where(M,with(C1,D1)))),

               select(from(B,where(N,with(C2,D2)))))

Q_{23}:   select A from M where C1 intersect select B from N where C2

E_{23}:   intersect(select(from(A,where(M,C1))),select(from(B,where(N,C2))))

Q_{24}:   select A from M where C1 with D1 intersect

       select B from N where C2 with D2

E_{24}:   intersect(select(from(A,where(M,with(C1,D1)))),

               select(from(B,where(N,with(C2,D2)))))

Q_{25}:   select A from M where C1 difference select B from N where C2

E_{25}:   difference(select(from(A,where(M,C1))),

   select(from(B,where(N,C2))))

Q_{26}:   select A from M where C1 with D1 difference

       select B from N where C2 with D2

E_{26}:   difference(select(from(A,where(M,with(C1,D1)))),

               select(from(B,where(N,with(C2,D2)))))

Let us look at an example.

Example 7.2

Consider the fuzzy query: Get candidates' names for candidates who are young with the degree of 0.9, or have had higher education, or live in the city company C3 is located in. The query could be expressed in FSQL as follows

SELECT Name FROM   candidates
WHERE Age = $Young WITH 0.9

UNION

SELECT Name FROM   background
WHERE Education = $HE

UNION   (Q7.1)

SELECT Name FROM   candidates
WHERE Address = (SELECT Address
FROM   company
WHERE   Cname = c3)

The internal representation of the query, that is the structure of the query, could be more easily visualized as the tree structure shown in Figure 7–4, where $Young and $HE are possibility distributions of young and higher education respectively.

Since the FSQL parser has a different entry for each possible FSQL query, unacceptable queries can be discarded on the grounds of a mismatch. This technique allows us to resolve query ambiguities with comparatively little effort.

7.4.2 Creation of Variables

The important technique of translating the FSQL function into the canonical logic representation is the creation of variables. Let us now consider how we can create a variable to stand for the values of an attribute specified in an FSQL query, and then the variable can be used to determine possible instantiation states for the attribute. Afterwards, all information about this will be derived from where the variable appears in the canonical logic expression. Basically, the value of a variable can be affected by knowledge about any of the positions in which that variable has appeared. The FSQL parser provides a way of generating such variables.

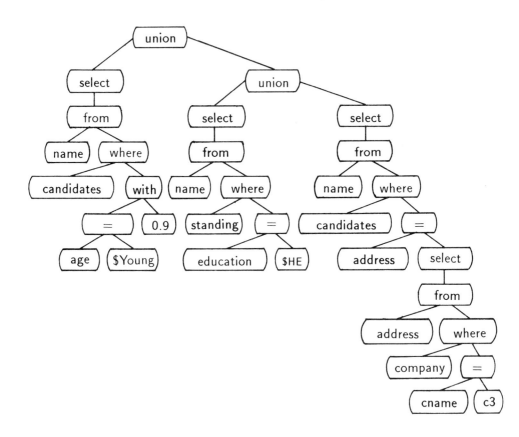

Figure 7–4 The Tree Structure of the Function of (Q7.1)

First of all, the predicate **user_head_xs** creates a set of variables to represent the target list specified in the SELECT statement of the outermost level fuzzy query block, if a retrieval operation is required. In the meantime, it keeps the heading required by the user for formatting the final answer to the query. The set of the variables will form the head H_i of the subquery SUB_i in the canonical logic expression.

In assimilating an FSQL function, we have the problem of dealing with the situation when a new attribute is discovered. If the attribute has been encountered before, then the created variable corresponding to the attribute is a join variable that will appear in the canonical logic form; otherwise, we must ensure that the new variable we assign to it does not accidentally coincide with one representing any other attribute. In both cases, it is important to keep the correspondence between the attributes and the variables. However, it is not always easy to maintain the correspondence. For instance, an extra variable should be introduced if a built-in function has been encountered.

While dealing with an attribute, it is helpful not only to remember whether the corresponding variable is desired by the user but also to understand whether the variable is a join variable or just an independent one. However, there is no need to classify variables into different types in the physical implementation since an FSQL query, with a fixed function or a function form, implies that attributes can be created step by step, while parsing.

Another important implementation technique is to decide when these variables are considered as real variables by the PROLOG system. Because of the fact that variables in PROLOG behave in a very active way, but are taken to be local to each clause (*i.e.* unrelated to variables in other clauses, even when their identifiers might coincide), it is sensible to postpone the conversion for as long as possible, both for the sake of efficiency and correspondence.

7.4.3 The Treatment of Conditions

In general, a fuzzy query block will be translated into a sub-query SUB_i located in the canonical logic form. The most difficult job in parsing an FSQL is to understand the WHERE conditions (and WITH degree) on which the answer to a fuzzy query is to be obtained.

Let us consider the following example:

Example 7.3

SELECT	attri11, attri21
FROM	relation1, relation2
WHERE	relation1.attri11 > relation2.attri21
AND	relation1.attri13 = 5
AND	relation.attri22 IN

      (SELECT   attri31

      FROM   relation3

      WHERE   attri32 = \$Young

      WITH   0.8)

WITH   0.9 ;

It is easy to see that there are three kinds of conditions:

(1) Join conditions. The comparison between two attributes belonging to different relations, such as

relation1.attri11 > relation2.attri21

(2) Chaining conditions. One of chaining operators ("IN", or "=", or "NOT_IN") is used in the comparison in order to select information from one relation based on the contents of another relation, such as

relation2.attri22 IN

    (SELECT attri31 FROM relation3

      WHERE attri32 = \$Young WITH 0.8)

(3) Simple conditions. Comparison with a constant (integer or atom), such as

relation1.attri13 = 5

Specifically, the parser provides a different entry for each possible combination of an arbitrary fuzzy query block specification. There are 13 cases of specification about fuzzy query blocks in our implementation. The recursive processing is accomplished by a matched predicate **get_sub_qs(Spec,Vars,FunDes)** in which the three arguments **Spec**, **Vars**, and **FunDes** must all be given:

Spec: Specification of the fuzzy query block.

Vars: Variables, which are going to match with the target list of the SELECT statement of the block.

FunDes: Function description from the outer level of the block.

What happens at execution time for the predicate **"get_sub_qs"** in dealing with the fuzzy query block is illustrated in Figure 7–5.

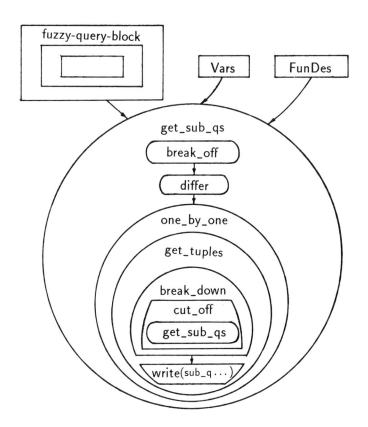

Figure 7–5 Compilation of a Fuzzy Query Block

A top level IF/PROLOG implementation corresponding to the recursive processing (including some necessary explanatory notes) is given below:

THE PARSER OF LANGUAGE FSQL

```
/*    FSQL step 1:   Accept an FSQL Query Into "q"   */

e :- accept_fsql, !, compiler.


accept_fsql :- nl, read_in(X), tell(q), accept(X), told.


accept([]) :- write('.'), nl.
accept([abort]) :-
        tell(q), told, nl,
        display('Please give your query again:'),
        nl, accept_fsql.
accept(X) :- write_into(X), read_in(Y), accept(Y).


write_into([]).
write_into([X|Y]) :- write(X), put(32), write_into(Y).

/*    FSQL step 2: Compiler_1 ---
                   From FSQL to Canonical Logic Form    */

compiler :-
        see(q), read(x), seen, see('/dev/tty'),
        X =.. [F,A|B], tell(que), !, parse(F,A,B),
        told, retractall(current_num(_,_)).

            /*   More than one block:
select ... UNION select ... UNION select ...    */

parse(union,select(A),[B]) :-
        !, user_head_xs(A,Xs), get_sub_qs(A,Xs,!), put(44),
        write('!;'), write(Xs), put(44), !, B =.. [I,J|K],
        sub_parse(I,J,K,Xs), put(44), write('!.'), nl.


sub_parse(select,J,[],Xs) :- !, get_sub_qs(J,Xs,!).
sub_parse(union,select(J),[K],Xs) :-
```

272

```
        get_sub_qs(J,Xs,!), put(44), write('!;'), write(Xs),
        put(44), !, K =.. [U,V|T], sub_parse(U,V,T,Xs).

/*    One block involving insert, delete or modify    */

parse(insert_into,:(N,New),[]) :-
        !, table(N,H), to_list(New,Ms), length(H,M), !,
        length(Ms,M), write(sub_q(N,Ms,[],[],[],asserta)),
        put(44), write('!.'), nl.
parse(modify,set(N,where((S=E,with(Z,D)),[]) :-
        !, gen_sym('X',X), to_list(Z,C), replace(X,S,E,E1),
        get_tuples(N,[S],[X],C,[],[u,X,E1],D),
        put(44), write('!.'), nl.
parse(modify,set(N,where(S=E,Z)),[]) :-
        !, gen_sym('X',X), to_list(Z,C), replace(X,S,E,E1),
        get_tuples(N,[S],[X],C,[],[u,X,E1]),
        put(44), write('!.'), nl.
parse(modify,set(N,S=E),[]) :-
        !, gen_sym('X',X), replace(X,S,E,E1),
        get_tuples(N,[S],[X],[],[],[u,X,E1]),
        put(44), write('!.'), nl.
parse(delete,where(N,with(Z,D)),[]) :-
        !, to_list(Z,C), get_tuples(N,[],[],C,[],retract,D),
        put(44), write('!.'), nl.
parse(delete,where(N,Z),[]) :-
        !, to_list(Z,C), get_tuples(N,[],[],C,[],retract),
        put(44), write('!.'), nl.
parse(delete,N,[]) :-
        !, table(N,H), length(H,M), clear_up(M,[],Ms),
        write(sub_q(N,Ms,[],[],[],retract)),
        put(44), write('!.'), nl.

/*    One block only: both SELECT--x--FROM--y1&y2--type and
                       SELECT--x--FROM--y--type    */

parse(select,A,[]) :-
```

273

```
                user_head_xs(A,Xs), !, get_sub_qs(A,Xs,!),
                put(44), write('!.'), nl.

/*    SELECT X FROM Y1,Y2 WHERE Z WITH D    */

get_sub_qs(from(X,where(and(Y1,Y2),with(Z,D))),Var,!)  :-
            !, to_list(and(Y1,Y2),Names),
            (X == '*', all_headings(Names,Cols); to_list(X,Cols)),
            to_list(Z,Conds), break_off(Cols,Var,Conds,S,V,F,FF,D),
            differ(Names,S,V,F,FF,R), one_by_one(R).

/*    SELECT X FROM Y1,Y2 WHERE Z    */

get_sub_qs(from(X,where(and(Y1,Y2),Z)),Var,!)  :-
            !, to_list(and(Y1,Y2),Names),
            (X == '*', all_headings(Names,Cols); to_list(X,Cols)),
            to_list(Z,Conds), break_off(Cols,Var,Conds,S,V,F,FF),
            differ(Names,S,V,F,FF,R), one_by_one(R).

/*    SELECT X FROM Y1,Y2    */

get_sub_qs(from(X,and(Y1,Y2)),V,!)  :-
            !, to_list(and(Y1,Y2),Names),
            (X == '*', all_headings(Names,Cols); to_list(X,Cols)),
            differ(Names,Cols,V,[],[],R), one_by_one(R).

/*    SELECT AVG(A) FROM N WHERE Z WITH D    */

get_sub_qs(from(X,where(N,with(Z,D))),[V],!)  :-
            functor(X,F,1), !, arg(1,X,A), gen_sym('X',M),
            to_list(Z,C), get_tuples(N,[A],[M],C,[],[F,M,V],D).

/*    SELECT AVG(A) FROM N WHERE Z    */

get_sub_qs(from(X,where(N,Z)),[V],!)  :-
            functor(X,F,1), !, arg(1,X,A), gen_sym('X',M),
            to_list(Z,C), get_tuples(N,[A],[M],C,[],[F,M,V]).

/*    SELECT X FROM N WHERE Z WITH D    */
```

274

```
get_sub_qs(from(X,where(N,with(Z,D)))),V,K)  :-
        !, (X == '*', table(N,S); to_list(X,S)),
        to_list(Z,C), get_tuples(N,S,V,C,[],K,D).

/*   SELECT X FROM N WHERE Z   */

get_sub_qs(from(X,where(N,Z)),V,K)  :-
        !, (X == '*', table(N,S); to_list(X,S)),
        to_list(Z,C), get_tuples(N,S,V,C,[],K).

/*   SELECT  dept,CNT(ename)  FROM  emp  GROUP_BY  dept
     WHERE   salary > 8000    WITH  0.9   */

get_sub_qs(from(and(G,H),
                group_by(N,where(G,with(Z,D))))),[X1,X2],!)  :-
        !, table(N,L), sort(L,[G],[X1],Ms1),
        write(sub_q(N,Ms1,[],[],[X1],[group,X1,X1],D)),
        put(44), functor(H,F,1), arg(1,H,A),
        gen_sym('X',M), to_list(Z,C),
        get_tuples(N,[G,A],[X1,M],C,[],[F,M,X2],D).

/*   SELECT  dept,CNT(ename)  FROM  emp  GROUP_BY  dept
     WHERE   salary>8000    */

get_sub_qs(from(and(G,H),group_by(N,where(G,Z))),[X1,X2],!)  :-
        !, table(N,L), sort(L,[G],[X1],Ms1),
        write(subq(N,Ms1,[],[],[X1],[group,X1,X1])), put(44),
        functor(H,F,1), arg(1,H,A), gen_sym('X',M), to_list(Z,C),
        get_tuples(N,[G,A],[X1,M],C,[],[F,M,X2]).

/*   SELECT S FROM N GROUP_BY G HAVING CNT(DD)>2   */

get_sub_qs(from(S,group_by(N,having(G,C))),[X|Xs],!)  :-
        !, to_list(S,[G|H]), table(N,L), sort(L,[G],[X],Ms1),
        write(sub_q(N,Ms1,[],[],[X],[group,X,X])),
        put(44), C =.. [F,A,B], A =.. [F1,DD],
        gen_sym('X',A1), gen_sym('X',A2),
        F2 =.. [F,A2,B], sort(L,[G,DD],[X,A1],Ms2),
```

```
        write(sub_q(N,Ms2,[],[F2],[X,A1],[F1,A1,A2])),
        to_function(H,Xs,N,L,G,X).

/*   SELECT G,CNT(A1),AVG(A2) FROM N GROUP_BY G   */

get_sub_qs(from(S,group_by(N,G),[X|Xs],!) :-
        to_list(S,[G|F]), table(N,L), sort(L,[G],[X],Ms),
        write(sub_q(N,Ms,[],[],[X],[group,X,X])),
        to_function(H,Xs,N,L,G,X).

/*   SELECT AVG(A) FROM N   */

get_sub_qs(from(X,N),[V],!) :-
        functor(X,F,1), !,    /* built-in function involved */
        arg(1,X,A), gen_sym('X',M),
        get_tuples(N,[A],[M],[],[],[F,M,V]).

/*   SELECT X FROM N}   */

get_sub_qs(from(X,N),V,K) :-
        (X == '*', table(N,S); to_list(X,S)),
        get_tuples(N,S,V,[],[],K).   /* K is '!' or 'not' */

to_function([],_,_,_,_,_) :- !.
to_function([A|B],[X1|Xs],N,L,G,X) :-
        put(44), A =.. [F,D], gen_sym('X',U),
        sort(L,[G,D],[X,U],Ms),
        write(sub_q(N,Ms,[],[],[X,U],[F,U,X1])),
        to_function(B,Xs,N,L,G,X).

/*   Given requested domains X, assert corresponding headings
in the current database and file "que" respectively.   */

user_head_xs(from(X,where(and(Y1,Y2),_)),Xs) :-
        head_xs(X,and(Y1,Y2),Xs).
user_head_xs(from(X,and(Y1,Y2)),Xs) :-
        head_xs(X,and(Y1,Y2),Xs).
user_head_xs(from(X,where(Y,_)),Xs) :-
```

```
          head_xs(X,Y,Xs).
user_head_xs(from(X,group_by(Y,_)),Xs) :-
          head_xs(X,Y,Xs).
user_head_xs(from(X,Y),Xs) :-
          head_xs(X,Y,Xs).
head_xs(X,and(Y1,Y2),Xs) :-
          !, to_list(and(Y1,Y2),Names),
          (X == '*', all_headings(Names,Cols); to_list(X,Cols)),
          (pure(Cols,D), asserta(user_h(D)), length(D,M),
          gen_var('X',M,Xs), write(Xs), put(44).
head_xs(*,N,Xs) :-
          table(N,H), asserta(user_h(H)), length(H,M),
          genvar('X',M,Xs), write(Xs), put(44).
head_xs(X,_,Xs) :-
          to_list(X,S), pure(S,H), asserta(user_h(H)),
          length(H,M), gen_var('X',M,Xs), write(Xs), put(44).

/*  Given a set of table names, obtain all headings each
    of which has its own table name at its beginning.   */

all_headings([],[]).
all_headings([A|B],H) :-
          table(A,H1), modifying(A,H1,H2),
          all_headings(B,H3), append(H2,H3,H).
modifying(_,[],[]).
modifying(A,[X,Y],[@(A,X)|Z) :-
          modifying(A,Y,Z).

/*  In "break_off(Cols,Xs,Conds,S,V,F,FF)",  cols, Xs  and
    Conds are given, S, V, F, FF are required. Here F means
    independent formulae, FF relevant formulae   */

break_off(S,V,[],S,V,[],[],Degr).
break_off(S1,V1,[A|B],S,V,F,[A1|FF],Degr) :-
          /* "A" is a join condition */
          A =.. [I,J,K], J = @(N1,D1), K = @(N2,D2), N1 /== N2, !,
```

```prolog
            (member(K,S1,M), member(Y,V1,M), S2 = S1, V1 = V2;
            gen_sym('X',Y), S2 = [K|S1], V2 = [Y|V1]),
            A1 =.. [I,J,Y], break_off(S2,V2,B,S,V,F,FF,Degr).
break_off(S1,V1,[A|B],S,V,[A|F],FF,Degr) :-
            /* "A" is a non-join condition */
            break_off(S1,V1,B,S,V,F,FF,Degr).
break_off(S,V,[],S,V,[],[]).
break_off(S1,V1,[A|B],S,V,F,[A1|FF]) :-
            /* "A" is a join condition */
            A =.. [I,J,K], J = @(N1,D1), K = @(N2,D2), N1 /== N2, !,
            (member(K,S1,M), member(Y,V1,M), S2 = S1,V1 = V2;
            gen_sym('X',Y), S2 = [K|S1], V2 = [Y|V1]),
            A1 =.. [I,J,Y], break_off(S2,V2,B,S,V,F,FF).
break_off(S1,V1,[A|B],S,V,[A|F],FF) :-
            /* "A" is a non-join condition */
            break_off(S1,V1,B,S,V,F,FF).
equal(N,H) :- table(N,H).
equal(T,H) :- to_list(T,H).

/*    In "differ(Names,S,V,F,FF,R)", Names, S, V, F, and
      FF are given, get R such that [(N1,S1,V1,F1,FF1),
      (N2,S2,V2,F2,FF2),...]. In terms of the table name
      N, to pick up its corresponding S1, V1, F1 and FF1
      from S, V, F, FF, and put the rest of F and FF into
      F2 and FF2 respectively.    */

differ([],_,_,_,_,[]).
differ([N1|N2],S,V,F,FF,[(N1,S1,V1,F1,FF1)|R]) :-
            table(N1,H), pick_s1_v1(N1,H,S,V,S1,V1),
            pick_f(N1,H,FF,FF1,FF2), pick_f(N1,H,F,F1,F2),
            differ(N2,S,V,F2,FF2,R).

/*    In the "pick_s1_v1(N,H,S,V,S1,V1)", given N,S,V,
      get S1 and V1 from S and V in terms of the table
      name N and his heading H.    */
```

```
pick_s1_v1(_,_,[],[],[],[]).
pick_s1_v1(N,H,[@(N,D)|T],[X|Y],[D|U],[X|V]) :-
        pick_s1_v1(N,H,T,Y,U,V).
pick_s1_v1(N,H,[D|T],[X|Y],[D|U],[X|V]) :-
        member(D,HO,pick_s1_v1(N,H,T,Y,U,V).
pick_s1_v1(N,H,[_|T],[_|Y],U,V) :-
        pick_s1_v1(N,H,T,Y,U,V).
pick_f(_,_,[],[],[]).
pick_f(N,H,[A|B],[A1|X],Y) :-
        A =.. [I,@(N,D),K],    /* A belongs to N */
        A1 =.. [I,D,K], pick_f(N,H,B,X,Y).
pick_f(N,H,[A|B],[A|X],Y) :-
        arg(1,A,D), member(D,H),    /* A belongs to N */
        pick_f(N,H,B,X,Y).
pick_f(N,H,[A|B],X,[A|Y]) :-
        pick_f(N,H,B,X,Y).    /* A does not belong to N */
one_by_one([N,S,V,F1,F2,Degr)|[]]) :-
        get_tuples(N,S,V,F1,F2,Degr,!).
one_by_one([(N,S,V,F1,F2,Degr)|B]) :-
        get_tuples(N,S,V,F1,F2,Degr,!),
        put(44), one_by_one(B).
one_by_one([N,S,V,F1,F2)|[]]) :-
        get_tuples(N,S,V,F1,F2,!).
one_by_one([(N,S,V,F1,F2)|B]) :-
        get_tuples(N,S,V,F1,F2,!),
        put(44), one_by_one(B).
get_tuples(N,S,V,C,F2,Sth,Degr) :-
        table(N,H), break_down(S,V,C,Ss,Vs,Fs1,F21,Degr),
        reform_f2(Ss,Vs,F2,Sss,Vss,F22), sort(H,Sss,Vss,Ms),
        append(F21,F22,Fs2), degree(Ms,Var),
        write(sub_q(N,Ms,Fs1,Fs2,Var,Sth,Degr)).
get_tuples(N,S,V,C,F2,Sth) :-
        table(N,H), break_down(S,V,C,Ss,Vs,Fs1,F21),
        reform_f2(Ss,Vs,F2,Sss,Vss,F22), sort(H,Sss,Vss,Ms),
```

```
          append(F21,F22,Fs2), degree(Ms,Var),
          write(sub_q(N,Ms,Fs1,Fs2,Var,Sth)).
```

/*   Given (1) the heading S1 and (2) variables V1 which
      are already involved before, and (3) specified
      conditions Cond, produce (1) a new heading S2, (2)
      variable V2, in which columns or values stated in
      Cond are included, (3) independent formulae Fs1 and
      (4) relevant formulae Fs2. For instance:
      ?-break_down([c,a],[x1,x2],[b>5,c>sth],S2,V2,Fs1,Fs2)
      then: S2=[b,c,a]; V2=[z1,x1,x2]; Fs1=[z1>5];
      Fs2=[x2>sth]. Here sth means to connect to another
      table.   */

```
break_down(S,V,[],S,V,[],[]) :-
          !.              /* boundary condition */
break_down(S1,V1,[A|B],S2,V2,Fs1,Fs2) :-
          A=..[I,J,K], !, Key_point(S1,V1,I,J,K,S,V,F1,F2), !,
          break_down(S,V,B,S2,V2,F12,F22),
          (F1 == !, Fs1 = F12; Fs1 = [F1|F12]),
          (F2 == !, Fs2 = F22; Fs2 = [F2|F22]).
break_down(S,V,[],S,V,[],[],Degr) :-
          !.              /* boundary condition */
break_down(S1,V1,[A|B],S2,V2,Fs1,Fs2,Degr) :-
          A =.. [I,J,K], !, Key_point(S1,V1,I,J,K,S,V,F1,F2), !,
          break_down(S,V,B,S2,V2,F12,F22,Degr),
          (F1 == !, Fs1 = F12; Fs1 = [F1|F12]),
          (F2 == !, Fs2 = F22; Fs2 = [F2|F22]).
key_point(S1,V1,I,J,select(K),S,V,F1,F2) :-
          cut_off(S1,V1,I,J,K,S,V,F1,F2).
key_point(S1,V1,I,J,K,S,V,F1,!) :-
          substitute_1(S1,V1,K,S2,V2,X),
          substitute_2(S2,V2,I,J,X,S,V,F1).
```

/*   "IN" and "="   */

```
cut_off(S,V,in,J,K,S1,V1,!,!) :-
```

```prolog
        to_list(J,L), subst(S,V,L,Xs,S1,V1),
        get_sub_qs(K,Xs,!), put(44).
cut_off(S,V,=,J,K,S1,V1,!,!) :-
        cut_off(S,V,in,J,K,S1,V1,!).

/*    NOT_IN    */

cut_off(S,V,not_in,J,K,S1,V1,!,!) :-
        to_list(J,L), subst(S,V,L,Xs,S1,V1),
        get_sub_qs(K,Xs,not), put(44).

/*    General Chaining    */

cut_off(S1,V1,I,J,K,S,V,F1,F2) :-
        member(J,S1,M), !, member(J1,V1,M),
        gen_sym('X',Y1), get_sub_qs(K,[Y1],!),
        put(44), substitute_2(S1,V1,=,J,J1,S,V,F1),
        F2 =.. [I,J1,Y1].
cut_off(S1,V1,I,J,K,S,V,F1,F2) :-
        !, gen_sym('X',Y1), gen_sym('X',Y2),
        get_sub_qs(K,[Y2],!), put(44),
        substitute_2(S1,V1,=,J,Y1,S,V,F1),
        F2 =.. [I,Y1,Y2].
reform_f2(S,V,[],S,V,[]) :-
        !.              /* boundary condition */
reform_f2(S,V,[A|B],S3,V3,Fs) :-
        A =.. [I,J,K], substitute_1(S,V,K,S1,V1,X),
        substitute_2(S1,V1,I,J,X,S2,V2,F1),
        reform_f2(S2,V2,B,S3,V3,F2),
        (F1 == !, Fs = F2; Fs = [F1|F2]).

/*    Firstly, consider K: given S, V, and K,
      obtain S1, V1, and X.    */

substitute_1(S,V,@(_,K),S,V,X) :-
        member(K,S,M), member(X,V,M).
substitute_1(S,V,@(_,K),[K|S],[X|V],X) :-
```

281

```
        gen_sym('X',X).
substitute_1(S,V,K,S,V,K).
```

```
/*    Secondly, consider I, J and X (new K) together:
      if the main word J happens to exist in S.
      ?-substitute_2([a,b],[x1,x2],>,a,3,S,V,F1)
      then S=[a,b], V=[x1,x2], F1=X1>3.   */
```

```
substitute_2(S,V,I,J,K,S,V,F1) :-
      member(J,S,M), member(J1,V,M),
      !, F1 =.. [I,J1,K].
```

```
/*    Substitute directly. For instance:
        ?-substitute_2([a,b],[x1,x2],=,c,5,S,V,F1)
      then S=[c,a,b],V=[5,x1,x2], F1=!.   */
```

```
substitute_2(S,V,=,J,K,[J|S],[K|V],!) :- !.
```

```
/*    In cond, J is a local one. For example:
        ?-substitute_2([a,b],[x1,x2],>,c,5,S,V,F1,F2)
      then S=[c,a,b]; V=[z1,x1,x2]; F1=z1>5.   */
```

```
substitute_2(S,V,I,J,K,[J|S],[Z,V],F1) :-
      !, gen_sym('X',Z), F1 =.. [I,Z,K].
```

Note that this program is only a part of the FSQL parser involving the three basic techniques of translating the FSQL expression into the canonical logic form. In the program, both the predicate "break_off" and the predicate "break_down" are used to cope with the WHERE statement in a fuzzy query block. The differences between them are as follows:

(a) The predicate "break_off" is used to break off a fuzzy query block in which the FROM statement contains several relations. As a result, by creating join variables, the join conditions specified in the WHERE statement will be replaced by relevant formulae. There are seven arguments associated with the predicate:

break_off(Attrs_1,Vars_1, Conds,Attrs_2,Vars_2,IndeFs,ReleFs,Degr)

Given attributes Attrs_1, variables Vars_1 which match with the attributes, and the conditions Conds specified in the WHERE statement, the predicate "break_off" parses the conditions Conds. The new list of attributes Attr_2 and their corresponding variables Vars_2 will be obtained. All conditions will be classified into independent formulae IndeFs and relevant formulae ReleFs. However, at this stage, the predicate ignores any chaining conditions and treats them as simple ones.

(b)   The predicate "break_down" is only used to break down a fuzzy query block in which the WHERE statement may contain chaining conditions. As a result, by creating join variables, the chaining conditions will be broken down into pseudo-independent formulae and relevant formulae. There are also eight arguments related to the predicate:

break_down(Attrs_1,Vars_1, Conds,Attrs_2,Var_2,IndeFs,ReleFs,Degr)

Given attributes Attrs_1 which have been encountered so far, variables Vars_1 which have been created, and the nonjoin conditions, the new list of attributes Attrs_2 and their corresponding variables Vars_2 will be obtained. All conditions will be classified into independent formulae IndeFs and relevant formulae ReleFs.

The function of the predicate "differ" is that, from the collection of all attributes S, variables V, nonjoin conditions F, and relevant formulae FF, which is the result of the execution of break_off, each relation picks up its own attributes S1, variables V1, nonjoin formulae F1, and relevant formulae FF1 respectively, then puts them into the box R in the particular order:

$$[(N1,S1,V1,F1,FF1),(N2,S2,F2,FF2),\ldots\ldots]$$

The box R will be dealt with by the predicate "one_by_one". As the subgoals of the predicate "one_by_one", the predicate "get_tuples" performs the writing of the query tuple in the canonical logic form. The predicate has seven arguments:

get_tuples(Name,Attrs_1, Vars_1,Conds,ReleFs,FunDes,Degr)

where:

Name	The fuzzy relation name.
Attrs_1	Attributes which have been encountered in the fuzzy relation.
Vars_1	Variables which correspond to attributes Attrs_1.
Conds	Nonjoin conditions (i.e. chaining conditions or simple conditions).
ReleFs	Relevant formulae, probably obtained from "break_off".
FunDes	Function description which may be any form given in Section 7.2.
Degr	Threshold level involved in the fuzzy query.

The relationship among subgoals of the predicate "get_tuples" is shown in Figure 7–6. By means of proper changing and sorting, the canonical form is obtained.

If there exists another nested chaining embedded in the chaining condition then the predicate "get_sub_qs" will be called again and again until the "break_off" and "break_down" processing hits the bottom of the recursion.

Finally, the f-PROLOG version of the original fuzzy query can be obtained from the canonical logic form by using the following IF/PROLOG implementation program.

```
/*   FSQL step 3: Compiler_2 ---
                From Canonical Logic Form to f-PROLOG    */

f_goals :-
        see(que), read(Q), seen, tell(query),
        set_up_a_goal(Q), told.

set_up_a_goal(Q) :-
        write('?-['), write_degr(Q), write(']-answer('),
        write_vars(Q), write(', ('), write_sub_goal(Q),
        write(')).'), nl.
set_up_a_goal((Q1,Q2)) :-
        order((Q1,Q2)), write('.'), nl.
```

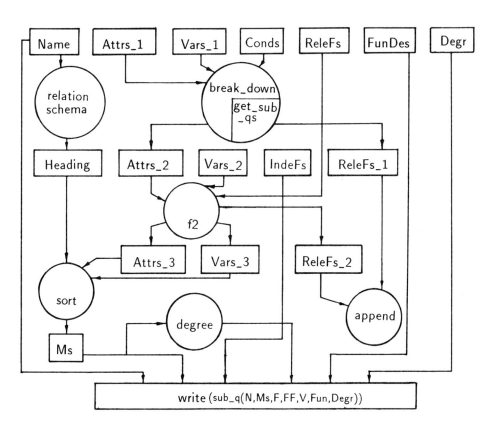

Figure 7–6 The Function of the Predicate "get_tuples".

```
set_up_a_goal((Q1;Q2)) :-
        set_up_a_goal(Q1), set_up_a_goal(Qs).


write_degr(sub_q(_,_,_,_,_,_),!)) :- write('1').
write_degr(sub_q(_,_,_,_,_,D),!) :- write(D).


write_vars(sub_q(N,_,_,_,_,_),!)) :- write(N).
write_vars(sub_q(N,_,_,_,_,_),!)) :- write(N).


write_sub_goal((sub_q(N,Ms,Fs,Fs2,_,Fu),!)) :-
        form_predicate(N,Ms,Fs1,Fu), write_args(Fs2).
write_sub_goal((sub_q(N1,M1,F1,F2,V1,S1),
                            sub_q(N2,M2,F3,F4,V2,S2),!)) :-
        form_predicate(N1,M1,F1,S1), put(44),
        form_predicate(N2,M2,F3,S2), put(44),
        append(F2,F4,F), (F == []; put(44), write_args(F)), !.
write_sub_goal((sub_q(N,Ms,Fs,Fs2,_,Fu,_),!)) :-
        form_predicate(N,Ms,Fs1,Fu), write_args(Fs2).
write_sub_goal((sub_q(N1,M1,F1,F2,V1,S,_1),
                            sub_q(N2,M2,F3,F4,V2,S2,_),!)) :-
        form_predicate(N1,M1,F1,S1), put(44),
        form_predicate(N2,M2,F3,S2), put(44),
        append(F2,F4,F), (F == []; put(44), write_args(F)), !.
write_sub_goal(Q) :-
        remove(Q,A,V,Q1,F2), write_sub_goal(Q1),
        (F2 == []; put(44), write_args(F2)).


write_args([]).
write_args([H|[]]) :-
        (H == #, write('_'); write(H)).
write_args([H|T]) :-
        (H == #, write('_,'); write(H),
        put(44)), write_args(T).
```

286

```
remove(!,_,_,!,_).
remove((T,Q),A,V,R,Fs2)} :-
        T == A, !, T = sub_q(N,Ms,Fs1,Fs2,_,Fu),
        form_predicate(N,Ms,Fs1,Fu), put(44),
        remove(Q,A,V,R,_).
remove((T,Q),A,V,(T1,R),F2) :-
        T = sub_q(N,Ms,Fs1,Fs2,Vs,Fu), subtract(Vs,V,V1),
        T1 = sub_q(N,Ms,Fs1,Fs2,V1,Fu), remove(Q,A,V,R,F2).


form_predicate(N,M,[],!) :-
        write(N), put(40), write_args(M), put(41).
form_predicate(N,M,F,!) :-
        form_predicate(N,M,[],!), write_args(F).
form_predicate(N,M,F,not) :-
        write('not ('), form_predicate(N,M,F,!), put(44).
form_predicate(N,M,[],S) :-
        atom(S),                /* S = asserta; retract */
        write(S), put(40), form_predicate(N,M,[],!), put(41).
form_predicate(N,M,F,retract) :-
        form_predicate(N,M,F,!), put(44),
        form_predicate(N,M,[],retract).
form_predicate(N,M,[],[K,X,G]) :-
        write(K), put(40), write(X), put(44),
        form_predicate(N,M,[],!), put(44), write(G), put(41).
form_predicate(N,M,F,[K,X,G]) :-
        write(K), put(40), write(X), write(',('),
        form_predicate(N,M,F,!), write('),'),
        write(G), put(41).
```

We conclude this chapter with a rather sophisticated example showing the original FSQL query and its canonical logic expression given by the FSQL parser.

Example 7.4

Suppose one wants to list the candidates' names and addresses for each candidate whose age is approximately equal to Smith's with the degree of 0.9. The FSQL expresses the fuzzy query thus:

> SELECT   Name, Address
> FROM   candidates
> WHERE   Age ~=
> >   (SELECT   Age
> >   FROM   candidates
> >   WHERE   Name = smith)
> WITH   0.9 ;

The canonical logic form deduced from the FSQL parser (Compiler_1) is

```
[X1,X3] &
sub_q(candidates,[X1,#,X2,X3],[],[X2 ~= S],[X1,X2,X3],0.9,!) &
sub_q(candidates,[smith,#,S,#],[],[],[S],!)  &
```

It can be seen that the nested fuzzy query is decomposed into a simple collection of fuzzy query tuples in its canonical form. Eventually, we obtain the f-PROLOG expression of the original fuzzy query from the FSQL parser (Compiler_2):

```
?-[0.9]-answer((X1,X3),
              (candidates(X1,_,X2,X3),
               candidates(smith,_,S,_),
               X2 ~= S)).
```

Chapter 8

THE TREATMENT OF INCOMPLETE INFORMATION AND SOFT CONSTRAINTS IN THE FPDB SYSTEM

In this chapter, we first examine the question of incomplete information in the FPDB system. We begin by defining the notions UNDECIDED, UNDEFINED and NULL, where UNDECIDED and UNDEFINED are regarded as special possibility distributions, and go on to discuss them, especially NULL values, in detail. Then we investigate consistency and soft integrity constraints in the FPDB system by means of examples expressed in FSQL.

8.1 Open and Closed World Assumptions

Some assumptions are often made when designing or using a database system. When representing fuzzy information in a fuzzy relational database system, two assumptions are possible: open and closed world assumptions.

(a) The 'open world assumption' corresponds to the fuzzy logic approach
to query evaluation: Given a fuzzy relational database and a query, the
only answers to the query are those which are obtained from proofs
of the query given database as hypotheses. With this definition we
could represent negative information explicitly, for example, by adding
assertions of form "not(P)".

(b) The 'closed world assumption' states that, if a tuple t of a relation R is
known, then it must be a member of R. Under this assumption, certain
answers are admitted as a result of failure to find a proof. More specifically, the notion of negative facts is accommodated by the definition
of satisfaction which states that $S_f \implies \neg A$ **iff** it is not the case that
$S_f \implies A$, where A is an atomic formula.

The appropriateness and formulation of these two assumptions depend on
the application, on the type of database system and on the database designer's
understanding of what the assumptions mean. The second approach presupposes
a complete knowledge of the domain being represented. For many fields of
application, this assumption is appropriate. For example, it is natural to assume
that the candidates named in the table **candidates** are the only candidates
there are. For such domains, an implicit representation is usually preferable, as
negative information generally out-numbers by far the positive information, and
it would be redundant to represent it explicitly when it can simply be established
by default.

8.2   Extension of the Sample Database

We have stated that a key aspect of the fuzzy relational database is that attribute
values need not be atomic. An attribute value d_{ij}, where i is the tuple index,
can be a subset of its domain set, D_j.

In the FPDB system, each fuzzy relation allows not only precise atomic values,
but also possibility distributions, particularly UNDECIDED, UNDEFINED,
and NULL as attribute values, for representing and manipulating fuzzy and

incomplete information. Fuzzy attribute values have been studied in the preceding chapters. To examine incomplete information in this chapter, we extend the "job-information-centre" database as shown in Figure 8–1:

candidates			
Name	**Sex**	**Age**	**Address**
Smith	Male	30	Newcastle
John	Male	ABOUT 28	Carlisle
Anna	Female	22	Penrith
Mary	Female	$Middle-aged	Carlisle
Jill	Female	30	Penrith
Susan	Female	ABOUT 28	Darlington
Tom	Male	24	Carlisle
Harry	Male	36	Darlington
Fred	Male	ABOUT 25	Darlington
Margaret	Female	20	Penrith
Andrew	Male	24	Carlisle
Barry	Male	33	Newcastle
Thomas	Male	31	Darlington
Martin	Male	$Young	Newcastle
Henry	Male	29	Penrith
Robert	Male	UNDECIDED	Newcastle
George	Male	$Young	NULL

background				
Name	**Education**	**Profession**	**Experience**	**Hobby**
Smith	University	Manager	2	Travelling
John	High-school	Assistant	6	Sports
Anna	High-school	Secretary	3	Singing
Mary	University	Technician	$Long	Cooking
Jill	Post-graduate	Manager	4	Travelling
Susan	University	Manager	1	Painting
Tom	University	Engineer	1	Singing
Harry	University	Manager	7	Reading
Fred	University	Technician	5	Sports
Margaret	High-school	Secretary	1	Dancing
Andrew	University	Engineer	2	Singing
Barry	Post-graduate	Engineer	6	Sports
Thomas	Post-graduate	Manager	3	Fishing
Martin	University	Engineer	2	Dancing
Henry	University	Clerk	8	Fishing
Robert	Post-graduate	Manager	UNDECIDED	NULL
George	UNDEFINED	UNDEFINED	UNDEFINED	NULL

ability				
Name	Intelligence	Initiative	SocialMaturity	Skill
Smith	VERY Good	Excellent	Excellent	VERY Good
John	FAIRLY Good	Good	VERY Good	Good
Anna	Good	VERY Good	Excellent	Good
Mary	VERY Good	Good	Good	Moderate
Jill	Excellent	Moderate	VERY Good	VERY Good
Susan	Good	VERY Good	VERY Good	Good
Tom	Moderate	Bad	Moderate	VERY Good
Harry	VERY Good	Moderate	Good	Good
Fred	Moderate	FAIRLY Good	Excellent	Bad
Margaret	Good	Moderate	Good	Bad
Andrew	Good	VERY Good	Moderate	Moderate
Barry	Good	Good	FAIRLY Good	Good
Thomas	Excellent	Good	Excellent	Moderate
Martin	Good	Moderate	Good	VERY Good
Henry	Moderate	Good	Good	Moderate
Robert	NULL	NULL	NULL	NULL
George	Bad	NULL	NULL	Bad

body			
Name	**Health**	**Height**	**Looks**
Smith	Good	$Tall	Good
John	Good	ABOUT 175	Good
Anna	Good	ABOUT 170	Good
Mary	Good	165	VERY Good
Jill	Good	174	Moderate
Susan	Moderate	$Short	Moderate
Tom	VERY Good	180	Moderate
Harry	Moderate	185	Good
Fred	Good	178	FAIRLY Good
Margaret	Good	170	Good
Andrew	VERY Good	$Short	Good
Barry	Good	169	FAIRLY Good
Thomas	Moderate	190	Moderate
Martin	VERY Good	171	Good
Henry	Good	173	Moderate
Robert	Good	$Tall	Moderate
George	NULL	ABOUT 170	Good

(1)   Information about Candidates

company				
Cname	**Location**	**President**	**Employees**	**Profit**
C1	Newcastle	David	400	300,000
C2	Carlistle	Edward	100	100,000
C3	Penrith	Felix	2000	1,000,000
C4	Darlington	Alice	800	NULL

job			
Position	**Cname**	**Salary**	**Benefits**
Manager	C1	12000	Good
Manager	C2	10000	VERY Good
Manager	C3	8000	Moderate
Manager	C4	10000	Bad
Engineer	C1	9000	Good
Engineer	C2	9000	Good
Engineer	C3	8000	Moderate
Engineer	C4	9000	Bad
Secretary	C1	7000	VERY Good
Secretary	C2	7000	Good
Secretary	C3	6000	Good
Secretary	C4	5000	Moderate
Technician	C1	6000	Moderate
Technician	C2	5000	Good
Technician	C3	4500	Moderate
Technician	C4	7000	Bad
Clerk	C1	7000	Moderate
Clerk	C2	7000	Moderate
Clerk	C3	6000	Moderate
Clerk	C4	5000	Bad
Assistant	C1	6000	Good
Assistant	C2	5000	FAIRLY Good
Assistant	C3	3000	Moderate
Assistant	C4	5000	Moderate

(2)   Information about Companies

relationship		
Name1	**Name2**	**Type**
Smith	Anna	Couple
Smith	Susan	Friend
Smith	Fred	Friend
Smith	Henry	Friend
Andrew	Smith	Friend
Barry	Smith	Friend
John	Smith	Friend
Anna	Mary	Friend
Tom	Susan	Couple
Jill	Harry	Friend
Thomas	Henry	Friend
Tom	Martin	Friend
Henry	Margaret	Friend
Harry	Anna	Friend
David	John	Relative
David	Margaret	Relative
Felix	Anna	Relative
Alice	Martin	Relative
Alice	Robert	NULL

location		
City1	**City2**	**Distance**
Newcastle	Carlisle	ABOUT 60
Newcastle	Penrith	45
Newcastle	Darlington	40
Carlisle	Penrith	23
Carlisle	Darlington	$Near
Penrith	Darlington	52

(3) Environment

Figure 8–1 The Extended Version of the
Job-information-centre Database

8.3 UNDECIDED and UNDEFINED as Possibility Distributions

We have two special possibility distributions which are well worth notice. One is a possibility distribution whose $\Pi_A(X)$ is identical to unity, *i.e.*

$$\pi_{A(X)}(u) = 1, \qquad \forall u \in \Omega \tag{8.1}$$

which is called UNDECIDED since it is possible that $A(X)$ could be any value in Ω and we cannot obtain any more information about $A(X)$ from the possibility distribution whose $\Pi_{A(X)}$ is identical to zero, *i.e.*

$$\pi_{A(X)}(u) = 0, \qquad \forall u \in \Omega \tag{8.2}$$

which is referred to as UNDEFINED because there is no possibility that the value of $A(X)$ could exist in the universe of discourse Ω.

These possibility distributions mentioned above are shown in Figure 8–2.

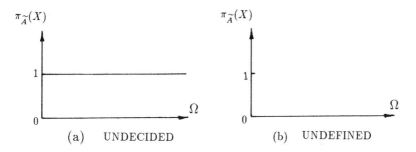

Figure 8–2   Possibility Distributions of Incomplete
Information: UNDECIDED and UNDEFINED

8.4 UNDECIDED, UNDEFINED and NULL as Attribute Values

Why do we need the concept of an UNDECIDED, UNDEFINED or NULL value? The short answer is that real-world information is frequently incomplete, and we need some way of handling such incompleteness in our formal system.

In fuzzy databases, the idea of incomplete information has most often been captured by the use of a value called NULL, usually interpreted as a value unknown to the database. The initial discussions of NULL values by Codd took the NULL value to mean unknown, *i.e.* any one of the values of the entire attribute domain [Codd, 1975]; it was similar to the UNDECIDED which we defined in the last section. Lipski extended the idea of Codd's NULL value by considering that a value though unknown is a specific subset of the universe of discourse [Lipski, 1979]. By allowing nonatomic values in the relational data model, Grant represents incomplete numeric and non-numeric data [Grant, 1979, 1980]. If the range of an unknown numeric item is known, then the pair of numbers representing the range is used.

However, it should be possible to represent situations of UNDEFINED, absolutely unknown and so on. For this reason, we present an approach dividing incomplete attribute values into three types: UNDECIDED, UNDEFINED and NULL.

We proceed to explain the attributes UNDECIDED and UNDEFINED. In the extended version of the "job-information-centre" database (see Figure 8–1), the value UNDECIDED in the attribute Age (see table **candidates**) means that we know Robert has an age, *i.e.* he is alive, but we do not know how old he is. Also for Robert, the value UNDECIDED in the attribute Experience (see table **background**) represents that he had experience of being manager, but we do not know how long it was. On the other hand, in the table **background**, the value UNDEFINED is permitted. For George, the value UNDEFINED in the attribute Education, Profession and Experience represents that he hasn't got any education, he is the jobless, and has no work experience, respectively.

Different from those, in the FPDB system, the NULL value means absolutely unknown, that is, we do not know even whether the attribute value is defined or not. For instance, in the extended version of the "job-information-centre" database (see Figure 8–1), NULL values in the attribute Hobby (see table **background**) mean that we do not know whether Robert and George have a hobby or not.

8.5 Handling UNDECIDED, UNDEFINED and NULL Values in FSQL

We have stated that not all the attributes in the FPDB system contain completely known values; some may be UNDECIDED, UNDEFINED or NULL. This section therefore presents a framework for dealing with them. It describes how UNDECIDED, UNDEFINED and NULL values affect expressions and aggregate functions; how to search for them; and how FSQL orders rows with them.

8.5.1 NULL Values in Expressions and Functions

When an expression or individual function refers to a column that contains a NULL value, the result may also be NULL.

First, let **op** denote any one of the comparison operators $=$, $/ =$, $<$, $>$, $=<$, $>=$, $>>$, $<<$, and $\tilde{} =$. What is the result of evaluating the comparison "x **op** y" if x or y, or both, happen to be NULL? Since by definition NULL represents absolutely unknown, we define the result in every case to be absolutely unknown (*i.e.* NULL) also, rather than truth values in the interval $[0, 1]$. To deal with NULL values properly, therefore, it is necessary to develop a revised version of the usual fuzzy logic in the FPDB system. It is our opinion that the absolutely unknown or NULL truth-value (ϕ for short) can reasonably be interpreted as "maybe."

It is an immediate consequence of the foregoing definition that the comparison "x **op** y" (**op** is one of the operators $=$, $/ =$, $<$, $>$, $=<$, $>=$, $>>$, $<<$, and $\tilde{} =$) evaluates to NULL if x or y or both happen to be NULL; *i.e.* the value of "NULL **op** NULL" is NULL rather than truth value 1. It follows that, taking **op** as equality, the comparison "$x = x$" does not necessarily yield the truth value 1, but may be absolutely unknown (*i.e.* NULL).

Similarly, if we let op denote any one of the arithmetic operators $+$, $-$, $*$, $/$, and let x and y denote two numerical values (or NULL), then the value of the arithmetic expression "x **op** y" is defined to be NULL if x is NULL or y is NULL or both. Unary $+$ and $-$ are treated analogously, *i.e.* if x is NULL, then $+x$ and $-x$ are also considered to be NULL. To illustrate how NULL values affect expressions, we present several examples below.

Example 8.1

Select all candidates who have a hobby of sports.

[**In FSQL**]

SELECT	Name
FROM	background
WHERE	Hobby = sports
WITH	F ;

[**In f-PROLOG**]

?–[F]–answer(Name ,
              (background(Name,_,_,_,sports))).

[**Result**]

Name	
John	1
Fred	1
Barry	1
Robert	ϕ
George	ϕ

Example 8.2

List per capita profit for each company.

[**In FSQL**]

SELECT	Cname, Employees, Profit, Profit/Employees
FROM	company ;

[**In f-PROLOG**]

?–answer((Cname,Employees,Profit,Profit/Employees),
          (company(Cname,_,_,Employees,Profit))).

[**Result**]

Cname	Employees	Profit	Profit/Employees
C1	400	300,000	750
C2	100	100,000	1000
C3	2000	1,000,000	500
C4	800	NULL	NULL

The expression Profit/Employees returns a NULL value for all companies who have a NULL profit (C4 in Example 8.2).

Aggregate functions that refer to NULL values do not simply return NULL values. In fact, NULL values are always eliminated from the argument to an FSQL built-in function such as SUM or AVG, except for the case of CNT(*), which counts all tuples including all-null tuples (every attribute value appearing in the tuples is NULL). Indeed, the SUM function, for example, is not truly a function that sums all the values in its argument; that is, the function reference SUM(Atr) is not semantically equivalent to the expression

$$a_1 + a_2 + \cdots + a_n$$

where a_1, a_2, ..., a_n are the values appearing in the attribute Atr at the time the function is evaluated.

Example 8.3

Find the sum, average of the profits of all companies appearing in the table **company.**

[In FSQL]

> SELECT SUM(Profit), AVG(Profit), CNT(*)
> FROM company ;

[In f-PROLOG]

> ?–answer((SUM,AVG,CNT),
>   (sum(Profit,company(_,_,_,_,Profit),SUM),
>   avg(Profit,company(_,_,_,_,Profit),AVG),
>   cnt(*,company(_,_,_,_,_),CNT))).

[Result]

SUM(Profit)	AVG(Profit)	CNT(*)
1,400,000	466,666.67	4

We see that, in the FPDB system, there is no guarantee that

$$AVG(X) = SUM(X)/CNT(*)$$

where X is an attribute name. For instance, in Example 8.3, AVG(Profit) is equal to SUM(Profit)/3 rather that SUM(Profit)/4, since there are three non-null values appearing in the column Profit.

As a special case, it is necessary to address the question of what would happen if the argument to a built-in function happens to be the empty set. In the case of CNT the result should clearly be zero; but what about the other functions? An aggregate function such as SUM or AVG may be applied to some attribute of some fuzzy relation, and that relation happens to be empty. For example, taking the query "List all companies for which the average employee salary is much greater than 5000 with the degree of 0.8," and consider what the system should do if it encounters a company that currently has no employees. FSQL takes the position that the result should be NULL in all cases other than CNT.

8.5.2 UNDECIDED and UNDEFINED in Expressions and Functions

We are now in a position to examine how UNDECIDED and UNDEFINED values affect expressions. For convenience in this discussion, we ignore NULL values, since we have stated that the result of an expression involving NULL values is also NULL.

Quite similarly, let op denote any one of the comparison operators ($=$, $/=$, $<$, $>$, $=<$, $>=$, $>>$, $<<$, and $~=$) or arithmetic operators ($+$, $-$, $*$, $/$). What is the result of evaluating the comparison "x op y" if x or y, or both, happen to be UNDECIDED or UNDEFINED?

According to the definitions of UNDECIDED and UNDEFINED themselves, FSQL takes the position that the result in every case is UNDECIDED/UNDEFIN if the expression contains UNDECIDED /UNDEFINED only, whereas the result in every case is NULL if the expression contains both UNDECIDED and UNDEFINED values.

To deal with UNDECIDED and UNDEFINED values properly, the fuzzy logic used in the FPDB system should be further developed; that is, we use "?" and "θ" to denote UNDECIDED and UNDEFINED respectively.

Example 8.4

Retrieve the name, sex, age, and education of all candidates who have ever been managers for over two years.

[**In FSQL**]

SELECT	Name, Sex, Age, Education
FROM	candidates, background
WHERE	Profession = manager
AND	Experience > 2
WITH	F ;

[**In f-PROLOG**]

```
?-[F]-answer((Name,Sex,Age,Education),
        (candidates(Name,Sex,Age,_),
        background(Name,Education,manager,Experience,_),
        Experience > 2)).
```

[**Result**]

Name	Sex	Age	Education	
Jill	Female	30	Post-graduate	1
Susan	Female	ABOUT 28	University	0.53
Harry	Male	36	University	1
Thomas	Male	31	Post-graduate	1
Robert	Male	UNDECIDED	Post-graduate	?

To aggregate functions, UNDECIDED and UNDEFINED values are treated as the same as NULL values in the calculations.

8.5.3 Search for UNDECIDED, UNDEFINED and NULL Values

We now introduce some additional functions to assist in searching for UNDECIDED, UNDEFINED and NULL values. First, it is necessary to define a truth-valued function IS_NULL.

Definition 8.1

IS_NULL is a truth-valued function in binary logic, whose argument is an arbitrary scalar expression involving attribute names (which can be qualified when necessary) and whose value is true (1) if that argument evaluates to NULL and false (0) otherwise.

To search for rows that contain NULL values in an attribute, we can use the WHERE statement of FSQL containing the condition "Attribute IS NULL" which is equivalent to the expression IS_NULL(Attribute).

Example 8.5

Display the background of all candidates whose hobby is absolutely unknown (NULL).

[In FSQL]

        SELECT   Name, Education, Profession, Experience, Hobby
        FROM   background
        WHERE   Hobby IS NULL ;

or

            SELECT   *
            FROM   background
            WHERE   Hobby IS NULL ;

[In f-PROLOG]

    ?–answer((Name,Education,Profession,Experience,Hobby),
          (background(Name,Education,Profession,Experience,Hobby),
          is_null(Hobby))).

or

    ?–answer(* ,
          (background(Name,Education,Profession,Experience,Hobby),
          is_null(Hobby))).

[Result]

Name	Education	Profession	Experience	Hobby
Robert	Post-graduate	Manager	UNDECIDED	NULL
George	UNDEFINED	UNDEFINED	UNDEFINED	NULL

Note that NULL values do not satisfy any condition other than IS NULL. That is why the user could not use the condition "Hobby = NULL" in the above example. In fact, the WHERE statement "WHERE Attribute = NULL" is illegal in FSQL.

Analogous to the function IS_NULL, the truth-valued functions IS_UNDECIDED and IS_UNDEFINED can be defined as follows.

Definition 8.2

IS_UNDECIDED (IS_UNDEFINED) is a truth-valued function in binary logic, whose argument is an arbitrary scalar expression involving (qualified or unqualified) attribute names and whose value is true (1) if that argument evaluates to UNDECIDED (UNDEFINED) and false (0) otherwise.

We present two examples to illustrate how to use the special functions: IS_UNDECIDED and IS_UNDEFINED.

Example 8.6

Show the background of all candidates whose age is unknown.

[In FSQL]

```
SELECT    Name, Education, Profession, Experience, Hobby
FROM      candidates, background
WHERE     IS_UNDECIDED(Age) ;
```

[In f-PROLOG]

```
?-answer((Name,Education,Profession,Experience,Hobby),
        (candidates(Name,_,Age,_),is_undecided(Age),
        background(Name,Education,Profession,Experience,Hobby))).
```

[Result]

Name	Education	Profession	Experience	Hobby
Robert	Post-graduate	Manager	UNDECIDED	NULL

Example 8.7

Retrieve the name, age, education and address of all candidates who were definitely unemployed.

[In FSQL]

SELECT	Name, Age, Education, Address
FROM	candidates, background
WHERE	IS_UNDEFINED(Profession) ;

[In f-PROLOG]

```
?–answer((Name,Age,Education,Address),
    (candidates(Name,_,Age,Address),
    background(Name,Education,Profession,_,_),
    is_undefined(Profession))).
```

[Result]

Name	Age	Education	Address
George	$Young	UNDEFINED	NULL

Keep in mind that the WHERE statements "WHERE Attribute = UNDECIDE" and "WHERE Attribute = UNDEFINED" are also illegal in FSQL.

8.5.4 Ordering Rows With UNDECIDED, UNDEFINED and NULL Values

When we use an ORDER_BY statement to sort columns (hard or softly) that contain incomplete information, such as UNDECIDED, UNDEFINED and NULL values, the NULL entries are always displayed first when they exist; the UNDEFIN entries are displayed second, and then the UNDECIDED entries are displayed, regardless of whether one specifies ascending or descending order.

Example 8.8

Get a table which consists of all companies, each one with its number of employees and its profit, ordered by the profits.

[In FSQL]

```
SELECT        Cname, Employees, Profit
FROM          company
ORDER_BY      Profit ;
```

[In f-PROLOG]

```
?-answer((Cname,Employees,Profit),
         (company(C,_,_,E,P),
          order(3,(C,E,P),(Cname,Employees,Profit)))).
```

[Result]

Cname	Employees	Profit
C4	800	NULL
C2	100	100,000
C1	400	300,000
C3	2000	1,000,000

Example 8.9

Get a table which consists of all candidates who live in Newcastle, each one with his/her age and hobby, ordered by the ages.

[In FSQL]

```
SELECT        Name, Age, Hobby
FROM          candidates, background
WHERE         candidates.Name = background.Name
AND           Address = newcastle
ORDER_BY      Age ;
```

[In f-PROLOG]

```
?-answer((Name,Age,Hobby),
         (background(N,_,_,_,H),
          candidates(N,_,A,newcastle),
          order(2,(N,A,H),(Name,Age,Hobby)))).
```

Name	Age	Hobby
Robert	UNDECIDED	NULL
Martin	$Young	Dancing
Smith	30	Travelling
Barry	33	Sports

8.6 Consistency and Soft Constraints in the FPDB System

We say that a fuzzy relational database is in a consistent state if it satisfies a collection of explicit fuzzy logical conditions which are called soft integrity constraints or fuzzy constraints. Some general types of soft constraints have been discussed which have to do with fuzzy functional dependencies and keys, aggregation, and so on. In addition, there are many other types of soft constraint which are specified by fuzzy logic expressions like the ones which appear in the WHERE statement of the fuzzy query block. In the FPDB system, soft integrity constraints are effectively checked after execution of each FSQL statement. If the base relation associated with an integrity constraint does not satisfy that constraint, then the FSQL statement has no effect. Let us consider several simple examples by using FSQL specifications.

Suppose that, in addition to the base relations specified in the "job-inform-ation-centre" database, the database also contains (at least temporarily) the relation **employee_c1(Name,Position,Education,Salary)** which consists of all employees of company C1 selected from the table **candidates**. We have

Example 8.10

The average value of salaries of all employees who have higher education is greater than the average value of salaries of all employees who have only high-school education. In FSQL this soft constraint is specified as follows:

```
ASSERT    CHECK_AVG  ON employee_c1 :
WHERE     (SELECT  AVG(Salary)
          FROM     employee_c1
          WHERE    Education  IN  (university,post-graduate))
               >  (SELECT   AVG(Salary)
                   FROM      employee_c1
                   WHERE     Education = high-school) ;
```

Example 8.11

Secretaries in company C1 must have higher education and must be young with
the degree of 0.9. The FPDB system specifies the soft constraints in terms of
FSQL as follows:

```
ASSERT    CHECK  ON employee_c1 :
WHERE     (SELECT  Name
          FROM     employee_c1
          WHERE    Position = secretary)  IN
                       (SELECT   Name
                        FROM      candidates, background
                        WHERE     Education = $HE
                        AND       Age = $Young
                        WITH      0.9) ;
```

Example 8.12

Each manager's age is less than the average value of all other employees in
company C1 with the degree of VERY possible. In FSQL, this soft constraint
is specified as:

```
ASSERT    CHECK_AVG  ON employee_c1 :
WHERE     (SELECT    Age
          FROM       employee_c1, candidates
          WHERE      employee_c1.Name = candidates.Name
          AND        Position = mamager) <
                     (SELECT    AVG(Age)
                     FROM       employee_c1,candidates
                     WHERE      employee_c1.Name =̇
                                candidates.Name
                     AND        Position /= manager)
WITH      VERY possible ;
```

Example 8.13

In company C1, the president's relatives will not be employed. In FSQL it is
specified as:

```
ASSERT    CHECK  ON employee_c1 :
WHERE     employee_c1.Name  NOT_IN
          (SELECT    Name1
          FROM       employee_c1, relationship
          WHERE      Type = relative
          AND        Name2 =
                     (SELECT    President
                     FROM       company
                     WHERE      Cname = c1)
          UNION
          (SELECT    Name2
          FROM       employee_c1, relationship
          WHERE      Type = relative
          AND        Name1 =
                     (SELECT    President
                     FROM       company
                     WHERE      Cname = c1)
```

From now on, we discuss consistency by introducing the concept of an FPDB
transaction.
```
```

A user interacts with the FPDB system specifying a sequence of FSQL statements which may be fuzzy queries or database updates. Such a sequence of actions is called an FPDB transaction (transaction for short) that the FPDB system treats as a single entity. It transforms one consistent database state into another database state which is also consistent. If a transaction does not have this property all its updates of the database are rejected. More specifically, FPDB ensures data consistency based on transactions: for every transaction, all of its operations are completed (made permanent in the database) or none of the operations are. If a system or user program (query or update expression) fails while a transaction is in progress, the database is automatically restored to the state it was in prior to the transaction starting.

For example, if money is to be deducted from one account and added to another account, then both updates should either succeed together or fail together. If an error occurs making the updates, neither update is made.

When a user's program fails, FPDB restores the data after detecting the error. When the operating system fails, the data are restored when FPDB is restarted.

A transaction may range from all the operations on the database for an entire program to a single FSQL update statement (INSERT, DELETE, or MODIFY). In many programs it is practical to divide the operations of a user's program into subsets of transactions. In these programs, the FSQL commands BEGIN_TRANSACTION and END_TRANSACTION are used to finish one transaction and begin another. The former makes the changes "permanent" and the later "undoes" all changes made in that transaction.

Example 8.14

The following is a transaction consisting of two update actions:

```
BEGIN_TRANSACTION
    DELECT    employee_c1
    WHERE     Position = manager
    AND       Name  IN
                    (SELECT    Name
                     FROM      employee_c1, candidates
                     WHERE     employee_c1.Name = candidates.Name
                     AND       Age =< 25
                     WITH      0.9) ;
    MODIFY    employee_c1
    SET       Salary = Salary * 1.1
    WHERE     Education = post-graduate
END_TRANSACTION
```

Chapter 9

APPLICATIONS OF THE FPDB SYSTEM

Database technology is one of the most significant features of the transition in computer applications: from "data processing" to "information processing" and eventually to "knowledge processing".

Applications of fuzzy relational databases may already be found in many different areas. From the viewpoint of system engineering, in the present chapter we demonstrate some principal fields of application of the FPDB system concerned with knowledge representation, decision making, expert systems, fuzzy control, fuzzy clustering and information retrieval (see Figure 9–1).

Now a summary is provided in order to give an assortment of particular, real world, applications where fuzzy relational databases have been utilized.

Knowledge Representation	Decision Making	Expert System	Fuzzy Control	Fuzzy Clustering and Information Retrieval
The FPDB Database System				

Figure 9–1   The Principal Applications of the FPDB System

In the initial section, some issues on knowledge representation will be discussed. We state that FPDB is a useful tool to manage large collections of fuzzy knowledge.

Section 9.2 examines the FPDB application in the area of decision making.

In discussing the framework of a decision making system, we will survey the behaviour of personnel evaluation as an example. In fact, there are many extensions of this application to scientific and commercial environments, such as policy preferences, medical decision making, economic forecasting, and so on. For instance, imagine a corporation that plans to establish an office or division at a new location. It is often the policy of corporations to select or transfer employees to establish a core group which is then augmented by new employees. The corporation goals are to select or transfer employees that will be of most benefit to the new organization and least disrupt their previous organization.

In Section 9.3, we examine the applicability of the FPDB system to building expert systems in the realm of analysis of manual lifting tasks. We will say that a great many applications of expert systems are in the fields of medical diagnosis, petroleum prospecting, pattern recognition, scientific analysis, financial management, engineering design, electronic trouble shooting, risk and damage assessment, and military defence systems, *etc.*

We also explore the use of the FPDB system for supporting fuzzy control systems, in Section 9.4. In this vein we will describe an experimental fuzzy control system for supporting traffic control of an expressway. There is no doubt that many other applications such as robotics control, feedback control systems, water purification process and boiler control, *etc.* can be handled with a similar approach.

One of the most immediate applications of the FPDB system, fuzzy clustering and information retrieval, will be discussed in Section 9.5. In this section, we will examine the "job-information-centre" database once again to discuss the usage of fuzzy clustering in FPDB. In our opinion, the FPDB system can be used directly as a library management system or other information retrieval system to improve retrieval efficiency.

Apart from those mentioned above, some potential applications of the FPDB system concern the following fields: artificial intelligence, image processing, biological sciences, geography, sociology, psychology, linguistics, semiotics, especially humane studies, soft science and some more restricted topics.

9.1 Knowledge Representation

A representation is defined as a set of conventions for describing things. Most people working in artificial intelligence agree that designing a good representation is one of the keys to solving difficult problems.

Knowledge is the symbolic representation of aspects of some named universe of discourse. It is generally of three types: facts, rules of good judgment (heuristics), and evaluations. Much problem-solving knowledge can be represented in the form of structures. Various knowledge representation approaches including natural language, logic (*e.g.*, formal logic, fuzzy logic, modal logic, *etc.*), production rules, networks and frames have been investigated. In fact, anyone desiring to create a knowledge base, regardless of the specific domain involved, must deal with the most fundamental problem: how do we represent human knowledge in terms of data structures that a machine can process?

To solve the problem, we must satisfy the modular requirement. During the development of the knowledge base, experts are unlikely to present all the facts and relationships necessary for expert performance in the domain. Being human, experts tend to forget or to simplify details about their knowledge, and the systems must augment their knowledge at a later time. Because knowledge imparted to the system is largely empirical and because knowledge in the domains is developing rapidly, systems need to make changes easily and in an incremental or modular fashion.

Thus, the knowledge system will support a high-level representation language whose primitive elements are the attributes and associations of a particular domain problem. In this section, we are concerned mainly with the use of the FPDB system.

We have mentioned that the relational approach to the representation of knowledge in computer systems was first developed by Codd [Codd, 1970]. However, knowledge engineering is a discipline devoted to integrating human knowledge in computer systems. A great deal of human knowledge is usually derived in fuzzy linguistic form from experts. In many fields, rules encoding chunks of knowledge are not totally certain most of the time, and make use of fuzzy predicates or categories in their expression. For this reason, a basic issue in the design of database or knowledge base is how to equip them with a capability for

315

treating fuzziness and uncertainty. The theory and techniques of fuzzy relational databases, particularly the FPDB system, offer a way to incorporate subjective evaluations in the fuzzy relational knowledge base, in which a linguistic variable differs from a numerical variable in that its values are not numbers but words. In our opinion the FPDB database system is a tool to achieve the goal of having manipulable natural language expressions.

Various advantages are claimed for the fuzzy relational approach compared with the use of others. For example:

(1) Due to the similarity between FPDB relations and mathematical fuzzy relations, well-defined operations from fuzzy relational theory can be used to process fuzzy relational knowledge bases. Such operations include fuzzy selection, projection, join, and some necessary fuzzy set operations such as union, intersection and difference, *etc.*

(2) Due to the well-defined nature of fuzzy relational operations, it is easier to construct general purpose query languages for querying fuzzy relational knowledge bases, such as FSQL.

(3) By using update operations (combined with retrieval operations when necessary), a fuzzy relational knowledge base can be expanded to include new types of knowledge more easily than other systems. For example, the addition of a column to a fuzzy relation is generally less troublesome than the addition of a field to a record type.

Note that in fuzzy relational database systems, we can represent entities and relationships between entities, but not much else. This does not mean to say that such systems are not important. Much of the knowledge which is required in the everyday management of organizations is of this simple nature. Consequently, we have given it wide coverage. Many knowledge bases will contain a large amount of simple knowledge (*i.e.* data), and the theory and techniques which have been developed in database technology to manage large collections of (fuzzy or nonfuzzy) data will have their use in knowledge base systems.

As a typical example, the "job-information-centre" has been represented in the FPDB system, and it has been investigated overall in the preceding chapters.

9.2 Decision Making in a Fuzzy Environment

Decision making is the essence of every human activity, both by individuals and groups and organizations. Most decision making processes proceed in a dynamic manner, *i.e.* decisions are made at sequential moments of time and influence both present and future outcomes. This is particularly true when some uncertainty is involved.

The real challenge is being able to deal with "softness" of system constraints, goals, behaviour, *etc.*, which is so strongly manifested in socioeconomic and other human-centred systems. An efficient tool for formulating and solving the decision making problems under fuzziness is the Bellman and Zadeh approach [Bellman and Zadeh, 1970] which has served as a point of departure for most of the authors in fuzzy decision theory. They consider a situation of decision making under certainty, in which, however, the objective function as well as the constraint(s) are fuzzy. The fuzzy objective function is characterized by its membership function and so are the constraints. Since we want to satisfy the objective function as well as the constraints, a decision in a fuzzy environment is defined by analogy to nonfuzzy environments as the selection of activities which simultaneously satisfy objective function(s) and constraints. According to the above definition, the decision in a fuzzy environment can therefore be roughly viewed as the intersection of fuzzy constraints and objective function(s). The relationship between constraints and fuzzy objective functions in a fuzzy environment is therefore fully symmetric; that is, there is no longer a difference between the former and the latter.

It is common in the process of decision making to call upon the advice of experts in pertinent areas. If the issues to be decided are very important and complex, a great many data and opinions may be gathered from various experts. Dealing with this mass of, often diverse, information requires a formally organized and mechanized system, and indeed the fuzzy relational database is highly appropriate in just such a situation. The general structure of a decision making system is suggested in Figure 9–2.

Here we will illustrate the use of the FPDB system in the issue of personnel evaluation. In this decision making example, the "job-information-centre" database is still available, provided we use the relation **opinions** (see Figure 9–3)

317

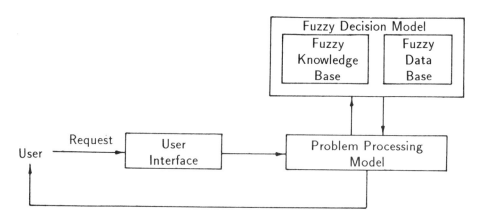

Figure 9–2 Decision Making System

instead of the relation **ability**. In addition, similarity relations are also required to complete the specification of the domains of Intelligence, SocialMaturity, and Skill in this application. This is shown in Figure 9–4.

We are assuming that the database would be used by presidents of given companies to assist in forming decisions on talent evaluation. We know that the database is not only an informational fact source on candidates but also contains the opinions of a group of presidents who impact the decisions to be made.

Now several specific queries using these relations will be presented, illustrating some typical uses for this fuzzy relational database. As usual, each query expressed in natural language is given first in each example. This statement is then followed by the FSQL and f-PROLOG expressions equivalent to the natural language query and then the final result. These queries will be of increasing complexity, representing various inquiries on the presidents' opinions of given candidates' abilities.

1.   What are David's views of Smith's abilities in intelligence, social maturity, and skill?

[In FSQL]

        SELECT   Intelligence, SocialMaturity, Skill
        FROM   opinions
        WHERE   President = david
        AND   Candidate = smith ;

opinions				
Candidate	**President**	**Intelligence**	**SocialMaturity**	**Skill**
Smith	David	Excellent	Excellent	Excellent
Smith	Edward	Bad	Excellent	Good
Smith	Felix	Good	Good	Good
Smith	Alice	Excellent	Good	Normal
John	David	Good	Excellent	Excellent
John	Edward	Good	Excellent	Good
John	Felix	Normal	Normal	Excellent
John	Alice	Excellent	Good	Good
Anna	David	Normal	Excellent	Bad
Anna	Edward	Excellent	Good	Bad
Anna	Felix	Excellent	Normal	Normal
Anna	Alice	Excellent	Excellent	Good
Mary	David	Bad	Excellent	Normal
Mary	Edward	Good	Good	Excellent
Mary	Felix	Normal	Good	Normal
Mary	Alice	Good	Good	Good

Figure 9–3   The Relation **opinions**

	Bad	Normal	Good	Excellent
Bad	1.0	0.5	0.2	0.0
Normal	0.5	1.0	0.7	0.3
Good	0.2	0.7	1.0	0.8
Excellent	0.0	0.3	0.8	1.0

Figure 9–4   Similarity Relations for the Domains of
Intelligence, SocialMaturity and Skill
in the Relation **opinions**

[In f-PROLOG]

> ?–answer((Intelligence,SocialMaturity,Skill),
>
> (opinions(smith,david,Intelligence,SocialMaturity,Skill))).

[Result]

Intelligence	SocialMaturity	Skill
Excellent	Excellent	Excellent

This query was a rather simple one, retrieving data just as stored in the base relations. The next example will build on the result of a given subquery and require the use of a threshold 0.8 approximately to represent the natural linguistic hedge "considerable".

2. Which companies' presidents are in considerable agreement with David on the skill of Smith?

[In FSQL]

```
SELECT    Cname, President
FROM      company
WHERE     President  IN
          (SELECT    President
           FROM      opinions
           WHERE     Candidate = smith
           AND       President / = david
           AND       Skill =
                     (SELECT    Skill
                      FROM      opinions
                      WHERE     Candidate = smith
                      AND       President = david)
           WITH      0.8) ;
```

[In f-PROLOG]

> ?–[0.8]–answer((Cname,President),
>
> (company(Cname,_,President,_,_),
>
> opinions(smith,President,_,_,Skill),
>
> opinions(smith,david,_,_,Ski),
>
> similar(Skill,Ski), President / = david)).

[**Result**]

Cname	President
C2	Edward
C3	Felix

This result shows that the presidents of companies C2 and C3 are in considerable agreement with David on Smith's skill. If we use social maturity instead of skill, we will obtain the following result from the example above.

Cname	President
C2	Edward
C3	Felix
C4	Alice

In the area of decision making, consensus measurements are extremely important for the use of fuzzy relational databases. The sample queries in the personnel evaluation example reflected the desire for an expression of agreement or consensus relative to topics of interest to a typical user. Aside from the actual answer relation returned for such queries, quantitative measures of the consensus can be developed.

In brief, databases, and particularly fuzzy relational database technology, are important prerequisites to decision making, because building a decision making system without existing databases and associated DBMSs will be extremely difficult.

9.3   Expert Systems

The past fifteen years has seen rapid growth in the field of expert systems and their applications. Some of these applications are in the fields of medical diagnosis, petroleum prospecting, pattern recognition, scientific analysis, and many other fields of application to knowledge engineering disciplines.

An expert system, as its name implies, can be defined as the embodiment within a computer of a knowledge-based component, from an expert skill, in such a form that the system provides the user with a facility for posing questions

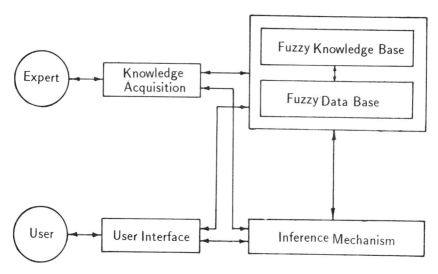

Figure 9–5 General Structure of a Fuzzy Expert System

and obtaining answers to questions relating to the information stored in its knowledge base.

In general, the structure of a fuzzy expert system is shown in Figure 9–5.

Knowledge acquisition is the intermediate process in which knowledge, usually in the form of problem descriptions, ad hoc rules, heuristics, empirical data, and relationships, is acquired from the expert.

The fuzzy knowledge base and fuzzy database contain all the knowledge (rules and facts) about a certain domain which has been entered either directly by the human expert or extracted indirectly via the system. Apart from special storage requirements and system-dependent structures, the knowledge base/ database can be exchanged in some expert systems. That is, there can be several knowledge bases/databases, each covering a different domain, which can be "plugged in" the "shell" of the remaining expert system.

The inference mechanism is a fuzzy engine for manipulating rules and facts from the fuzzy knowledge base and fuzzy database, and it can form inferences and draw conclusions. The conclusions can be deduced in a number of ways which depend on the structure of the engine.

Much of the information used in knowledge-based expert systems arises from human thought and the cognition process, and as such it is uncertain, fuzzy and even incomplete. We will say that the theory and techniques of fuzzy relational databases, particularly the FPDB system, will play an important role, in the characterization and the management of fuzziness and incompleteness for the design of expert systems. The elasticity of FPDB avoids the rigidity of conventional approaches. Human inference is inherently elastic, and conventional computer operation is rigid. In the light of fuzzy sets and fuzzy logic, the FPDB system provides an interface between these elastic and rigid domains. Specifically, in the elastic domain we use linguistic values represented by possibility distributions, while in the rigid domain we tend to use real numbers. In this system, gradual transitions from membership to nonmembership are formed. We use modifiers such as *'very'*, *'more or less'*, *'fairly'*, ..., *'slightly'* and so forth to modify the meaning of the fuzzy values.

As an example, we now discuss a fuzzy expert system for the analysis of manual lifting tasks (LIFTING) developed by utilizing the FPDB system.

1. The structure of LIFTING

Similar to the others, the LIFTING system consists of three major components:

(a)   a user interface

(b)   a fuzzy knowledge base

(c)   a fuzzy inference mechanism

The fuzzy knowledge base, written using the FPDB database and f-PROLOG, provides the expertise of the system. The fuzzy inference engine used in LIFTING is the f-PROLOG system. From f-PROLOG, the LIFTING system has the ability to incorporate the degree of certainty the user may have in his evaluation concerning a specific value of the relevant variable.

2. The fuzzy knowledge base

The fuzzy knowledge base of the LIFTING system consists of a total of 149 f-Rules. 85 f-Rules relate to risk analysis, while 64 f-Rules are used to produce explanations of the inference process as well as messages regarding the potential for job redesign, which are communicated to the user through an explanation mode. The problem of risk analysis is divided into two parts: (1) analysis of the task-related risk; (2) analysis of the operator-related risk.

The task-related risk mode assesses the potential risk of low back disability to a 'young healthy male' using only the task variables. An 'ideal worker' is characterized as being strong, fit and of general good health. These characteristics provide the worker with a low risk profile.

The operator-related risk refers to the specific worker. The use of task variables in combination with worker characteristics allow for the systematic analysis of the worker-lifting system. In addition, the above procedure can aid in better matching the job demands to the worker's abilities.

The most influential factors for the task and work variables used as possible inputs to the system are as follows: (i) load size, (ii) frequency of lift, (iii) horizontal distance from the body, and (iv) height of lift. Since load size is a central issue in lifting tasks, the knowledge base was designed with load size as the primary influence on the potential risk.

The worker characteristics selected for use in the knowledge base include: (i) muscular strength, (ii) fitness, (iii) age. Since research has shown that strength is directly linked to the amount of weight a person can lift safely, workers' strength is given highest priority. Similarly, as frequency of lift increases, the aerobic capacity of a person becomes more critical. Therefore, fitness, as an indirect measure of aerobic capacity, is also included. Lastly, since strength and aerobic capacity are both functions of age, the age of a worker is also considered.

3. Linguistic values of task and worker variables

In order to account for the natural fuzziness inherent in the task and operator variables, linguistic representations of these variables are used. The linguistic values of such variables are represented by means of possibility distributions.

The first linguistic variable, the load size, has linguistic values:

$$\{\ldots, very\text{-}light, light, medium, heavy, very\text{-}heavy, \ldots\}$$

where

$$
\begin{aligned}
very\text{-}light &= \{1/1, 0.8/2, 0.6/5, 0.5/8, 0.2/10, 0.1/15\}, \\
light &= \{1/1, 0.8/8, 0.5/10, 0.2/15, 0.1/17.5\}, \\
medium &= \{0.1/5, 0.5/10, 0.8/12.5, 1/17.5, 0.75/25, 0.5/25, 0.1/30\}, \\
heavy &= \{0.2/20, 0.5/23, 0.75/25, 1.0/32, 0.75/36, 0.5/38, 0.3/40\}, \\
very\text{-}heavy &= \{0.1/30, 0.5/38, 0.8/42, 0.9/44, 1/46, 1/55\}.
\end{aligned}
$$

The frequency of lift has linguistic values:

324

$$\{\ldots, \textit{very-low}, \textit{low}, \textit{medium}, \textit{high}, \textit{very-high}, \ldots\}.$$

The height of lift consists of six general categories:

(1) floor-to-knuckle,   (2) floor-to-shoulder,

(3) floor-to-reach,   (4) knuckle-to-shoulder,

(5) knuckle-to-reach,   (6) shoulder-to-reach;

these sufficiently cover the range of lifting heights.

The horizontal distance from the body is classified as *very-close*, *close*, *medium*, *far*, *very-far*, and so on. These linguistic values can be defined in a similar way to that shown above.

On the other hand, the operator variable strength is divided into: *average*, *strong*, and *very-strong*, etc. The operator-fitness variable related to the aerobic capacity can be: *average*, *good*, and *excellent*, etc. Lastly, the values selected for the variable operator-age are: *young*, *middle-aged*, and *old*, etc.

4.   f-Rules in the fuzzy knowledge base

In the fuzzy knowledge base, the first 32 f-Rules are task-related risk rules. In some rules, all four task variables are required in order to deduce a conclusion as given below:

high_task_risk :–[p]–
    load_size($Very-heavy), frequency($Medium),
    horizontal_distance($Close), height($Low).

where 'p' is the abbreviation for the linguistic truth value "possible" (see Section 3.8). It means that if the load is very heavy, frequency of lift is medium, horizontal distance away from the body is close, and height of lift is low, then "the task risk is high" is possible/true.

At other times, only two or three variables are sufficient to reach a conclusion. For example:

high_task_risk :–[VERY p]–
    load_size($Very-heavy), frequency($High).

This means that, if the load is very heavy and frequency of lift is high, then "the task risk is high" is very possible/true.

On the other hand, three of four similar task-related rules are combined into groups to aid in assessing the operator-related risk. The various combinations of operator characteristics were examined for their effect on the overall risk. In general, we have

$$\text{high\_operator\_risk} :-[f]-$$
$$\text{task\_risk}(A), \text{operator\_strength}(B1),$$
$$\text{operator\_fitness}(B2), \text{operator\_age}(B3).$$

where f is a linguistic implication strength, such as possible, VERY possible, FAIRLY possible *etc.*, while A, B1, B2, and B3 are in $\{\ldots, very\ impossible,$ *impossible, notvery possible, moreorless possible, possible, very possible, ...*$\}$, $\{\ldots, average, strong, very\ strong, \ldots\}$, $\{\ldots, average, good, excellent, \ldots\}$ and $\{young,\ middle\text{-}aged,\ old\}$ respectively. For instance, if a task risk is medium and the operator capacities are adequate, the operator risk would remain medium. If the critical operator capacities are better than those required for the job, the operator risk would decrease, possibly to less than medium. If the critical operator capacities are below the demands of the job, the operator risk would increase to more than medium.

9.4   Fuzzy Logical Control

The fuzzy logical control systems and expert systems discussed in the preceding section have one thing in common, i.e. both want to model human experts' experience and their decision making behaviour. However, clear differences between them also exist:

(1)   The existing fuzzy logical control systems originated in control engineering rather than in artificial intelligence.

(2)   Fuzzy logical control models are all rule-based systems.

(3)   By contrast to expert systems, fuzzy logical control systems serve almost exclusively the control of technological production systems, and hence their domains are even narrower than those of expert systems.

(4)   In general, the rules of fuzzy logical control systems are not extracted from the human expert through the system but formulated explicitly by the system designer.

(5)   Finally, because of their purpose, their inputs are normally observations of technological systems and their outputs control statements.

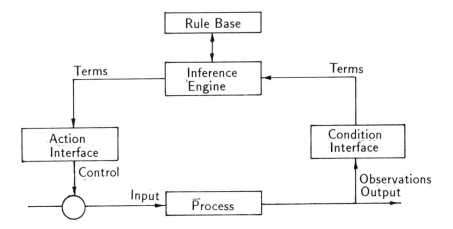

Figure 9-6 Fuzzy Logical Controller

The structure of a fuzzy logical control system is depicted in Figure 9-6.

The essential design requirements in a fuzzy logical control system are as follows:

(a) Define input and control variables; that is, determine which states of the process will be observed and which control actions are to be considered.

(b) Define the condition interface; that is, fix the way in which observations of the process are expressed as possibility distributions.

(c) Design the rule base; that is, determine which rules are to be applied under which conditions.

(d) Design the inference engine; that is, supply the inference mechanism to perform fuzzy reasoning. This will generally lead to fuzzy outputs.

(e) Determine rules according to which fuzzy control statements can be transformed into crisp control actions.

For the purpose of illustrating these questions in the FPDB environment, we use the traffic (on-ramp) control model as an example [Sasaki and Akiyama, 1988]. The solutions of this approach are not used directly for the actual decision process of traffic control, and are usually only applied to help the operator's decision process.

1. System Structure

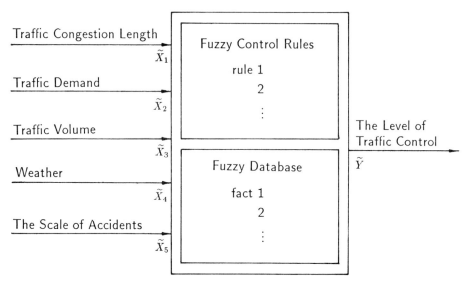

Figure 9–7   Fuzzy Traffic Control Process

There are problems that should be considered in describing the traffic control decision process by fuzzy inference; particularly, in a fuzzy inference process, input and output are each fuzzy linguistic variables. Two important transformation steps are considered as follows:

(i)   The process that transforms the actual data as information into the input data of fuzzy inference.

(ii)   The process that transforms the output of fuzzy inference into the actual traffic control action. It means that the actual on-ramp control is put into force by some control pattern which is selected according to the control level.

Figure 9–7 illustrates the fuzzy traffic control model.

2. Fuzzy Data

The data should be selected to explain the judgment of the operator. There is much complicated data, and information is gathered to help judgment in the field. For actual traffic control many kinds of data such as traffic volume, weather, and the scale of accidents, *etc.* are necessary, but since this is an example to illustrate the role of FPDB in this field, only two factors are selected, to simplify the model in the discussion.

(i) The length of traffic congestion

This is the most typical variable that shows the present state of traffic congestion. The data are obtained by traffic detectors and displayed on a CRT at every operating time (*e.g.* three minutes). They always form useful information to the operator. The length of traffic congestion is obtained at 500 *metre* intervals, which means that, if the actual traffic congestion length is 3.2 *km*, for example, the operators can only get information that traffic congestion is from 3 *km* to 3.5 *km*, or *about* 3 *km* long.

(ii) Expected traffic demand

The operator makes a judgment not only from the data obtained every operating time but also from past experience. In particular, operators have their own expected traffic demand from their daily experience.

3. Fuzzy Control Processes

(1) Fuzzy Control Rules

Fuzzy Control Rules define the action of the model. It means the operator's judgment process is expressed by these f-Rules (see Chapter 3). Two points are considered to make rules:

RULE 1: level_low :-[1]- con_short.

RULE 2: level_low :-[0.9]- con_medium, dem_small.

RULE 3: level_medium :-[1]- con_medium, dem_medium.

RULE 4: level_high :-[0.9]- con_medium, dem_big.

RULE 5: level_high :-[1]- con_long.

Figure 9–8 Fuzzy Control Rules

(i) An operator makes judgments mainly according to the congestion length. The number of categories that they recognize is at most three. They are 'con_long', 'con_medium', and 'con_short'. If the length of congestion becomes longer, they feel that stronger traffic control will become necessary.

(ii) An operator has also three categories for recognition of traffic demand. This variable should be considered when the congestion length is medium. The traffic condition changes according to change in traffic demand when the length of congestion is not stable.

These results are ascertained by a questionnaire to the operators. After consideration, the f-Rules shown in Figure 9–8 are determined.

(2) Possibility Distributions

Fuzzy linguistic values 'con_long', 'con_medium', and 'con_short', etc. can be described by possibility distributions

$$\Pi_{con\_long}(x) = Long,$$
$$\Pi_{con\_medium}(x) = Medium,$$
$$\Pi_{con\_short}(x) = Short,$$

implying that

$$\text{Poss}\{con\_long = x\} = \mu_{Long}(x),$$
$$\text{Poss}\{con\_medium = x\} = \mu_{Medium}(x),$$
$$\text{Poss}\{con\_short = x\} = \mu_{Short}(x),$$

where the shapes of the membership functions are shown in Figure 9–9. Other fuzzy linguistic values such as dem_big, dem_medium, dem_small, $level\_low$, $level\_medium$, and $level\_high$ can be defined by analogy.

(3) Determination of Control Level

Fuzzy inference can be formulated by f-PROLOG, in which the relationship between input and output is calculated by the min-max rule. At every operating time, several f-Rules may be satisfied simultaneously. The conclusion with the greatest degree of truth will always be selected as the final result output. Many approaches are further used to transform the output distribution to one crisp control value. After considering some techniques, the expected value of the fuzzy

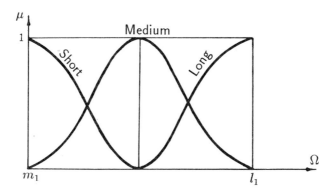

Figure 9-9 Example of Membership Function

output distribution is regarded as the determined control level in our method. The point is conceived to be decided under consideration of all rules with fuzzy implication attenuation.

9.5 Fuzzy Clustering and Information Retrieval

The principal objective of clustering techniques is to partition a given data set into so-called homogeneous clusters. For instance, it is often used in classifying weather situations. The word homogeneous means that all points in the same group are close to each other, and are not close to points in the other groups. Clustering algorithms may be used to build pattern classes or to reduce the size of a data set while retaining relevant information. In classical algorithms it is implicitly assumed that disjoint clusters exist in the set of data. However, the separation of clusters is a fuzzy concept, and the representation of clusters by fuzzy sets may seem more appropriate in certain situations.

One of the most immediate applications of FPDB is fuzzy clustering; it permits elastic soft methods to set the cluster boundary in a gradually changed "buffer zone", since fuzzy set theory has given birth to several interesting fuzzy clustering techniques. In the present section, however, we are not going to study fuzzy clustering algorithms, such as fuzzy ISODATA, fuzzy partition, and graph-theoretic methods, *etc.*, which can be seen in the literature [Zimmermann,

1985; Dubois and Prade, 1980], but we pay attention to its usage in the field of information retrieval.

An information retrieval system compares the specification of required items with the description of stored items and retrieves or lists all the items that match in some defined way that specification. An example of a fuzzy system describing an information retrieval process can be found in [Negoita, 1981]. We are concerned here with the clustering aspect of the problem.

Let X be a set of documents. A fuzzy set on X is interpreted as a fuzzy cluster of documents. Let Y be a set of descriptors y_j, $j = 1, 2, \ldots, n$. A document $x \in X$ is described as

$$x = (y_1(x), y_2(x), \ldots, y_n(x))$$

where

$$y_j(x) = \begin{cases} 1, & y_j \text{ is present in } x; \\ 0, & y_j \text{ is not present in } x. \end{cases}$$

The probability that the descriptor y_j is present in any document of the cluster i is denoted P_{ij}. The membership function of the cluster i is μ_i such that [Negoita, 1973]

$$\mu_i(x) = \frac{\sum_{j=1}^{n} P_{ij} y_j(x)}{\sum_{j=1}^{n} y_j(x)}.$$

A reasonable necessary condition for a clustering algorithm used for structuring the storage of documents is that every document should be assigned to at least one cluster. To take into account all the clusters, a document x is assigned to the cluster i as soon as

$$\mu_i(x) \geq \min_{j,k} \max_{x \in X} \min\{\mu_j(x), \mu_k(x)\}.$$

In our opinion, similarity relations are quite useful in representing the similarity of documents. When a similarity relation Sim on the set A is given, let λ be a certain value in $[0, 1]$; we may define:

For any $x, y \in A$, if $Sim(x, y) \geq \lambda$, then x and y are in the same cluster; otherwise, they are not in the same cluster.

We can thus cluster the set A. Specifically, let

$$A = \{a_1, a_2, a_3, a_4, a_5\}$$

$$Sim = \begin{pmatrix} 1 & 0.70 & 0.95 & 0.80 & 0.80 \\ 0.70 & 1 & 0.70 & 0.70 & 0.70 \\ 0.95 & 0.70 & 1 & 0.80 & 0.80 \\ 0.80 & 0.70 & 0.80 & 1 & 0.90 \\ 0.80 & 0.70 & 0.80 & 0.90 & 1 \end{pmatrix}$$

When $\lambda = 1$, A is clustered as:

$$\{a_1\}, \{a_2\}, \{a_3\}, \{a_4\}, \{a_5\}.$$

When $\lambda = 0.95$, A is clustered as:

$$\{a_1, a_3\}, \{a_2\}, \{a_4\}, \{a_5\}.$$

When $\lambda = 0.90$, A is clustered as:

$$\{a_1, a_3\}, \{a_2\}, \{a_4, a_5\}.$$

When $\lambda = 0.80$, A is clustered as:

$$\{a_1, a_3, a_4, a_5\}, \{a_2\}.$$

When $\lambda = 0.70$, A is clustered as itself:

$$\{a_1, a_2, a_3, a_4, a_5\}.$$

We see that the result of the fuzzy clustering is relative to the threshold λ. The greater the value of λ, the more the number of clusters. A series of clusters can be obtained by using different λ. It is shown in Figure 9–10.

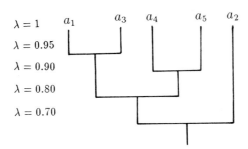

Figure 9–10   The Example of Fuzzy Clustering

The advantage of this clustering approach is that the value of λ can be modified according to different requirements. It is not necessary to accurately estimate how many clusters should be obtained.

We can see that the example of fuzzy clustering mentioned above can be dealt with immediately by means of FPDB operations. In this case, the set $A = \{a_1, a_2, a_3, a_4, a_5\}$ can be seen as a one-ary relation R:

A
a_1
a_2
a_3
a_4
a_5

Of course, the similarity relation Sim defined above is also required.

By typing the retrieval operation

SELECT	A	
FROM	R	
WHERE	A $= a_1$	(Q9.1)
WITH	1 ;	

we have the result:

A
a_1

If we use a_2, a_3, a_4 and a_5 instead of a_1 in WHERE clause respectively, we will obtain the results:

A	A	A	A
a_2	a_3	a_4	a_5

This corresponds to the case $\lambda = 1$ of the clustering procedures shown in Figure 9–10. In such a case, the set of all points is clustered into five partitions: $\{a_1\}$, $\{a_2\}$, $\{a_3\}$, $\{a_4\}$ and $\{a_5\}$.

Let $\lambda = 0.95$, we have the following retrieval operation:

SELECT   A

FROM   R   (Q9.2)

WHERE $A = a_1$

WITH   0.95 ;

it concludes that

A
a_1
a_3

Similarly, if we use a_2, a_3, a_4 and a_5 instead of a_1 in WHERE clause respectively, we will obtain the results:

A	A	A	A
a_2	a_1	a_4	a_5
	a_3		

Note that, when we use a_1 and a_3 respectively, (Q9.2) reaches the same result. Thus, the number of clusters of the set of all points has changed, to four: $\{a_1, a_3\}$, $\{a_2\}$, $\{a_4\}$ and $\{a_5\}$.

By analogy, if we use $\lambda = 0.9$ or $\lambda = 0.8$, the set of all points will be clustered into three partitions: $\{a_1, a_3\}$, $\{a_2\}$ and $\{a_4, a_5\}$, or two partitions: $\{a_1, a_3, a_4, a_5\}$ and $\{a_2\}$. Finally, if we use $\lambda = 0.7$, the set of all points is clustered as itself, with only one partition: $\{a_1, a_2, a_3, a_4, a_5\}$. This corresponds to the case $\lambda = 0.7$ of the example shown in Figure 9–10.

To facilitate the applications of fuzzy clustering and information retrieval, a CLUSTER statement has been built in FSQL. A second order predicate 'cluster(N,S,T)' is correspondingly implemented in f-PROLOG, where N is the N-th element of the set S, and T is a threshold value. Consequently, the example shown in Figure 9–10 can be handled easily by using

SELECT   A

FROM   R

CLUSTER   A

WITH $\langle degree \rangle$;

with different values of ⟨degree⟩.

As a result, clusters of similar documents can be considered. For example, we consider the "job-information-centre" database again. In the following retrieval operations represented by FSQL (and f-PROLOG) expressions referred to fuzzy clustering, the similarity relation shown in Figure 9–11 is required.

	6000	7000	9000	12000
6000	1.0	0.85	0.5	0.3
7000	0.85	1.0	0.7	0.4
9000	0.5	0.7	1.0	0.6
12000	0.3	0.4	0.6	1.0

Figure 9–11   Similarity Relation for the Domain
of Salary in the Relation **job**.

1.   Partition the positions of company C1 into clusters, such that people
     at all positions within any one partition can earn the same salary.
[In FSQL]

```
SELECT    Position
FROM      job
WHERE     Cname = c1
CLUSTER   Salary
WITH      1 ;
```

[In f-PROLOG]

```
?–answer(Position,
         (job(Position,c1,Salary,_), cluster(2,(Position,Salary),1))).
```

[Result]

Position	Position	Position	Position
Manager	Engineer	Secretary	Technician
		Clerk	Assistant

In such a case, all positions of company C1 are clustered into four partitions. Let $\lambda = 0.85$, then we have the following.

2. Partition the positions of company C1 into clusters, such that people at all positions within any one partition can earn salaries close to each other, with the confidence degree of 0.85.

[In FSQL]

SELECT	Position
FROM	job
WHERE	Cname = c1
CLUSTER	Salary
WITH	0.85 ;

[In f-PROLOG]

?–[0.85]–answer(Position,
     (job(Position,c1,Salary,_), cluster(2,(Position,Salary),0.85))).

[Result]

Position	Position	Position
Manager	Engineer	Secretary
		Technician
		Clerk
		Assistant

In this case, the number of clusters of all positions of company C1 has changed, to three.

Similarly, if we further reduce the threshold value, the number of clusters will be fewer. Finally, if we use $\lambda = 0.3$, the result is

Position
Manager
Engineer
Secretary
Technician
Clerk
Assistant

In this case, all positions of company C1 are clustered as itself, with only one partition.

337

Chapter 10

CONCLUDING REMARKS

10.1   Conclusions

This book deals with a new field, which is the integration and intersection of many disciplines, especially fuzzy set theory, logic programming and fuzzy information processing. These disciplines are pending further development both in theories and techniques. Many scientists have contributed to this progress, and most achievements are theoretical. In this book an attempt has been made to incorporate the recent advances in both theory and applications. Comparatively speaking, we have not put the stress on the mathematical hypotheses and the corresponding proofs in the present book; the aim of this volume is to emphasize applications and logic principles rather than mathematical theory, in order to make progress in engineering and applications by utilizing fully theoretical achievements to hand. The intention is to avoid the appearance of a recipe book, with many special formulae set out for types of problems.

Most such publications so far are collections of papers. Although there exist several such monographs, the links between chapters and sections are often loose. We have endeavoured to achieve a balance between theory and applications based upon a prerequisite of a course in fuzzy set theory, logic programming and relational databases, and we hope that the book has indeed given some of the flavour of the kinds of problems in these fields.

This book is structured, in an attempt to discuss every aspect closely, around a typical sample database (job-information-centre). Throughout the book we have demonstrated each new idea by examples in the particular environment.

Only by solving a large number of exercises can the reader be expected to develop an understanding of the basic concepts of fuzzy PROLOG relational database systems. Thereby the readers will get an integrated image.

Techniques of artificial intelligence have been combined with fuzzy relational database systems. Fuzzy logic has been used in the FPDB system not only as the programming tool, but also as a database formalism.

In this book, we pay most attention to fuzzy relational databases. The authors have a realistic outlook to fashionable new words such as 'knowledge engineering', 'distributed expert system', 'meta-knowledge representation', 'man-machine engineering', *etc.* In our opinion, the FPDB system can be used as a basis of such new areas of computer science and technology, no matter what the architecture of the new generation computers, decision support system, or man-machine engineering. They will not make good progress before the problems of fuzzy databases are really solved. On the other hand, based on f-Horn clause logic [Liu and Li, 1988(a)] and fuzzy linguistic logic [Zadeh, 1975], the authors have developed a new fuzzy logic programming language f-PROLOG, hence the logic foundation of the FPDB system is guaranteed. Note that the f in an f-Goal corresponds to the λ in the λ-level-set which can be seen as a threshold. Furthermore, the value of f can be linguistic when necessary. Thus, the naturalness of the man-machine interface is improved.

Investigation shows that there may be a few fuzzy relations in the database. The attribute values of the database may also be fuzzy data or in a natural linguistic format. Soft constraints on some relations are allowed as well as hard constraints in the FPDB system. An important thing is that, both in the FPDB system and the f-PROLOG system proposed by the authors, the following important assumptions are made:

1. The majority of relations in the database are nonfuzzy; most of the f-Rules in an f-PROLOG program are involved in the implication strength 1.

2. The minority of relations in the database are fuzzy; a few of the f-Rules in an f-PROLOG program have implication strengths which are less than 1.

3. A tiny minority of information in both of the fuzzy relational database and the fuzzy logic program is incomplete.

In addition, the authors consider that the solution reached by fuzzy systems may not be the optimum. However, seeking satisfactory results is our purpose. Obviously, it is quite different from those conventional approaches which are popular in the field of fuzzy systems. In the light of these important assumptions, the FPDB system is practical. In a word, we admit fuzziness, but we don't think anything is vague. We allow incompleteness, but we don't believe that information is fragmentary. In a fuzzy system, although the optimum solution may exist, we pay particular attention to seeking the satisfactory conclusion. In this way, we may select distinct threshold values so as to get a series of solutions with different levels of confidence. We believe such a procedure of man-machine interaction is heuristic to the users.

In the FPDB system, all real base relations are represented by extended conventional relations, since all the base relations which are originally fuzzy can be equivalently transformed into extended conventional relations by allowing fuzzy attribute values. This is one of the important contributions of this work. As a result, the great difficulty of compelling designers or users to give the numerical measure of each tuple belonging to a certain relation is overcome.

It is a mistake that the original meaning of grades of membership as estimates of possibilities becames a "black box" in the minds of most subjects such that only numerical values of the grades of membership are remembered, their more detailed meaning being lost in the course of time. Our approach differs from others in that it takes up the fuzzy subject of thought processes that do not fit into the relational database framework. We have found a connection between the use of linguistic values in natural language on the one hand, and numerical membership values on the other hand. As a result, fuzzy values, even fuzzy linguistic values could be handled as well as nonfuzzy values in the relational database model, which is mathematically well-defined and simulates information processing in natural language communication. Since fuzzy linguistic values are allowed, the expression of membership functions becomes implicit. For this reason, the user interface is improved, because the user usually prefers to input queries by using linguistic values instead of numerical membership values.

The operations on base relations often produce fuzzy virtual relations since the conditional expressions will often be fuzzily satisfied in a degree which is in the interval $[0, 1]$. As a result, the theory of fuzzy relational operations including fuzzy relational algebra and fuzzy relational calculus is proposed. Especially for treating fuzzy comparison, the concept of the degree of coincidence, and the corresponding fuzzy comparison operators have been defined. Furthermore, an approach to fuzzy sorting is suggested.

In virtual relations, the degree of satisfaction is just the degree of truth. Let t be a tuple in the fuzzy relation $R(A_1, A_2, \ldots, A_n)$, then

$$\mu_R(t) = \min\{\mu_{A_i}(t)|i = 1, 2, \ldots, n\}.$$

Thus the correspondence between the fuzzy relational database and the fuzzy logic is established.

Another contribution of this work is that we present the high level fuzzy relational query language FSQL for the first time. Because of the attractive features of standard SQL it is incumbent upon us to install it into our database system. In terms of our implementation we call the marriage of SQL and fuzzy linguistic logic FSQL. This language is exactly like the standard SQL in form, and the standard SQL is a special case of FSQL. However, owing to introducing the WITH statement, and allowing fuzzy conditional expressions, fuzzy aggregate functions, especially fuzzy linguistic values, *etc.*, it is closer to the natural language (English), and hence a better interface to casual users is provided. So far as we know, this is the best query language at present. One of the important strategies for parsing an FSQL query into the f-PROLOG form is that structured keywords in FSQL are considered as operators in PROLOG by declaring them in advance. Another important technique in writing the parser of FSQL is the creation of variables, which are used to determine possible instantiation states for attributes.

Note that, in the FPDB system, three kinds of incomplete information UNDECIDED, UNDEFINED and NULL are distinguished. The advantage is that each incomplete value has a special meaning, not simply unknown. UNDECIDED means that the attribute value is defined and it could be any value in the domain. UNDEFINED means there is no possibility that the attribute value could exist in the domain. NULL is a special value for representing the situation that we do not know even whether the attribute value is defined or not.

Based on the "job-information-centre" database, the usefulness of FPDB is introduced from different aspects. Particularly, we have found a number of applications in such fields as knowledge engineering, decision support systems, expert systems, fuzzy control and **fuzzy** clustering, where fuzzy data play an important role in nature.

At the beginning of the present book, the authors made a penetrating analysis of the nature and properties of the membership function and its digital characteristics such as the mathematical expected value, variance, moment, fuzzy expected value, and so on. We have come to the conclusions that:

- The grade of membership $\mu_A(x)$ of an element x to a fuzzy set $\tilde{A}$ is numerically equal to the degree of truth v of the fuzzy predicate "x is $\tilde{A}$" describing the fuzzy set $\tilde{A}$ applies to the element x, *i.e.*

$$\mu_{\tilde{A}}(x) = \alpha \iff \text{is}(x, \tilde{A}) \leftarrow (\alpha) - .$$

- The membership function is not a primitive concept. A membership value is generally not absolutely defined. It seems more important to become aware of how the human mind manipulates names of fuzzy sets than to figure out precisely numerical grades of membership since the perception process itself is fuzzy. As soon as it has a good shape, it can be considered as a satisfactory approximation. In other words, the construction of a membership function is more a justification of a shape than a quantitative estimation procedure.

- The membership function is perceived more like a continuum and differentiable, and to have an S shape or a bell shape rather than a discrete set of membership values, although it may be sampled for practical purposes. In addition, a slight modification of the membership values does not drastically affect the rough shape of the result of a set operation.

- On the whole, ordinary membership functions will be sufficient for an approximate quantitative representation of this intrinsically qualitative notion; that is, gradual category membership. To take into account the imprecision of membership functions, we may think of using **Type 2** fuzzy sets. The parameters of higher order fuzzy sets tolerate less precise estimation.

- A few operations on membership functions, such as ordering, minimization, maximization, negation, *etc.* are certainly meaningful. However, many

342

mathematical or set operations and their composition on membership functions are meaningless.

- Besides the <u>mathematical</u> expected <u>value</u>, <u>variance</u>, <u>moment</u>, and <u>fuzzy</u> <u>expected</u> <u>value</u>, many other digital characteristics of the possibility distribution, such as the area, $hgt(\tilde{A})$—height of the fuzzy set $\tilde{A}$, the point of the maximum value, are also quite useful. Particularly, slope, k, is a digital characteristic for decrease in membership with increasing distance from the point of the maximum value. It yields $k > 0$ and for $k \to \infty$ we get the nonfuzzy possibility distribution as a special case.

10.2 Recommendation for Future Studies

The experimental version of FPDB has been implemented in IF/PROLOG associated with the C language. It was a rather ambitious project at the time, involving the implementation of a fuzzy logic programming language f-PROLOG and a high level fuzzy query language FSQL. There are several directions in which both the theories and techniques we have described could be extended. The developments of immediate practical importance for database interfaces and management systems are now illustrated as follows.

f-PROLOG is a generalization of the standard PROLOG interpreter, while the conventional PROLOG system is the special case. Because of the similarity in syntax, f-PROLOG can run binary PROLOG programs written in Edinburgh syntax, such as IF/PROLOG, with very little alteration. All of the sample programs from the IF/PROLOG handbook have been run using f-PROLOG. Nevertheless, it is possible that the system could be made more efficient by intelligent backtracking techniques, and could reduce execution time by pruning the search tree. These possibilities are currently under investigation. To give better portability, the f-PROLOG system is now being developed entirely in C language. The revised version will consist of the linguistic extension proposed in Section 3.8, in which linguistic values can be dealt with as well as the numerical values.

The present f-PROLOG interpreter is available to run on a wide variety of present day computers, and useful programs can be written without waiting for the so called fifth generation computers. However, the architecture of present day computers is beginning to show its limitations. Similar to the conventional PROLOG language, significant improvements in the man-machine interface and in software productivity are needed, but are not being achieved as fast as would be hoped for using present day machines. Especially, using only software techniques, inference speed is still limited. On the other hand, we know that the key premise of logic programming is that computation is controlled inference. This view of computation is proving exceedingly fruitful, as we believe the FPDB project demonstrates. It leads naturally to the idea that we should design computers as inference machines. In the Fifth Generation Computer System Project in Japan, a PROLOG machine has been implemented in order to overcome these increasingly serious limitations. This is a good start toward this future architecture. In the authors' opinion, the development of a fuzzy PROLOG machine, and other fuzzy inference machines, is a hopeful direction in the new generation computer research.

Performance is an important concern in the design and implementation of fuzzy relational databases. Many software optimization techniques have been utlized for finding proper order in accessing relations related to a fuzzy query. However, moving data between main memory and secondary storage is a very time-consuming task, especially when large quantities of data are involved. There is obviously a place for associative hardware (a fuzzy database machine) to optimize retrieval speed. As a result, we present a general proposal for bridging the gap between a fuzzy PROLOG system and a fuzzy relational database machine.

f-PROLOG so far is a sequential inference language. In other words, rigid sequence is hidden in the execution mechanism of f-PROLOG. It internally supports depth-first control strategy, from left to right. Hence the language is mainly suitable for running on current computers.

Current computers use a so-called von Neumann architecture, where a single central processing unit performs each step of a calculation serially, one step after another. When large amounts of data are to be processed, this one-step-at-a-time processing is too slow. Parallel processing techniques provide an alternative which allows large problems to be solved faster, based on the premise that dividing a problem into smaller parts will yield faster results.

Scientific and engineering problems in the next decade will require an increase in speed of at least two orders of magnitude over the fastest current machines such as the Cray-2. Most experts agree that some form of parallel processing must be implemented to meet these demands.

The application requirements of a computer determine the most appropriate type of architecture. Von Neumann architectures are appropriate for data processing tasks with procedural languages. Supercomputers, designed for solving large scale numerical calculations in engineering and science, utilize single assignment languages. Fifth Generation computers, on the other hand, are aimed at knowledge-based systems applications operating with inference languages.

The declarative semantics of f-PROLOG ensure that the same results could be obtained even if subgoals in an f-Goal are executed in different sequences, and GOTO statements and assignment statements are abolished through unification. It shows that the static structure of programs and their dynamic execution procedures are consistent. As a result, we say that f-PROLOG is naturally well suited to parallel programming and therefore an excellent candidate for powerful future computers incorporating parallel processing.

·Since new generation computers with multi-processors are being developed, parallel fuzzy PROLOG becomes possible. In fact, even on von Neumann computers, parallel f-PROLOG could be developed by applying virtual parallel processes and multi-job operations. In addition, parallel f-PROLOG tends toward combining with object-oriented programming, data flow languages, fuzzy relational databases and distributed computer systems, *etc.*

AND-parallels and OR-parallels could be developed in logic programming languages. Compared with conventional PROLOG, many more OR-parallels are involved in the f-PROLOG language. It has been proved that the cost of developing OR-parallels is much less than that of developing AND-parallels. So the research of parallel fuzzy PROLOG is even more significant.

In the FPDB system, redundancy should be reduced as far as possible. In a nonfuzzy relational database, a tuple is redundant if it is exactly the same as another tuple. Any operation over a nonfuzzy relation at least implicitly entails removing redundant tuples. In a fuzzy relational database, the redundancy is an elastic measure. In the sense of Buckles and Petry [Buckles and Petry, 1982], a fuzzy tuple is redundant if it can be merged with another through the set union of corresponding domain values. The merging of tuples, however, is subject to constraints on the similarity thresholds. Two tuples t_i and t_j are redundant if

345

their degree of similarity is greater than a certain threshold. Other measures such as semantic distances can be also used to define the notion of redundancy.

The lack of redundant tuples in an ordinary relational database is tantamount to the absence of multiple occurrences of the same tuple. In a fuzzy relational database, if two tuples are redundant, we prefer to remove the more vague tuple in order to induce a unique outcome. However, which one is more vague or more precise between two fuzzy tuples? This question leads to an interesting topic.

We should enhance both the practicality and the expressive power of the FPDB system, for example, by allowing more aggregate functions to be applied to the query output, or installing new query languages into the system. In our opinion, FQBE (Fuzzy Query By Example) and other types of languages could be designed and implemented entirely in PROLOG. As a matter of fact, different types of users have very different needs and skills. The choice of a language will depend upon the human circumstance of its intended use. Consequently, a universal interface supporting a variety of high-level query languages is needed. In such an environment, all kinds of users could have a common understanding of the data, and communicate with one or another query language about the database.

There is no doubt that natural language is the ideal database language. A number of developments of natural language based computer systems such as ROBOT [Harris, 1977], QPROC [Wallace and West, 1983] are highly encouraging. We hope our work will encourage extensive investigation of this feature for future versions of the FPDB system.

There is no question that the problem of missing information is an important one. In the FPDB system, we have defined three incomplete values: UNDECIDED, UNDEFINED and NULL. It is much better than only using NULL as "unknown". But even so, we admit that this may not be the best, or the only way, at least. We expect our method to be helpful so that further research on this, or alternatives, will lead to more satisfactory approaches.

In recent years, distributed databases have become an important area of information processing, and it is easy to foresee that their importance will rapidly grow. There are both organizational and technological reasons for this trend: distributed databases eliminate many of the shortcomings of centralized databases and fit more naturally in the decentralized structures of many or-

346

ganizations. In our view, the availability of fuzzy relational databases, such as FPDB, and of computer networks, will give rise to a new field—fuzzy distributed databases. Completely new problems will be faced for designing and implementing a distributed database, and a great deal of research work should be done in order to solve them. This research work will constitute a new discipline having its own theories and technology.

REFERENCES

Astrahan, M. M. and Lorie, R. A. "SEQUEL–XRM: A Relational System." *Proc. ACM Pacific Regional Conference*, San Francisco, California, 1975.

Baldwin, J. F. "Fuzzy Logic and Fuzzy Reasoning." *J. Man-Machine Stud.* 11, 1979, 465-480.

Baldwin, J. F. and Zhou, S. Q. "A Fuzzy Relational Inference Language." *J. FSS.* 14, 1984, 155–174.

Bellman, R. and Zadeh, L. A. "Decision-Making in a Fuzzy Environment." *Mgt. Sci.* 17, 1970, 141–164.

Bellman, R. and Giertz, M. "On the Analytic Formalism of the Theory of Fuzzy Sets." *Inf. Sci.* 5, 1973, 149–156.

Bruynooghe, M. "The Memory Management of PROLOG Implementations." in: *Logic Programming* (Clark, K. L. and Tarnlund, S. A. Eds.), Academic Press, New York, 1982, 83–98.

Buckles, B. P. and Petry, F. E. "A Fuzzy Representation of Data for Relational Databases." *J. FSS.* 7, 1982a, 213–226.

Buckles, B. P. and Petry, F. E. "Fuzzy Databases and their Application." in: *Fuzzy Information and Decision Processes* (Gupta, M. M. and Sanchez, E. Eds.), North-Holland, 1982b, 361–371.

Chamberlin, D. D. and Boyce, R. F. "SEQUEL: A Structured English Query Language." *Proc. ACM SIGMOD Workshop on Data Description, Access, and Control*, Ann Arbor, Mich., 1974.

Chanas, S. and Nowakowski, M. "Single Value Simulation of Fuzzy Variable." *J. FSS.* 25, 1988, 43–57.

Chang, C. L. and Lee, R. C. T. "Symbolic Logic and Mechanical Theorem Proving." Academic Press, New York, 1973.

Codd, E. F. "A Relational Model of Data for Large Shared Data Banks." *Communications of the ACM*, 6, 1970, 377–387.

Codd, E. F. "Relational Completeness of Data Base Sublanguages." *Data Base Systems, Courant Computer Science Symposia Series*, 6, 1972, Prentice-Hall.

Codd, E. F. "Understanding Relations." *FDT Bull. ACM-SIGMOD* 7, 1975, 23–28.

Date, C. J. "An Introduction to Database Systems." Third Edition, Addison-Wesley Publishing Company, 1981.

Date, C. J. "Relational Database: Selected Writings." Addison-Wesley Publishing Company, 1986.

De Luca, A. and Termini, S. "A Definition of a Nonprobabilistic Entropy in the Setting of Fuzzy Sets Theory." *Inf. Control* 20, 1972, 301–312.

Dubois, D. and Prade, H. "Fuzzy Sets and Systems: Theory and Applications." Academic Press, New York, 1980.

Fagin, R. "Multivalued Dependencies and a New Normal Form for Relational Databases." *ACM Trans. Database Systems* 2, 1977, 262–278.

Giles, R. "Lukasiewicz Logic and Fuzzy Theory." *J. Man-Machine Stud.* 8, 1976, 313–327.

Giles, R. "A Formal System for Fuzzy Reasoning." *J. FSS.* 2, 1979, 233–257.

Giles, R. "The Concept of Grade of Membership." *J. FSS.* 25, 1988, 297–323.

Grant, J. "Null Values in a Relational Database." *Inform. Process. Lett.* 6, 1977, 156–157.

Grant, J. "Incomplete Information in a Relational Database." *Fundamenta Informaticae* 3, 1980, 363–378.

Gupta, M. M. and Sanchez, E. "Fuzzy Information and Decision Processes." North-Holland, 1982.

Hamacher, H. "Uber Logische Aggregationen nicht-binär expliziter Entscheidungskriterien." Frankfurt/Main, 1978.

Harris, L. R. "User Oriented Database Query with the Robot Natural Language Query System." *J. Man-Machine Stud.* 9, 1977, 697–713.

Hisdal, E. "Are Grades of Membership Probabilities?" *J. FSS.* 25, 1988, 325–348.

Holsapple, C. W. and Whinston, A. B. "Decision Support Systems: Theory and Application." Springer-Verlag, 1987.

Horn, A. "On Sentences Which are True of Direct Unions of Algebra." *J. Symbolic Logic* 16, 1951, 14–21.

Kalbfleish, J. G. "Probability and Statistical Inference." Second Edition, Springer-Verlag, New York, 1985.

Kanal, L. N. and Lemmer, J. F. "Uncertainty in Artificial Intelligence." North-Holland, 1986.

Kowalski, R. A. "Predicate Logic as Programming Language." *Proc.* IFIP 74, North-Holland, Amsterdam, 1974, 569–574.

Kowalski, R. A. "Logic for Problem Solving." North-Holland, New York, 1979.

Lee, R. C. T. "Fuzzy Logic and Resolution Principle." *J. Assoc. Comput. Mach.* 19, 1972, 109–119.

Li, Deyi "A PROLOG Database System." Research Studies Press, England, 1984.

Lipski, W. "On Databases with Incomplete Information." *J. ACM.* 28, 1981, 41–70.

Liu, Dongbo and Li, Deyi "Fuzzy Reasoning Based on f-Horn Clause Rules." *Proc. of 1st Int. Workshop on Algebraic and Logic Programming,* Akademie-Verlag, Berlin, 1988a, 214–222.

Liu, Dongbo and Li, Deyi "Fuzzy PROLOG Language and Expert Systems." *Mini-Micro Computer Systems* 5, 1988b, 26–31.

Liu, Dongbo and Li, Deyi "A New Fuzzy Inference Language f-PROLOG." *Computer Engineering* 1, 1989a, 23–27.

Liu, Dongbo and Li, Deyi "Quantitative Development of Logic Reasoning Theory." *Chinese J. Computers* 10, 1989b, 796–799.

Liu, Dongbo and Li, Deyi "Fuzzy Proof Theory." *J. Computer Science and Technology* 1, 1990.

Malvache, N. and Willaeys, D. "The Use of Fuzzy Sets for the Treatment of Fuzzy Information by Computer." *J. FSS.* 5, 1981, 323–327.

Mizumoto, M. and Tanaka, K. "Some Properties of Fuzzy Sets of Type 2." *Inform. and Control* 31, 1976, 312–340.

Negoita, C. V. "On the Application of the Fuzzy Sets Separation Theorem for Automatic Classification in Information Retrieval Systems." *Inf. Sci.* 5, 1973, 279–286.

Negoita, C. V. "Fuzzy Systems." Abacus Press, 1981.

Prade, H. and Negoita, C. V. "Fuzzy Logic in Knowledge Engineering." Verlag TUV Rheinland, Koln, 1986.

Raju, K. V. S. V. N. and Majumdar, A. K. "The Study of Joins in Fuzzy Relational Databases." *J. FSS.* 21, 1987, 19–34.

Rescher, N. "Plausible Reasoning." Amsterdam: Van Gorcum, 1976.

Rissanen, J. "Independent Components of Relations." *ACM Trans. Database Systems* 2, 1977, 317–325.

Sanchez, E. "Inverses of Fuzzy Relations: Application to Possibility Distributions and Medical Diagnosis." *Proc. IEEE Conf. Decision Control*, New Orleans 2, 1977, 1384–1389.

Sasaki, T. and Akiyama, T. "Traffic Control Process of Expressway by Fuzzy Logic." *J. FSS.* 26, 1988, 165–178.

Schafer, G. "A Mathematical Theory of Evidence." Princeton, New Jersey: Princeton University Press, 1976.

Schneider, M. and Kandel, A. "Applications of Fuzzy Expected Intervals to Fuzzy Expert Systems." *J. Expert Systems* 1, 1988a, 169–186.

Schneider, M. and Kandel, A. "Properties of the Fuzzy Expected Value and the Fuzzy Expected Interval." *J. FSS.* 26, 1988b, 373–385.

Shortliffe, E. H. "MYCIN: Computer Based Medical Consultation." Elsevier, New York, 1976.

Silvert, W. "Symmetric Summation: A Class of Operations on Fuzzy Sets." *IEEE Trans. on Systems, Man and Cyb.* 9, 1979, 657.

Umano, M. "Freedom-0: A Fuzzy Database System." in: *Fuzzy Information and Decision Processes* (Gupta, M. M. and Sanchez, E. Eds.), North-Holland, 1982, 339–347.

van Emden, M. H. "An Interpreting Algorithm for Prolog Programs." in: *Implementations of PROLOG* (Campbell, J. A. Ed.), Ellis Horwood, Chichester, 1984, 93–110.

van Emden, M. H. "Quantitative Deduction and its Fixpoint Theory." *J. Logic Programming* 1, 1986, 37–53.

Wallace, M. G. and West, V. "QPROC: a natural language database enquiry system implemented in PROLOG." *ICL Technical Journal*, November, 1983, 393–407.

Yarger, R. R. "On a General Class of Fuzzy Connectives." *J. FSS.* 3, 1980, 235–242.

Zadeh, L. A. "Fuzzy Sets." *Inform. and Control* 8, 1965, 338–353.

Zadeh, L. A. "Similarity Relations and Fuzzy Orderings." *Inf. Sci.* 3, 1970, 177–206.

Zadeh, L. A. "Outline of a New Approach to the Analysis of Complex Systems and Decision Processes." *IEEE Trans. on Systems, Man, and Cybernetics* SMC-3, 1973, 28–44.

Zadeh, L. A. "The Concept of a Linguistic Variable and its Application to Approximate Reasoning." *Int. Sci.* 8, 1975a.

Zadeh, L. A. "The Concept of a Linguistic Variable and its Application to Approximate Reasoning." *Int. Sci.* 9, 1975b.

Zadeh, L. A. "Calculus of Fuzzy Restrictions." in: *Fuzzy Sets and Their Applications to Cognitive and Decision Processes* (Zadeh, L. A., Fu, K.

S., Tanaka, K. and Shimura, M. Eds.), Academic Press, New York, 1975c, 1–39.

Zadeh, L. A. "Fuzzy Sets as a Basis for a Theory of Possibility." *J. FSS.* 1, 1978a, 3–28.

Zadeh, L. A. "PRUF—A Meaning Representation Language for Natural Languages." *J. Man-Machine Stud.* 10, 1978b, 395–460.

Zadeh, L. A. "Possibility Theory and Soft Data Analysis." in: *Mathematical Frontiers of the Social and Policy Sciences Boulder* (Cobb, L. and Thrall, R. M. Eds), CO 1981, 69–129.

Zadeh, L. A. "Fuzzy probabilities." *Information Processing and Management* 19, 1984, 148–153.

Zimmermann, H. J. and Zysno, P. "Latent Connectives in Human Decision Making." *J. FSS.* 4, 1980, 37–51.

Zimmermann, H. J. "Fuzzy Set Theory—and Its Application." Kluwer-Nijhof Publishing, 1985.

Appendix 1

SYSTEM PREDICATES AND PRECEDENCES OF OPERATORS

1.1 BUILT-IN PREDICATES AND FUNCTIONS IN f-PROLOG

(1) The List of Conventional Predicates in f-PROLOG

!

This is called 'cut', and discards all choice points created since the parent goal started execution. The cut affects all clauses of the parent goal.

abolish(H)

This removes all clauses which have the head **H**.

abort

This aborts all current executions.

add(A,B,X)

X = A + B.

ancestor(G)

This unifies goal **G** with the parent goal of the current goal. **G** must be instantiated to a goal atom or structure and its arguments may be uninstantiated.

ancestors(GL)

This unifies goal-list **GL** with a list of all the parent goals of the current goal. Note that it must be called as a subgoal.

append(L1,L2,L3)

List **L3** is the concatenation of the list **L2** and list **L1**. At least one argument must be instantiated. If any one or two arguments of it are instantiated, then the third argument or the second and third arguments are unified with the appropriate result(s).If all three arguments are instantiated f-PROLOG attempts to prove the statement.

arg(N,T,A)

This succeeds if the **N**-th argument in term **T** is **A**.

assert(C)

This inserts a clause **C** in the current database.

asserta(C)

This inserts a clause **C** in the database before any other stored clauses for the corresponding predicate.

asserta(H,B)

This inserts a clause with head **H** and body **B** in the database before any other stored clauses for the corresponding predicate.

assertz(C)

This inserts a clause **C** in the database after all other stored clauses for the corresponding predicate.

assertz(H,B)

This inserts a clause with head **H** and body **B** in the database after all other stored clauses for the corresponding predicate.

atom(T)

This is true if **T** is currently instantiated to an atom, *i.e.* a nonvariable term of arity 0.

atomic(T)

This succeeds if **T** is currently instantiated to an atom or an integer.

atomic_length(T,Length)

This unifies **Length** with the number of characters in term **T** where **T** is an atom or arithmetical expression.

break

This gets a new invocation of the top level interpreter.

bye

This terminates the f-PROLOG session, if you are at the top interpreter level. If you are in a **break**, **bye** returns you to the prior level.

bye is equivalent to the **end_of_file** key(s) and end. **bye** may be used within programs as it is used at the interpreter level.

call(G)

This causes the goal **G** to be evaluated.

char_code(Ch,Cc)

If **Ch** is an atom of length 1 then **Cc** is unified with its ASCII code. If **Ch** is a variable, then the character represented by the given ASCII charcode **Cc** is unified with **Ch**.

clause(H,B)

This succeeds if there is a clause in the database with head **H** and body **B**.

clear_eol

This clears the screen from the cursor to the end of line.

clear_eos

This clears the screen from the cursor to the end of screen.

cls

This clears the screen.

close(F)

File **F**, currently open for input or output, is closed. **F** must be an atom. Fails if file **F** is not open.

compare(C,T1,T2)

Comparing the terms **T1** and **T2** returns the result comparison, for which the only possible values are:

> '=' if **T1** is identical to **T2**
> '<' if **T1** is before **T2** in the standard order
> '>' if **T1** is after **T2** in the standard order

compare(=,T1,T2) is equivalent to **T1 == T2**

The standard order is:

variable	are in an unknown order
numbers	normal numeric order
atoms	in alphabetical order or ASCII order
terms	ordered first by arity, then by the name of the functor (in alphabetical or ASCII code order), then by the arguments (note that an argument may be a term and then the same rules are applied recursively).

concat(L,A)

The elements of the list are concatenated in the order of their occurrence in the list **L** and unified with the atom **A**.

The elements of the list may be atoms and arithmetical expressions, but not structures. Arithmetic expressions are evaluated and the result is converted to an atom.

concat(L,Separator,A)

This is similar to the above, except that the atom in **Separator** is inserted between the elements of **L**.

consult(F)

Enter all clauses from the file **F** into the database.

debug

This switches the debugger on. More information is now retained for debugging purposes, and therefore execution requires more space. For large programs, you may need to allocate more stack area on invoking f-PROLOG. This can be done without losing the current program state via **save_system(F)** and **load_system(F)**.

debugging

This outputs the list of current active spy points.

decompcons(A,L)

The atom **A** is decomposed into a list of characters and the result is unified with **L**, *i.e.* **L** is a list of the characters of **A**.

delete(Elt,L1,L2)

This deletes one element **Elt** from the list **L1** and unifies it with **L2**.

deny(H,B)

This removes a clause from the database which has head **H** and body **B**.

digit(T)

This succeeds if **T** is an atom consisting of a single character, and the character is a digit.

display(T)

This writes the term **T** to the CURRENT output stream. Its format does not put quotation marks around atoms.

displayq(T)

This writes the term **T** to the CURRENT output stream. Its format puts quotation marks around atoms.

div(A,B,X)

X = A / B.

end

This terminates the f-PROLOG session if you are at the interpreter level. If you have used break to enter a new interpreter loop, **end** brings you back to the prior level. It is equivalent to **bye**.

exists(F,Permission)

This succeeds if the file **F** exists and has the specified **Permission**. **F** must be an atom and so must be in quotation marks if the file name contains special characters like '/' or '%'. **Permission** must be either the atom "r" or the atom "w", for read and write permission respectively.

exit

This returns f-PROLOG to the operating system.

fail

Always fails.

files

This lists all files currently known to f-PROLOG on the CURRENT output stream, giving access mode and type of every file.

functor(T,Fn,N)

This succeeds if **T** is a term whose functor is **Fn** and arity **N**.

get(X)

This unifies **X** with the ASCII code of the next nonblank printable character from the CURRENT input stream.

get0(X)

This unifies **X** with the ASCII code (0–255) of the next character from the CURRENT input stream.

getchar(S,N,Ch)

Character **Ch** is unified with the N-th character of String **S**.

get_home(Line Column)

This retrieves the co-ordinates of the home position of the terminal screen.

index(S,Ss,Pos)

The first occurrence of the substring **Ss** in the string **S** is searched for, and **Pos** is unified with the first position of this occurrence. The procedure fails if there is no such substring. **S** and **Ss** may be atoms or arithmetical expressions. In the latter case it is evaluated during execution.

integer(T)

This is true if **T** is currently instantiated to an integer.

is(X,E) or **X is E**

X is assigned by **E**.

length(L,M)

This succeeds if the length of the list **L** is **M**.

length_dist(L,M)

This succeeds if the number of distinct items of the list **L** is **M**.

letter(T)

This succeeds if **T** is an atom which is a single character, and the character is a letter a–z, or **A–Z**.

listing(H)

This lists all user clauses in the database with the head **H**.

listall

This lists all clauses in the current database.

load(F)

This reads an f-PROLOG program into the current database, where **F** specifies the file to be loaded. It succeeds if there exists a file named **F**.

lower_upper(Low,Up)

The atom **Low** is raised to uppercase or the atom **Up** is transformed to lower-case.

make_atom(T,A)

This converts the term **T** to an atom string and unifies it with **A**.

make_number(T,N)

This converts the value of **T** to a number and unifies it with **N**.

member(Elt,L)

This succeeds if element **Elt** is a member of list **L**. If **Elt** is uninstantiated it generates the elements of **L** via backtracking.

mod(A,B,X)

X = A mod B.

move_cursor(Line,Column)

This places the cursor at the specified screen location.

mult(A,B,X)

X = A * B.

name(A,Ch)

If **A** is an atom, a list of the ASCII codes of the characters making up the atom is returned. If **A** is uninstantiated, **Ch** must be instantiated to a list of ASCII character codes and **A** is formed from these character codes.

nl

A new line is written to the CURRENT output stream.

nl(N)

N new lines are written to the CURRENT output stream.

nodebug

This removes all the current spy points.

nonvar(T)

This succeeds if **T** is currently instantiated to a non-variable term.

nospy(P)

This releases spy points on predicate **P** during debugging.

not(G)

If **G** succeeds, then **not(G)** fails; if **G** fails, **not(G)** succeeds.

notrace

Tracing is turned off by calling **notrace**.

number(N,L)

If number **N** is an integer or real number then it converts the number to a list of ASCII character codes and unifies it with **L**. If **N** is uninstantiated, **L** must be instantiated to a list of ASCII character codes representing digits, then the number formed from the character codes is unified with **N**.

numeric(T)

This succeeds if **T** is a real or integer number.

op(Pre,Ty,Op)

This defines **Op** as an operator with the specified type of **Ty** and precedence of **Pre**. The precedence **Pre** must be an integer between 0 and 1200. The higher the number the lower the precedence. The op-type **Ty** must be one of the atoms xf, yf, fy, fx, yfx, xfx, xfy. The operator **Op** is the symbol for the operator itself.

outpos(Col)

This unifies (returns) **Col** with the current column-position of the cursor, always an integer.

outtab(N)

This requires an integer or an expression that evaluates to an integer as **N**. The cursor is moved to the column given by **N**. If **N** is less than the current column, the cursor is moved to the next line.If **N** is larger than the line length, the cursor is moved over to column "**N mod line-length**", and down "**N div length**" (integer division) lines.

perm(L,PL)

This permutes the list **L**. The first permutation is the unchanged list. Then one element after the other is permuted.

pipe(X)

This creates a pipe named **X** (atom).

portraycl(C)

This writes out the clause **C** on the current output.

portraygoals(G)

This writes out the goals **G** on the current output.

print(T)

This writes out the term or term list **T** on the same line to the current output stream.

printr(T)

This is similar to the **print(T)**, except that it terminates the line with a carriage return.

put(Cc)

The ASCII character corresponding to the value of **Cc** is output to the CURRENT output stream.

putc(C)

This succeeds by writing the character **C** to the current output stream. If **C** is a variable, it must be instantiated to a character.

read(X)

This reads the next term from the current input stream and unifies it with X.

real(T)

This is true if **T** is a real number.

reconsult(F)

This instructs the interpreter to read in the program contained in the file **F**. This is like **consult(F)** except that the definition of any procedure in the reconsulted file replaces any clauses for that procedure already present in the database.

This is a built-in predicate which always succeeds. After a "fail" f-PROLOG returns to the last clause solved successfully, and attempts to find another solution. If repeat was the last successful clause in a procedure, in effect it has an "infinite number of solutions" and an infinite sequence of backtracking choices is generated.

retract(C)

This removes the first clause in the database that matches the clause **C**.

retractall(P)

This removes all clauses in the database that match the specific predicate **P**.

retractop(Pre,Ty,Op)

363

The definition of the operator **Op** is removed from the database. **Pre** must be instantiated to a number between 0 and 1200. **Ty** must be instantiated to one of these atoms: xf, yf, fy, fx, xfx, yfx, or xfy. **Op** must be instantiated to an existing operator symbol.

save(F)

This saves the current database to the file named in **F**.

see(F)

This causes file **F** to become the current input stream. f-PROLOG input is now taken from the file named **F** instead of the currently defined input stream; the next read, get0 or get reads from file **F**.

seeing(F)

This unifies **F** with name of the current input file. This is useful to save the current name while temporarily reading from another file.

seen

This closes the current input stream. The standard input stream, called user, cannot be closed.

set_home(Line,Column)

This defines the cursor home position of the screen. This home position can be found with **get_home(Line,Column)**.

setprompt(S)

This sets the f-PROLOG prompt to the string **S**.

skip(C)

This reads and discards characters from the CURRENT input stream until the character is read that matches the value of **C** (ASCII). It does not backtrack.

sort(L1,L2)

The elements of the **L1** are sorted into standard order yielding the list **L2**. Repeated items are deleted during the sorting process.

spy(P)

This puts a spy point on predicate **P**.

struct(T)

This succeeds if **T** is an f-PROLOG structure.

sub(A,B,X)

X = A - B.

system

This allows users to interact with the operating system without leaving the f-PROLOG session.

system(Cmd)

This cause the operating system to execute the command **Cmd**.

system_date(Date)

The current date is given in **Date** as a six digit number of the form 'ddmmyy' where dd means day, mm means month and yy means year.

system_time(Time)

The current time is given in **Time** as a six digit number of the form 'hhmmss' where hh means hours, mm means minutes and ss means seconds.

tab(Count)

Output **N** spaces to the CURRENT output stream, where **N** is value of **Count**. **Count** may be an arithmetical expression, since it is evaluated.

tell(F)

This causes file **F** to become the CURRENT output stream.

telling(F)

This instantiates **F** with the name of the CURRENT output file.

told

This closes the CURRENT output stream and directs output back to STANDARD output.

trace

This switches tracing on. Its output is printed on the STANDARD error stream (usually the screen).

trace(F)

This causes file **F** to become the CURRENT error stream. Exception messages and the trace protocol are written to CURRENT error and are now directed to this file.

traced

This closes the current error stream and directs the error stream back to STANDARD error.

traceput(C)

The character with ASCII code **C** is printed to the CURRENT error stream, usually the screen.

tracing(F)

This instantiates **F** with the name of the current error file.

trimcore

This releases unwanted space to the operating system.

true

Always succeeds.

unload(F)

This removes only those clauses that were originally loaded from file **F**.

var(T)

This succeeds if **T** is currently uninstantiated.

write(T)

This writes **T** to the current output stream.

writeq(T)

This writes **T** to the current output stream, and its format puts in quotation marks around atoms.

X , Y

Fuzzy logic expression **X and Y**.

X ; Y

Fuzzy logic expression **X or Y**.

X == Y

This succeeds if the terms currently instantiated to **X** and **Y** are literally identical. (In particular, variables in equivalent positions in the two terms must be identical.)

X /== Y

This succeeds if the terms currently instantiated to **X** and **Y** are not literally identical.

X < Y

Value of **X** is less than value of **Y**.

X > Y

Value of **X** is greater than value of **Y**.

X =< Y

Value of **X** is less than or equal to value of **Y**.

X >= Y

Value of **X** is greater than or equal to value of **Y**.

X = Y

Values of **X** and **Y** are equal.

X /= Y

Values of **X** and **Y** are not equal.

(2)   The List of Fuzzy Predicates in the f-PROLOG

fuzzy_eq(X,Y)   or   **X ˜= Y**

X is approximately equal to **Y**, and vice versa.

much_gt(X,Y)   or   **X >> Y**

X is much greater than **Y**.

much_ls(X,Y)   or   **X << Y**

X is much smaller than **Y**.

similar(X,Y)

X is similar to **Y**, and vice versa.

(3)   The Second Order Predicates in f-PROLOG

answer(Results,(Q))

This executes the query **Q** and, concludes the **Results**. Particularly, if **Results** is storage, then it executes the storage statement **Q**.

all(Answer,Q,Set_of_answers)

This executes the query **Q** and, for each solution, saves the value of **Answer**. It finally builds a set of all answers and matches this set with **Set_of_answers**.

avg(X,G,R)

R is the average value of column **X** in the base relation.

cnt(X,G,R)

This counts the numbers **R** in column **X**, where **X** is an attribute in the base relation **G**.

group(N,G,N)

This conceptually rearranges the base relation **G** into groups such that in any group all tuples have the same value for the grouped attribute **N**.

max(X,G,R)

This produces the maximum value **R** in the column **X**, where **X** is an attribute in the base relation **G**.

min(X,G,R)

This produces the minimum value **R** in the column **X**, where **X** is an attribute in the base relation **G**.

modify(Old,G,New)

This replaces an instantiated tuple **G** in the database by a new tuple which is the same as **G** except that the occurrence of **Old** becomes **New**.

order(N,S,G)

Given a set of attributes **S**, this orders all solutions by the N-th attribute in **S** and produces the ordered set in **G**.

sum(X,G,R)

R is the sum value of column **X** in the base relation **G**.

(4)   The Table of Built-in Functions in f-PROLOG

Functions	Result is $\cdots$
abs(E)	absolute value
acos(E)	arccosine
asin(E)	arcsine
atan(E)	arctangent
ceil(E)	round up (real number)
cos(E)	cosine
cosh(E)	hyperbolic cosine
exp(E)	exponential
float(E)	return real number
floor(E)	convert to integer
ln(E)	natural logarithm
log(E)	logarithm to base 10
sign(E)	sign
sin(E)	sine
sinh(E)	hyperbolic sine
sqrt(E)	square root
tan(E)	tangent
tanh(E)	hyperbolic tangent
trunc(E)	convert to integer by truncation

300	xfx	mod
400	yfx	$*$, $/$
500	yfx	$+$, $-$
700	xfx	$=$, $/=$, $>$, $<$, $>=$, $=<$, $==$, $/==$, $=:=$, $=..$
		$\tilde{}=$, $>>$, $<<$, is , in , not_in
900	fy	not
930	xfy	and , or
940	yfx	having
950	yfx	where , with
960	yfx	group_by
970	yfx	from , set , ':'
980	fx	select , modify , delete , insert_into
990	xfy	union , intersect , difference
1000	xfy	,
1100	xfy	;
1200	xfx	:–[,]–
1200	fx	?–

Appendix 2

OFTEN USED MEMBERSHIP FUNCTIONS IN FPDB

1. The membership function of the fuzzy comparison operator:
    $>>$ (**much greater than**)

$$\mu_{>>}(x,y) \;=\; \begin{cases} 0, & x \le y; \\ \left[1 + c\,(x-y)^{-2}\right]^{-1}, & x > y. \end{cases} \qquad (c>0).$$

Particularly, for "Salary", $c = 2.25 \times 10^6$. It is shown in Figure 1.

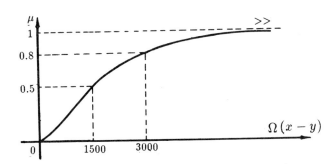

Figure 1

2. The membership function of the fuzzy comparison operator:
$<<$ (**much less than**)

$$\mu_{<<}(x,y) = \begin{cases} \left[1 + c\,(y-x)^{-2}\right]^{-1}, & x < y. \\ 0, & x \ge y; \end{cases} \qquad (c > 0).$$

Particularly, for "Salary", $c = 2.25 \times 10^6$. Figure 2 illustrates the membership function for $c = 2.25 \times 10^6$.

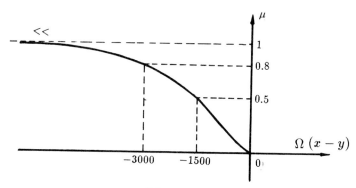

Figure 2

3. The membership function of the fuzzy comparison operator:
$\tilde{=}$ (**approximately equal to**)

$$\mu_{\tilde{=}}(x,y) = e^{-c|x-y|} \qquad (c > 0).$$

For "Age", $c = 2.23 \times 10^{-1}$. It is depicted in Figure 3.

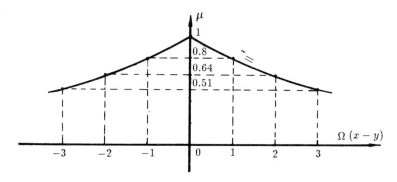

Figure 3

372

For "Salary", $c = 1.053 \times 10^{-3}$. Figure 4 depicts the membership function for $c = 1.053 \times 10^{-3}$.

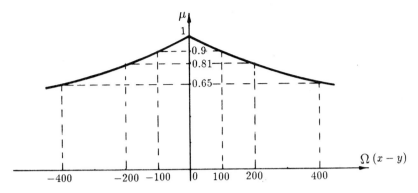

Figure 4

4. The membership functions of the terms: *young*, *middle-aged* and *old* (consider $x \in \Omega = [0, 200]$).

$$\mu_{young}(x) = \begin{cases} 1, & 0 \le x \le 25; \\ \left[1 + \left(\frac{x-25}{5}\right)^2\right]^{-1}, & 25 < x \le 200. \end{cases}$$

$$\mu_{middle-aged}(x) = \begin{cases} 0, & 0 \le x \le 25; \\ \frac{1}{2} + \frac{1}{2}\sin\frac{\pi}{10}(x - 50), & 25 < x \le 35; \\ 1, & 35 < x \le 45; \\ \frac{1}{2} - \frac{1}{2}\sin\frac{\pi}{10}(x - 50), & 45 < x \le 55; \\ 0, & 55 < x \le 200. \end{cases}$$

$$\mu_{old}(x) = \begin{cases} 0, & 0 \le x \le 50; \\ \left[1 + \left(\frac{x-50}{5}\right)^{-2}\right]^{-1}, & 50 < x \le 200. \end{cases}$$

Figure 5, 6 and 7 depict the membership functions above respectively.

373

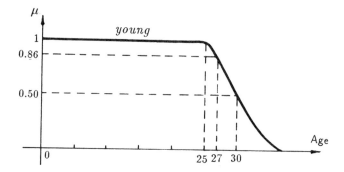

Figure 5

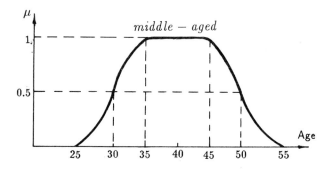

Figure 6

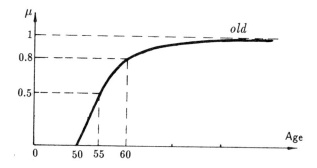

Figure 7

5. The membership function of the fuzzy operator: *about*

$$\mu_{about\ x_0}(x) \;=\; e^{-c(x-x_0)^2}, \qquad (c > 0).$$

374

For "Age", $c = 1.62 \times 10^{-1}$. It is shown in Figure 8.

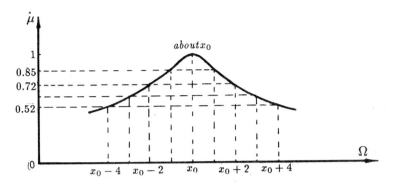

Figure 8

6.   The membership function of the terms: *near* and *far*

$$\mu_{near}(x) = \begin{cases} 1, & x \le \alpha; \\ e^{-k(x-\alpha)^2}, & x > \alpha. \end{cases} \qquad (k > 0).$$

For "Distance", $\alpha = 20$ (*miles*), $k = 2.3 \times 10^{-2}$. It is illustrated in Figure 9.

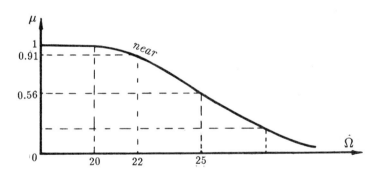

Figure 9

$$\mu_{far}(x) = \begin{cases} 0, & x \le \alpha; \\ 1 - e^{-k(x-\alpha)^2}, & x > \alpha. \end{cases} \qquad (k > 0).$$

For "Distance", $\alpha = 40$ (*miles*), $k = 3.28 \times 10^{-2}$. It is shown in Figure 10.

375

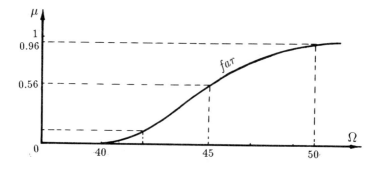

Figure 10

7. The membership function of the terms: *possible,
very possible, fairly possible, almost definite,
almost impossible* and *definite*

$$\mu_{possible}(x) = \begin{cases} 0, & 0 \le x \le 0.5; \\ 2\left(\frac{x-0.5}{0.2}\right)^2, & 0.5 < x \le 0.6; \\ 1 - 2\left(\frac{x-0.7}{0.2}\right)^2, & 0.6 < x \le 0.8; \\ 2\left(\frac{0.9-x}{0.2}\right)^2, & 0.8 < x \le 0.9; \\ 0, & 0.9 < x \le 1. \end{cases}$$

$$\mu_{very\,possible}(x) = \mu_{possible}^2(x-0.1) = \begin{cases} 0, & 0 \le x \le 0.6; \\ 4\left(\frac{x-0.6}{0.2}\right)^4, & 0.6 < x \le 0.7; \\ \left[1 - 2\left(\frac{x-0.8}{0.2}\right)^2\right]^2, & 0.7 < x \le 0.9; \\ 4\left(\frac{1-x}{0.2}\right)^4, & 0.9 < x \le 1. \end{cases}$$

$$\mu_{fairly\,possible}(x) = \mu_{possible}^{\frac{1}{2}}(x+0.1) = \begin{cases} 0, & 0 \le x \le 0.4; \\ \sqrt{2}\left(\frac{x-0.4}{0.2}\right), & 0.4 < x \le 0.5; \\ \sqrt{1 - 2\left(\frac{x-0.6}{0.2}\right)^2}, & 0.5 < x \le 0.7; \\ \sqrt{2}\left(\frac{0.8-x}{0.2}\right), & 0.7 < x \le 0.8; \\ 0, & 0.8 < x \le 1. \end{cases}$$

$$\mu_{almost\,definite}(x) = \begin{cases} 0, & 0 \le x \le 0.8; \\ 2\left(\frac{x-0.8}{0.2}\right)^2, & 0.8 < x \le 0.9; \\ 1 - 2\left(\frac{x-1}{0.2}\right)^2, & 0.9 < x \le 1. \end{cases}$$

376

$$\mu_{almost\ impossible}(x) = \begin{cases} 1 - 2\left(\frac{x}{0.2}\right)^2, & 0 \leq x \leq 0.1; \\ 2\left(\frac{0.2-x}{0.2}\right)^2, & 0.1 < x \leq 0.2; \\ 0, & 0.2 < x \leq 1. \end{cases}$$

$$\mu_{definite}(x) = \begin{cases} 1, & x = 1; \\ 0, & x \neq 1. \end{cases}$$

Figure 11 sketches the above.

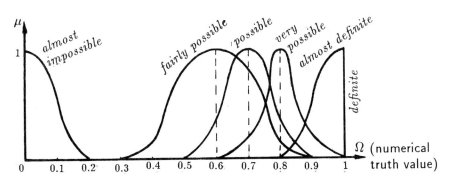

Figure 11

8. The membership function of the terms: *excellent, good, moderate,* and *bad*

$$\mu_{excellent}(x) = 1 - e^{-\left(\frac{0.5}{|1-x|}\right)^{2.5}}.$$

$$\mu_{good}(x) = 1 - e^{-\left(\frac{0.25}{|0.4-x|}\right)^{2.5}}.$$

$$\mu_{moderate}(x) = 1 - e^{-5|x|}.$$

$$\mu_{bad}(x) = 1 - e^{-\left(\frac{0.25}{|-0.4-x|}\right)^{2.5}}.$$

Figure 12 depicts the above.

377

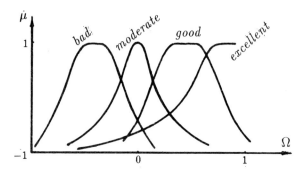

Figure 12

9. The membership function of the terms: *high*

$$\mu_{high}(x) = \begin{cases} 0, & x \le \alpha; \\ \left[1 + \left(\frac{x-\alpha}{c}\right)^{-2}\right]^{-1}, & x > \alpha. \end{cases} \qquad (c > 0).$$

For "Salary", $\alpha = 5000$ (\$), $c = 2 \times 10^3$ (see Figure 13).

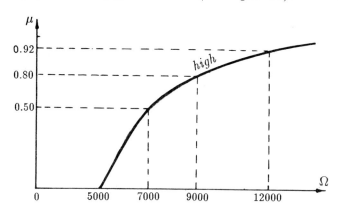

Figure 13

10. The membership function of the terms: *long*

$$\mu_{long}(x) = \begin{cases} 0, & 0 \le x \le 2; \\ \left[1 + \left(\frac{x-2}{c}\right)^{-2}\right]^{-1}, & x > 2. \end{cases} \qquad (c > 0).$$

378

For "Experience", $c = 2$ (see **Figure 14**).

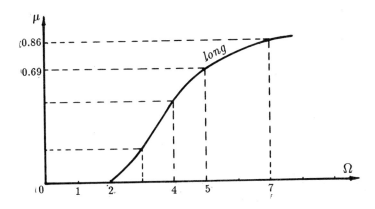

Figure 14

Appendix 3

QUESTION-ANSWERING EXAMPLES
WITH THE FPDB SYSTEM

Based on the "job-information-centre" database (see Figure 8–1), here we attempt to offer some of the kinds of fuzzy queries successfully run by FPDB under VAX/VMS on VAX-11/780. The examples below show the fuzzy query, its representations in FSQL, f-PROLOG, and the actual answer.

Query 1:   Get full details of all companies.

[In FSQL]

> SELECT   *
> FROM   company ;

or

> SELECT   Cname, Address, President, Employees, Profit
> FROM   company ;

[In f-PROLOG]

> ?–answer(* ,
>   (company(Cname,Address,President,Employees,Profit))).

or

> ?–answer((Cname,Address,President,Employees,Profit),
>   (company(Cname,Address,President,Employees,Profit))).

[Result]

Cname	Address	President	Employees	Profit
C1	Newcastle	David	400	300,000
C2	Carlistle	Edward	100	100,000
C3	Penrith	Felix	2000	1,000,000
C4	Darlington	Alice	800	NULL

Query 2: Get a table of candidate names, ages, and looks.

[In FSQL]

```
SELECT    Name, Age, Looks
FROM      candidates, body
WHERE     candidates.Name = body.Name ;
```

[In f-PROLOG]

```
?-answer((Name,Age,Looks),
         (candidates(Name,_,Age,_),
          body(Name,_,_,Looks))).
```

[Result]

Name	Age	Looks
Smith	30	Good
John	ABOUT 28	Good
Anna	22	Good
Mary	$Middle-aged	VERY Good
Jill	30	Ordinary
Susan	ABOUT 28	Ordinary
Tom	24	Ordinary
Harry	36	Good
Fred	ABOUT 25	FAIRLY Good
Margaret	20	Good
Andrew	24	Good
Barry	33	FAIRLY Good
Thomas	31	Ordinary
Martin	$Young	Good
Henry	29	Ordinary
Robert	UNDECIDED	Ordinary
George	$Young	Good

Query 3: Select those tuples from the table **candidates** which very possibly represent young persons.

[In FSQL]

SELECT   *
FROM   candidates
WHERE   Age = $Young
WITH   VERY possible ;

[In f-PROLOG]

?–[VERY p]–answer((Name,Sex,Age,Address),
         (candidates(Name,Sex,Age,Address))).

[Result]

Name	Sex	Age	Address
Anna	Female	22	Penrith
Tom	Male	24	Carlisle
Margaret	Female	20	Penrith
Andrew	Male	24	Carlisle
Martin	Male	$Young	Newcastle
George	Male	$Young	NULL

Query 4: List a table which consists of all candidates, each one with his/her age.

[In FSQL]

SELECT   Name, Age
FROM   candidates ;

[In f-PROLOG]

?–answer((Name,Age),
       (candidates(Name,_,Age,_))).

[Result]

Name	Age
Smith	30
John	ABOUT 28
Anna	22
Mary	$Middle-aged
Jill	30
Susan	ABOUT 28
Tom	24
Harry	36
Fred	ABOUT 25
Margaret	20
Andrew	24
Barry	33
Thomas	31
Martin	$Young
Henry	29
Robert	UNDECIDED
George	$Young

Query 5: Get an alphabetical listing of candidates, each one with his/her sex.

[In FSQL]

```
SELECT      Name, Sex
FROM        candidates
ORDER_BY    Name ;
```

[In f-PROLOG]

```
?–answer((Name,Sex),
        (candidates(N,S,_,_),
        order(1,(N,S),(Name,Sex)))).
```

[Result]

Name	Sex
Andrew	Male
Anna	Female
Barry	Male
Fred	Male
George	Male
Harry	Male
Henry	Male
Jill	Female
John	Male
Margaret	Female
Martin	Male
Mary	Female
Robert	Male
Smith	Male
Susan	Female
Thomas	Male
Tom	Male

Query 6: Get a list of candidates who have a university education, ordered by their ages, each one with his/her age and address.

[In FSQL]

SELECT	Name, Age, Address
FROM	candidates, background
WHERE	Education = university
ORDER_BY	Age ;

[In f-PROLOG]

```
?-answer((Name,Age,Address),
        (background(N,university,_,_,_),
        candidate(N,_,A,Add),
        order(2,(N,A,Add),(Name,Age,Address)))).
```

[Result]

Name	Age	Address
Martin	$Young	Newcastle
Tom	24	Carlisle
Andrew	24	Carlisle
Fred	ABOUT 25	Darlington
Susan	ABOUT 28	Darlington
Henry	29	Penrith
Smith	30	Newcastle
Harry	36	Darlington
Mary	$Middle-aged	Carlisle

Query 7: Show all young candidates, with the confidence degree of 0.9, who have never been engineers.

[In FSQL]

```
SELECT      Name
FROM        candidates
WHERE       Age = $Young
WITH        0.9

DIFFERENCE

SELECT      Name
FROM        background
WHERE       Profession = engineer ;
```

or

```
SELECT   Name
FROM     candidates
WHERE    Age = $Young
         Name  NOT_IN
             (SELECT   Name
              FROM     background
              WHERE    Profession = engineer)
WITH     0.9 ;
```

[In f-PROLOG]

```
?–[0.9]–answer( Name ,
          (candidates(Name,$Young,_,_),
           not(background(Name,engineer,_,_,_))))).
```

[Result]

Name
Anna
Margaret
George

Query 8:   Get a table of names of candidates who are very possibly young, ordered by names.

[In FSQL]

```
SELECT     Name
FROM       candidates
WHERE      Age = $Young
WITH       VERY possible
ORDER_BY   Name ;
```

[In f-PROLOG]

```
?-[VERY p]-answer( Name ,
              (candidates(N,_,$Young,_),
               order(1,N,Name))).
```

[Result]

Name
Andrew
Anna
George
Margaret
Martin
Tom

Query 9:   Construct a table of names of candidates who are definitely young male.

[In FSQL]

```
SELECT    Name
FROM      candidates
WHERE     Sex = male
AND       Age = $Young
WITH      1 ;
```

?-[1]-answer(Name ,
          (candidates(Name,male,$Young,_))).

[Result]

Name
Tom
Andrew
Martin
George

Query 10: Get a table of candidates who are middle-aged with the confidence degree of ABOUT 0.9.

[In FSQL]

SELECT	Name
FROM	candidates
WHERE	Age = $Middle-aged
WITH	ABOUT 0.9 ;

[In f-PROLOG]

?-[ABOUT 0.9]-answer(Name ,
          (candidates(Name,_,$Middle-aged,_))).

[Result]

Name
Mary
Harry

Query 11: Retrieve the name, sex, education and address of all candidates who have been secretaries and are very possibly young.

[In FSQL]

SELECT	Name, Sex, Education, Address
FROM	candidates, background
WHERE	Age = $Young
AND	Profession = secretary
WITH	VERY possible ;

[In f-PROLOG]

> ?–[VERY p]–answer((Name,Sex,Education,Address),
>   (candidates(Name,Sex,$Young,Address),
>   background(Name,secretary,_,_,_))).

[Result]

Name
Anna
Margaret

Query 12: Retrieve the companies in which the candidate Smith may get a high salary.

[In FSQL]

SELECT	Cname
FROM	background, job
WHERE	Name = smith
AND	background.Professon = job.Position
AND	job.Salary = $High
WITH	F ;

or

SELECT	Cname	
FROM	job	
WHERE	Salary = $High	
AND	Position =	
	(SELECT	Profession
	FROM	background
	WHERE	Name = smith
	WITH	F) ;

[In f-PROLOG]

> ?–[F]–answer(Cname ,
>   (background(smith,_,P,_,_),
>   job(P,Cname,$High,_))).

[Result]

Cname	
C1	0.92
C2	0.86
C3	0.70
C4	0.86

Query 13: Suppose that, in addition to the relations specified in the "job-information-centre" database, the database also contains the relation employee(Name,Sex,Age, Health,Height). Insert into the relation **employee** selected tuples from the relation **candidates** and **body**.

[In FSQL]

INSERT_INTO	employee
SELECT	Name, Sex, Age, Health, Height
FROM	candidates, body
WHERE	candidates.Name = body.Name ;

[In f-PROLOG]

```
?-answer( storage ,
        (candidates(Name,Sex,Age,_),
        body(Name,Health,Height,_),
        asserta(employee(Name,Sex,Age,Health,Height))))).
```

Query 14: Delete the candidate Smith from the relation **candidates**.

[In FSQL]

DELETE	candidates
WHERE	Name = smith ;

[In f-PROLOG]

```
?-answer( storage ,
        (retract(candidates(smith,_,_,_)))))·
```

Query 15: Change the president of company C1 to Taylor.

[In FSQL]

MODIFY	company
SET	President = taylor
WHERE	Cname = c1 ;

    ?–answer(storage ,

          (modify(President,company(c1,_,President,_,_), taylor))).

Query 16:   Double the salaries of all engineers and managers working in a big company with the degree of 0.9.

[In FSQL]

MODIFY	job
SET	Salary = Salary * 2
WHERE	Position IN (engineer,manager)
AND	Cname IN

                (SELECT   Cname

                 FROM   company

                 WHERE   Employees = \$Big

                 WITH   0.9) ;

[In f-PROLOG]

    ?–answer(storage ,

          (modify(Salary,job(Position,Cname,Salary,_),Salary * 2),

          (Position == engineer; Position == manager),

          company(Cname,_,_,\$Big,_))).

Query 17:   Get the total number of candidates.

[In FSQL]

                SELECT   CNT(*)

                FROM   candidates ;

[In f-PROLOG]

    ?–answer(CNT ,

          (cnt(*,candidates(_,_,_,_),CNT))).

[Result]

CNT(*)
17

Query 18:   How many different addresses are shown in the table **candidates** ?

[In FSQL]

```
SELECT    CNT(Address)
FROM      candidates ;
```

[In f-PROLOG]

```
?–answer( CNT ,
        (cnt(Address,candidates(_,_,_,Address),CNT))).
```

[Result]

CNT(Address)
4

Query 19: How many girls who are young with the degree of 0.9 are in the **candidates** table ?

[In FSQL]

```
SELECT    CNT(Name)
FROM      candidates
WHERE     Age = $Young
AND       Sex = female
WITH      0.9 ;
```

[In f-PROLOG]

```
?–[0.9]–answer( CNT ,
        (cnt(Name,candidates(Name,female,$Young,_),CNT))).
```

[Result]

CNT(Name)
2

Query 20: Get numbers of those candidates, for each candidate whose age is greater than or equal to 25 with the confidence degree of 0.9.

[In FSQL]

```
SELECT    CNT(Name)
FROM      candidates
WHERE     Age >= 25
WITH      0.9 ;
```

[In f-PROLOG]

> ?–[0.9]–answer(CNT ,
>> (cnt(Name,candidates(Name,_,Age,_),CNT),
>> Age >= 25)).

[Result]

CNT(Name)
9

Query 21: Get the greatest and the least value of candidate ages.

[In FSQL]

> SELECT   MAX(Age), MIN(Age)
> FROM   candidates ;

[In f-PROLOG]

> ?–answer((MAX,MIN),
>> (max(Age,candidates(_,_,Age,_),MAX),
>> min(Age,candidates(_,_,Age,_),MIN))).

[Result]

MAX(Age)	MIN(Age)
$Middle-aged	20

Query 22: Get the average age of female candidates.

[In FSQL]

> SELECT   AVG(Age)
> FROM   candidates
> WHERE   Sex = female ;

[In f-PROLOG]

> ?–answer(AVG ,
>> (avg(Age,candidates(_,female,Age,_),AVG))).

[Result]

AVG(Age)
27.81

Query 23:   Get candidate names for each candidate whose age
is very possibly less than the average of all
candidates who live in Carlisle.

[In FSQL]

```
SELECT   Name
FROM     candidates
WHERE    Age <
              (SELECT   AVG(Age)
               FROM     candidates
               WHERE    Address = carlisle)
WITH     VERY possible ;
```

[In f-PROLOG]

```
?-[VERY p]-answer( Name ,
              (candidates(Name,_,Age,_),
               avg(Age, candidates(_,_,_,carlisle),AVG),
               Age < AVG)).
```

[Result]

Name
Anna
Tom
Margaret
Andrew
Martin
George

Query 24:   Who is the tallest among young male candidates with
the confidence degree of 0.9 ?

[In FSQL]

```
SELECT    Name
FROM      candidates, body
WHERE     Sex = male
AND       Height =
                    (SELECT    MAX(Height)
                     FROM      candidates, body
                     WHERE     Sex = male
                     AND       Age = $Young
                     WITH      0.9)
AND       Age = $Young
WITH      0.9 ;
```

[In f-PROLOG]

```
?-[0.9]-answer( Name ,
               (candidates(Name,male,$Young,_),
                body(Name,_,MAX,_),
                max(Height,(body(Name,_,Height,_),
                            candidates(Name,male,$Young,_)),MAX))).
```

[Result]

Name
Tom

Query 25: Get the total numbers and average ages of male candidates and female candidates respectively.

[In FSQL]

```
SELECT    Sex, CNT(Name), AVG(Age)
FROM      candidates
GROUP_BY  Sex ;
```

[In f-PROLOG]

```
?-answer((Sex,CNT,AVG),
        (group(Sex,candidates(_,Sex,_,_),Sex),
         cnt(Name,candidates(Name,Sex,_,_),CNT),
         avg(Age,candidates(_,Sex,Age,_),AVG))).
```

[Result]

394

Sex	CNT(Name)	AVG(Age)
Male	12	29.80
Female	5	27.81

Query 26: For each profession, get the profession name and the total number of candidates who are in that profession.

[In FSQL]

```
SELECT      Profession, CNT(Profession)
FROM        background
GROUP_BY    Profession ;
```

[In f-PROLOG]

```
?-answer((Profession,CNT),
    (group(Profession, background(_,_,Profession,_,_),Profession),
    cnt(Profession, background(_,_,Profession,_,_),CNT))).
```

[Result]

Profession	CNT(Profession)
Manager	6
Assistant	1
Secretary	2
Technician	2
Engineer	4
Clerk	1
UNDEFINED	1

Query 27: Get the profession names of all the professions in which more than two candidates are in that profession.

[In FSQL]

```
SELECT      Profession
FROM        background
GROUP_BY    Profession
HAVING      CNT(Profession) > 2 ;
```

[In f-PROLOG]

?–answer(Profession ,
  (group(Profession, background(_,_,Profession,_,_),Profession),
  cnt(Profession, background(_,_,Profession,_,_),CNT),
  CNT > 2)).

[Result]

Profession	CNT(Profession)
Manager	6
Engineer	4

Query 28: How many positions will pay much more than $4000 with the degree of 0.8 in each company ?

[In FSQL]

SELECT	Cname, CNT(Position)
FROM	job
GROUP_BY	Cname
WHERE	Salary >> 4000
WITH	0.8 ;

[In f-PROLOG]

?–[0.8]–answer((Cname,CNT),
  (group(Cname,job(_,Cname,_,_),Cname),
  cnt(Position,(job(Position,Cname,Salary,_),
  Salary >> 4000),Position))).

[Result]

Cname	CNT(Position)
C1	4
C2	4
C3	2
C4	3

Query 29: Select all candidates who like sports.

[In FSQL]

```
         SELECT   Name
         FROM     background
         WHERE    Hobby = sports
         WITH     F ;
```

[In f-PROLOG]

```
?–[F]–answer( Name ,
            (background(Name,_,_,_,sports))).
```

[Result]

Name	
John	1.00
Fred	1.00
Barry	1.00
Robert	ϕ
George	ϕ

Query 30:   List per capita profit for each company.

[In FSQL]

```
SELECT   Cname, Employees, Profit, Profit/Employees
FROM     company ;
```

[In f-PROLOG]

```
?–answer((Cname,Employees,Profit,Profit/Employees),
         (company(Cname,_,_,Employees,Profit))).
```

[Result]

Cname	Employees	Profit	Profit/Employees
C1	400	300,000	750
C2	100	100,000	1000
C3	2000	1,000,000	500
C4	800	NULL	NULL

Query 31:   Find the sum and average of the profits of all companies appearing in the table **company**.

[In FSQL]

```
            SELECT    SUM(Profit), AVG(Profit), CNT(*)
            FROM      company ;
```

[In f-PROLOG]

```
?–answer((SUM,AVG,CNT),
        (sum(Profit,company(_,_,_,_,Profit),SUM),
         avg(Profit,company(_,_,_,_,Profit),AVG),
         cnt(*,company(_,_,_,_,_),CNT))).
```

[Result]

SUM(Profit)	AVG(Profit)	CNT(*)
1,400,000	466666.67	4

Query 32: Retrieve the name, sex, age, and education of all candidates who have ever been managers for over two years.

[In FSQL]

```
            SELECT    Name, Sex, Age, Education
            FROM      candidates, background
            WHERE     Experience > 2
            AND       Profession = manager
            WITH      F ;
```

[In f-PROLOG]

```
?–[F]–answer((Name,Sex,Age,Education),
        (candidates(Name,Sex,Age,_),
         background(Name,Education,manager,Experience,_),
         Experience > 2)).
```

[Result]

Name	Sex	Age	Education	
Jill	Female	30	Post-graduate	1.00
Susan	Female	ABOUT 28	University	0.53
Harry	Male	36	University	1.00
Thomas	Male	31	Post-graduate	1.00
Robert	Male	UNDECIDED	Post-graduate	?

398

Query 33: Display the background of all candidates whose hobby is absolutely unknown (NULL).

[In FSQL]

```
SELECT    Name, Education, Profession, Experience, Hobby
FROM      background
WHERE     IS_NULL(Hobby) ;
```

or

```
SELECT      *
FROM      background
WHERE     IS_NULL(Hobby) ;
```

[In f-PROLOG]

```
?-answer((Name,Education,Profession,Experience,Hobby),
         (background(Name,Education,Profession,Experience,Hobby),
         is_null(Hobby))).
```

or

```
?-answer( * ,
         (background(Name,Education,Profession,Experience,Hobby),
         is_null(Hobby))).
```

[Result]

Name	Education	Profession	Experience	Hobby
Robert	Post-graduate	Manager	UNDECIDED	NULL
George	UNDEFINED	UNDEFINED	UNDEFINED	NULL

Query 34: Show the background of all candidates whose age is unknown.

[In FSQL]

```
SELECT    Name, Education, Profession, Experience, Hobby
FROM      candidates, background
WHERE     IS_UNDECIDED(Age) ;
```

[In f-PROLOG]

```
?-answer((Name,Education,Profession,Experience,Hobby),
         (candidates(Name,_,Age,_),is_undecided(Age),
         background(Name,Education,Profession,Experience,Hobby))).
```

399

Name	Education	Profession	Experience	Hobby
Robert	Post-graduate	Manager	UNDECIDED	NULL

Query 35: Retrieve the name, age, education and address of all candidates who were definitely unemployed.

[In FSQL]

SELECT	Name, Age, Education, Address
FROM	candidates, background
WHERE	IS_UNDEFINED(Profession) ;

[In f-PROLOG]

?–answer((Name,Age,Education,Address),
        (candidates(Name,_,Age,Address),
        background(Name,Education,Profession,_,_),
        is_undefined(Profession))).

[Result]

Name	Age	Education	Address
George	$Young	UNDEFINED	NULL

Query 36: Get a table which consists of all companies, each one with its number of employees and its profit, ordered by the profits.

[In FSQL]

SELECT	Cname, Employees, Profit
FROM	company
ORDER_BY	Profit ;

[In f-PROLOG]

?–answer((Cname,Employees,Profit),
        (company(C,_,_,E,P),
        order(3,(C,E,P),(Cname,Employees,Profit))))).

[Result]

Cname	Employees	Profit
C4	800	NULL
C2	100	100,000
C1	400	300,000
C3	2000	1,000,000

Query 37: Get a table which consists of all candidates who live in Newcastle, each one with his (or her) age and hobby, ordered by the ages.

[In FSQL]

SELECT	Name, Age, Hobby
FROM	candidates, background
WHERE	candidates.Name = background.Name
ORDER_BY	Age ;

[In f-PROLOG]

```
?-answer((Name,Age,Hobby),
         (candidates(N,_,A,_),
          background(N,_,_,_,H),
          order(2,(N,A,H),(Name,Age,Hobby)))).
```

[Result]

Name	Age	Hobby
Robert	UNDECIDED	NULL
Martin	$Young	Dancing
Smith	30	Travelling
Barry	33	Sports

Query 38: Select all candidates whose age is greater than or equal to 25.

[In FSQL]

SELECT	Name
FROM	candidates
WHERE	Age >= 25
WITH	F ;

[In f-PROLOG]

```
?-[F]-answer( Name ,
            (candidates(Name,_,Age,_),
            Age >= 25 )).
```

[Result]

Name	
Smith	1.00
John	1.00
Mary	1.00
Jill	1.00
Susan	1.00
Harry	1.00
Fred	0.50
Barry	1.00
Thomas	1.00
Henry	1.00
Robert	?

Query 39: Select all candidates whose age is greater than or equal to 25 with the confidence degree of 0.5.

[In FSQL]

```
SELECT   Name
FROM     candidates
WHERE    Age >= 25
WITH     0.5 ;
```

[In f-PROLOG]

```
?-[0.5]-answer( Name ,
              (candidates(Name,_,Age,_),
              Age >= 25 )).
```

[Result]

Name
Smith
John
Mary
Jill
Susan
Harry
Fred
Barry
Thomas
Henry

Query 40: Show all candidates who are very possibly about 25 years old.

[In FSQL]

```
SELECT   Name
FROM     candidates
WHERE    Age = ABOUT 25
WITH     VERY possible ;
```

[In f-PROLOG]

```
?-[VERY p]-answer( Name ,
          (candidates(Name,_,ABOUT 25,_))).
```

[Result]

Name
Tom
Fred
Andrew

Query 41: List all candidates who have had a university education or above.

[In FSQL]

```
           SELECT   Name
           FROM     background
           WHERE    Education = university
            OR      Education = post-graduate
           WITH     F ;
```

[In f-PROLOG]

> ?–[F]–answer(Name ,
>   (background(Name,university,_,_,_);
>   background(Name,post-graduate,_,_,_)))).

[Result]

Name	
Smith	1.00
Mary	1.00
Jill	1.00
Susan	1.00
Tom	1.00
Harry	1.00
Fred	1.00
Andrew	1.00
Barry	1.00
Thomas	1.00
Martin	1.00
Henry	1.00
Robert	1.00
George	θ

Query 42: Get the names of all candidates who are young with the confidence degree of 0.9.

[In FSQL]

```
           SELECT   Name
           FROM     candidates
           WHERE    Age = $Young
           WITH     0.9 ;
```

[In f-PROLOG]

404

$$?-[0.9]-answer(Name,(candidates(Name,\_,\$Young,\_))).$$

[Result]

Name
Tom
Fred
Andrew

Query 43:   Retrieve the names and addresses of all candidates who were definitely unemployed.

[In FSQL]

```
SELECT   Name, Address
FROM     candidates, background
WHERE    IS_UNDEFINED(Profession) ;
```

[In f-PROLOG]

```
?-answer((Name,Address),
        (candidates(Name,_,_,Address),
        background(Name,_,Profession,_,_)
        is_undefined(Profession))).
```

[Result]

Name	Address
George	NULL

Query 44:   Delete all young candidates who live in Newcastle or Darlington with the confidence degree of VERY possible.

[In FSQL]

```
DELETE   candidates
WHERE    Age = $Young
AND      Address IN (newcastle,darlington)
WITH     VERY possible ;
```

[In f-PROLOG]

?-[VERY p]-answer(storage ,
                (retract(candidates(_,_,$Young,newcastle)),
                 retract(candidates(_,_,$Young,darlington))))).

Query 45:   Insert two tuples ⟨Richard,Male,ABOUT 28,Carlisle⟩
and ⟨David,Male,30,Penrith⟩ into the relation
candidates.

[In FSQL]

INSERT_INTO   candidates(Name,Sex,Age,Address) :
                 ⟨richard,male,ABOUT 28,carlisle⟩
                 ⟨david,male,30,penrith⟩ ;

or

INSERT_INTO   candidates :
                 ⟨richard,male,ABOUT 28,carlisle⟩
                 ⟨david,male,30,penrith⟩ ;

[In f-PROLOG]

?-answer(storage ,
        (asserta(candidates(richard,male,ABOUT 28,carlisle),
         asserta(candidates(david,male,30,penrith)))).

Query 46:   Change the address of Mary to Newcastle.

[In FSQL]

MODIFY   candidates
SET   Address = newcastle
WHERE   Name = mary

[In f-PROLOG]

?-answer(storage ,
        (modify(Address, candidates(mary,_,_,Address),newcastle))).

Query 47:   Retrieve the name and age of the youngest candidate.

[In FSQL]

SELECT   Name, Age
FROM   candidates
WHERE   Age =
                 (SELECT   MIN(Age)
                  FROM   candidates) ;

?-answer((Name,MIN),
              (min(Age,candidates(_,_,Age,_),MIN),
              candidates(Name,_,MIN,_))).

[Result]

Name	Age
Margaret	20

Query 48: Retrieve the names of all secretaries who are young girls with the confidence degree of 0.8.

[In FSQL]

```
SELECT    Name
FROM      background
WHERE     Profession = secretary
AND       Name  IN
              (SELECT   Name
              FROM      candidates
              WHERE     Sex = female
              AND       Age = $Young
              WITH      0.8) ;
```

[In f-PROLOG]

?-[0.8]-answer(Name ,
              (candidates(Name,female,$Young,_),
              background(Name,_,secretary,_))).

[Result]

Name
Anna
Margaret

Query 49: Find all candidates whose addresses are the same as company C1.

[In FSQL]

```
SELECT   Name
FROM     candidates, company
WHERE    Cname = c1
AND      candidates.Address = company.Address
WITH     F ;
```

[In f-PROLOG]

```
?-[F]-answer( Name ,
        (candidates(Name,_,_,_,Address1),
        company(c1,Address2,_), Address1 = Address2)).
```

[Result]

Name	
Smith	1.00
Barry	1.00
Martin	1.00
Robert	1.00
George	ϕ

Query 50:   Find all couples of which both definitely have had higher education.

[In FSQL]

```
SELECT   Name1, Name2
FROM     relationship
WHERE    Type = couple
AND      Name1  IN
                (SELECT   Name
                 FROM     candidates
                 WHERE    Education = $HE
                 WITH     1)
AND      Name2  IN
                (SELECT   Name
                 FROM     candidates
                 WHERE    Education = $HE
                 WITH     1) ;
```

[In f-PROLOG]

```
?-answer((Name1,Name2),
         (relationship(Name1,Name2,couple),
         candidates(Name1,_,_,$HE,_),
         candidates(Name2,_,_,$HE,_))).
```

[Result]

Name1	Name2
Tom	Susan

Query 51: Construct a table of young candidates (with the degree of 0.9) who are managers or engineers or secretaries.

[In FSQL]

```
SELECT   Name
FROM     background
WHERE    Profession IN (manager,engineer,secretary)
AND      Name IN
              (SELECT   Name
               FROM     candidates
               WHERE    Age = $Young
               WITH     0.9) ;
```

[In f-PROLOG]

```
?-[0.9]-answer( Name ,
         (candidates(Name,_,$Young,_),
         (background(Name,manager,_,_,_,);
         background(Name,engineer,_,_,_);
         background(Name,secretary,_,_,_))))).
```

[Result]

Name
Anna
Tom
Margaret
Andrew
Martin

409

Query 52: Show all pairs of candidates who are friends and are approximately of the same age with the degree of 0.8.

[In FSQL]

```
SELECT    Name1, Name2
FROM      relationship
WHERE     Type = friend
AND       Name1 IN
                (SELECT  Name
                 FROM    candidates
                 WHERE   Age ˜=
                            (SELECT  Age
                             FROM    candidates
                             WHERE   Name = Name2
                             WITH    0.8))
WITH      0.8 ;
```

[In f-PROLOG]

```
?-[0.8]-answer((Name1,Name2),
            (relationship(Name1,Name2,friend),
            candidates(Name1,_,Age1,_,_),
            candidates(Name2,_,Age2,_,_),
            Age1 ˜= Age2)).
```

[Result]

Name1	Name2
Smith	Henry
Thomas	Henry
Tom	Martin

Query 53: Find all pairs of friends in which both have had a university education.

[In FSQL]

410

```
SELECT    Name1, Name2
FROM      relationship
WHERE     Type = friend
AND       Name1 IN
                  (SELECT    Name
                   FROM      background
                   WHERE     Education = university)
AND       Name2 IN
                  (SELECT    Name
                   FROM      background
                   WHERE     Education = university)
```

[In f-PROLOG]

?-[F]-answer((Name1,Name2),
            (relationship(Name1,Name2,friend),
            background(Name1,university,_,_,_),
            background(Name2,university,_,_,_))).

[Result]

Name1	Name2
Smith	Susan
Smith	Fred
Smith	Henry
Andrew	Smith
Tom	Martin

Query 54: Which candidate in Carlisle is younger than Fred with the confidence degree of 0.8.

[In FSQL]

```
SELECT    Name
FROM      candidates
WHERE     Address = carlisle
AND       Age <
                  (SELECT    Age
                   FROM      candidates
                   WHERE     Name = fred)
WITH      0.8 ;
```

411

[In f-PROLOG]

?–[0.8]–answer(Name ,
            (candidates(Name,_,Age,_,carlisle),
            candidates(fred,_,Age1,_,_),
            Age < Age1)).

[Result]

Name
John
Mary

Query 55: Retrieve the names of all candidates who have very good looks and intelligence (but not excellent).

[In FSQL]

SELECT	Name
FROM	body
WHERE	Looks = VERY good
WITH	F

INTERSECT

SELECT	Name
FROM	ability
WHERE	Intelligence = VERY good
WITH	F ;

or

SELECT	Name
FROM	body
WHERE	Looks = VERY good
AND	Name IN

(SELECT	Name
FROM	ability
WHERE	Intelligence = VERY good
WITH	F)

WITH	F ;

[In f-PROLOG]

412

?–[F]–answer(Name ,
                (body(Name,_,_,VERY good),
                ability(Name,VERY good,_,_,_)))).

[Result]

Name	
Smith	0.80
Anna	0.80
Mary	1.00
Harry	0.80
Margaret	0.80
Andrew	0.80
Martin	0.80

Query 56:   Retrieve the names and addresses of all candidates
who are relatives of company C1's president, and
live far from the company C1.

[In FSQL]

```
SELECT    Name, Address
FROM      candidates
WHERE     Name  IN
              (SELECT   Name1
               FROM     relationship
               WHERE    Type = relative
               AND      Name2 =
                            (SELECT   President
                             FROM     company
                             WHERE    Cname = c1)
          UNION
               (SELECT   Name2
                FROM     relationship
                WHERE    Type = relative
                AND      Name1 =
                             (SELECT   President
                              FROM     company
                              WHERE    Cname = c1))
```

AND   Address IN
                (SELECT   City1
                 FROM   location
                 WHERE   Distance = $Far
                 AND   City2 =
                                (SELECT   Location
                                 FROM   company
                                 WHERE   Cname = c1)
                 WITH   F)
            UNION
                (SELECT   City2
                 FROM   location
                 WHERE   Distance = $Far
                 AND   City1 =
                                (SELECT   Location
                                 FROM   company
                                 WHERE   Cname = c1)
                 WITH   F)
     WITH   F ;

[In f-PROLOG]

```
?-[F]-answer((Name,Address),
        (candidates(Name,_,_,_,Address),
         (relationship(Name,President,friend);
          relationship(President,Name,friend)),
         company(c1,Location,_,_,_),
         (location(Location,Address,$Far);
          location(Address,Location,$Far)))).
```

[Result]

Name	Address	
John	Carlisle	0.99
Margaret	Penrith	0.56

Query 57: Retrieve the name,profession and age of Smith's wife.

[In FSQL]

```
SELECT    Name, Profession, Age
FROM      candidates, background
WHERE     Name  IN
              (SELECT    Name2
               FROM      relationship
               WHERE     Type = couple
               AND       Name1 = smith

          UNION

              (SELECT    Name1
               FROM      relationship
               WHERE     Type = couple
               AND       Name2 = smith) ;
```

[In f-PROLOG]

```
?-answer((Name,Profession,Age),
         (candidates(Name,_,Age,_),
          background(Name,_,Profession,_,_),
          (relationship(Name,smith,couple);
           relationship(smith,Name,couple))))).
```

[Result]

Name	Profession	Age
Anna	Secretary	22

Query 58: Find the salaries of all candidates who are young secretaries or clerks, if they are employed in company C1.

[In FSQL]

```
SELECT    Name, Salary
FROM      candidates, background, job
WHERE     Age = $Young
AND       Profession  IN  (secretary, clerk)
AND       Cname = c1
WITH      F ;
```

[In f-PROLOG]

415

?–[F]–answer((Name,Salary),
            (candidates(Name,_,$Young,_),
             (background(Name,_,secretary,_,_);
              background(Name,_,clerk,_,_)),
             job(_,c1,Salary,_))).

[Result]

Name	Salary	
Anna	7000	1.00
Margaret	7000	1.00

Query 59: Retrieve the name, addresse, education, and intelligence, of all young candidates who are a president's relative.

[In FSQL]

SELECT	Name, Address, Education, Intelligence
FROM	candidates, background, ability
WHERE	Age = $Young
AND	candidates.Name IN

(SELECT	Name1	
FROM	relationship	
WHERE	Type = relative	
AND	Name2 IN	
	(SELECT	President
	FROM	company))
UNION		
(SELECT	Name2	
FROM	relationship	
WHERE	Type = relative	
AND	Name1 IN	
	(SELECT	President
	FROM	company))

WITH	F ;

[In f-PROLOG]

?-[F]-answer((Name,Address,Education,Intelligence),
              (candidates(Name,_,$Young,_),
              (relationship(Name,President,relative);
              relationship(President,Name,relative)),
              company(_,_,President,_,_))).

[Result]

Name	Address	Education	Intelligence	
Margaret	Penrith	High-school	Good	1.00
Anna	Penrith	High-school	Good	1.00
Martin	Newcastle	University	Good	1.00
Robert	Newcastle	Post-graduate	NULL	ϕ

Query 60: Show all pairs of candidates who are friends with
each other, and are approximately of the same age.

[In FSQL]

```
SELECT    Name1, Name2
FROM      relationship
WHERE     Type = friend
AND       Name1  IN
              (SELECT    Name
               FROM      candidates
               WHERE     Age ~=
                             (SELECT    Age
                              FROM      candidates
                              WHERE     Name = Name2)
               WITH       F)
UNION
SELECT    Name1, Name2
FROM      relationship
WHERE     Type = friend
```

```
AND     Name2  IN
                (SELECT  Name
                 FROM    candidates
                 WHERE   Age ~=
                              (SELECT  Age
                               FROM    candidates
                               WHERE   Name = Name1)
                 WITH    F) ;
```

[In f-PROLOG]

```
?-[F]-answer((Name1,Name2),
          ((relationship(Name1,Name2,friend);
           relationship(Name2,Name1,friend)),
           candidates(Name1,_,Age1,_),
           candidates(Name2,_,Age2,_),
           Age1 ~= Age2)).
```

[Result]

Name1	Name2	
Smith	Susan	0.52
Smith	Henry	0.80
John	Smith	0.52
Thomas	Henry	0.64
Tom	Martin	1.00

Query 61: Retrieve the name, sex, education and health of all candidates who are young with the degree of ABOUT 0.8.

[In FSQL]

```
SELECT  Name, Sex, Education, Health
FROM    candidates, background, body
WHERE   Age = $Young
WITH    ABOUT 0.8 ;
```

[In f-PROLOG]

?–[ABOUT 0.8]–answer((Name,Sex,Education,Health),
(candidates(Name,Sex,$Young,_),
background(Name,Education,_,_,_),
body(Name,Health,_,_))).

[Result]

Name	Sex	Education	Health
Anna	Female	High-school	Good
Tom	Male	University	VERY Good
Margaret	Male	High-school	Good
Andrew	Male	University	VERY Good
Martin	Male	University	VERY Good
George	Male	UNDEFINED	NULL

Query 62: Retrieve the name and address of all candidates who are relatives of company C1's president, and are fairly intelligent.

[In FSQL]

```
SELECT    Name, Address
FROM      candidates, ability
WHERE     Intelligence = FAIRLY good
AND       Name  IN
          (SELECT    Name1
           FROM      relationship
           WHERE     Type = relative
           AND       Name2  IN  (SELECT    President
                                 FROM      company
                                 WHERE     Cname = c1))
          UNION
          (SELECT    Name2
           FROM      relationship
           WHERE     Type = relative
           AND       Name1  IN  (SELECT    President
                                 FROM      company
                                 WHERE     Cname = c1)) ;
WITH      F ;
```

[In f-PROLOG]

```
?-[F]-answer((Name,Address),
             (candidates(Name,_,_,Address),
              ability(Name,FAIRLY good,_,_,_),
              company(c1,_,President,_,_),
              (relationship(Name,President,relative);
               relationship(President,Name,relative))))).
```

[Result]

Name	Address	
John	Carlisle	1.00
Margaret	Penrith	0.80

Query 63: Retrieve the name, intelligence, initiative and social maturity of all candidates who have been managers for a long time and whose addresses are different from the company C1's.

[In FSQL]

```
SELECT    Name, Intelligence, Initiative, SocialMaturity
FROM      candidates, ability
WHERE     candidates.Name  IN
               (SELECT    Name
                FROM      background
                WHERE     Profession = manager
                AND       Experience = $Long
                WITH      F)
AND       candidates.Address /=
               (SELECT    Location
                FROM      company
                WHERE     name = c1)
WITH      F ;
```

[In f-PROLOG]

?–[F]–answer((Name,Intelligence,Initiative,SocialMaturity),
      (candidates(Name,_,_,Address),
      ability(Name,Intelligence,Initiative,SocialMaturity),
      background(Name,_,manager,$Long,_),
      company(c1,Location,_,_,_),
      Address /== Location)).

[Result]

Name	Intelligence	Initiative	SocialMaturity	
Jill	Excellent	Moderate	VERY Good	0.50
Harry	VERY Good	Moderate	Good	0.86

Index

rules 88
rule base 76

satisfactory solution 162-164
second normal form (2NF) 147
second order predicates 368-369
semantic distance 221
selection 152, 153, 189, 208
SELECT-FROM-WHERE block 178
single value simulation 241
similarity measure 219
similarity relations 160
simple condition 270
storage statements 195
soft constraint 308-312
soft sciences 2, 11
structures 87
SEQUEL 178
SQL 17, 177-182

term 81
third normal form (3NF) 148
three-valued logic 99
truth table 99
tuple 138
two-valued logic 99
type 2 fuzzy set 32, 57-60
type II f-Rule 130

uncertainty 1-9
UNDECIDED 18, 297-308
UNDEFINED 18, 297-308
unification 89
unified universe of discourse 43

union 150, 193, 206
union-compatible 150

very 72-74
variable 87
variance 66, 68
virtual database 251, 252
virtual relation 203-205

weak equality 218
weak inclusion 218
weighted Hamming distance 221
well formed formula (WFF) 81

λ-level-set 62-64
λ-level-relation 209